INFORMATION NETWORK AND DATA COMMUNICATION, III

INFORMATION NETWORK AND DATA COMMUNICATION, III

Proceedings of the IFIP TC6 International Conference on
Information Network and Data Communication
Lillehammer, Norway, 26–29 March, 1990

Edited by

DIPAK KHAKHAR
IB-ADB
Lund University
Lund, Sweden

FRANK ELIASSEN
Department of Computer Science
University of Tromso
Tromso, Norway

1990

NORTH-HOLLAND
AMSTERDAM · NEW YORK · OXFORD · TOKYO

ELSEVIER SCIENCE PUBLISHERS B.V.
Sara Burgerhartstraat 25
P.O. Box 211, 1000 AE Amsterdam, The Netherlands

Distributors for the United States and Canada:
ELSEVIER SCIENCE PUBLISHING COMPANY INC.
655 Avenue of the Americas
New York, N.Y. 10010, U.S.A.

Library of Congress Cataloging-in-Publication Data

IFIP TC 6 International Conference on Information Network and Data
   Communication (3rd : 1990 : Lillehammer, Norway)
   Information network and data communication, III : proceedings of
the IFIP TC6 International Conference on Information Network and
Data Communication, Lillehammer, Norway, 26-29 March, 1990 / edited
by Dipak Khakhar, Frank Eliassen.
      p.   cm.
   Includes bibliographical references.
   ISBN 0-444-88696-6
   1. Computer networks--Congresses. 2. Data transmission systems-
-Congresses.   I. Khakhar, Dipak, 1943-   . II. Eliassen, Frank.
III. International Federation for Information Research. Technical
Committee 6.   IV. Title.
TK5105.5.I3422   1990
006.3--dc20   90-38331
                                                            CIP

ISBN: 0 444 88696 6

Printed in The Netherlands.

PREFACE

The contents of this book are the papers presented at the third International Conference on Information Network and Data Communication.The conference was held in the township of Lillehammer in Norway and was organized by the computer societies in Norway (Den Norske Dataforening) and Sweden (Dataföreningen).

The main theme of the conference was the application of open standards in corporate information systems. Information systems is an important corporate resource recognized at the highest level of coporate management. In order to make better use of extremely rapid technical development, there is a need for cooperating open information systems together with appropriate communication structures. The application of standards for networking and for information exchange and access, is mandatory for reaching such a goal. The conference identified important considerations for formulating a successful information processing and communicatuions strategy, presented critical technical managerial issues, and described new and soon-to-be available communication facilities.

Looking back at a decade with OSI, one can safely conclude that the OSI reference model has had a major impact on distributed system design. However, it is concluded in one of the contributed papers of this conference, that it is now high time to review and evaluate the OSI reference model, its services and protocols in light of new network technologies and new distributed system requirements that have appeared after its publication. Beyond this the conference covered a number of current aspects and issues in data communication such as network management, high capacity networks, network security, data communication as a competitive advantage, integrating heterogeneous distributed systems, message handling systems, mobile communication and VAN services. Morever, the conference examined issues, prospects and consequences of the European movement towards a competitive telecommunication market.

A great deal of work goes into organizing a conference of this magnitude. We warmly thank all of you who contributed and so made this conference possible. In particular we would like to thank Ellen Bøhler and Ann-Kristin Moe Rustad for their enormous effort in organizing the conference. We would also like to thank the companies who generously supported the conference. Without their contribution it would have been impossible to hold such an event.

Frank Eliassen and Dipak Khakhar

PROGRAMME COMMITTEE

Frank Eliassen (N), Chaiman
Dipak Khakhar (S), Vice-Chairman
Kjell Å. Bringsrud (N)
Jan Ekberg (SF)
Terje Grimstad (N)
Jan Guettler (N)
Villy B. Iversen (DK)
Morten Paulsen (N)
Knut Smaaland (N)
Terje Tøndel (N)

ORGANIZING COMMITTEE

Nils Bull (N), Chairman
Ellen Bøhler (N)
Erik Bergersen (N)
Dipak Khakhar (S)
Berit Mørk (N)
Agneta Qwerin (S)

ACKNOWLEDGEMENTS

INDC-90 thanks the following corporations for their generous contribution:

Digital Equipment Corporation A/S, Norway
Ericsson Radio Systems, Sweden
Ericsson Telecom A/S, Norway
IBM Norway
Norsk Data A/S, Norway
Norsk Hydro a.s., Hydro Data
Norwegian Telecommunication Administration
Siemens A/S, Norway
Swedish Telecom
Telesoft AB, Sweden
TBK A/S, Norway

TABLE OF CONTENTS

Information Network and Data Communication, III
D. Khakhar and F. Eliassen (Editors)
Elsevier Science Publishers B.V. (North-Holland)
© IFIP, 1990

10 YEARS WITH OSI

A. Danthine

Institut Montefiore, Université de Liège, B - 4000 Liège, Belgium.

After a review of the basic concepts behind the OSI Reference Model, the paper shows the robustness of this model which has been able to absorb new technologies with minor modifications. The inflation of standards which followed the acceptance of the OSI RM was a real danger and the paper surveys the works of manufacturer's and user's associations, as well as standardisation bodies to achieve implementable protocol suites, known as profiles or functional standards. The possibility of revisiting the base standards is discussed as well as the possible aggregation of layers in profiles.

The third part of the paper is devoted to the evaluation of what the OSI may offer as communication support to the distributed systems taking into account the requirements in terms of transparency, management and performance.

1. INTRODUCTION

It is now becoming more and more difficult to find a manufacturer which has not yet indicated its support to the OSI. Some have clearly indicated their willingness to migrate to the OSI architecture and its protocol suite, others have announced OSI application gateways to open their system while preserving their proprietary network architecture.

The same consensus is found among many users who are looking into OSI as the only way to go for interoperability.

Even the success of TCP/IP did not prevent the DoD to announce in September 1986 its future migration to the OSI world.

Does such a consensus mean that the OSI Reference Model is perfect and the OSI standards are complete, widely available and offering levels of performance higher than expected ? Not exactly so.

But taking into account the complexity of the problem, the investments in manpower which have been done already within all the standardisation bodies and the dynamic which has been created around OSI, it is difficult to imagine a way-out.

But following OSI does not mean rejecting necessary moves to follow the evolution of the technologies and of the applications. The OSI world has already been able to generate not only lots of standards but also a lot of corrective actions.

To survey the ten years of OSI, we will divide its evolution into two phases and try to express the pros and cons arguments about what has been achieved during this decade.

2

2. THE FIRST PHASE

2.1. The OSI Reference Model.

The starting point is this OSI Reference Model [Zimmerman, 80] developed at the end of the seventies. At that time, the communication infrastructure was made of switched lines, leased lines and packet switching networks and this is clearly visible in the model.

The basic concepts behind the OSI RM are layering and transparency. The layering was the cornerstone of the control of the complexity. An open system is viewed as being logically composed of an ordered set of subsystems. Subsystems of the same rank form the (N)-layer of the architecture. An (N+1)-entity request (N)-services via an (N)-SAP which permits the (N+1)-entity to interact with an (N)-entity in the (N)-layer. The (N)-services are provided to (N+1)-entities using the (N)-functions performed within the (N)-layer and the services available from the next lower layer. One important point is that the initial OSI RM considered that all associations between (N)-SAPs had to be *"connections"*.

The OSI RM not only defines the principles of operation of open systems organised in layers but introduces the thirteen principles to be used to make specific choice for the layers and their contents [Danthine, 89]. Applying these principles, and taking into account the communication environments and its existing standards, the final choice was the well known seven layers.

It is important to stress that the OSI RM has become the framework for all works on network architectures as well as for the teaching of networks in the universities. Study of any proprietary network architecture is done today using the OSI RM as reference.

2.2. The Robustness of the OSI RM

The communication environment, when the OSI RM was introduced, was dominated by switched lines, leased lines and packet switching networks. This is obvious from the functions associated with the three lower layers of the model.
The first serious challenge to the OSI RM came from the emergence of the local area network (LAN) technology. How do the LANs fit the OSI RM and its layers ?

No doubt that a physical layer was needed as well as a data link layer as LANs transmit data using a classical frame structure involving source and destination addresses as well as some Frame Check Sequence and Control information required for error detection and in some cases error recovery.

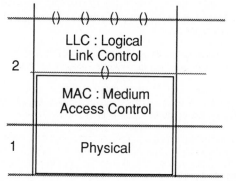

Fig.1 *The LAN in the OSI Reference Model*

The layer 3 is more difficult. If intranet routing is considered as the main function of the layer 3, it is clear that layer 3 is not needed due to the existence of a physical medium to which all systems are connected and which provides a direct link between any two points. But, if we look into X.25 packet level, we must recognise that the layer 3 function is not only the intranet routing but also the multiplexing of virtual connections on a single access line.

However the IEEE 802 Committee decided to provide a sub-addressing in the layer 2 through the Logical Link Control (LLC). The LLC sublayer is placed on top of the Medium Access Control (MAC) sublayer. Every open system has one MAC address (often called the physical address) but through the LLC offers to its processes a set of SAPs (fig.1).

Furthermore, the IEEE 802 based its works on the idea of the same LLC sublayer on top of any MAC sublayer.
The LLC is providing three types of service;
- type 1 : unacknowledged connectionless service
- type 2 : connection-mode service
and more recently
- type 3 : acknowledged connectionless service.

A comparison between the service primitives of the connection-mode *network* Service (ISO 8348) and the service primitives of the connection-mode *LLC* service (ISO 8802-2) is not without interest and the difference may be related to the very different communication environments (X.25 versus LAN) as well as to the evolution of the standardisation Committee, about the interest of some parameters for some service primitives.

The difference of the levels of these two services may be traced to the routing functions which, at the beginning, were not foreseen in the LANs. The repeater is a layer 1 entity repeating at the bit level with no routing or switching functions. But what about the bridge?

A bridge between two LANs of the same type is just doing a routing function based on the learned knowledge of the location of the systems on the two LANs. This routing function is based on the frame destination address and belongs to the MAC sublayer.

If we reviewed all the moves which finally ended up with the LAN model in the OSI RM (fig 1), we would not find a principle of layering which has been violated, but here these principles did not convey the same result. From that point of view, the OSI RM looks robust even if, at the end of the process, the LAN world and the X.25 world are offering different architectural views.

It is however clear that the types of services offered by the layer 2 of the LANs may be considered as very stable and with very little dependence to the technology of the LAN itself.

It will be also very interesting to see if the broadband ISDN will be able to fit into this architectural model or if it will offer the same architectural view than the X.25 world.

Having to deal with architectural differences on one side and with difference of services on the other side, the complexity of the network layer is not surprising as it has to deal with connectionless and connection-mode services in all the possible interplays.

Another aspect of the robustness of the OSI RM is related to the transport layer, one of the most stable layers.

The five classes of transport protocols have been specified to offer the same quality of service to the transport users even when the network services are very different. However the concept of connection is so deeply rooted in the model that although many people believe that the class 4 (TP4) was specially designed for connectionless networks, it is described in the standard assuming a **"connection-mode** network service with unacceptable residual error rate" on network connection (ISO 8073 -1986, page 7).

In fact, the designers of TP4 had in mind the characteristics of the low speed "datagram" networks of the 1970's, and the protocol is certainly not optimised for the high quality connectionless service of modern high speed LANs. It is unfortunate that, instead of promoting TP4 on top of **connectionless** network service based on LANs, the standardisation groups have not worked out a new version of the TP, reassessing the various mechanisms with the new environment.

2.3. The Inflation of Standards.

The OSI RM is a framework allowing the specification of protocol entities in the various layers. Those who were afraid of the lack of standards to fill the OSI RM may now begin to relax. The complete list of the ISO standards from DP to IS about the OSI RM, its services and its protocols included, in September 1989, 282 items.

3. THE SECOND PHASE

1984 is a turning point in the development of OSI : it sees the stabilisation of the 5 lower layers including transport and session. From this year the effort is now almost exclusively put on presentation and application layers without enough consideration on possible evolution necessary in the lower layers in order to provide more adequate or performant services. The number of subjects dealt with in parallel increase steadily with the difficult problem of integrating the work of CCITT which has, in the 1984 version of X.400, somewhat diverged from the ISO model and anticipated protocols of layers 6 and 7.

1984 is also a turning year because, in January, 12 European manufacturers, which had the year before created the Standards Promotion and Application Group (SPAG), publicly took a commitment to offer products implementing OSI protocols. In the same year, a few manufacturers announced products. UK Government recommended an OSI intercept strategy and IBM announced an OSI competence centre in La Gaude. At the end of the year, SPAG published its Guide to the Use of Standards which established a typology of profiles which is at the origin of the Functional Standards. The SPAG regularly updates its GUS [GUS, 87].

In 1984, also, the OSI work is reallocated in ISO ; transport is given to the Transmission Subcommittee TC 97/SC 6 and layers 5 to 7 subjects are reassigned to groups in a new SC 21 replacing the original SC 16.

At this point the right structure was set to proceed parallel developments of "generic" parts of the model (presentation, ASCE, addressing, ..) and applications of use to the end users (message handling, file transfer, virtual terminal and, more recently, transaction processing).

Outside ISO, the emphasis was on the following points :
- functional standards
- conformance
- procurements

Very little was done on **global performances**, though the session as it is presently was often perceived as restraining performances.

Today the range of networks goes from a single LAN with a few dozens of workstations, to a broad site involving a few dozens of LANs and a few thousands of systems, to the multi-site enterprise communication systems involving, through WANs, the federation of local facilities. Last but not least, we have to consider also networks involving hundreds of sites connected by all the communication facilities available on the wide area to provide multi-corporate

services such as Message Handling Systems or EDI (Electronic Data Interchange). This wide range of goals has raised questions in many people's mind :
- Is it reasonable to believe that the same Reference Model will apply to the single LAN and to the network which grew up from the ARPANET to reach today an internet of a thousand networks ?
- Is it possible to envisage a perfect interoperability of all these communication systems involving a lot of heterogeneous equipments ?
- Are users ready to trade performances for global interoperability or is OSI world ready to provide interoperability with performances ?

3.1. The Search for Simplification

If the OSI Reference Model was more and more widely accepted, very soon people discovered that OSI standards as such were not a precise enough basis for interoperability. Compromises in the standards design led to too many options or parameters and the layer independence led to too many combinations. Even the users perceived the danger of jeopardising the interoperability of equipments.

The MAP initiative which began in 1982 and the TOP initiative were based on two basic principles:
- to select a protocol suite from layer 7 to layer 1 in order to achieve a coherent open system.
- to freeze each selected protocol by reducing the number of options and by setting some of the available parameters.

Though the General Motors MAP project was the first big group to select its required subset of protocols and options in the OSI stack, SPAG had certainly the merit to introduce the concept of profiles which encompasses several layers and to determine the transport service as the hinge between Transport matters (T profiles) and Application matters (A profiles).

The rationale for the introduction of a class of Telecommunication functions is that the user of an end-system is isolated from the characteristics of the telecommunications facility being used for a particular instance of communication with another end-system.

The split between the functions of the Application Class and those in the Telecommunication Class is located at the OSI Transport Service boundary and the Transport Protocol itself is included as part of the Telecommunication Class of Functional Standards.

It is clear that the level of the split is a basic choice. The fact that we have a unique definition of a connection-mode transport service is certainly an important point for supporting that choice. Another possible choice would be to locate the split at the Network Service Boundary and to leave the transport protocol in the Application Class, i.e. in the end-systems.

The work of SPAG was contributed to CEN-CENELEC which published in 1984 a survey on the standards for a European Information Technology programme and joined with CEPT in 1985 in the Information Technology Subcommittee. The first PreENV were published in March 1986.

The trend launched by SPAG in Europe was followed by COS in US and POSI in Japan. The CEN-CENELEC activities in Europe was followed by the NBS (now NITS) with its Implementation Agreements and to complete the picture, one must mention the GOSIP (Government OSI Procurement) initiated by the US Government and quickly followed by UK, Canada, Sweden, France and the CEC.

In parallel the CEC launched in 1985 an important programme on conformance testing (CTS).

3.2. The Functional Standards

The CEN/CENELEC work is based on the same principles as MAP and TOP but the scope is wider. Following SPAG, CEN/CENELEC is not only interested in profiles called now functional standards, involving a complete seven layers protocols stack but *also by functional standards involving only the lower layers that are needed to provide a given level of service.*

A functional standard is a document which includes among other things
- a simple definition of the function
- an illustration of the scenario within which the function is applicable
- a single working set of standards, including precise references to the actual texts of the standards being used
- specifications of the application of each referenced standard covering **recommendation on the choice of classes of subsets, and on the selection of options, range of parameter value, etc.**

One may however question the rationale behind an activity process where first Standardisation Committees are working hard to produce standards with a lot of options and a lot of protocol mechanisms and where later on other Standardisation Committees are working hard also to select options and protocol mechanisms in order to achieve a "functional standard" in an application oriented environment.

The session protocol of the ISO is a good example of an "extended" work on a standard where a lot of situations have been thought of and a lot of mechanisms and options have been introduced. The Committee has been trying to define a protocol for all possible situations and one may say that they succeeded. However it will be surprising to see a lot of implementations of the complete session. The Session protocol looks more like a "shopping list" where standardisation committees working with an application requirement in mind will be able to select and to specify a "functional standard".

This two-steps process is time consuming and it is therefore not surprising that in Melbourne, the CCITT decided to try to accelerate the standardisation process for which the grain of time is today 4 years.

CEN/CENELEC actions ultimately create European Prestandards known as ENVs, which will become EN.

3.3. The SPAG and the Distributed Systems

SPAG tries to integrate as much as possible its works and the works of CEN/CENELEC/CEPT/ITSTC but has also introduced profiles (SPAG did not adopt the term Functional Standard) such as R/31 (fig. 2).

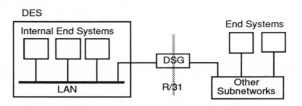

Fig.2. *Distributed End System (DES) and Distributed System Gateway (DSG)*

A Distributed End System (DES) is the denomination used to designate a distributed system using a LAN as communication medium and adopting a Telecommunication profile. Inside the

DES, all stations or systems are end-systems with respect to every other station on the LAN but not vis-à-vis the attached subnetworks. However the whole LAN is an end-system vis-à-vis the attached subnetworks through the Distributed System Gateway (DSG). The functionality of the DSG is that of a relay in the Connection-mode Transport Service, responsible for establishing and maintaining the integrity of a transport connection between the end-systems and providing transport class conversion between Class 4 on the LAN side or Class 0 or 2 on the WAN side. This DSG is based on ECMA TR/21 protocol.

3.4. The Corporation for Open Systems (COS)

The Corporation for Open Systems (COS) approved in April 1988 its Profile Specification (PS) version 1.1. This document specifies the subset of the OSI base standards *which will be tested in the COS testing programme.*

The included applications are File Transfer and Electronic Mail. Lower layer protocol combinations selected to support these applications allow communication over complex configurations involving concatenated LAN and/or WAN subnetworks as well as simple configurations based on a single subnetwork (fig. 3).

The protocol combinations in the lower layers offer alternatives providing the Connectionless Network Service (CLNS) and the Connection-mode Network Service (CONS). An interworking function allowing communication between CONS and CLNS based systems is required but no solution to this problem has achieved acceptance.

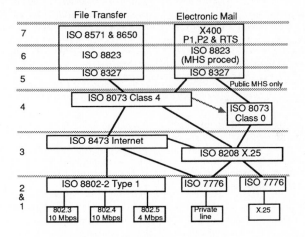

Fig. 3. *COS Protocol Overview*

The COS PS consists almost entirely of references to other documents. The COS PS may be thought of the top document of a three levels hierarchy. The second level is the NBS Workshop Implementation Agreements and the bottom level consists of the base standards. The pace of the updates of the COS PS is high as the average interval between versions should be 12 months.

We would like to reproduce here part of the philosophy of the Profile Specification of COS :"*The profiles specified in this document are restricted in scope to achieve a manageable set of testable standards. Selection of the COS profiles was guided by a belief that excessive complexity is a major threat to the success of OSI and ISDN. Purchasing, implementing, and testing OSI/ISDN systems all become more difficult as alternatives proliferate. COS has attempted to avoid complexity by choosing a small number of protocol combinations from the large set available in the base standards. The temptation to add protocol combinations has been balanced by concern about the negative effect of a confusing array of protocols and protocol options. ..."*

The COS protocol overview (fig. 3) allows to define the profiles for the COS end-system as well as the profiles for the COS intermediate system. For these relay systems, only the connectionless has been defined and no relay in the transport layer has been introduced. For the transport layer, the COS PS put more emphasis on TP 4 than the SPAG GUS.

3.5. The TCP/IP success

It is during the second phase where we have seen a lot of activities going on to define Profiles, Functional Standards and Implementation Agreements that TCP/IP has been more and more successful.

TCP/IP may be considered as a de-facto Profile or de-facto Functional Standard. One element of its success is related to the integration of the network protocol in the kernel of the UNIX system.

TCP/IP has influenced some of the protocols and some of the profiles of the OSI world. It is however unlikely that TCP/IP will be able to resist, in the long run, to the trend to an OSI world.

It is however important that the experience gains through TCP/IP will not be lost for the OSI. Recent change in the transport protocol of TCP/IP [Van Jacobson, 88] has been introduced to overcome congestion collapses which happen in the TCP/IP world. These congestion collapses are not at all excluded in an OSI environment and it is therefore important to integrate new mechanisms to avoid problems which will come when the size and the heterogeneity of the networks will reach a certain level.

3.6. Aggregation of Layers

The overall trend in the OSI environment is to define functional standards or profiles. By doing so and due to the mechanisms used to create these profiles, a protocol belonging to a protocol suite in a given profile may not be able to interoperate with the same protocol belonging to another profile. Therefore one of the advantages of the layering is lost. If we take into account the performance aspect it may be interesting to merge several layers of a protocol suite into a single "superlayer".

There exist one extreme example of aggregation of layers: the miniMAP. The real time constraint has been at the origin of the aggregation of layers 6 to 3 into a null layer. This collapsed architecture is today known as EPA (Enhanced Performance Architecture).

Another example of integration of layers is given in [Danthine, 88b].

Collapsing several layers into a superlayer is not the only way to improve the performance in using a protocol suite. Implementation techniques are also very important [Watson, 87] but aggregation of layers will allow to go further in the process of protocol simplification for instance by the elimination of redundant mechanisms and will be beneficial for the performance.

3.7. Revisiting the Base Standards ?

If we consider all the profiles, functional standards, or implementation agreements, it is clear that there are differences between them, but it is clear also that there is an extremely strong convergent view between them.

If we compare a given base standard to the union of the choices of all the profiles, functional standards and implementation agreements, it is obvious that many subsets of the base standard have not been considered by anyone whereas other subsets have been considered almost by all. A typical case is 802.4 for which only two subsets have been considered in the functional standard approach.

It is of course possible to leave the base standard as it is but it is also possible to acknowledge the results of the work of people looking into implementation aspects. This will mean to revisit the base standards and to suppress from it all the subsets, parameters, sets of values, which have not been found of interest by any. But we are probably dreaming...

4. WORKSTATION ACCESS RATE ON LAN

The LANs have offered, to the workstations, a *potential* bandwidth several orders of magnitude higher than the bandwidth available with classical twisted pairs communication.

In the last five years, we have seen a tremendous evolution of the available workstation access rate to the LAN. The third generation of Ethernet controllers are offering today an access rate, at the MAC interface, which is now a sizable part of the Ethernet bandwidth.

In the last five years, we have also seen a tremendous evolution of the required access rate to the LAN due to increased use of graphics and to the development of new applications in a more bandwidth demanding environment such as X-Windows

However, the increase of the MAC access rate through more carefully designed controllers has not been followed by an increase of the access rate *seen from the application*. The protocols of layers 3 and 4 are responsible for part of the bandwidth reduction provided to the application levels.

TP4 was not designed to be implemented on top of the connectionless network service offered by the LANs. Even if many mechanisms existing in TP4 are useful in the connectionless environment, it is important to stress that a protocol which would have been designed for the new LAN environment would have been different from TP4.

Some drawbacks of TP4 are also present in TCP/IP which is also introducing drastic reduction of throughput for equipments such as file servers and graphics workstations which require more and more access rate to the communication network.

It will be naive to believe that the solution lies in the increase of the speed of the LAN and that replacing Ethernet (802.3) controllers by FDDI controllers will solve the problem.

This situation will still be more unacceptable when high performance FDDI controllers will be available. Many workstations will not be able to benefit from the increased bandwidth due to the bottleneck created by the transport and network layers.

No standard is available today which specify a transport protocol designed for the high speed environment. The eXpress Transport Protocol (XTP) is an example of the trend to develop a new transport protocol for the high speed environment [Chesson, 88]. If such a protocol is standardised by an ANSI Committee, it may later on become an ISO standard and be another example of a protocol entirely standardised in the US and finally adopted by the European Companies.

FDDI is another example of such a path of action and the net result is the competitive edge gained by US companies. Some are developing the chip set, some others are developing the FDDI controllers and some workstation manufacturers such as Apollo and Sun are already testing these new controllers. It will be of interest to see how long we will have to wait to

10

have equivalent announcement from European Manufacturers.

The problem of performance of the TP4 and of the layer 3 protocols that we have already today with existing LANs such as Ethernet or the Token Ring at 16 Mbps will also arise tomorrow with the FDDI network or with any high speed LAN such as LION and BWN [Danthine, 89]. They will also appear when the broadband ISDN access will be provided. Today, no stable transport protocol is available to be put on top of any of these very high speed communication services.

5. B-ISDN

CCITT has agreed that the Broadband-ISDN would be implemented by the "Asynchronous Transfer Mode" (ATM). ATM is a packet oriented transfer mode, which has been simplified in order to support a high bandwidth information flow. No error control is performed on a link by link basis, the simplification being possible due to the high quality of the medium (optical fibre). Services needing an error-free transmission would perform end-to-end error recovery.

In ATM, the multiplexed information flow is organised in fixed size blocks, called cells; this allows easier packet processing. A cell consists of a user information field and a header; the primary role of the header is to identify cells belonging to the same "Virtual Channel" on an asynchronous time division multiplex. Cells are assigned on demand, depending on the source activity and the available resource. Cell sequence integrity on a virtual channel is guaranteed by the ATM network.

ATM is a connection-oriented technique : header values are assigned to each section of a connection at call set-up and released at the end of the call. Signalling and user information, are carried on separate virtual channels (outband signalling). The main purpose of the connection set up is to define the virtual channel before actual transfer of user information i.e. preestablish the route to the destination and reserve the bandwidth required by the source. During the user information transfer phase, simple fixed routing occurs. The call is accepted only when the resources have been reserved, thus, no flow control is required on a link by link basis. The bandwidth allocation process must guarantee that the cell loss rate due to internal congestion in the switch remains under an acceptable value.

ATM is designed to offer a flexible transfer capability common to all services, i.e. without any predefined fixed bitrate channel structure. This is commonly referred to as "ATM bearer service".

5.2. MANs

The introduction of ATM exchanges as a product may not envisaged before 1995. However in the mean time, an urgent need exists to have broadband networks which would interconnect LANs over large distances, e.g. a city. This is the purpose of the introduction of Metropolitan Area Networks (MANs) supporting, as a first priority, connectionless service i.e. "supporting the transfer of variable length packet data that can tolerate variable end-to-end delivery delay but requiring error detection functions" (such as the MAC of 802.x LANs). Given the ultimate deployment of B-ISDN, it is highly desirable that deployed MANs be able of graceful evolution to B-ISDN. That means that besides the connectionless service support, MANs should be able to support (possibly in a later phase) the following types of services too :
- Isochronous service, supporting the transparent transfer of data with guaranteed bandwidth and constant low end-to-end delay, without any error detection capabilities; this service would provide a stream-mode access to the higher layer, (suitable for voice and image).
- Connection oriented non isochronous, supporting the transfer over a virtual channel of information flows segmented into fixed length cells having no specified inter-arrival time, (suitable for easy interconnection with B-ISDN).

The IEEE 802.6 committee is in charge of MAN standardisation. In that context, the DQDB MAN (Distributed Queued Dual Bus) is a strong candidate that fits the philosophy stated here above; it has now reached its final approbation phase in the 802.6 Working Group and it is expected to be approved by IEEE standards Board in spring 1990. DQDB has a "slot" structure (data structure at the lowest level) very similar to the one of the ATM cells and intended for easy interconnection of DQDB and ATM.

5.3. ATM and the OSI reference model

B-ISDN is being built following network layering principles and a protocol reference model has been introduced and is currently being further elaborated.

Up to now, very little attention and work has been paid to the mapping of the B-ISDN stack onto the OSI one. One major obvious characteristic departing from OSI is that ATM, being connection oriented *with outband signalling*, different vertical subdivisions ("planes") may be needed for the representation of the B-ISDN stack :
- the user plane is used for the actual user information flow
- the control plane is used for the signalling related to the virtual channel establishment and release and it obviously contains routing functions.
- the management plane for Operation and Maintenance is also foreseen (as in OSI).

The ATM layer (bearer service) is commonly viewed as being the physical layer of OSI, since once the virtual channel is set, it can be considered as a point to point connection (a sort of "virtual circuit") with no functionality related to the OSI layers above the physical layer.

Identifying the layer 2 in B-ISDN is a bit more difficult. The features provided in the ATM adaptation layer would correspond to layer two of OSI. Although the adaptation layer itself is subdivided into two sublayers, it is not clear whether (and how) the LLC and MAC layers issued from the LAN environment can directly apply to the B-ISDN environment.

For the interconnection of MANs with the ATM network, it has to be investigated to what extent the network layer is involved, especially when considering the trend to have DQDB slots as compatible as possible to ATM cells.

6. COMMUNICATION SUPPORT FOR DISTRIBUTED SYSTEMS

The OSI RM deals essentially with end-systems and its main goal is **connectivity**. A user in an end-system which interacts with another user in another end-system is aware of the fact that the destination is in another end-system.

In the following, we will use the term Distributed System to designate either a distributed operating system or a distributed service. But, in both cases, the key concept is **transparency.** This means that the user in a distributed system is not aware of the distributed character.

OSI is offering also distributed services but without transparency.

6.1. The Client-Server Model

In the OSI RM, it is basically assumed that two application processes which are communicating are symmetric even if in practice this assumption is sometimes violated. For distributed systems, we will directly use an asymmetric model, the Client-Server Model. In this model, the Client sends a request and the Server sends a reply.

To achieve the full transparency, the Client must ignore that the Server is not colocated to him. Therefore, the communication between Client and Server must not be based on the I/O model but on a Remote Procedure Call (RPC) model (fig.4). In this model, the Client machine will send a message to the Server machine but the Client needs not be aware of it. In practice, the Client Process initiates the action by a procedure call to a Client stub which is a special procedure in the Client machine which will hide to the Client the existence of the network. The Client stub will collect the parameters associated with the procedure call and pack them into a message in an operation known as parameter marshalling. After the message has been constructed, it will be sent to the Server stub using a transfer service.

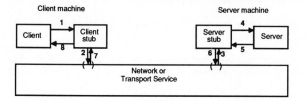

Fig. 4. *Remote Procedure Call in the Client-Server Model*

When the message arrives to the Server, it is passed to the Server stub which unmarshalls the parameters. The Server stub then calls the Server procedure passing the parameters in a standard way. For the Server, this procedure call looks completely local as it obeys all the standard rules.

When the Server has completed its work, it returns the result, if any, to the Server stub which then marshals the result into a message sent back to the Client stub. Finally, the Client stub returns to its caller and any value returned by the Server is passed to the Client.

Many RPC systems are assuming in *the application layer* the existence of a communication sublayer offering, to the client and the server stubs, the basic transfer service involving a communication protocol . Such a protocol introduces some of the functionalities of the session and the transport layer and *access directly the network or data link service without going through the OSI protocol stack*. By so doing, the designers try to minimise end-to-end overheads such as connection management, buffer copying and process scheduling. The REX protocol of ANSA [Herbert, 88] & [ANSA, 89] is a good example of such a trend.

We had already this kind of situation with X.400 where the RTS sublayer was providing the communication service to the MTA but here the RTS was using the service provided by the session and the transport layers(with TP0 on X.25 and TP4 on LAN) but at the cost of functions duplication [Danthine, 88b]

6.2. Binding or not Binding

Coming back to the description of the functioning of the Remote Procedure Call, one may ask how the Client stub knows who it has to call through the transport or the network service ? To solve this problem, Birrell and Nelson [1984] have introduced a scheme involving a specialised kind of data base system (fig.5). When a server is booted, it registers with the data base system by a message containing its name and a unique identifier (random n-bit integer). This registration is done by having the server call a procedure "export" handled by the stub which adds, to the information given by the Server, the NSAP or the TSAP which has to be used to reach the Server through the Server stub.

Later, when a Client makes its first call, its stub has to locate the Server. The Client stub sends the Server name to the data base system which returns the NSAP or the TSAP and the unique identifier. At that point, the **binding** is done.

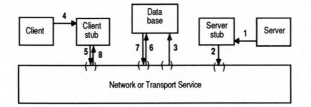

Fig.5. *Client Server Binding via Data Base*

As the unique identifier must be included in each RPC call, a crash of the Server will request a reboot and a new identifier. This means that any attempt to use the old one will fail making the Client stub aware of the crash and forcing to rebind.

In some distributed services such as the Network File System (NFS) of SUN, one tries to avoid any binding by using a stateless protocol. In that case, the parameters of each procedure call contain all the information necessary to complete the call and the server does not keep track of any passed request. This makes the crash recovery very easy. In case of a crash, the Client has to wait until the reboot is done and the Server is again available.

It is clear that the usability of a distributed system is directly related to the performances of the underlying transfer service. This is a reason why, some systems like NFS are based on a connectionless network service rather than on a connection - mode transport service.

6.3. OSI and the Distributed Systems

In the OSI RM, the key concept is connectivity and it is the rule rather than the exception that two end-systems in communication will belong to different administration domains.

Distributed systems are in general heavily managed and therefore not very open. From the previous section, one may get the impression that the only thing that OSI will be able to contribute in the distributed systems area is the connection - mode transport service inside the administration domain. Today, even the connectionless network service has not been considered as a level of service available alone in the profile of functional standard.

To open a distributed system, the first approach is to take the distributed system as a single end-system and to open it by a gateway. In section 3.3, we introduced DSG, a transport level gateway. Such a solution will not be usable with NFS which is not based on a transport service and which will require an application gateway.

Many distributed applications will not require a communication based only on a connection-mode transport service and will consider also the possibility to use a connectionless network service. In MHS, the communication between UAs provided by the MTS is connectionless.

The OSI model, originally developed for providing communication between heterogeneous computer systems, has been enhanced by layer 7 service elements like Transaction Processing, in order to provide interworking between distributed applications. After having added more and more application oriented service elements to layer 7, it became a mess. Several attempts has been made to tidy up layer 7.

OSI conforming systems are not the only communication systems. Almost every computer manufacturer has its own one. Therefore it may not be desirable to base distributed processing support only on OSI. As a consequence organisations like ANSA tried to establish a frame work for distributed processing. ECMA TC32-TG2 deals with open distributed processing. Since 1988, ISO has established the working group ISO/IEC JTC1/SC21/WG7 for **Open**

Distributed Processing (ODP). The aim of this working group is to develop a basic reference model (framework) for building distributed multimedia application.

6.4. Heterogeneous Communication

One obvious characteristic of computer networks is that they link together various kinds of computers : different machines will be purchased from different manufacturers as price/performance ratios evolve; each manufacturer will introduce new designs to keep up with the progress of technology; special purpose machines will be built for specific applications. In short, competition leads to progress through diversity.

Diversity, however, has its cost : applications can no longer communicate by copying fragments of data from their memory to the network, or to files : the structure of the data would be lost, as the binary representation of the same high level construct will vary in different systems. Binary incompatibility derives from three major causes :
- different hardware designs lead to different choices of word length, bit orders or floating point representation;
- different programming languages will use different data representation constructs, e.g. for character strings or variable size arrays;
- different compilers of the same languages may make different choices e.g. for the internal representation of "packed arrays of Boolean" or for the alignment of components to word boundaries within constructs.

Diversity also has its advantages, and freezing research on CPU design, programming languages or compilers is certainly not an option. The networking software has to adapt by providing what the OSI reference model calls a presentation service.

In RPC system, homogeneity may allow to use simple convention but this is not anymore the case with heterogeneous systems which require the full consideration of the presentation mechanism.

Within the ISO framework, the presentation service uses the ASN-1 language, an upward compatible evolution of the CCITT recommendation X.409, which clearly separates data specification, i.e. the definition of an abstract syntax, from data encoding according to a transfer syntax. Although the usage of a particular description language, like ASN-1, has almost no impact on performances, the particularities of the ASN-1 "basic encoding rules" (BER), i.e. the standard transfer syntax, make it very slow to encode and decode : experiments made at INRIA demonstrate that it can be as much as 20 times slower to encode data in ASN-1/BER than to simply copy them : data elements are encoded with a "T-L-V" recursive scheme where "T" represents the type of data field, "L" its length, and "V" the actual data value; almost all fields have a variable-size encoding, with a requirement to use exactly the minimum of bytes necessary to convey the value.

When high speed networks will be available tomorrow, the speed of demanding applications like fast transactions or multimedia conferencing is likely to be limited by the processing power of the end systems. In the presentation layer, every byte of the message will have to be processed. Hence, we can probably not accept the poor performances introduced by the byte oriented T-L-V encodings.

Another problem posed by the actual OSI protocols is the "double copying" which is very often required.

In homogeneous RPC system based on a transfer layer accessing directly the network controller, it may be possible to avoid or reduce the double copying. Furthermore, the retransmission, if needed, may take place from the original data and not from temporary memory.

In heterogeneous RPC or in the general case of heterogeneous computer systems, the data are first encoded by copying them in an encoding buffer in application memory, and are then passed to the transmission control which will copy them again in some transport control buffers; on then other path, they will be copied again from the transport buffers to the application memory, where the decoding will be done. This poor interaction results from the complexity of the protocols, which does not allow to consider them as a simple "filter". It results in particular from the intricate architecture of the OSI upper layers, where the synchronisation functions are accomplished by common application service elements (CASE), above the presentation layer, by using session services realised by the session protocol. The presentation filter would be required to decode some, but not all, of the data, which will be passed at various places of session protocol data units; the session protocol itself being encoded by a protocol similar to ASN-1/BER. In any case, the efficiency of the "filter" approach would be jeopardised by the strong octet per octet structure of the ASN-1/BER

Last but not least, we realise that the high speed presentation functions will be best realised by hardware. This is made difficult by the very structure of the presentation layer, which requires a complete knowledge of the data syntax and of the local representation choices.

7. CONCLUSION

The advent of high speed communication media such as HSLAN, MAN and B-ISDN on one side and the requirement of low response time for distributed applications more and more demanding in terms of graphics and friendly interfaces require a re-examination of the OSI RM and of its protocols in order to keep the promises of the Open Systems without jeopardising the performances.

Two basic trends exist today.

The first one attempts to develop new transport (and network) protocol taking into account the new media and looking at the start at the possibility of implementing it on silicon.

The second one attempts to develop an application communication sublayer accessing directly the network or data link service in order to achieve low response time and high throughput. In doing so, some functionalities of the transport and the session layers are integrated in this sublayer.

If the first attempt succeeds, will the second one be still necessary ?

It is also important to stress that with heterogeneous systems, the coding and decoding of the PDU using for instance ASN.1 compiler is a basic factor in the reduction of the throughput and in the increase of the response time.

To complete this state-of-the-art report, it is essential to stress that the formal description techniques are evolving from an academic environment to the industrial world due to the efforts done to build support tools and to define methodology allowing to proceed from the formal specifications to an implementation. However no OSI protocol have yet been designed using FDT from the very beginning.

All these conclusions indicate that the time has come to revisit the OSI RM, its services and protocols.

8. REFERENCES

[ANSA 89]
   ANSA reference manual, APM Ltd., Poseidon House, Castle Park, Cambridge, UK 1989.
[Birrell, 84]
   BIRRELL A.D., NELSON B.J., **Implementing Remote Procedure Calls,** *ACM on Computer*

Systems, 2 (1), February 1984, pp 39-59

[Cheriton, 86]

CHERITON D., **VMTP : a transport protocol for the next generation of communication systems**, *Proceedings of SIGCOMM 86*, ACM Computer Communication Review, Vol. 16, N° 3, (1986), pp.406-415.

[Chesson, 88]

CHESSON G., **XTP/PE overview**, *13th Conference on Local Computer Networks*, IEEE Computer Society (Oct. 1988), pp.292-296.

[Danthine, 88a]

DANTHINE A.,HAUZEUR B.,HENQUET P.,CONSTANTINIDIS C., FAGNOULE D. & CORNETTE V. **Corporate Communication System by LAN Interconnection**, *Information Technology for Organisational Systems*, EURINFO 88,Athens, H.-J. Bullinger et al. Ed., Elsevier (North Holland), pp 315-326

[Danthine, 88b]

DANTHINE A.,GODELAINE P., **MHS in a Corporate Communication System Offering Internet Service** *Message Handling Systems and Distributed Applications.* Costa Mesa, October 10-12, 1988, Stefferud E., Jacobsen O.J. & Schicker P. Ed., Elsevier (North Holland), pp 305-320

[Danthine, 89]

DANTHINE A. **Communication Support for Distributed Systems - OSI versus Special Protocols** *IFIP Congress' 89 - Information Processing 89* San Francisco Ritter G.X. Ed., Elsevier (North Holland), pp 181-190

[GUS, 87]

Guide to the Use of Standards, Standards Promotion and Application Group (SPAG), North-Holland, 1987

[Herbert, 88]

HERBERT A., **Communications Aspects in ANSA**, *Computer Standards & Interfaces*, 8 (1988), pp 49-56

[ISO, 81]

ISO, **Open System Interconnection - Basic Reference Model** , *ISO IS 7498*, 1981 (see also Computer Networks 5, 1981, pp.81-118)

[Van Jacobsen, 88]

VAN JACOBSON, **Congestion Avoidance and Control,** May 1988, 27 p.

[Watson, 87]

WATSON R.W., **Gaining Efficiency in Transport Services by Appropriate Design and Implementation Choices,** *ACM Trans. Comp. Systems*, Vol. 5, n°2, May 1987, pp. 97-120

[Zimmerman, 80]

ZIMMERMAN H, **The ISO Model of Architecture for Open Systems Interconnection,** *I.E.E.E. Trans. Commun.*, COM-28, 4 (Apr. 1980) pp 425-432

Information Network and Data Communication, III
D. Khakhar and F. Eliassen (Editors)
Elsevier Science Publishers B.V. (North-Holland)
IFIP, 1990

TUTORIAL on SECURITY IN APPLICATION PROTOCOLS

JOHN G ROSS

Director & Principal Consultant
Security & Standards Consultancy Ltd
38 Quilp Drive
Chelmsford
Essex
England CM1 4YA

1. INTRODUCTION

With the widespread dependence on Information Technology in
Commerce, Industry and Government, and the increasing inter-
connectivity that is becoming feasible with the use of open
system standards, the need to take special measures to
preserve the security of information is becoming more and more
pressing. No longer can information systems be considered as
isolated units where the handling of information can be
policed easily. Already, many cases have appeared in the
press of "hackers" abusing information systems and causing
loss of valuable resources through remote access via data
networks. Furthermore, as the need for human intervention
reduces, the potential for abuse going on unchecked becomes
larger and larger.

The requirements for security in different environments will
vary greatly not only in degree but also in the type of
protection needed. For example, many commercial systems are
more concerned with the "integrity" of the information (for
example ensuring that the financial value has not been
changed) rather than the confidentiality or privacy of the
information which is the primary concern of many military
systems. In addition, the placement to security measures to
provide the required protection depends on the areas of
vulnerability to threats. For example, if a particular link
of a network goes over a radio link whilst the rest of the
network is installed in a restricted areas then measures may
need to be directed only at that link. Whereas, when using a
public network end to end security measures may need to be
taken to protect against threats across the whole network.

This paper is a short tutorial on security in application protocols and open distributed systems. It starts with a description of an architecture to meet the differing security requirements and vulnerabilities for Open Systems Interconnection (OSI) [1]. This architecture, which has been recently ratified as an international standard (ISO 7498-2) forming part of the Basic Reference Model for OSI, provides the conceptual basis for the provision of security in an OSI environment. It identifies the differing categories of security services, their placement within the 7 layers of the OSI Reference Model and the measures (security mechanisms) that can be taken to counter vulnerabilities relating to specific layers.

Following on from the description of these general architectural concepts, this paper examines the security vulnerabilities of a specific application of OSI, that is electronic message handling systems. It outlines the security measures included the CCITT 1988 recommendations for Message Handling Systems [2] which counter the identified vulnerabilities. The CCITT standard defines several mechanisms which as a whole are designed to counter all identified vulnerabilities, for a full tutorial reference should be made to X.402 and its annexes. A great deal of the X.400 mechanisms, particularly to provide authentication are based on the X.509 Authentication Framework. For a full tutorial on the authentication methodologies employed in X.509, reference should be made to that standard. It is not the intention of this paper to repeat tutorial information which exists in the above standards, but to add value to the existing tutorial information in the base standard. One mechanism in particular, is examined in more detail: security labelling. This mechanism, although originating from the military need to provide confidentiality in a multi-level secure environment, can equally be applied to provide integrity controls within a single security level for commercial security.

This paper assumes an outline knowledge of the OSI Reference Model and the structure of X.400 Messaging systems. One of the objectives of this paper is to highlight the importance of detailing a security policy, so that any security measures are directed to meet the protection needs most effectively and efficiently. The OSI security architecture provides a useful basis for describing these needs, and through examination of the X.400 recommendations for security an example of how this can be achieved for Message Handling Systems is given.

2. BASIC SECURITY CONCEPTS

Before examining the security of OSI, X.400 and X.509 it is useful to place this within a more general context. There are aspects of security which are outside the concern of the IT system itself.

These include physical security measures, such as physical control of access to computing facilities, personnel security including vetting of key staff, procedural security and documentation. Although they do not directly impact on the communications or the operation of IT systems, these measures need to be considered alongside measures within OSI and X.400 protocols in providing information security.

Within IT systems security issues are specifically concerned with Electronic Information Security (EIS) which overlap wholly or partly with OSI, X.400 and X.509 security. These security issues are specifically in the areas of communications (sometimes called COMSEC) and computing (sometimes called COMPUSEC). COMSEC is specifically concerned with vulnerabilities within the communications and provides protection against data as it passes through communication links and equipment. Link encryption is a measure that is commonly associated with COMSEC. COMPUSEC is specifically concerned with countering vulnerabilities within the computer systems themselves. Use of access vulnerabilities within the computer systems themselves. Use of access control lists and passwords are some of the measures commonly used in COMPUSEC.

OSI and X.400 security, although they are commonly associated with communications, cover both COMSEC and COMPUSEC issues. These protocols, in particular those concerned with X.400, X.500 and the higher levels of OSI, are not only concerned with communications but result in the manipulation of information within the computer systems. Thus not only does the communication of information need to be protected, but also information, which can be remotely operated on via communication protocols, needs to be protected within the end computer systems.

3. OSI SECURITY ARCHITECTURE

If security measures are to be effective they must be directed at the particular security concerns and vulnerabilities of the IT environment. There is no point in protecting the confidentiality of information where the main concern is that the information has no been falsified. Also, for example, where a particular link is vulnerable to external threats security measures need only be directed at protecting that part of the network.

3.1. Basic Areas of Concern

The OSI Security Architecture [1] provides the basis for describing the different security concerns and placing those concerns within the OSI 7 layer Reference Model to provide protection against different areas o vulnerability. The OSI Security Architecture identifies five basic areas of security concern:

Confidentiality: information is not made available to unauthorised individuals, also commonly called privacy.

Integrity: information has not been altered or destroyed in an unauthorised manner.

Authentication: corroboration that an identity associated with information is as claimed.

Access Control: the prevention of unauthorised use of a resource (eg a data item or computing resource).

Non-repudiation: prevention of denial that a party has participated in an exchange of information.

3.2. Refinement into Security Services

The details of the security provisions depend on the form of the communication service being provided. In particular, different forms of protection can be provided on a stream of data passing through a connection, to individual data packets sent via a connectionless communication service. Therefore in application to OSI, the OSI Security Architecture refines these "areas" into a number of Security Services which relate to different aspect of the OSI communication service.

3.2.1 Confidentiality and Integrity Security Services

The Confidentiality and Integrity Security Services are refined in terms of the scope of transmission covered by such protection: a whole connection, a connectionless data unit or selective field. In addition, the Connection Integrity service is further refined into with and without recovery. A further confidentiality service, Traffic Flow Confidentiality, protects against inference of information from observation of traffic flows.

TABLE – OSI SECURITY SERVICES

	LAYER						
	1	2	3	4	5	6	7
Authentication							
Peer			Y	Y			Y
Data Origin			Y	Y			Y
Access Control			Y	Y			Y
Confidentiality							
Connection	Y	Y	Y	Y		Y	Y
Connectionless		Y	Y	Y		Y	Y
Selective Field						Y	Y
Traffic Flow	Y		Y				Y
Integrity							
Connection with Recovery				Y			Y
Connection without recovery			Y	Y			Y
Connection Selective Field							Y
Connectionless			Y	Y			Y
Connectionless Selective Field							Y
Non Repudiation							
Origin							Y
Delivery							Y

3.2.2. Authentication Security Services

Two forms of Authentication Security Services are defined. One, Data Origin Authentication, identifies the origin of a particular data item or individual data packet. The other, Peer Entity Authentication, identifies the two ends of a connection to each other.

3.2.3. Access Control Security Service

There is no refinement of the Access Control Security Service.

3.2.4. Non-Repudiation Security Services

Two forms of Non-repudiation are given. One gives proof of origin of a particular item of data, the other proof of delivery.

3.3 Protection Against Vulnerabilities within the 7 Layer Model

The OSI Security Architecture identifies to which layers of the OSI Reference Model these Security Services may be applied (see table). On first examination this may seem to be over complex. However, this can be broken down into protection against vulnerabilities in 3 basic areas of vulnerability:

vulnerabilities on an individual link

vulnerabilities to end to end communications

COMSEC and COMPUSEC vulnerabilities on application specific data

Depending on the communications environment (point to point/ broadcast, connection/connectionless) these different vulnerabilities may be protected at different levels in seven layers of the OSI reference model.

3.3.1. Vulnerabilities on an Individual Link

The main concern considered of to relate specifically to an individual link is confidentiality. That is confidentiality both against direct observation of data as well as indirect observation of traffic flows. In the case of point to point links this is provided at the physical layer. However, for broadcast networks, where addressing and media access information needs to be sent in clear form, this may be provided at the link layer.

3.3.2. Vulnerabilities to End to End Communications

This covers all areas of security, except non-repudiation providing protection against threats such as masquerading and modification of data, as well as protection against observation of data in transfer. Not only are individual links to be protected but also threats in intermediate packet switches and relay systems are countered.

The security services providing end to end protection may be provided either in the network layer or within the transport layer. It is considered that for profiles with connection based communications at the network layer, the security services are best provided at the network layer; for profiles with connectionless at the network layer and connection based communication at the transport layer, these security services could be provided in the transport layer.

Where a sub-network, which interconnects other sub-networks to form an internet, is particularly vulnerable to attack (eg if using a public wide area network to interconnect private LANs), rather than using end to end protection services between the end systems the security services might be applied just across the individual sub-network. In this case it is likely that the same network layer security services would be used as for full end to end protection.

3.3.3 Vulnerabilities on Application Specific Data

This covers both COMSEC type security of data in transfer (primarily Confidentiality and Integrity), as well as the basis for COMPUSEC protection on data and resources within a system (primarily Authentication and Access Control). The functionality for the Confidentiality and Integrity Services applies to data in transfer is divided between the Presentation layer, but the control of functions (eg selection of keys) is left to the Application layer. Further protocols, either specific to an application or within a application or within a application service element common to a number of application protocols, are provided in the application layer for Authentication and Access Control.

3.4. Vulnerabilities Outside of Peer to Peer OSI Communications

The OSI Security Architecture concentrates on security services providing protection related to direct peer to peer communications. However, where more than two parties are involved in exchanging information further protection facilities may be required to protect against vulnerabilities on data passing through third parties without depending on the internal security of that third party.

Consider, for example, a third party file store which two other parties use for sharing information but do not wish to trust to maintain the confidentiality and integrity of the information through internal COMPUSEC access control mechanisms. This can be achieved through use of cryptographic mechanisms to transform the data before transfer to the file store using keys unknown to the untrussed file store. However, since the OSI Confidentiality Integrity Services only apply to data in transfer, if such protection is required further security measures are needed outside the OSI security services (ie within the OSI application).

This vulnerability may occur in other application systems where data is transferred via third parties. Another prime example of this is message handling. This paper now goes on to describe the provision of such security within the CCITT X.400 Recommendations for Message Handling Systems.

4. X.400 SECURITY

INTRODUCTION

In 1988 CCITT revised its X.400 Recommendations for Message Handling Systems [2]. This 1988 version of X.400 was also published by ISO as an international standard for Message Oriented Text Interchange Systems (MOTIS). The revision of X.400 included the definition of security services and mechanisms to protect against the specific vulnerabilities of message handling systems following the X.400 Recommendations. As described previously, the OSI Security Services protects data on interactions between two peer communication systems. However, alternative protective measure are required where intermediate message handling systems are considered vulnerable.

The 1988 X.400 goes much further than the OSI Security Architecture. It defines not only Security Services appropriate to the message handling services defined in X.400 but also includes protocol elements especially for security and defines some specific mechanisms for security appropriate to the multi-domain environment that X.400 supports.

4.1. Vulnerabilities

The X.400 Recommendations identifies some of specific threats against which message handling could be vulnerable unless specific measures are taken; the threats include:

Masquerading: an entity successfully pretending to be a different entity

Message replay: a message is repeated or replayed out of its proper context

Modification: information lost or modified without detection

Denial of service: the entity fails to perform its function, or prevents other entities from performing their function

Repudiation: the denial of submitting, receiving, or originating a message

Leakage of information: the acquisition of information by an unauthorised party

Traffic analysis: the deduction of information from the size, route or rate of messages.

4.2. X.400 Security Model

In a similar way to the OSI Security Architecture Security Services, the general security concerns of Confidentiality, Integrity, Authentication, Access Control and Non-repudiation may be related to the particular features of Message Handling Systems to provide a number of security services for X.400. These services are specified in the form of an abstract model. This security model, like the OSI security architecture, provides a framework for describing the security services that counter the potential vulnerabilities of MHS. Depending on the perceived threats, certain of the MHS security services can be selected to counter the MHS's vulnerability to the threat. These security services are supported through the use of service elements of the Message Transfer Service message envelope.

The X.400 (88) security services are capable of supporting a wide range of security policies. The X.400 (88) security services selected as part of EIS measures necessary in order to fulfil a security policy will depend on individual applications and the levels of trust placed in parts of the system. An X.400 component of the security policy therefore must define how the risks to and exposure of assets can be reduced to an acceptable level.

The X.400 security services are as described below. It should be noted that they are grouped in a way slightly different

from that given in the X.400 Recommendations to aid comparison
with the OSI Security Architecture.

4.3. X.400 Authentication Security Services

X.400 refers to three forms of authentication, Origin
Authentication, Peer Entity Authentication and Proof of
Delivery/Submission. The first two have close counterparts in
the OSI security architecture.

The first security service, Origin Authentication, is
equivalent to the OSI Data Origin Authentication service but,
but unlike the OSI equivalent applies across multiple
messaging system outside the peer level communications. It
provides corroboration of the originator of data not only to
the final recipient (or recipients), but also to intermediate
messaging systems which handle the message in transfer. Three
different forms of origin security service are identified
relating to three different forms of "messaging data": the
message (ie messages which contains user data), the probe and
report (both of which contain information about the operation
of messaging).

The next security service, Peer Entity Authentication, is the
same service as provided in the OSI application layer.

The Proof of Submission Security Service provides the
originator with a means of corroborating that a message has
been submitted a messaging system which has taken on
responsibility for transfer. The Proof of Delivery Security
Service provides the originator with corroboration that a
message has been delivered from the viewpoint of the message
transfer service. It should be noted that the Proof of
Delivery does not necessarily imply that the final recipient
has received and accepted the message. Thus this service is
different from Non-repudiation.

Simple authentication based on passwords is provided on some
of the authentication services but the major authentication
mechanisms in X.400 are based on asymmetric encryption
techniques, with certificates which may be used to convey a
verified copy of the public-asymmetric-encryption-key of the
subject of the certificate. Tokens are used to exchange
security other related information (such as time-stamp). The
token itself being protected by encryption and digital
signature techniques. The techniques are specified in detail
in CCITT Recommendation X.411. In general these techniques,
are based on the X.509 authentication framework called strong
authentication.

4.4. X.509 Authentication Framework

Strong authentication in X.509 is based on public key crypto systems (PKCS). A prerequisite of the PKCS in X.509 is that the encipherment/decipherment must have mutual properties. That means that both keys in the key pair can be used for encipherment. If the secret key is used for encipherment then the public key is used for decipherment and vice versa. Encipherment using the secret key provides what is commonly known as a "digital signature", as only the user in possession of the secret key could have encrypted the information.

If the public key is used for encipherment and the secret key used for decipherment. This method provides confidentiality, as only the recipient user has the key to decipher the information. The foundation on which X.509 authentication is based is that the secret key is always kept SECRET, and the public key is available to any one participating in strong authentication. Users public keys are protected by means of a certificate. Certificates are generated, and protected by certification authorities.

Copies of certificates can be distributed to users via the X.500 Directory Information Base.

4.5. X.509 Security Token

The X.509 Authentication Framework relays of the exchange of security tokens for strong authentication. A security token is a collection of security and identity information which can be both signed (by the digital signature mechanism) and encrypted. Tokens are exchanged at the time authentication, which can be one-way, two-way or three-way.

One-way authentication involves the transfer of a security token from the originator to the recipient. It only verifies the originator.

Two-way authentication involves the exchange of security token between the originator and recipient. It verifies both the originator and recipient.

Both one-way and two-way authentication rely on the use of random numbers and time-stamps being included in the security data.

Three-way authentication is an extension to two-way authentication where the time-sharp may be zero, on the random number for uniqueness. However, this method has several known differences.

In most cases X.500 relies on two-way authentication for peer-entity authentication between MHS objects. One-way authentication is used for message, probe and report origin authentication, because X.400 is generically a connectionless application. In X.400 authentication of originator and recipient is provided separately. In the first case one-way authentication of messages and in the second case one-way authentication of reports or rely messages.

X.509 (88) is an authentication mechanism based exclusively on asymmetric techniques, where as X.400 security token can be symmetric or asymmetric.

The use of symmetric encryption techniques for authentication purposes is for further study, this is primarily because the existing X.509 authentication framework relies on one algorithm CCITT are committed to study other asymmetric and symmetric encryption techniques as authentication mechanisms for future versions of the standard.

4.6. X.400 Access Control Security Services

This is provided by two "layers" of service. Both of these services are related to a specific access control technique: security labelling, and security context. The first service, the Message Security Labelling Security Service, involves labelling individual messages with a security classification and restricting the flow of messages based on this classification. The second service, the Security Context Security Service, involves establishing a set of classifications between communicating peers. Messages may only flow between communicating peers if the classification given in it's security label is within the security context of the association between the peers.

4.7. X.400 Confidentiality Services

Three Confidentiality services are described in X.400. Firstly, a Connection Confidentiality service, which protects all communications between peers and is the direct equivalent of the OSI security service. Connection Confidentiality is provided by invoking this underlying OSI security service. Next Content Confidentiality provides for confidentiality of the message content to the originator and designated recipients. Finally, the Message Flow Confidentiality service provides a form of Traffic Flow Confidentiality. Only a limited form of this security service is provided by X.400.

The Content Confidentiality service uses encipherment to separate the information in the message by making it unintelligible to a third party. Several encipherment methods can be used including symmetric and asymmetric algorithms. Using content confidentiality the service is end to end between the originator and recipient. The message content is unintelligible to intermediate messaging systems. A secret key used for decipherment may be carried within a "sealed token" which can only be opened by the final recipient. This token may also be used to convey other security relevant information between the originator and recipient such as a security classification for use outside the message handling environment, and encipherment keys.

4.8. X.400 Integrity Services

A Connection Integrity Security Service protects all messages passing between peers and is provided via the underlying OSI service as in the case of Confidentiality. Content Integrity provides for the integrity of an individual message. The Message Sequence Integrity protects a sequence of messages against re-ordering or replay.

The primary integrity service of X.400 (88), is content integrity. This provides assurance that either the message contents have not been changed by third party, or if alterations have been made, the recipient is aware that it has taken place, and can therefore take appropriate action.

The service uses check-sums generated using a cryptographic algorithm. The content integrity service operates end to end between User Agents. The content integrity security element is used to compute a content integrity check as a function of the entire message content. Depending on the method used to compute the content integrity check, a secret key may be required, which may be confidentially sent to the message recipient using the message argument confidentiality security element in the message token (ie the "sealed token" described above).

4.9. X.400 Non-Repudiation Services

Three non-repudiation services are provided: Origin, Submission and Delivery. Unlike the Proof of Origin and Submission services the proof cannot be revoked, the non-repudiation services do not demand/require any additional mechanisms to be implemented. They use existing authentication mechanisms, such as: Content Integrity, Proof of Delivery and Proof of Submission. These mechanisms become non-repudiation when a third party is involved, such as the generation of certificates by a CA or a trusted notarization service.

5. SECURITY LABELLING

APPLICATION

Security Labelling, the binding of a security classification to a data or processing object, is a technique which has its origins in the military world for the provision of multi-level separation of sensitive information. The US Department of Defence Trusted Computer System Evaluation Criteria [4] includes the provision of such separation as one of the basic requirements of its more secure systems (B1 and above). Multi-level security is primarily concerned with providing vertical separation of information for confidentiality between different levels of clearance.

As described in [5] commercial systems are more concerned with the horizontal separation of roles which may perform different operations on the same information, thereby providing integrity. Rather than restricting flow of information between strongly bound compartments commercial systems are mor e concerned with ensuring that information relating to sensitive operations (eg financial transactions) only come via the path "designated" to carry such messages. Thus in commercial systems messages are mor likely to labelled relating to its role rather than a clearance level. In this case there would not be a clear separation or hierarchy between different roles.

5.1. X.400 Security Labelling

In X.400(88) security labels are assigned to every entity of the message handling system, such as MTA'S (Message Transfer Agent) MS's (Message Store) and UA's (User Agent). Labels are also assigned to every submit, transfer and delivery data unit, such as messages, probes and reports.

All X.400 entities are assigned a set of security labels, which are registered via the administration ports. This registration of each connected entity is primarily used to define the classifications or clearance levels of the entity. Before entities can submit, transfer or deliver, the entities are required to form a bind. During binding the security clearance levels of the entities are checked against the levels of transfer which are expected to take place under the bind. This sets up a security context for the period of the bind, which in effect establishes the range of security labels which can be submitted, delivered or transferred using that bind.

5.2. Labelling Entities

The security classifications of entities are established by the Register function of the Message Transfer Services (MTS)and the MS-Register function of the Message Store (MS).

The ability to set up security contexts which relate to the security labels of message, probes, and reports, has several benefits. Firstly security context can be used to effect route control. An MTA may be connected to several MTA's for the purpose of message relay, each MTA interconnection may establish varying levels of security context. It would therefore be possible for a trusted MTA to route a "secret" message to another MTA for which "secret" security context had been established, but it would not route the message if only an unclassified security context existed.

Security contexts are also very useful to control delivery or retrieval ports. For example, assume the scenario of a remote user with a UA implemented on a personal computer. The user would expect to be able to retrieve messages via a message store from any PC with the UA capability. However the user may not want all his personal and private information to be mode available in a public environment, restricting access to his personal data to his private office. The security context which would be established between the UA and the MS would in the above case be dependent on the physical location of the terminal acting as the User Agent.

5.3. Labelling information

In X.400 (88) secure messaging all information, such as messages, probes and reports may be associated with a security label. This label is used to specify the classification of the message. Trusted MTA, MS and UA will enforce logical separation in accordance with the classification in the security label. During submission, transfer, delivery or retrieval it is important that the label is not changed by a third party. The integrity of the label is therefore important. It is also important that a label is correctly associated with the message, probe or report for which it pertains. This is sometimes called label binding. In X.400 (1988) both the integrity protection and the binding of the label to the message is achieved via the message token. The message token can be protected by the integrity and confidentiality mechanisms. The X.400 (88) message token is protected end to end (User Agent to User Agent), and therefore not visible or usable by the message transfer service (MTS).

If the MTS requires a label binding facility, this can be

provided by the X.400 (88) service, Message Origin Authentication check. This security service uses asymmetric encryption techniques where the public key is held by all the MTS's along the route.

6. CONCLUSIONS

The OSI Security Architecture, together with the X.400 and X.509 security facilities, provide a flexible basis for meeting the specific security requirements for a very wide range of environments. Firstly, by clearly separating out the different security concerns such as integrity and confidentiality and applying them to specific communication services the security measures are directly targeted. Thus the overheads for the provision of security are minimised. Secondly, the security services can be directed at the specific area of vulnerability.

In general terms the higher the layer, either OSI or X.400/X.509 the more specific a security service is to particular application data but more points of vulnerability are covered. Looking at the one extreme, Physical Layer security only protects a single link, by covers all data passing through that link. At the other end X.400 content Confidentiality and Integrity Security Services, only protects the message contents but covers vulnerabilities in all the message handling systems and links between them which handled that specific message.

It is only by fully analyzing the security requirements of any communication system and identifying the particular areas of vulnerability to threats, within the context of a general security policy, can the appropriate security service be identified. By defining an EIS (COMSEC and COMPUSEC) security policy in terms of abstract security services, independent of the mechanism to be used, the systems provider is given greater flexibility to choose the most appropriate mechanism with out effecting the basic policy.

Work is in progress to define standard protocols and mechanism for security in the OSI environment, called "Security Frameworks". These should be agreed over the next few years. As described briefly in this paper, the protocols and mechanisms for X.400 and X.509 have already been defined. X.400 and X.500 introduces a number of approaches to security many of which are likely to be adopted within OSI. In particular, the technique of security labelling provides a useful basis for security that may have wider applicability than at present.

It is considered that by adopting the security standards that have already emerged and will emerge over the next few years, very effective protection can be provided to communication systems. Provided that care is taken in selecting the appropriate security services this protection can be provided with the minimal overhead. **However, this paper highlights that this can only be achieved by proper analysis of security concerns and vulnerabilities, as part of a full risk analysis, to form the basis of a comprehensive security policy covering all facets of security.**

REFERENCES

[1]   Information Processing Systems-Open Systems Interconnection-Basic Reference Model Part 2-Security Architecture ISO 7498-2 1988

[2]   Recommendations for Message Handling: CCITT X.400(1988)
    or
        Message Oriented Text Interchange Systems (MOTIS): ISO 10021

[3]   Recommendations for Directory Authentication Framework: CCITT X.509 (1988)

[4]   Department of Defence Trusted Computer System Evaluation Criteria DOD-5200.28-STD

[5]   "A comparison of Commercial and Military Computer Security Policies" Clark& Wilson, IEEE Symposium on Security and Privacy 1987

[6]   "Security in X.400 Messaging" J Ross & R Cocks, Online Conference on Message Handling Systems, October 1986

[7]   "Security standards for OSI and X.400 "Nick Pope & John Ross, Corporate Computer Security Conference, February 1989

Information Network and Data Communication, III
D. Khakhar and F. Eliassen (Editors)
Elsevier Science Publishers B.V. (North-Holland)
IFIP, 1990

TUTORIAL on X.500 - THE DIRECTORY

David W Chadwick

**IT Institute
University of Salford
Salford M5 4WT
England**

1   THE MODEL OF THE DIRECTORY

The Directory is a collection of one or more open systems, whose
application entities are called Directory System Agents (DSAs). These
DSAs cooperate to hold information about a set of objects of interest to
users of the Directory. The users of the Directory, either people or
computer programs, can access this information via a Directory User Agent
(DUA), which is also an application entity (see Figure 1.)

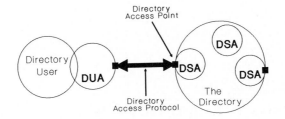
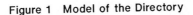

Figure 1   Model of the Directory

If all the Directory information - from the perspective of the users - is
stored in a single DSA, that DSA is said to be **stand-alone**.   If the
Directory comprises more than one DSA, the Directory is said to be
distributed.   In the main, a DUA is shielded from knowing the structure
of the Directory, and need only know a single **Access Point** into the
Directory.

An Access Point is defined as the name and address of a DSA.   In ISO-ese,
this is the Application Entity Title and Presentation Address of a DSA.

A DSA may offer zero, one or more Access Points into the Directory.   A
DUA and DSA may be in the same or different open systems.   If in
different open systems, they communicate using the Directory Access
Protocol (DAP).

----

2   THE INFORMATION MODEL

2.1 Objects, Entries and Attributes

The complete set of information held by the Directory, which is
accessible via the services provided by the Directory, is called the
Directory Information Base (DIB).   The DIB holds information about
objects which are of interest to users of the directory.   These objects
might typically be associated with information processing systems or
telecommunications.   The directory objects may not have a one to one
correspondence with real world things, but can have a many to one or one
to many relationship.   For example, a directory object may be a mailing
list containing the names of many real people, or alternatively a real
person may be present in the Directory as both an organisational person
object and a residential person object.

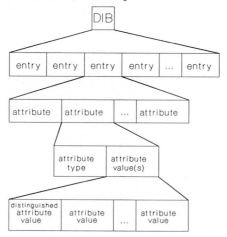

Figure 2   The Information Model

Each (directory) object is distinguished from all other objects in the
Directory by its **name**.   The information about each named object is held
in the DIB as a single **entry** (see Figure 2).   Each entry consists of a
set of **attributes**.   An attribute describes a particular characteristic
of the object.   Examples of attributes might be: for a person (object),
his telephone number (attribute); for an application entity (object), its
presentation address (attribute).

Each entry has one special attribute, called its object class, which
indicates what type of object it is.   This is part of the Directory
schema (see section 2.5).   Part 7 of the Directory Standard [1]
standardises several object classes which have general applicability
(examples here include: Application Entity, Person, DSA, and Country).

An attribute is comprised of an **attribute type** and a series of one or
more **attribute values**.   Part 6 of the Standard defines several attribute

types of general applicability. e.g. Presentation address, country name and telephone number. Each entry has part of its name (its Relative Distinguished Name - see section 2.2) stored as one or more attributes, and the values of these are termed **distinguished values**.

2.2 **Names and the DIT**

As stated above, each object known to the Directory is distinguished from all other objects by its name. Thus each object, or entry, is said to have a **Distinguished Name**. The names of entries held in the DIB are built up in a hierarchical manner, using a tree structure. Thus each entry takes the name of its parent (or superior), and has appended to it a **relative distinguished name** to uniquely identify it from all of its peers. The DIB can therefore be represented as a Directory Information Tree (DIT), in which each node represents a directory entry, and each arc a relative distinguished name (RDN), see figure 3. A RDN is syntactically a set of attributes types and values and this information is held in the entry along with all the other attributes.

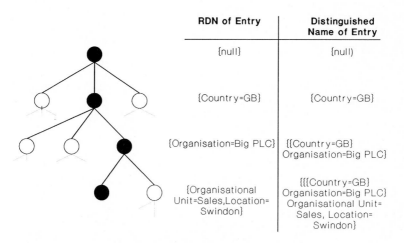

	RDN of Entry	Distinguished Name of Entry
	{null}	{null)
	{Country=GB}	{Country=GB}
	{Organisation=Big PLC}	{{Country=GB} Organisation=Big PLC}
	{Organisational Unit=Sales,Location= Swindon}	{{{Country=GB} Organisation=Big PLC} Organisational Unit= Sales, Location= Swindon}

Figure 3   A Hypothetical DIT, showing the relationship of RDN's to Distinguished Names

The only entry allowed to have a null distinguished name and RDN is the root entry, but this entry is only for convenience and does not represent a real directory object. Entries which do not have subordinate entries are termed **leaf entries**, entries which do have, are termed **non-leaf entries**.

2.3 Aliases

An object may be known by more than one name, depending upon its role or
referenced context, for example, the author could be known by his name as
an employee of Salford University (i.e. Country = GB, Organisation =
Salford University, Organisational Unit = IT Institute, Personal Name =
David Chadwick), or by his role within BSI (i.e. Country = GB,
Organisation = BSI, Organisational Unit = IST21/Panel4, Directories
Rapporteur = David Chadwick). To allow for this, the concept of aliases
has been introduced into the Directory model of names. Each directory
object only has one distinguished name, and therefore one entry in the
DIB, but it may have one or more alternate alias names. Each alias name
has a corresponding alias entry, which contains a pointer to the object
entry, as shown in figure 4 below. (The pointer is actually the
distinguished name of the object entry which it points to.) Alias
entries have a special object class of 'alias', to distinguish them from
object entries. All alias entries are leaf entries in the DIT.

In figure 4, there is a directory entry for the R&D organisational unit
of organisation PLC in the United States. The name of the R&D
organisational unit of PLC in the UK is an alias name for the US entry
(ie the alias entry contains the pointer (C=US, O=PLCinc, OU=R&D)). All
information pertaining to the R&D unit is held in the US entry. Anyone
referencing the alias name in the UK will be automatically re-routed to
the US entry by the Directory, through a process termed **alias
dereferencing** (see section 5.1.1).

An alias may not point to another alias. However, if an alias points to a
non-leaf object in the DIT, this object may have an alias subordinate.
It is thus possible that the Directory may need to dereference more than
one alias whilst navigating to the final object entry.

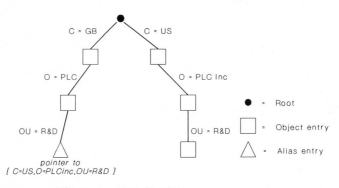

Figure 4   Alias Entries

2.4 Purported Names and Name Resolution

A directory user will generally give a purported name as input to a
directory service. A purported name is syntactically a name (i.e. a
sequence of RDNs) but it may or may not name an actual entry in the DIT.
Name Resolution is a procedure carried out by the Directory, which
determines if the name is valid, i.e. it unambiguously identifies a
single entry in the DIT. Logically, name resolution is the process of
sequentially matching each RDN in a purported name to an arc in the DIT,
beginning at the root and working downwards in the DIT. If an alias is
encountered, this is dereferenced and name resolution recommences again
from the root, with the name pointed to in the alias entry. A complete
description of alias dereferencing and name resolution in the distributed
directory is described later in section 5.1.

2.5 Directory Schema

The Directory schema specifies a set rules which govern : the syntax
that attribute values may have, the number of values that an attribute
type may have, the attributes that an object may have, and the structure
of the DIT - including the allowable RDNs of entries (see Figure 5). The
standard defines what an attribute syntax and an attribute type are
comprised of and Part 6 standardises various attribute types and syntaxes
that have general applicability. The standard also defines what an
object class is comprised of, and Part 7 standardises various useful
object classes. However, the standard does not currently define
precisely what a DIT structure rule is, nor does it define any useful DIT
structures of general applicability. Instead, it is left up to a local
implementation or administrator to determine the structure of the portion
of the DIT that a given DSA will hold, and annex B of Part 7 merely
suggests recommended DIT structures and name forms.

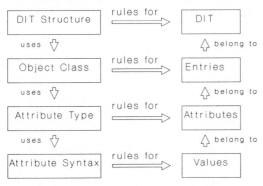

Figure 5 The Directory Schema

3 THE DIRECTORY SERVICES

The Directory Services are provided by using the Remote Operations
Service defined in X.219/ISO 9072. This provides a request-response type
service between two parties that have formed an association via a BIND
operation. The procedures for distributed operation in Part 4 of the
Directory (X.518) describe how the directory services may be realised to
the directory user through arbitrarily many participating DSAs, each
bound together with a ROS association (see sections 4 and 5).

Directory operations either succeed or fail. If they succeed, a result
is returned, which may contain further information. If they fail, an
error diagnostic is returned. Part 3 of the Directory (X.511) details the
services, the results and the error diagnostics.

3.1 The Read Operation

The Read Operation is used to read information about an object from its
directory entry. The input arguments are a purported name and an
indication of which entry information is to be read. The latter argument
enables the enquirer to specify whether all the information is to be
read, or just a subset of the attribute types and values.

The result of the operation yields the distinguished name of the entry,
plus the requested attribute types and values.

3.2 The Compare Operation

The Compare Operation is used to compare the purported value of an
attribute with those actually existing in the entry. The input arguments
are a purported name, and an attribute value assertion. The operation
result returns the distinguished name of the entry (only if one or more
aliases were dereferenced) and a TRUE or FALSE indication, signifying if
the attribute value is actually present or not in the entry.

3.3 The List Operation

The List Operation is used to list the immediate subordinates of an
entry. The input argument is a purported name. The result of the
operation carries the distinguished name of the entry (only if one or
more aliases were dereferenced), plus the relative distinguished names of
the subordinates. Under certain circumstances (see section 5.2.1), the
list may be incomplete. This occurs when the subordinates of an entry
exist in one or more different DSAs from that of the entry, and the
parent DSA is unable or unwilling to chain the request onwards. In this
case, referrals (Access Points) to the other DSA's will be returned
instead of the names of the subordinates.

3.4 The Search Operation

The Search Operation is used to search portions of the DIT, and to
return selected information about selected entries. It is potentially a
very powerful operation. The input arguments identify: the base entry
from which the search is to start, the portion of DIT to be searched, the

criteria (filter) for selecting entries, whether aliases are to be searched, and what information should be returned from the selected entries.

The base entry argument is a purported name. The portion of DIT to be searched may be one of: base entry only, immediate subordinates of the base entry only, and base entry plus its entire subtree.

The filter applies certain tests to an entry to determine if it is selected or not. The tests are applied to attributes within the entry, and test for such things as: if an attribute type is present, or if an attribute value lies within a given range. The aliases argument dictates whether or not aliases, which are subordinate to the base entry, should be dereferenced and the search continued from those entries.

Finally, how much entry information should be returned is specified. This can be all the information, or just a specified subset of attribute types and values.

The result returns the distinguished name of the base entry (only if one of more aliases were dereferenced in reaching it), plus the distinguished name of every selected entry along with the requested entry information.

3.5 The Abandon Operation

The Abandon Operation allows the user to abandon any of the above operations, if he is no longer interested in obtaining the result. The abandon operation has just one argument, which identifies the operation to be abandoned. The abandon operation is not guaranteed to always work, and the Directory may refuse (fail) the abandon request. As an analogy, consider throwing a stone into the middle of a pond, from which waves ripple outwards. The stone represents the initial operation, and the ripples represent chained operations. Throwing in a second stone, representing the abandon operation, will not cause the original ripples to be stilled. Similarly, the Directory (a DSA) may not wish, or be able, to abandon an operation which has already been chained to other DSA's.

3.6 The Modify Operations

These operations may modify entries within the DIT. However, the operations have, as currently defined, certain limitations, some of which are the subject of extension work. The limitations are as follows: it is not possible to abandon these operations once they have been started; the operation argument must contain the distinguished name of the entry to be modified, and must not contain embedded aliases; and the named entry must reside in the same DSA as its superior, (except for Modify Entry).

Successful modify operations do not return any entry information.

3.6.1 The Add Entry Operation

This operation allows a leaf entry to be added to the DIT, although some restrictions are currently imposed on its applicability. The operation argument contains the distinguished name of the entry plus its associated attribute information. The entry to be added may be an object entry or an alias entry.

3.6.1.1 Restrictions to the Add Entry Operation

The current restrictions to Add Entry are imposed when more than one DSA would be affected by the operation. This might be the case when : a parent does not know the names of its children residing in other DSA's (so called non-specific subordinate knowledge references are in use - see section 4.2.3), or the entry is needed to be added to a different DSA from that of its parent. In the former case, the Add Entry cannot be performed without the child DSAs being contacted first, in order to ensure that the new name is not a duplication.

3.6.2 The Remove Entry Operation

This operation allows a leaf entry to be deleted from the Directory, although one restriction currently limits its applicability. The operation argument contains the distinguished name of the entry to be removed. The entry to be removed may be an object entry or an alias entry.

3.6.2.1 Restriction to the Remove Entry Operation

The current restriction to Remove Entry is imposed when more than one DSA would be affected by the operation. This will be the case when the leaf entry is in a different DSA from its parent.

3.6.3 The Modify RDN Operation

This operation is used to change the relative distinguished name of a leaf entry, although some restrictions are imposed on its applicability. The operation arguments are the distinguished name of the entry, the new RDN, and an indication of whether the old RDN attribute values should be deleted from the entry information or not.

3.6.3.1 Restrictions to the Modify RDN Operation

The current restrictions to Modify RDN are imposed when more than one DSA would be affected by the operation. This might be the case when : the parent of an entry is in a different DSA from the entry, or the parent doesn't know the names of its children held in remote DSA's because non-specific subordinate references are in use (it cannot thus modify the name of its local child as it might duplicate a remote name).

3.6.4 The Modify Entry Operation

This operation allows entry information to be modified in the following ways: new attributes or attribute values may be added, and existing

attributes or attribute values may be deleted. Any number of
modifications may be specified in one operation, but all must be allowed,
or none will be made. The operation is thus atomic. It is not allowed
to modify the distinguished attribute values (i.e. the RDN) of the entry
by this operation. An alias entry may be modified by this operation, by
altering the pointer attribute which points to the distinguished name of
an entry.

The operation arguments are the distinguished name of the entry to be
modified, plus the sequence of modifications to be made.

4   THE MODEL OF THE DISTRIBUTED DIRECTORY

A DSA has the responsibility for carrying out a request on behalf of the
DUA which contacts it. The DSA may or may not have the required
information in its local database. If it does not have, the Directory
standard defines three modes of interaction for retrieving the
information.   DSAs communicate with each other using the Directory
System Protocol (DSP), through DSA Access Points (see Figure 6). In the
first mode of interaction, termed **chaining**, the DSA passes, or chains,
the request onto another DSA which it knows is better able to service the
request. The final chain may be of arbitrary length, and depends upon the
location of the desired information, and the willingness of intermediary
DSAs to chain. DSAs are able to chain, because they maintain **knowledge
references** which define the location of parts of the directory
information (see section 4.2).

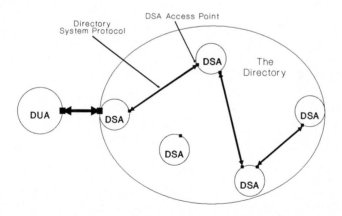

Figure 6   The Distributed Directory, showing Chaining

The second mode of interaction, termed multicasting, is similar to
chaining, but in this case the multi-casting DSA is not sure which DSA,
from a set of possible DSAs, is most likely to have the information.
Therefore, an identical request is sent to all the DSAs in the set.
Multicasting is used when a DSA encounters a non-specific subordinate
reference.

In the final mode of interaction, termed referrals, the DSA does not propagate the request to another DSA, but rather returns the Access Point to the other DSA back to the requestor.   (The requestor may be a DUA or another DSA.)   The requestor may then continue to service the request, by contacting the Access Point directly (see Figure 7).

It is important to realise that each of these modes can occur in any combination e.g. chaining followed by referral followed by multi-casting etc.

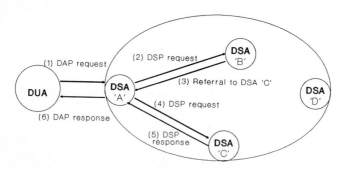

Figure 7 Referral passed back to a DSA and acted upon

4.1 Naming Contexts

When the DIT is distributed between many DSAs, the unit of distribution is termed a **naming context**. A naming context is defined as a subtree of the DIT, which starts at a given vertex and extends downwards to leaf or non-leaf vertices. Subordinate of the non-leaf vertices denote the start of further naming contexts, and are referenced from the original naming context by knowledge references. A naming context comprises:

> . a context prefix (this is the distinguished name of the given vertex)
> . a set of entries, which form a subtree with the given vertex at its root
> . a complete set of knowledge references to the subordinate naming contexts.

There is no limit to how many naming contexts a DSA may hold.

4.2 Types of Knowledge Reference

In general, a knowledge reference comprises of two components:

> . the (relative) name of an entry

.   the Access Point of the DSA holding the entry

The exact form of the (relative) name of an entry, determines the type of the knowledge reference.

The following types of knowledge reference are specified in the Directory Standard:

4.2.1 Superior Reference

This is a knowledge reference which points "upwards" in the DIT to a DSA which holds a naming context whose context prefix has less RDNs than the context prefix with fewest RDNs held by this DSA.

The knowledge reference consists simply of:

.   an Access Point to a DSA

For completeness, it may be thought of as also containing the name of the root of the DIT, which is null. Superior references are mandatory for all but first level DSAs (see section 4.3).

4.2.2 Subordinate Reference

This is a knowledge reference which points "downwards" in the DIT, to a DSA which holds a naming context immediately subordinate to one held by this DSA.

A subordinate reference consists of:

.   the RDN of the immediate subordinate DIT entry
.   the Access Point of the DSA

4.2.3 Non-Specific Subordinate Reference

This knowledge reference also points "downwards" in the DIT, to a DSA which is known to hold one or more subordinate naming contexts, but the specific RDNs of the context prefices are not known.

A non-specific subordinate reference thus consists of:

.   an Access Point to a DSA

For completeness, it may be thought of as also containing a wildcard RDN (meaning 'any').

Every DSA must mandatorily hold a complete set of subordinate or non specific subordinate references to each subordinate naming context.

4.2.4 Cross Reference

This type of knowledge reference points "crossways" in the DIT, and serves to optimise Distributed Name Resolution - by negating the necessity to first proceed up to the root, and then down to the required entry. Cross references are optional, and comprise:

. a context prefix
. the Access Point of the DSA holding the naming context

4.3 First Level DSAs

The Directory Standard recognises that no DSA administration will be prepared to hold the root entry of the DIT, and thus be responsible for participating in distributed name resolution for a significant proportion of all queries worldwide. Simililarly, all other DSA administrations would not be prepared to make international calls to this one root DSA in order to get their queries resolved.

If a root DSA did exist, it would hold the root naming context. From the earlier definition, this can be seen to comprise the root entry plus a complete set of subordinate or non-specific subordinate references to all naming contexts immediately subordinate to the root. Since a root entry will not actually exist, the root naming context will only comprise of knowledge references. Thus, any DSA which holds the root naming context will be capable of acting as the root in Distributed Name Resolution. Such DSAs are termed First Level DSAs, and will usually be DSAs holding naming contexts immediately subordinate to the root (eg DSAs holding country entries).

First level DSAs, during distributed name resolution, will be able to locate the DSA which holds the entry corresponding to the initial RDN of any purported name presented to them, or will be able to diagnose a name error.

5 REALISING THE SERVICE IN A DISTRIBUTED DIRECTORY SYSTEM

In order for an operation to be carried out, there are essentially two phases:

i)   Locate the DSA which holds the entry specified by the purported name.
ii)   Evaluate the specified operation.

i) above is termed Distributed Name Resolution, and ii) above is termed Operation Evaluation.

5.1 Distributed Name Resolution

Arbitrarily many DSAs are typically involved in distributed name resolution. Each DSA that is passed the request (by referrals, chaining or multicasting), can typically only perform a fraction of the name resolution. Thus each subsequent DSA in the processing needs to know how much name resolution was performed by the previous DSA, and also what action is expected of it. This is achieved by including state information in the protocol (both the DSP and DAP), which describes the progress of the operation. The arguement, called Operation Progress, indicates whether distributed name resolution either hasn't started, or is progressing, or has finished. If 'progressing', it also indicates which RDN in the purported name is to be resolved next.

Upon receiving a request, a DSA determines the current progress of the operation and then compares the purported name against the context prefices of the naming contexts that it holds, to see if it has a match. If it has a sufficient match, it will compare the RDNs of entries that it holds with the remaining RDNs in the purported name. This may eventually lead to the whole purported name being matched (success), or to a conclusion that the purported name is wrong, or to a subordinate (or non-specific subordinate) reference being found.

In the event of a reference being found, the operation may be chained (or multicast) to the next DSA, by using the Access Point information contained in the subordinate (or non-specific subordinate) reference. Alternatively, a referral may be returned to the requestor, so that it may continue the processing. A referral contains an Access Point and Operation Progress arguements. In both cases, the Operation Progress argument is suitably updated ready for the next DSA.

If the DSA didn't get a sufficient match with its context prefices, then a non-first level DSA will either forward the request to the DSA in its superior reference, or return an error to the caller, depending upon the value of the operation progress argument. A first level DSA will be able to determine if the name is an error, or if a subordinate of the root has a matching initial RDN. In the later case, the first level DSA will forward the request to the DSA holding the subordinate, or return to the caller a referral to the DSA.

5.1.1 Alias Dereferencing

If, during distributed name resolution, an alias entry is encountered, this will need to be dereferenced. Alias dereferencing is the process of creating a new purported name from the old purported name and the alias pointer. This is accomplished by replacing the alias entry name component at the beginning of the purported name, with the pointer (which itself is a distinguished name) contained in the alias entry. For example, in Figure 4, a purported name of {C=GB,O=PLC, OU=R&D, PN=Jim Smith} would be converted into {C=US, O=PLCinc, OU=R&D, PN=Jim Smith} through alias dereferencing.

5.2 Operation Evaluation

Operations which can be evaluated by the manipulation of just one entry, are relatively straight forward, because only one DSA is involved. Such operations are Read, Compare, and Modify Entry. The DSA will perform the operation and return the result (or an error) to the requestor.

Operations which potentially involve more than one DSA are more complex to evaluate. If operations only read multiple entries, then concurrency control is not a problem, one only needs to consider locating the different entries/DSAs. Such operations are the Search and List operations. If operations potentially involves writing to more than one

DSA, then concurrency and committment control are important if distributed database consistency is to be maintained. Due to their complexity, these features are only just now being standardised as addenda, and therefore some limitations exist in the 1988 versions of the AddEntry, Remove Entry and Modify RDN operations, which ensure that they can be carried out entirely within one DSA. That being the case, these latter operations, from a distributed directory perspective, equate to the single entry operations like Read. The limitations currently applying to the Modify operations are detailed in section 3.6.

5.2.1 **The List Operation**

If the purported name and all its children reside in one DSA, then this also evaluates like a single entry operation. If one or more of the children reside in one or more other DSAs, then sub-requests will need to be passed to the Access Points of all the relevant subordinate and non-specific subordinate references. The Operation Progress argument in the protocol of the sub-requests is set to "completed", to indicate that the purported name has already been found, and that only the children of it are being sought. The sub-requests will return the names of the children, and the original DSA will then collate the returned names with those that it holds, to form the complete result of the operation.

If the DSA is unwilling or unable to chain (or multicast) the request to the subordinate DSAs, the DSA will return a **partial result**, which contains the names of the children that the DSA holds, plus referrals to the subordinate DSAs.

5.2.2 **The Search Operation**

From a distributed directory perspective, this is currently the most complex operation of all to evaluate. It is initially evaluated in the same way as a List operation, but if any alias entries are encountered, these may need to be dereferenced, and the search continued with the subtree rooted on the new purported name.

If a "whole subtree" search is requested, then as each child is identified, a new sub-request is formed, using the childs name as the new purported name. In this way, the purported name is incremented each time a level of the tree is descended. This happens recursively until leaf entries are encountered. A single search operation thus produces a cascade effect, with the original purported name forming the root from which multiple sub-requests fan out to the leaves of DIT, reaching every DSA that holds any of the intermediate entries. As the results ripple back from the leaves, each DSA holding a non-leaf entry needs to collate the incoming results with the set of results that it holds, to form of a new set of results which it relays to its superior DSA. The DSA holding the purported name will eventually receive a set of results which it can collate into the final answer.

Subtree searches can therefore be very time consuming, costly and generate large volumes of data, unless the initial filter is carefully specified.

Any DSA which does not wish to chain (or multicast) sub-requests onto subordinate DSAs, may instead return a partial result, which will contain referrals to the subordinate DSAs.

6 SECURITY IN THE DIRECTORY

Part 8 of the Directory Standard [1], defines how the Directory may be used to provide services for authenticating users. A user may be (some other part of) the Directory itself, or it may be another application, e.g. Message Handling (X.400) or file transfer (FTAM). Two sets of procedures are defined, termed simple and strong authentication, which offer differing degrees of security. These are described more fully in Ross [2].

6.1 The Proposed Draft Addendum on Access Controls

The Access Control addendum to the Information Framework [1] specifies a generally applicable basic access control scheme, but it also has the hooks built in to allow for more sophisticated or private access control schemes to operate in different portions of the DIT.

The access control addendum describes five components of the model:

- the protected items (what is being protected)
- the permissions (against which type of access)
- the user classes (by whom)
- the scope of an access control attribute (definition of Directory Access Control Domains)
- which permissions are required for each of the Directory abstract services

Access control information will be stored as operational attributes within existing Directory entries, and in newly defined sub-entries.

6.1.1 The Protected Items

A protected item can be an entry (or more precisely the RDN of an entry), the attributes within an entry, or specific values of an attribute. It is thus possible to allow a user class to, for example, have modify rights to (the RDN of) an entry, or to be able to read a specific attribute value, or to be able to add any new attribute to an entry.

6.1.2 The Permissions

Five basic permissions are defined: compare, read, add, modify and delete, and these should be self explanatory. When an access control attribute is added to an entry, the permissions are defined as being granted or denied. It is thus possible for example, to explicitly deny modify access to a particular user class, whilst simultaneously explicitly granting read access to the same user class.

Two further permissions are also defined in the PDAD, manage and administer, and these have to do with controlling access to the access control attribute. However, it is currently a matter of debate as to what the final format and semantics of these two permissions will be.

6.1.3 The User Classes

User class is a choice between : the distinguished name of a single user, a group of users (such as a membership list), a subtree of the DIT (such as an organisational unit), this entry (which means the distinguished name of the entry containing this access control attribute), and all users not explicitly named elsewhere in other access control values covering the protected item.

6.1.4 Directory Access Control Domains (DACDs)

The information framework is being extended to allow for subtree entries (or sub-entries) and operational attributes. Subtree entries are entries which describe subtrees of the DIT, and attributes attached to them are to be treated as being logically attached to every entry contained in the subtree definition. Access control domains are one type of sub-entry, and an access control attribute which is placed in this type of sub-entry will be effective for the entire subtree which the sub-entry defines. Thus, for example, an organisational unit DACD sub-entry with a read permission set for a particular group of users will allow all users in the group to read the specified attributes for all DIT entries in the organisational unit.

Operational attributes are a new type of attribute that are used by the Directory in order to perform the defined abstract services. They are not returned when a user performs a 'Read all attributes' operation. Access control attributes are just one example of operational attributes.

Directory access control domains can have two types of access control attribute; either default or absolute. Absolute DACD attributes over-ride access control attributes held within entries that fall within the scope of the domain, whereas default DACD attributes do not, and would only come into effect if absolute DACD and entry access control information were absent.

DACDs can be nested, so that, for example, organisations might set up default or absolute access control attributes, which an organisational unit might supplement with additional grants or denials, before a user finally sets the access control attributes on his or her own entry. In this way superiors can enforce security policies onto their subordinates, which are uninfringeable.

6.1.5 Permissions for Directory Operations

There are two stages in the execution of an operation by the Directory. Firstly, there is distributed name resolution, in which the Directory navigates to the DSA holding the entry, and secondly there is operation evaluation.

In order to perform name resolution, a user needs, as a minimum, compare permissions on each of the RDN terms in the purported name. Without this access, name resolution will fail, because the user has insufficient access rights to determine if the name exists or not.

Once the correct DSA has been found, the user then needs the appropriate permission for operation evaluation to proceed. For example, in order to modify an entry, the user will need add delete and modify permissions on the appropriate (non-naming) attributes, and to read an entry, the user will need read permission on all the attributes. The draft addendum lists all the permissions that are required in order for each abstract service to be correctly performed. If a user does not have permission to read a particular attribute then the Directory will behave, to this user, as if the attribute does not exist.

7   REFERENCES

[1] The Directory Documents	CCITT Number	ISO Number
Overview of Concepts, Models and Services	X.500	9594-1
Models	X.501	9594-2
Abstract Service Definition	X.511	9594-3
Procedures for distributed Operations	X.518	9594-4
Protocol Specifications	X.519	9594-5
Selected Attribute Types	X.520	9594-6
Selected Object Classes	X.521	9594-7
Authentication Framework	X.509	9594-8
Addendum 1 - Access Control		9594-2:1988/PDAD 1

[2] Ross J. Tutorial on Security in Application Protocols and Distributed Systems, this volume.

Information Network and Data Communication, III
D. Khakhar and F. Eliassen (Editors)
Elsevier Science Publishers B.V. (North-Holland)
© IFIP, 1990

COMMERCIAL DEVELOPMENTS TOWARDS OSI MANAGEMENT

Kimberly W. Kappel

Georgia Institute of Technology
School of Information and Computer Science
Atlanta, Georgia 30332

This paper describes commercial network management activities towards providing integrated network management based on OSI management. It relates these efforts to those taking place within the standards groups and the key implementors' groups. The framework and concepts of the OSI management model are outlined to understand their applicability to the commercial efforts. The network management architectures of AT&T, Digital Equipment Corporation, IBM and the OSI/NM Forum are used to analyze the direction of commercial applications working towards the realization of OSI management. Problems with current commercial approaches are considered.

1 INTRODUCTION

One of the most active areas of research and product development within the computer and communications industries is that of network management. The rapid rise of network management to critical status is primarily based on the need to manage all aspects of corporate information and communications networks as an integrated asset. This requirement has become known as "enterprise management". An enterprise is "an organization which operates one or more communications networks, and wants to apply consistent network management policies and procedures, using interoperable management solutions, to meet some common business objectives" [13]. Enterprise management has become synonymous with the ability to manage all elements within a network in an integrated, uniform, and consistent manner, including communications systems and distributed enterprise applications.

In the mid-1980's, users and vendors started discussing "integrated network management" as a solution to the tactical needs of network operations centers. These needs were largely focused on maintaining an operational network through consolidation of equipment failure and performance messages. Subsequently, users and vendors have become much more sophisticated and demanding in their requirements for seamless and transparent integration of network management applications running on different computers and supplied by different vendors. The ability for these network management systems and applications to exchange management data via a common management protocol is referred to as *interoperable network management*.

This paper gives a brief overview of the activities of the many standardization and implementors' agreement efforts directed towards integrated network management, a description of OSI management, and then describes the proposed solutions of the major, commercial vendors to the problems of enterprise management. The architectures of the commercial offerings, as well as the impact of groups like the OSI/Network Management Forum and the United States' National Institute for Standards and Technology (NIST) NMSIG are analyzed as they apply to the realization of OSI management.

2 NETWORK MANAGEMENT STANDARDS EFFORTS

There are many ongoing efforts, under the auspices of ISO, CCITT, IEEE and various vendor groups, to define industry standards for interoperable network management. These activities include definition of the protocols, message sets, management information and managed objects. There is some amount of overlap with the current structure of the work towards network management standards. The X3 Strategy Planning Committee of the American National Standards Institute (ANSI) issued a report in June of 1989 which concluded that that there is overlap in the technical work of these efforts [1]. Additionally, this report points out that the creation of each new group to focus on network management standards efforts does not necessarily result in the availability of additional personnel resources to perform the work. Therefore, the effectiveness of all efforts are diluted by the additions of new groups for vendors to participate in.

2.1 ISO OSI Management

After the development of the OSI Basic Reference Model (the seven layer model for computer communication), the International Standards Organization (ISO) realized that management of these interconnected and communicating distributed systems would be necessary. SC21/WG4 was established in March of 1985 to develop standards for the management of OSI [7]. Their focus is on management of OSI components - OSI layer entities and OSI applications. These emerging standards for OSI management will not be complete until sometime in the 1992 time-frame (see Figure 2).

At this time, there are several components of OSI management that are currently well understood and stable. A model for OSI management is described in the Management Framework [10] and in the Systems Management Overview [11]. They describe a basic architectural model for OSI management and define management requirements by identifying five specific management functional areas:

- Fault Management
- Accounting Management
- Security Management
- Configuration Management
- Performance Management

The framework identifies *systems management* as the mechanism for monitoring, control and coordination of managed objects through the use of application layer systems management protocols to be exchanged between management processes and defines a Management Information Base (MIB) as a conceptual repository of management information concerning managed objects [7].

ISO SC21/WG4 is developing the standards for the systems management protocols which are used to exchange and manipulate management information and the standards for defining the structure of management information. The process of moving a document to the status of international standard is, however, a fairly lengthy, labor-intensive and political effort to attain consensus between all participating national bodies.

2.1.1 OSI Management Concepts

The following concepts from the OSI management efforts of SC21/WG4 have been incorporated into the commercial architectures for network management products and solutions. There are many other concepts and principles defined within the total scope of OSI management, but these are the key contributors to the commercial efforts.

• Management Information and Managed Objects

The subject of OSI management communications is management information. The information relates to the resources being managed and is described using managed objects. The OSI management approach utilizes object oriented design concepts and the principles of object classes and attributes to define management information.

• Systems Management and Manager-Agent Interaction

Within OSI management, systems management is itself a distributed application which defines a structure for the communication of management information. Management activities are effected by managing processes communicating with agent processes to manipulate the managed objects. Each managed object has defined attributes, valid operations and notification the object may emit. Systems management is accomplished by Common Management Information Protocol and Services (CMIP/S) exchanges concerning managed objects to perform management functions.

Figure 1 - OSI Management Model

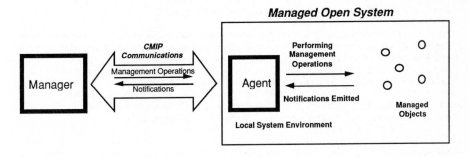

Figure 2 - Projected Timetables for OSI Management Standards from SC21/WG4

	DP	DIS	IS
• OSI Management Framework	09/86	06/87	10/88
• Common Management Information Service		09/88	09/89
• Common Management Information Protocol		09/88	09/89
• Systems Management			
• Overview	12/88	08/89	08/90
• Object Management	12/88	07/89	07/90
• State Management	12/88	04/90	04/91
• Relationship Management	12/88	04/90	04/91
• Error Reporting and Information Retrieval Function	12/88	04/90	04/91
• Management Service Control	12/88	04/90	04/91
• Confidence and Diagnostic Testing	10/89	07/90	07/91
• Log Control	10/89	07/90	07/91
• Structure of Management Information			
• Management Information Model	05/89	04/90	04/91
• Definitions of Support Objects	12/88	04/90	04/91
• Definitions of Management Attributes	12/88	04/90	04/91
• Guidelines for Managed Objects Definitions	10/89	09/90	09/91

DP=Draft Proposal, DIS=Draft Int'l Std IS=Int'l Std

2.2 Other Standards Efforts

There are other groups within ISO which are focused on the issues associated with management of the protocol layers. SC21/WG5 is attempting to define the management information relevant to the operation and management of the Session, Presentation and Application layers of the Basic Reference Model. Another group is working on the Network and Transport layers.

CCITT has produced recommendation M.30, Telecommunications Management Network, which defines a conceptual framework for management of network elements. It is very closely related to OSI management standards and draws heavily from the Systems Management concepts within ISO.

There are a series of IEEE standards which define network management for local area systems. IEEE 802.1 provides an overview of the family of 802 standards, describes the relationship of IEEE work to the OSI Basic Reference Models, and explains the relationship of these standards to higher layer protocols. Specification 802.1B defines an architecture and protocol for the management of IEEE 802 LANS. Other IEEE projects (802.2, 802.3, 802.4 and 802.5) are attempting to define layer-specific manageable objects. All of these projects are targeted to become ISO standards.

2.3 Implementors' Agreements

There are at least two implementors' groups working to develop agreements for the implementation of interoperable network management products. These groups have major impacts on products which are developed because standards are not intended to be implemented in the form in which they are published. They contain options and choices which must be made to form a *profile*. In the case of OSI management, the profiles must also specify the definitions of the objects that will be managed through the use of the protocols and message sets. These implementors' agreements specify the choices for each available option, thereby allowing for implementations by different vendors to interoperate properly.

2.3.1 OSI/Network Management Forum

The OSI/Network Management Forum (OSI/NMF) is an international consortium of over 120 telecommunications carriers and equipment manufacturers and computer systems vendors, formed in July of 1988, with the principle objective of promoting the use of and accelerating the development of OSI-based network management protocol standards. It is the most prominent of implementors' groups primarily because of the companies involved in its formation (AT&T, British Telecom, Northern Telecom Inc., Telecom Canada, Hewlett-Packard, Amdahl, and Unisys), and the relatively quick progress which it has made towards achieving its goals.

The OSI/NMF delivered public specifications for its interoperable architecture, protocol, application message set, and object templates based on ISO documents in various stages of becoming IS within its first eighteen months. The OSI/NMF has stated that they will base their solutions on current work in ISO, but they will fill in the gaps where work within ISO has not progressed sufficiently to produce products. This gives them the necessary leeway to progress without waiting for the complete suite of standards.

This group is particularly influential for the following reasons:

- Its membership includes all of the key data and voice vendors.

- The technical talent is considered to be the best available in the industry and draws from resources also involved in CCITT, IEEE, NIST NMSIG and other network management efforts. There are several ISO editors involved in the OSI/NMF efforts.

- They will bring products to market in late 1990 which allow users to implement interoperable network management strategies.

- They have the financial and technical resource to influence the direction of ISO.

2.3.2 US GOSIP

Effective in August 1992, the United States government will base all of its network management purchases on conformance to implementors' agreements which make up the Government OSI Profile (GOSIP). Within the US, the federal government is a major purchaser of networking components which will result in the GOSIP specifications becoming a major influence on vendors.

The GOSIP specifications are based on implementors' agreements developed at the OSI Implementors Workshop (OIW). Within the OIW, there is a Network Management Special Interest Group (NMSIG) developing the specifications for network management. The NMSIG membership is made up of over 120 organizations drawn from 13 countries, of which about one third can be considered to represent users. This makes the NMSIG unique from the other groups which have been described, because they are generally made up of vendors.

2.4.3 OSI/NMF VS. NMSIG

The work of the NMSIG and the OSI/NMF is very similar - *develop agreements for the implementation OSI management in a relatively short time-frame*. The key difference is that the OSI/NMF can make decisions on which directions they think ISO is likely to move in. They do this knowing that they may have to backtrack at a later date in order to achieve conformance with the final standards. The NMSIG is much more bounded to base their agreements on work which is considered to be stable within the ISO efforts.

3 COMMERCIAL USE OF STANDARDS

Many of the major telecommunications and computer vendors are already announcing OSI-based network management products even though the standards are several years from completion. The vendors are under pressure from the user community for a solution(s) to the integrated, enterprise-oriented network management problem. This user influence is propelling OSI management to the mainstream of product development in spite of the fact that the standards are not complete. The vendors are claiming OSI management as the basis for their product architectures because they realize that communications standards are required to provide integrated network management in a multivendor environment. They may not actually implement OSI management within their proprietary network management systems, but they will offer it as an interface to their system.

It is not yet clear whether the emerging concepts and standards of the OSI management efforts have driven the user expectations and requirements or whether the opposite is true. It is clear that user requirements have outpaced the availability of these standards and products which conform to them. The widespread publicity concerning the development of the OSI management standards has led the user and vendor communities to designate OSI-based network management as one of the primary differentiating factors amongst vendors.

The adoption of standards is not enough to ensure interoperability, however, because standards are designed for broad applicability and identify options for vendors to select. Standards do not specify conformance testing requirements and verify that vendors apply conformance testing to their products.

4 COMMERCIAL PRODUCTS

During the past two years, there have been many announcements and deliveries of architectures and products for enterprise network management. For most commercial implementations, enterprise management is accomplished by integrating the functionality provided by different management systems which control the physical and logical network components. These management systems are generally technology related and their sphere of management influence is limited to a particular networking technology, vendors' product, or sub-network of the overall corporate network.

The key to a vendor's strategy to providing enterprise management is the *architecture* of their solution. An architecture is a "a means of organizing and representing knowledge within a given field of application" [12]. Architectures generally provide a model which identifies the system components and interfaces. A network management architecture should provide a structure for consistent and flexible implementations of a set of functions and services to manage the networks and provide for meeting the user requirements of management.

3.1 AT&T

AT&T is a founding member of the OSI/NMF and has developed an OSI management-based architecture for providing end-to-end integrated management called the Unified Network Management Architecture (UNMA). The UNMA architecture is three-tiered and hierarchical (Figure 3). The network elements form the first tier and include the networking equipment and services in customer locations, local exchange carriers, and the AT&T interexchange network. Element Management Systems (EMS) are the second tier and they handle the operations, administration, maintenance and/or provisioning of one or more instantiations of a network element. The EMS function is typically provided by a network management system that was created specifically to manage the network elements under its control. The integrating network management system is the third tier. It is the system that will provide overall, end-to-end network management of the full set of elements that comprise the network.

UNMA is an open architecture in that the interface method between the tiers and between peer elements of the same tier for level two and three is based on CMIP. AT&T calls their version of this protocol NMP for Network Management Protocol. NMP includes a set of message specifications which will expand over time to eventually include all of the needed management functions: fault management, configuration and name management, accounting management, performance management, security management, and network planning.

Figure 3 - UNMA Architecture

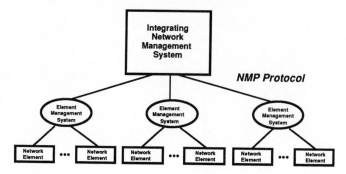

3.2 Digital Equipment Corporation

Digital Equipment Corporation's architecture for integrated, OSI-based network management is called the Enterprise Management Architecture (EMA). Digital defines the term *enterprise network* to mean "complex, multivendor communications and processing environments" [3].

The primary goal of EMA is to provide an "integrated, extensible management framework for current and future enterprise environments" [3]. EMA includes a management framework and architectural models and defines interfaces which are open to standards-based and proprietary products. EMA is a distributed management system which can have several active management centers, called directors. The components of EMA are:

• **Directory - Entity Framework** which defines the structure of management interfaces and interactions between directors. The director-entity relationship is very tightly based on the OSI concept of managers and agents.

Figure 4 - EMA Director - Entity Model

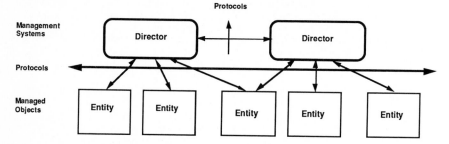

Directors may be arranged in a peer-to-peer or hierarchical architecture.
Entities may be managed by more than one director.

• **Entity model** which provides the mechanism to define the management information and operations of managed objects. An entity is divided into a managed object and an agent. The agent provides the management interface to directors.

Figure 5 - EMA Entity Model

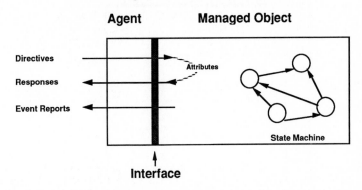

• **Director model** which defines a modular platform for the management of any type of managed object and support for the high-level management applications. A director provides an interface between a network manager and the network. The core of the director model is the management information repository. The management solution is very flexible and designed by selecting "plug-in" modules which provide for multi-vendor access, presentation services, and the desired management applications or functions.

Figure 6 - EMA Director Model

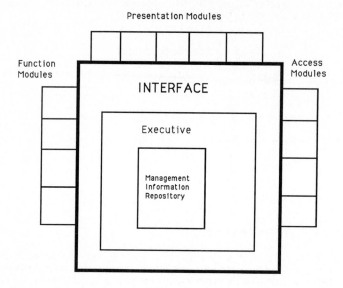

3.3 IBM

IBM was the first vendor to announce an integrated network management solution. The unveiling of Netview in 1986 created what many have called a defacto standard for integrated network management.

IBM's architectural goal is to permit cooperative participation by other vendors in the management of networks composed of SNA and non-SNA components. IBM calls this approach Open Network Management [8]. Three basic network management roles are identified in the architecture to allow for the monitoring of SNA and non-SNA elements. *Focal points* are used for all information resources of the enterprise. The network management focal point serves as the centralized system for network management. The primary, although not only, IBM focal point product is Netview. *Entry points* are the collection points for SNA devices. *Service points* are concentrating points within the architecture and are used to funnel multiple non-SNA streams into focal points. Netview/PC is a service point product and, essentially, acts as a network management gateway for non-SNA network elements.

In February of 1990, IBM announced its OSI management interface to Netview. It provides an interface to Netview which uses the OSI management standards.

63

Figure 7 - IBM Architecture

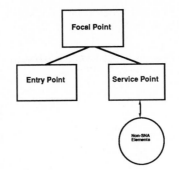

3.4 OSI/Network Management Forum

The architecture of the OSI/NMF is based on the concept of peer-to-peer interoperable network management. One of the founding principles of the OSI/NMF is that each member vendor will have a "level playing field" for providing network management functionality in a multivendor environment. OSI/NMF members believe that the management solution that is provided by their own network management system will be judged by the users on the basis of its capability to act as a "manager of managers". This concept of competitive differentiation is very important within their interoperable architecture. The OSI/NMF architecture for interoperable network management consists of the following components (all definitions are taken from the OSI/NMF Glossary [13]):

• **Interoperable Interface**

The interoperable interface is the formally defined set of protocols, procedures, message formats and semantics to communicate between OSI/NMF member network management systems.

• **Conformant Management Entity**

A CME is a real open system which supports the OSI/NMF interoperable interface.

• **Management Network**

The management network is the network through which CMEs communicate for the purposes of network management.

• **Management Solution**

A management solution is the total set of resources and facilities provided for network management purposes.

• **Managed Elements**

A managed element is a physical or logical resource that is to bemanaged, but exists independently of its need to be managed.

Figure 8 - OSI/NMF Architecture

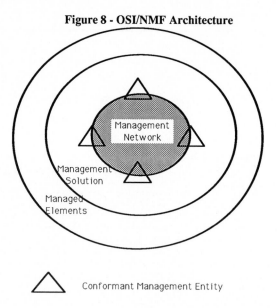

The CMEs communicate using the management network, which is made up of elements which also reside in the communications network and must be managed. The CMEs provide a view of managed elements under their management control to other CMEs through the interoperable interface into the management network. The management solution of each vendor may be proprietary, as long as the objects exposed on the interoperable interface conform to the OSI/NMF agreements.

4 PROBLEMS

4.1 Focus on Interoperability Instead of Solutions

The architectures described in the previous section provide the basic model and framework for interoperable network management. The vendors are focused on establishing the required components of the interoperable solution, but also on establishing their control of the management solution of any given customer. From a user's perspective, however, there is little value derived solely from the implementation of interoperable protocols.

This ability to exchange network management data is really just the *starting* point for solving the problems of the operator of today's complex networks. A typical network has multiple network management systems, each supplied by a different vendor with a different user interface. In fact, one recent survey of network operators revealed that over 50% of all networks have more than one network management system [5]. The implementation of the interoperable protocol allows these network management systems to exchange data. This does not really solve many of the problems of the network operator. The real value of interoperability lies in the applications that are built to run on top of the interoperable interface and provide solutions.

4.2 Lack of User Input

There has been little effort spent on establishing the user requirements of interoperable network management. There have been many surveys of user needs conducted, primarily by trade publications and analyst groups, but this information is not being funnelled into the standards and implementors' groups which are specifying the network management standards.

In many cases, vendors are compelled to keep their products functionally equivalent to their competitors, even if the functions provided are not the right ones. For example, a recent analyst report states that graphical user interfaces are not a priority for the network operators [5]. According to this report, network operators feel that graphics is not required in order to meet their tactical needs; that graphics is basically a "upper management toy".

4.3 Lack of Integration

Initial attempts at developing integrated network management systems have not resulted in full command and control capabilities through a single, top-level system. Each architecture described requires terminal access to lower-level management systems in order to completely control the network elements. The job of managing networks still requires highly skilled personnel and the ability to move between each vendors' particular language and style of interface.

Network management integration needs to be built into each component of the network. This would allow for different vendors' network elements to be managed by another vendors' network management system. This was the original intent of the OSI management model, but vendors are not willing to give up network management control of the elements that they provide.

5 CONCLUSIONS

The integration of LAN, WAN, data, voice, and distributed computing applications will be the major focal point of networking in the 1990s. Many users feel more strongly about the need for integrated network management than the need for more advancements in internetworking and termination technologies [4]. The key influences in the future for the design of new networks and the evolution of existing networks will be the ability to seamlessly integrate manageable components into an enterprise network which is based on standards.

The effects of these influences (integration, standards-based and manageable components) are already evident by the amount of effort the vendors are putting into integrated network management. Many vendors have based their solution(s) on OSI management or provided an interface to OSI management. The commercial products of today do not, however, provide for total systems management and the required solutions. Since 5-8% of a telecommunications department budget is spent on network management, this will force users to put pressure on the vendors to provide better solutions in a shorter time period [5].

Many problems with the progress toward OSI management are due to the approach of the standards efforts, as opposed to the resulting architectures and products. These include the lack of a detailed and achievable work plan by ISO, duplication of efforts by standards and implementors' groups, and lack of understanding of user requirements of interoperable network management.

In spite of these problems, interoperable network management based on OSI management is becoming a reality and should be widely implemented within the next five years.

REFERENCES

[1] ANSI X3/Strategy Planning Committee, "Report on Network Management", August 28, 1988.
[2] Datapro Research, *AT&T Unified Network Management Architecture (UNMA)*, CMS20-0460101, 1989.
[3] Digital Equipment Corporation, *Enterprise Management Architecture - General Description*, EK-DEMAR-GD-001, 1989.
[4] Enslow, Dr. Philip, Ronald Hutchins, Kimberly Kappel, "Future Campus Networks - A Vision of the Future", GIT 36-662, February 1990.
[5] Forrester Research Inc., *The Network Strategy*, "Net Management Update", Vol. 3, No. 88, July 1989.
[6] Kappel, Kimberly W., "The True Value of Interoperability", *Network Management Perspective*, January 1990, pp 13-15.
[7] Kobayashi, Yoshikazu, "Standardization Issues in Integrated Network Management", *Integrated Network Management I*, North Holland, Proceedings of the First International Symposium on Integrated Network Management, pp. 79-92, IFIP, 1989.
[8] Schultze, Flemming, "IBM Network Management - Architecture and Implementation", *Information Network and Data Communication II*, pp. 145-160, North Holland, IFIP, 1988.
[9] LaBarre, Lee and Dr. Paul J. Brusil, "Network Management Models Drive Standards", *The Network Management Journal,* Vol I, Fall 1989, pp35-52, The MITRE Corporation.
[10] ISO/IEC 7498-4:1989,"Information processing systems - Open Systems Interconnection - Basic Reference Model - Part 4: Management Framework".
[11] ISO/IEC JTC 1/SC21 , "2ND DP 10040: Information Processing Systems - OSI - Systems Management Overview", December 1989.
[12] OSI/Network Management Forum, *Forum Architecture,* Issue 1, January 1990.
[13] OSI/Network Management Forum, *Forum Glossary,* Issue 1, January 1990.

Information Network and Data Communication, III
D. Khakhar and F. Eliassen (Editors)
Elsevier Science Publishers B.V. (North-Holland)
© IFIP, 1990

Network Management in Heterogeneous Networks for Factory Automation

Martin Bosch, Georg Rößler, Werner Schollenberger

Institute of Communications Switching and Data Technics
University of Stuttgart
Stuttgart, Federal Republic of Germany

In factory automation, network management is one of the most important problems of communication, today. Without an effective network management, standardized protocol profiles will not be accepted by the majority of users. Especially, the management of heterogeneous networks is still not treated by standardization committees. This paper describes a Network Management Gateway, which will be a necessary component in future factories, when standardized and proprietary networks have to work together forming one large distributed system.

1. Introduction

The process of integrating all computers and controllers of a company to a large distributed system is in full swing. It will lead to a Computer Integrated Manufacturing (CIM), which is necessary in modern factory automation to react flexibly enough on changes dictated by the market. Besides the material flow, the information flow grows more and more important. This information is usually transmitted via Local Area Networks (LANs). The International Organization for Standardization (ISO) has developed the Basic Reference Model for Open Systems Interconnection (OSI) [2] as a framework for communication protocols. Due to some missing standardized protocols in the application system, various proprietary protocol profiles have been developed. To overcome their incompatibility, Interworking Units (IWUs) are necessary between each pair of communicating LANs. The costs of IWUs are immense and usually they lead to a reduced performance and functionality. Therefore, a standardized protocol profile like the Manufacturing Automation Protocol (MAP) [8] is absolutely necessary in the factory of the future.

At least for a transitional period, the MAP profile, as well as one or more proprietary protocol profiles will be used simultaneously in a company. To overcome the resulting communication barriers, specific IWUs to MAP (*MAP–Gateways*) are necessary. An example for a *MAP–Gateway*, including a performance evaluation, has been presented in [1].

With the growing size, sensitivity and importance of LANs for factory automation, another problem becomes increasingly important: the management of these networks, which will represent the backbone of factory automation in future. This network management becomes more difficult by the heterogenity of networks mentioned above. In a heterogeneous environment specific *Network Management Gateways* are necessary to allow an overall network management by dedicated manager stations.

2. General Aspects of Network Management

2.1. Purpose of Network Management

The primary goal of network management is to guarantee a certain quality of service for the whole network to which the following aspects contribute:

- availability,
- reliability,
- data throughput,
- utilization of the network resources,
- security.

The network to be managed can be regarded as a distributed system consisting of stations and their interconnection paths. Network management disregards the role of a station in the production process and is restricted to its communication resources. The information about these resources relevant for network management is comprised in the term Managed Object (MO). All management operations refer to Managed Objects. Although in open systems the communication protocols are well standardized, the stations themselves remain inhomogeneous resulting in different Managed Objects.

Network management involves

- planning,
- initialization,
- monitoring (recognition of overload situations),
- maintenance,
- fault diagnosis and repair,
- support on configuration changes,
- performance optimization.

It includes human activities and must be individually adapted to each network. Figure 1 shows the general logical structure of network management. It consists of the Network Administrator, usually a human being, a User Interface (Management Console) and the Management System providing a set of services to the Network Administrator and being able to handle some management functions automatically. Today it seems to be impossible for the Management System to cope with all situations occuring in normal operation of the network. An essential aspect of network management is the transfer of management information. This is done by the Management Information Service (MIS).

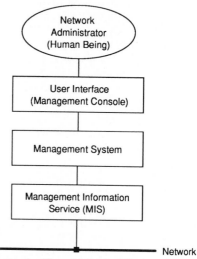

Figure 1 : General Logical Structure

For network management in open systems it is not sufficient to standardize communication services for the exchange of management data, but a common representation and understanding of these data is necessary. In addition, the management system must be able to perform operations on resources of remote stations in order to assist the Network Administrator efficiently. These issues are the goal of various ISO standardization activities. An abstract model of OSI Management is defined in the OSI Management Framework [3]. Other standards deal with the application layer communication services for network management [4, 5] and the representation of management information [6, 7]. The following section gives a brief overview to the principles and ideas of OSI Management.

2.2. Network Management in OSI

2.2.1. Architecture

Managed Objects are the target of all OSI Management operations. Altogether they form a conceptual database called Management Information Base (MIB). The MIB is distributed over all stations in the network. The location of Managed Objects corresponds to the location of the related resources. A Managed Object consists of

- Attributes,
- Events,
- Actions,
- other Managed Objects being contained in this object.

A Managed Object instance is defined by its name (Object Identifier) and its type (Object Class), which includes the possible operations on it and its attributes as well as all fault situations. Attributes represent values of the related resource which can be read and set by the manager. Events are predefined messages which will be reported from the managed station to the manager in case of relevant state transitions. They are related to attributes. Actions can be initiated in the managed stations. This enables the manager to request an open system to initialize its communication resources, to reset itself or to perform some test functions like echotests to other stations.

A Managed Object can contain further Managed Objects in addition to its attributes, events, and actions. This leads to a hierarchical structure in which the highest level is an object of class SYSTEM representing the whole station. The addressing scheme of Managed Objects is a tree structure, the Containment Tree.

As shown in Figure 2, OSI standardizes three levels of management communication

- (N)–Layer Operation,
- (N)–Layer Management,
- Systems Management.

(N)–Layer Operation provides mechanisms for monitoring and controlling of a single instance of communication via normal (N)–layer protocols between Layer Entities (LEs). (N)–Layer Management addresses several (N)–layer instances and provides mechanisms to monitor and control Managed Objects of one layer. Management operations restricted to layer N can be executed by a (N)–Layer Management Entity (LME) using (N)–Layer Management protocols. The End System to Intermediate System routing exchange protocol for use in conjunction with the protocol providing the connectionless–mode network service (ES/IS Protocol) is an example for a (N)–Layer Management protocol. The most important and powerful mechanism for monitoring and controlling Managed Objects within an open system is Systems Management. It is the only way to manage multiple layers and requires the availability of all seven layers of the protocol stack.

The only instance having access to management data of all layers of one station is the Systems Management Application Process (SMAP). It carries out Systems Management operations and is based on a specific Application Layer Management Service, provided by the Systems Management Application Entity (SMAE) using Systems Management protocols.

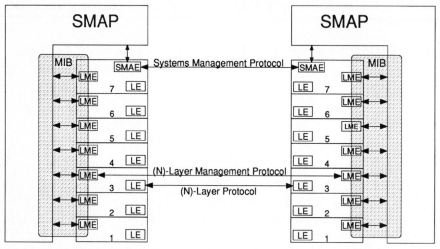

Figure 2 : Communication Model of OSI Management

2.2.2. Systems Management

Individual application processes on individual stations share the task of network management as depicted in Figure 3. They can be divided into manager processes (managers), initiating management activities and agent processes (agents), which have access to local Managed Objects and serve as peer entities for the manager. Every station with full communication capabilities holds one agent responsible for the Managed Objects of this station. Every operation on Managed Objects is invoked by a manager and performed by the agent concerned.

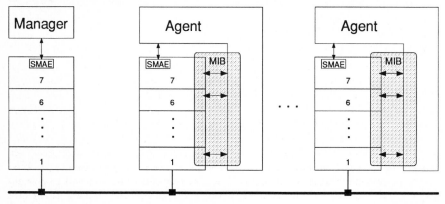

Figure 3 : Manager — Agent Relationship

Figure 4 shows the structure of a SMAE. The communication between managers and agents is performed by the exchange of Management Directives. For this purpose, the application layer provides the SMAE. The interface to the SMAP is realized in the Systems Management Application Service Element (SMASE), which defines a specific set of primitives for each management functional area (refer to subsection 2.2.3.). These primitives can be directly mapped onto primitives of the Common Management Information Service Element (CMISE), which is standardized in [4] together with the related Common Management Information Protocol (CMIP) standardized in [5].

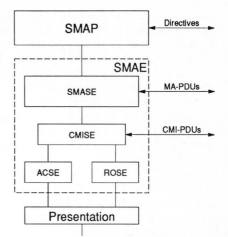

Figure 4 : Structure of the SMAE

The SMASE employs some parameters not used by the CMISE. The CMISE is based on the Application Service Elements ACSE (Association Control Service Element) for the control of CMIS associations and ROSE (Remote Operations Service Element) for the execution of remote operations. CMIS is a connection oriented service. It defines primitives to

- control the establishment and termination of CMIS associations,
- manipulate Managed Objects,
- report on events,
- initiate actions on remote stations.

The complexity of this service is not caused by a large number of service primitives as in the Manufacturing Message Specification (MMS), but by the number of Managed Objects with their individual definitions. For each primitive the CMISE can act as an invoker or as a performer. The role of each communication instance is negotiated during connection establishment. The primitives to control CMIS associations are

- M–INITIALIZE (association establishment),
- M–TERMINATE (normal termination),
- M–ABORT (abnormal termination).

The modification of Managed Objects is usually invoked by the manager and performed by the agent. The primitives to be used are

- M–GET (read one or several attributes),
- M–CANCEL–GET (abort a pending M–GET activity),
- M–SET (change an attribute),
- M–CREATE (create a new incarnation of a Managed Object),
- M–DELETE (delete an incarnation of a Managed Object).

The primitives mentioned above have additional parameters to specify the range of attributes (scope and filtering) and the behavior in case of errors (synchronization). With the scope parameter a set of Managed Objects is selected, which can be the specified object itself, the n-th level below the specified object in the Containment Tree or the whole subtree. The filtering parameter allows the expression of conditions attributes have to satisfy to get selected. The results of a M–GET request are transmitted via M–GET response primitives. Only the attribute values of one Managed Object can be returned with one Protocol Data Unit (PDU). In case of the selection of multiple objects, several linked response PDUs are transmitted (linked reply).

To inform the manager of certain events in its station, the agent uses the primitive M–EVENT–REPORT, which is related to a Managed Object. The information carried by this PDU depends strongly on the definition of the event.

M–ACTION enables the manager to initiate specific predefined actions in the remote station. The positive acknowledgement of a M–ACTION request indicates only the acceptance by the agent. The results of the action are transmitted in a M–EVENT–REPORT message.

2.2.3. Management Functions

In OSI standardization the different network management requirements are classified into five groups named Specific Management Functional Areas (SMFAs):

- Fault Management,
- Configuration Management,
- Performance Management,
- Security Management,
- Accounting Management.

Fault Management is the set of facilities which enables the detection, isolation and correction of abnormal operation of the network. The functions for Confidence and Diagnostic Testing (CDT) are a subset of these facilities. CDT defines actions to test the connectivity to other stations, e.g. connectivity test (test, whether station A is able to establish a connection to station B), connection saturation test (test, how many connections can be established between stations A and B simultaneously) and data saturation test (determine the maximal data throughput over one connection between stations A and B).

All functions dealing with network configuration as well as the addressing and controlling of Managed Objects refer to Configuration Management. Object Management as a subset of Configuration Management defines functions to get and set attributes of Managed Objects for configuration purposes. The function Enrol Object introduces a new Managed Object to the manager. Since a whole station is represented as one Managed Object of class SYSTEM, Enrol Object allows the introduction of a new station to the manager. On the other hand a Managed Object can be deactivated with the function Deenrol Object.

Performance Management is the set of facilities needed to evaluate the effectiveness of communication activities. They are used to gather statistical data about Managed Objects for planning and analysis purposes. A subset of this function is Workload Monitoring. It defines thresholds for attributes which are supervised by the agent, e.g. the rate of the number of PDUs sent by one layer. Each threshold is related to an event which is reported to the manager if the corresponding attribute exceeds the defined limit.

For the remaining functional areas standardization has just begun, therefore they are rarely implemented today. The facilities of Accounting Management enable charges to be assigned to the usage of Managed Objects. This includes the combination of costs where multiple Managed Objects are involved to provide a special service. Security

Management addresses the protection of information and communication resources from damage and misuse by unauthorized individuals.

3. Interconnection of Heterogeneous Networks

3.1. Principles of Internetworking

In this section it is assumed that the protocol profiles of the networks to be interconnected use identical protocols at and above a specific layer N. The coupling layer of the IWU, as depicted in Figure 5, may then be layer N-1 or above. The protocols of the lower layers 1 to N-1 are independent of each other. The protocols above the IWU's coupling layer have an end–to–end significance.

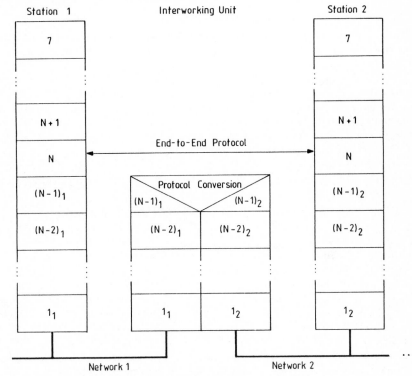

Figure 5 : Internetworking by Protocol Conversion

The networks are usually interconnected at the last different layer N-1 by protocol conversion. The protocol conversion software performs a mapping between service primitives of the two different N-1 protocols in the IWU. Sometimes the lack of a corresponding service primitive in the other protocol can be overcome by adequate sequences of available primitives. The entities of layer N-1 in the IWU may be identical to the corresponding entities in the other stations, respectively. Alternatively a specific layer N-1 entity for the IWU can be used, which performs a direct mapping of PDUs without using service primitives. The advantage of protocol conversion at layer N-1 is the end–to–end protocol at layer N and the minimal number of layers in the IWU, which results in a

74

minimal transfer time through this device. The existing stations at the interconnected networks 1 and 2 may remain unchanged.

As an alternative to protocol conversion, internetworking may be realized with the help of a global sublayer, by a common protocol in all stations or via transit systems by encapsulation of PDUs.

IWUs may be classified according to their coupling layer. A repeater is a physical layer IWU, which allows an extension of the limited size of a LAN. A bridge interconnects usually LANs on the Media Access Control (MAC) sublayer of the data link layer. On the network layer routers may be used, for example to interconnect LANs via Wide Area Networks (WANs). Internetworking on the transport layer or above is done by gateways.

3.2. Network Management in Heterogeneous Networks

Concerning the network management in a heterogeneous environment, a specific *Network Management Gateway* is necessary besides the IWU necessary for information flow. This *Network Management Gateway* may either be implemented as a dedicated device, or on the same computer as the IWU for the information flow. It should be transparent, so that the manager stations do not become aware of its existence. The concept of having manager stations in each subnetwork will not be considered here, since only one Management Domain is supported in today's manager stations. Additionally, some changes would be necessary in the manager stations implemented according to the OSI philosophy, which contradicts the principle of transparency mentioned above. Instead, we assume to have one or a few manager stations in a standardized OSI compatible network, which will manage the OSI compatible network and the adjacent proprietary networks as well.

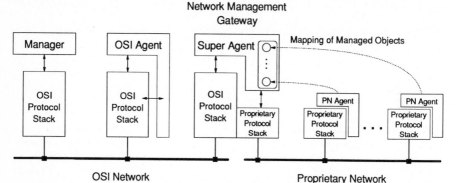

Figure 6 : Network Management via a Network Management Gateway

The *Network Management Gateway* behaves as a manager station from the point of view of its related proprietary stations. Consequently, all proprietary stations must have a Proprietary Network (PN) agent including variables corresponding to Managed Objects, which can be addressed by the *Network Management Gateway*. These variables must be mapped onto Managed Objects or their attributes in the OSI compatible network by the *Network Management Gateway*. As for other IWUs, a loss of functionality can usually not be avoided due to different sets of objects. This mapping can be seen to be located on top of the application layer. The functionality of OSI agents for stations of the proprietary network is located in the *Network Management Gateway*, as depicted in Figure 6. Therefore, a manager station has to address the *Network Management Gateway* instead of the related proprietary station.

In the *Network Management Gateway* arriving management PDUs have to be converted and then routed to the related PN agent process with the help of an alias address. There are various parameters, which are more or less useful for this routing process. The user information field of the M–INITIALIZE service should not be used as an alias address, to prevent the manager stations from filling this parameter, which would contradict the principle of transparency. In the MAC sublayer the least significant bit of the destination address could be used for alias addressing. With this bit a group address can be indicated. If the *Network Management Gateway* receives all packets with MAC addresses corresponding to the MAC addresses of its related proprietary stations but this bit set to one, the destination address of the target station can easily be determined by an inversion of the least significant bit. The drawback of this addressing scheme is the limited number of allowed group addresses in the *Network Management Gateway* due to the time needed to compare the MAC address of each arriving PDU to all stored group addresses. Another addressing variant is the use of separate Service Access Points (SAPs) at and above an arbitrary layer for each addressed agent. However, this would not be possible at the data link layer in our implementation. In some implementations this would also result in many protocol stacks above the layer where this is done, one for every administered proprietary station. The most adequate addressing concept, however, is the following: One *super agent* in the *Network Management Gateway* contains one Managed Object of class SYSTEM for each related proprietary station. This Managed Object will be addressed directly by a manager and can therefore be considered as the needed alias address. A second agent is responsible for the *Network Management Gateway* itself.

4. Network Management Gateway Design and Implementation

The prototype implementation of the *Network Management Gateway* has been designed to connect two different proprietary networks to an OSI environment for management purposes. In a first phase, the interconnection to one proprietary network has been implemented, the interconnection to the second proprietary network will be done in a second step.

4.1. Protocol Stacks of the Different Networks

Both proprietary networks use an OSI transport system. Therefore, all three networks can share the same physical medium. In the first proprietary network, the transport system is the iNA 960 software on the corresponding communication board from Intel which includes the Network Management Facility (NMF). This NMF consists of a small agent on each system and allows management data exchange based on the transport system. For the layers 1 to 4, attributes, e.g. counters, are defined to achieve network management. In the terminology of the NMF, these attributes are called *NMF objects*. In order not to confound them with the Managed Objects in OSI, these parameters will be called attributes. This convention makes sense, since the *NMF objects* usually represent OSI attributes. The protocol stack above the transport system contains non–OSI protocols and provides no management capabilities. The second proprietary network uses another implementation of the transport system. The higher layers are also different from OSI. On each system in the second proprietary network an agent resides to exchange management data using a proprietary protocol. In this network, management information is available for all layers of the protocol stack. In Figure 7 the protocol stacks of one manager station in the OSI environment, of the *Network Management Gateway*, and of one station of each proprietary network are depicted as far as they are related to network management.

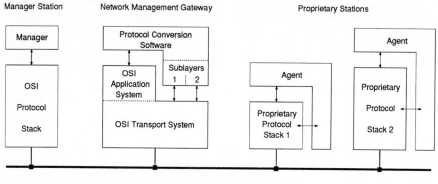

Figure 7 : Protocol Stacks of the Different Networks

4.2. Functionality of the Network Management Gateway

Figure 7 illustrates the functionality of the gateway. The gateway has to convert the CMIS M–GET and M–SET services to the corresponding services in the proprietary networks. Many attributes defined in OSI management are not supported in the proprietary networks but can be stored or calculated using other attributes in the gateway. Examples for these kinds of attributes are thresholds and rates. As the agents in the proprietary networks do not generate event reports, the *Network Management Gateway* has to generate them instantaneously on occurrence of specific events. To recognize these events, the gateway polls several attributes and notifies the manager of irregular or critical workload conditions. The agents in the proprietary networks do not support actions like performing echotests or opening connections for test purposes. The gateway realizes these actions if the results are meaningful to the manager and cannot be misinterpreted.

The gateway must contain both the OSI protocol stack including the CMISE to communicate with the manager and the protocol stacks of the proprietary networks as far as they are necessary for management purposes. Communication in the proprietary networks is based on the common transport system. For each proprietary network, the protocol conversion software contains one sublayer to meet the specific requirements of the networks. On top of these sublayers a common interface for both networks provides a simple and more comfortable access to both proprietary networks. The protocol conversion is done between this interface and that to CMIS.

4.3. Software Structure

As mentioned in section 2.2. network management makes intensive use of data, while the number of service primitives is comparatively small. Therefore, one of the main problems to be solved was to find data structures suitable for both the data contained in the MIB as defined in OSI and the requirements of the proprietary networks. In OSI management, the data are stored in the Containment Tree in a hierarchical manner. In contrast, the attributes available in the proprietary networks are stored in a kind of linear list with some additional information about the relations between the attributes. These relations are reflected in the numbers employed to identify them. To solve this incompatibility, one hierarchically structured Containment Tree is used with only one Managed Object of each class as a model for all stations in a proprietary network. For each station, the values of all attributes are stored in a data structure containing a few different lists. The model Containment Tree contains no management information but references, where to find the information requested in the data structure. After the protocol conversion software has been started, it reads the necessary information to fill the Containment Tree for each proprietary network from a file. With this method, the relations between the Managed Objects and attributes standardized in OSI and the attributes of the proprietary networks can be modified without changing and recompiling the software.

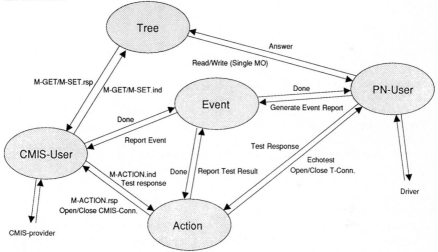

Figure 8 : Protocol Conversion Software Structure

Figure 8 gives an overview of the tasks in the protocol conversion software. The following section describes the functions of the different tasks and the messages they exchange.

The CMIS User Task provides the interface to the OSI protocol stack. The first function of this task is to establish and terminate CMIS associations to communicate with manager stations. Secondly, it enrols each station reporting the Managed Object of class SYSTEM to the managers at the beginning of the management activities. If a station of the proprietary network is shut down, the task deenrols the corresponding SYSTEM Managed Object. The third function is to distribute CMIS PDUs to other tasks to be processed there and to complete the answers of the other tasks to pass them to the CMIS provider.

The Tree Task handles M–GET and M–SET PDUs. It has to evaluate the Managed Objects and attributes from the PDU and has to determine the station and the attributes affected in the proprietary network. To do this, it also processes scope and filter parameters. The treatment of the PDU results in a request to the Proprietary Network User Task containing the operations required and a list of attributes. The answer to this request is employed to complete the corresponding CMIS response PDU. The task generates a linked reply, if multiple Managed Objects are affected. The Tree Task intensively uses the Containment Tree and also the data of the stations to accomplish its function.

The purpose of the Proprietary Network User Task is to provide a simple and comfortable interface for the Tree Task to the proprietary networks. As a normal result of a request from the Tree Task, the task updates the attributes in the station data and returns a list of the updated attributes. Internally, it polls certain attributes if required and supervises the corresponding thresholds. If an attribute value exceeds a threshold, the task notifies this to the Event Task.

The Event Task completes the information received from the Proprietary Network User Task in order to form a CMIS M-EVENT-REPORT PDU. This PDU is passed to the CMIS User Task to be sent to the managers.

The Action Task determines whether the result of the test described in the M-ACTION PDU is meaningful in a heterogeneous environment for the manager stations. If not, it rejects the request, otherwise it initiates the action, e.g. an echotest to a specific station, and activates the Event Task to report the test result to the manager.

4.4. Implementation Aspects

The interconnection software is implemented on an Intel 310 computer with the operating system iRMX II. This operating system is a real time multitasking operating system with priority based preemptive scheduling. The tasks in the system pass data segments to each other via mailboxes. To avoid inconsistencies in the global data used by different tasks, the mechanisms for mutual exclusion provided by the operating system are used. The tasks of the protocol conversion software are implemented in C and integrated after a stand-alone test of each task.

5. Conclusion

After an introduction into factory automation, where the necessity of an overall network management can be recognized, we have described the current state of network management and its philosophy in standardization. Specific problems of heterogeneous networks have been summarized. The main focus of this paper has been a *Network Management Gateway* for factory automation. The development of this gateway has been supported by the Commission of the European Communities (CEC) within the framework of the project *Communications Network for Manufacturing Applications* (CNMA), which is a part of the European Strategic Program for Research and Development in Information Technology (ESPRIT). The *Network Management Gateway* extends the management of the standardized CNMA network to stations in a proprietary network. We have described its protocol architecture and functionality as well as the resulting protocol conversion software structure. This gateway will be demonstrated at the University of Stuttgart in the experimental pilot of the CNMA project.

Acknowledgement

The authors would like to thank all the students who have been involved in the implementation of the *Network Management Gateway*.

References

[1] Martin Bosch; "Design, Implementation, Modelling and Simulation of a MAP-Gateway for Flexible Manufacturing", Modelling the Innovation: Communications, Automation and Information Systems, Rome, March 21 - 23, 1990

[2] ISO 7498; "Information Processing Systems — Open Systems Interconnection — Basic Reference Model", November 1983

[3] ISO 7498-4; "Information Processing Systems — Open Systems Interconnection — Basic Reference Model — Part 4: Management Framework", January 1988

[4] ISO DIS 9595-2; "Information Processing Systems — Open Systems Interconnection — Management Information Service Definition — Part 2: Common Management Information Service", 1989

[5] ISO DIS 9596-2 "Information Processing Systems — Open Systems Interconnection — Management Information Protocol — Part 2: Common Management Information Protocol", 1989

[6] ISO DP 10040; "Information Processing Systems — Open Systems Interconnection — Systems Management Overview", 1989

[7] ISO DP 10165; "Information Processing Systems — Open Systems Interconnection — Structure of Management Information", 1989

[8] MAP; "Manufacturing Automation Protocol", Version 3.0, General Motors, Warren/Michigan, April 7, 1987

Information Network and Data Communication, III
D. Khakhar and F. Eliassen (Editors)
Elsevier Science Publishers B.V. (North-Holland)
© IFIP, 1990

USING KNOWLEDGE BASED SYSTEMS IN TELECOMMUNICATION
MANAGEMENT NETWORKS

David LUNDBERG

TeleLOGIC AB
BOX 4148
203 12 Malmö
SWEDEN

Telecommunication management networks (TMNs) are used to control and
manage the operation of telecommunication networks. Knowledge based system
(KBS) techniques have been applied in these systems and in several applications,
but usually KBSs have been built in isolation, *i.e.* not as an integrated part of the
TMN. In order for a new generation of more advanced TMNs to become possible,
the integration with KBS is necessary. To be able to move towards integration,
KBS techniques must be taken into account already when system architectures,
concepts and environments are discussed. This paper proposes a general concept
for TMN where KBS techniques are integrated. The result is a knowledge based
telecommunication management network (KBTMN).

1. INTRODUCTION

The development of TMNs managing large and complex networks has enforced the use of
new techniques. Advanced information processing (AIP) techniques are used in many TMNs.
Advanced man-machine interfaces (MMIs), database systems and KBS are some examples of
AIP techniques. KBS are used to help TMN system users to manage the growing complexity
of telecommunication networks. KBSs can be used to handle both routine work to off-load
the users and to support the users carrying out their tasks.

Traditionally TMNs have been built without consideration of KBS techniques. Complex
tasks, difficult to solve using traditional programming techniques, are not supported by the
system. Later on, when experience has been gathered through use of the system and when
experts have become available, the idea of KBSs sometimes surfaces. Then knowledge based
systems supporting the users may be implemented as a supplement to the TMN.

The KBTMN concept presented in this paper represents an attempt to integrate KBS
techniques into TMNs at all stages of their life-cycle. The concept forms a platform to base
TMN applications on. The platform hides things like distribution and the use of several
knowledge representation formalisms. The concept also focuses the TMN system design on
KBS tools and techniques at an early stage of system development. The idea is to introduce

new technologies in TMNs and connect them together in a natural way. A more extensive description of the concept can be found in [Lundberg - 1989].

2. TELECOMMUNICATION MANAGEMENT NETWORKS

Today large telecommunication networks can be controlled and managed by one distributed TMN. Vast amounts of data and information are collected and the tasks to perform are growing increasingly complex. TMNs must be able to solve problems in a fast and accurate manner. Various user groups must be supported by the TMN, for example customers, operators, network planners and maintenance personnel. The different demands of these users must be taken into account when developing TMNs.

There are two main objectives of TMNs:

1. They should maintain efficient, reliable operation of the managed objects during both normal and exceptional conditions.

2. They should increase performance in terms of both quality and quantity of the managed objects.

A variety of tasks are handled or supported by TMNs. The most important ones are:

- Monitoring

- Operational control

- Diagnosis

- Maintenance and repair

- Planning

- Design and construction

- Administration

3. KNOWLEDGE BASED SYSTEMS

Knowledge based systems (KBSs) or expert systems is an area of AI that has grown rapidly during the last few years. The basic definition of a KBS is a system that solves problems within a specific, limited domain that normally would require human expertise. KBSs are best suited for problems that can not be solved using algorithmic methods.

In KBSs knowledge is regarded as separate from the rest of the program code, making it possible to change and manipulate the knowledge without interfering with the programs themselves. Due to this, a basic characteristic of KBSs is the knowledge representation formalism used. Rules is the most common formalism, but there are others, for example logic, procedures, scripts and objects.

In recent years it has become possible to develop real-time KBSs. These systems may for example have the capabilities to reason using temporal data, use non-monotonic reasoning (*i.e.* be able to retract conclusions if the prerequisites change during problem solving) or fulfil high performance demands.

There is a second generation KBSs evolving, the principle characteristic of which is a separation between deep, model based knowledge and shallow, heuristic knowledge [Ventakatasubramanian - 1987]. This makes it possible for the system to handle new unexpected problems, using general models of the current domain.

Several tools have been developed to support KBS development. Some tools that can be used for KBS applications in the TMN domain are G2, for real-time applications, MUSE, a tool-kit for development of medium-scale applications in the area of real-time and embedded systems and Nexpert Object a hybrid system that combines object-oriented and rule-based knowledge representations.

4. KNOWLEDGE BASED SYSTEMS IN TELECOMMUNICATION MANAGEMENT NETWORKS

There are a variety of applications for KBSs in TMNs and the technique has been successfully employed in several systems. Some examples are listed below.

Monitoring
KBSs for monitoring gives network operators help to observe the process and to suggest corrective actions when something goes wrong. Especially in rapidly changing processes, KBSs have a great potential. [Ross, Covo, Hart - 1988].

Operational Control
Operational control of telecommunication networks can be for example traffic routing. This is a real-time domain requiring high performance. One example of KBSs in traffic routing is given in [Jimenez - 1988].

Diagnosis
Diagnosis is by far the most common application of KBS in TMN. In diagnosis there are very few algorithms. Instead it is based on heuristics and experience, which can be implemented in KBSs. One examples is SHOOTX [Koseki - 1988], a diagnosis system for digital switching systems.

Maintenance & Repair
Some examples of KBSs in maintenance and repair are COMPASS [Prerau - 1985], a maintenance system for switching equipment and Starkeeper [Marques - 1988], a real-time network troubleshooter.

84

Planning
Planning is a suitable task for KBSs, but so far there have been very few applications in TMN.

Design & Configuration
Designing a telecommunication network and making reconfigurations of it is a task based on knowledge abut the network. There are some examples of KBS is this domain. See for example [Ferguson, Zlatin - 1988].

Administration
Administration of telecommunication networks comprises task like customer billing and customer query handling. Some examples of KBS applications in administration systems can be found in [Lundberg - 1988-1].

Most applications of KBSs in TMN are stand-alone systems where KBSs are built as a complement to existing TMNs. This is mainly due to a lack of useful programming languages and tools for KBS development in environments suitable for TMNs. This situation has to an extent changed in recent years and it is now possible to integrate KBS, *i.e.* develop embedded KBSs. Much can be gained merely by this integration of knowledge into the system. The integration of KBS functionality into TMNs, leading to a KBTMN is pictured in figure 1.

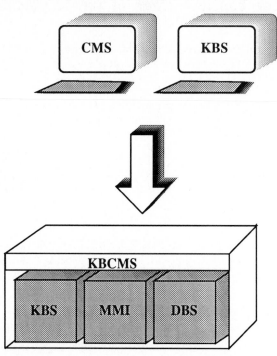

Figure 1:   The idea behind the KBTMN: KBSs should not be isolated systems, they should be an integrated part of TMNs together with other techniques like MMI and databases.

5. A CONCEPT FOR KNOWLEDGE BASED TMNs

The KBTMN concept is based on the acceptance of KBS as a possible technique to integrate into TMNs. This entails incorporation of the technique at the first system design stages. System models include KBSs as well as other AIP techniques. The basic idea behind the concept is the modularisation of KBS components, which facilitates development of KBS applications.

Our concept for KBTMNs is presented in figure 2.

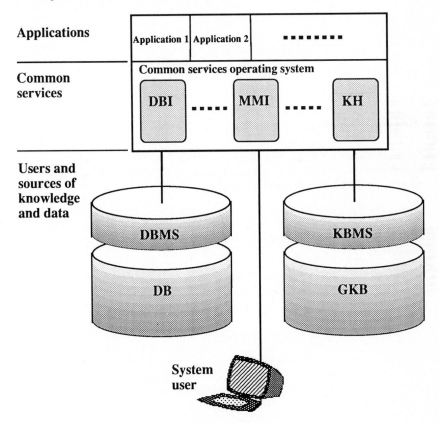

Figure 2:   A concept for TMNs, including KBS, databases and MMI.

Three main parts can be distinguished in the concept:

- applications
- common services

- users and sources of knowledge and data

Databases, database management systems (DBMS), MMIs, etc., which are parts of the concept, are used in most TMNs today. These parts are not discussed in this paper, instead the integration of KBS into the system is the main focus.

The KBTMN concept is further treated in [Lundberg - 1989], where it is applied to the general domain of control and management systems.

5.1 The General Knowledge Base (GKB)

The word general in general knowledge base reflects the fact that it contains knowledge from several domains, i.e. knowledge not specific to any particular application, task or user. More than one application in the TMN should be able to use knowledge stored in this knowledge base.

A general knowledge base has certain characteristics making it different from ordinary knowledge bases. The following are the main properties:

- General knowledge bases may comprise knowledge from several domains. A number of domain models have to be used to capture all knowledge needed. Inconsistencies are unavoidable when having many models describing a domain.

- Knowledge from several domains can usually not be captured using one single knowledge representation formalism. A general knowledge base typically supports several formalisms. Indeed, some set of knowledge may be implemented multiple times in different formalisms.

- General knowledge bases are often distributed because of the nature of the system they are implemented in (for example distributed TMNs).

5.2 The Knowledge Base Management System (KBMS)

KBMSs are built to handle the complexity of a general knowledge base and they should provide two main interfaces to the general knowledge base. One interface to the knowledge handler, i.e. the interface to the rest of the KBTMN system, and one to the knowledge base designer (see figure 3).

These two types of GKB users will pose different requirement on the KBMS. To manage this KBMSs have a structure comprising three abstraction levels: the implementation level, the engineering level and the knowledge level. These levels are described in [Brachman, Levesque - 1986]. The knowledge level handles the communication to the knowledge handler and the engineering level the communication to a knowledge base designer. Another pertinent attempt to model a knowledge base is found in [Bernus, Letray - 1987],where a four level model of knowledge representation is proposed.

Figure 3:   Two main interfaces to the general knowledge base (GKB) exist: The interface to
             the system designers and the interface to the knowledge handler.

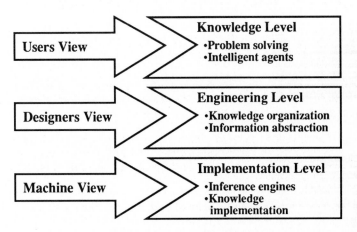

Figure 4:   A system like a KBMS can be viewed at a variety of levels. Three of these levels
             are the implementation level, the engineering level and the knowledge level.

The borders between the three levels are not completely strict.

5.3   The Knowledge Handler (KH)

The knowledge handler is a part of the common services operating system. As the name hints
at, the knowledge handler should take care of requests for knowledge coming from different
parts of the TMN. Requests for knowledge can come from system users, the MMI, various
applications, *etc.* The knowledge handler must not only be able to handle simple questions
involving knowledge and direct them to the KBMS, it must also be able to resolve
complicated questions involving both data and knowledge. Because of the separation of data
and knowledge on two logically different storage media, the knowledge handler must act as a
mediator. When the techniques have been further developed it is presumably possible to fuse
data and knowledge bases. But as long as knowledge bases can not fulfil the high per-

formance requirements often posed on databases and databases do not have the expressive power needed, they must be separated.

The knowledge handler has the role of an expert on distributed problem solving. This task is based on knowledge from several domains. The knowledge handler must at least contain a model of available resources in the system and their functionality. General knowledge of problem solving is also necessary to include in the knowledge handler. This knowledge is used to structure complex problems into simpler tasks before handling by knowledge bases or databases.

Knowledge transformation is another task for the knowledge handler. Depending on the properties of the knowledge, various models of the current domain are possible. The choice of model is often guided by user demands. Network operators, for example, will presumably use other models of a network than a network planner. Applications developed to support various user groups will use models and languages adapted to the specific users. Requests sent from applications may have to be transformed to fit other domain models before they can be further treated. Transformations can be simple, like translating from one term to another, for example meters to yards, but more complicated cases are possible, like transforming a functional description of a system error to a physical description denoting malfunctioning components. Functional and physical views of broadband telecommunication networks are treated in [Lundberg, Gardiner, Meroni, Spencer - 1988].

There are three main types of transformations in the KBTMN concept:

1. Transformations between two models in the general knowledge base.
2. Transformations from deep models in the general knowledge base to compiled knowledge in applications.
3. Transformations from deep models in the general knowledge base to databases fulfilling special requirements, for example real-time demands.

These types of transformations are depicted in figure 5.

One important motive for using knowledge transformations is the possibility to have improved performance in KBSs. A number of system users do not have to access knowledge from the same knowledge base, containing deep knowledge. Instead they can have a dedicated KBS or database with compiled knowledge. Knowledge transformations serve the distributed KBSs with new knowledge in case of refinements and changes of the general knowledge base.

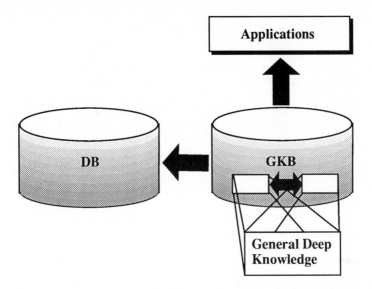

Figure 5:   Three types of transformations (depicted by the black arrows) can be
            distinguished in the KBTMN concept. Transformations between two deep
            models, a deep model and compiled knowledge and transformations between deep
            models and databases.

5.4 Applications

Functions and facilities of the TMN, are implemented as applications on top of the TMN
common services operating system. Applications treated here are of two kinds: applications
where KBS techniques are dominating and applications where KBS is used as a tool to solve
individual tasks involving knowledge. In both cases the KBTMN concept will provide several
features facilitating the use of KBS techniques. The concept of course also supports
applications with no KBSs.

Through the knowledge handler, applications can get help with tasks involving knowledge.
The knowledge handler takes care of the tasks and directs them to the general knowledge
base, the database, other applications or the MMI.

Adding KBS facilities to the common services will facilitate implementation of KBS in
applications. The applications will be able to access knowledge via the use of suitable
languages and formalisms and do not have to handle and store all knowledge themselves. A
great advantage is that tight integration of KBS applications with the rest of the system is
possible. The knowledge will mainly be handled in the general knowledge base and the knowledge handler. These two components may have to use dedicated AI software and hardware,
but applications can be implemented using ordinary techniques.

5.5 The Common Services Interface (CSI)

The interface between applications and common services (CSI) has an important role. Applications will not utilize the common service resources directly. Instead the common service interface should offer applications a model of the system in order to facilitate communication. This model is in a language rich enough to carry information and knowledge on various levels of abstraction. This language is called CSL (Common Services Language) and it is based on well-known concepts from AI, for example object models and first order logic. The KBMS or DBMS translates CSL into the actual implementation formalisms before the task is processed by knowledge bases or databases. CSL can be regarded as an extended SQL that enables communication with knowledge bases. CSL is also used as an information carrier within the common services architecture, for example between resources like knowledge bases and databases.

5.6 Realizations of the Concept

The concept presented in this paper is in part developed within the European collaboration project ADVANCE which is a part of RACE (R&D in Advanced Communication technologies in Europe). In ADVANCE concepts like this is studied in order to support the development of advanced network and customer administration systems for the evolving IBCN (Integrated Broadband Communication Network). Our work in this project is towards realisation of the knowledge handler module of the concept and specification of the applications to common service interaction language (CSL). A prototype is under construction in order to validate the basic ideas of this concept.

At Telelogic another prototype based on the concept has been developed. The designer interface of a KBMS is implemented and a physical network model is generated as a Prolog knowledge base. This network knowledge base is then used as a base for application development. This prototype will be used in future experiments with the concept. If other models are added, for example a functional network model, it will be possible to study the use of knowledge transformation between deep models. Network models can also be used to generate different applications, fulfilling different requirements, for example to generate real-time databases.

REFERENCES

Bernus, P., Letray, Z.: Intelligent Systems Interconnection: What Should come After Open Systems Interconnection? *Intelligent CAD Systems I: Theoretical and Methodological Aspects*. Springer Verlag, 1987.

Brachman, R. J., Levesque, H. J.: The Knowledge Level of a KBMS. *On Knowledge Base Management Systems*. Springer Verlag, 1986.

Ferguson, I. A., Zlatin, D. R.: Knowledge Structures for Communication Networks Design and Sales. *IEEE Network*, September 1988, 1988.

Jimenez, S.: The Application of Expert Systems to Network Traffic Management in Telecom Australia. *Telecommuncation journal of Australia*, 1988.

Koseki, Y.: SHOOTX: A multiple knowledge based diagnosis expert system for NEAX61 ESS. ISS 1988, 1988.

Lundberg, D.: Applicability of KBS to ADVANCE. RACE/ADVANCE, 1988-1.

Lundberg, D.: A Concept for Knowledge Based Support Systems in Network and Customer Administration Systems. Telelogic, 1988-2.

Lundberg, D., Gardiner, P., Meroni, M., Spencer, D.: Representing NCAS (Network and Customer Administration System) Knowledge. RACE/ADVANCE, 1988.

Lundberg, D.: Knowledge Based Control and Management Systems. Telelogic, 1989.

Marques, T.: A symptom-driven expert system for isolating and correcting network faults. *IEEE Communications*, 1988.

Prerau, D.: The Compass expert system: Verification, technology transfer and expansion. ISS, 1985.

Ross, M. J., Covo, A. A., Hart, C. D.: An AI-Based Network Management System. IEEE, Conference on computers and communications, 1988.

Ventakatasubramanian: An object-oriented two-tier architecture for integrating compiled and deep-level knowledge. 1987.

Information Network and Data Communication, III
D. Khakhar and F. Eliassen (Editors)
Elsevier Science Publishers B.V. (North-Holland)
© IFIP, 1990

SUPPORT TO NETWORK MANAGEMENT

Liane Margarida Rockenbach Tarouco

Institute of Informatics
Federal University of Rio Grande do Sul
Porto Alegre, RS, BRAZIL

The paper discusses approaches to the network management problem, showing alternative ways to support the network management activity. Special attention is dedicated to the management of a computer network comprised of open systems, in the sense defined by OSI. The standardization efforts developed by ISO, aiming at network management services on an OSI environment are described, with emphasis in fault management. An expert system to support the network management of an OSI environment is sketched.

1. INTRODUCTION

The successful operation of a computer network relies on its ability to detect and isolate faults and problems that may occur. Fault management procedures typically require that the faults be diagnosed and localized as precisely and efficiently as possible, to ensure that proper corrective action, including reconfiguration, is taken. The automatical diagnose of system malfunctions is highly desirable specially when timely and efficient, to reduce the impact of faults and of testing procedures on the system performance. Consequently, a rising interest in network management has been generated by a need to expand staff knowledge and to install tools capable of providing support to the network management activity.

Nowadays, this is accomplished through the use of realtime displays, while gathering the historical data needed either for performance analysis or for trend evaluation, or, still, to identify problem areas. A network management system can collect performance information and generate use statistics for every line, device, or system within the network. However, as a result of the significant increase in size and complexity of modern networks, there is a definite need for new management tools and techniques whereby networks can be used more effectively. These mechanisms must be able to deal with both the network physical entities (e.g. modems, multiplexers) and the network logical entities (e.g. session service access points, application programs).

A network management system must generate status and control information on a real-time basis, which will assist in the daily operation and support of the network, instead of just providing periodical reports of traffic and events. The amount of information provided must be reasonable; an excess of reported events or too much irrelevant information can prevent the network operator from understanding what is wrong in the network or what is causing it.

On the other hand, it is also important for the management system to deal with many kinds of network components, at least the most common ones. Users use to put together a network from a variety of those, but there is a trend whereby networks become growingly based on main architectures, like IBM's SNA. IBM developed an integration of its network management tools, under the Net View designation. An alternative architecture is OSI (Open Systems Interconnection). The trickle of products conforming the Open Systems Interconnect model - standards that enable computers from different vendors to communicate - may become a more substantial flow as more vendors announce products that conform to OSI specifications.

However, fully distributed network management functions in a large standardized network are still required. ISO/IEC JTC1/SC 21 is working on OSI Management Framework, describing the model and structure of OSI Management in a way that supplements and clarifies management's description contain in ISO 7498, the Basic Reference Model of Open Systems Interconnection (OSI).

This paper reports the efforts on network management standardization in an OSI environment, as well as some developments in network management support. A diagnosis protocol is also described, containing fault diagnosis capabilities. Finally, the paper points out to an expert system designed to advise fault management on an OSI management environment.

2. OSI MANAGEMENT ENVIRONMENT

OSI users need standard management activities, which are easy to use, in order to plan, organize, supervise, and control the communication service; it should be pointed out that, because the OSI environment is probably heterogeneous, this need is critical. OSI standardization has reached the point where implementation agreements are in place for all seven layers, products are on the market, or soon will be, supporting electronic mail and file transfer applications over a variety of local and wide-area networks.

There are requirements for:
—allocation, deallocation, access control and
      status indication of communications-objects;
—configuration management
—activation and deactivation;
—monitoring;
—appropriate command and response languages;
—time determination.

It is also important to rely on flexibility, to accommodate changing and new applications as a consequence of changing requirements. It means requirements for reconfiguration and handling of names and their synonyms.

Open systems must support their applications in a secure and predictable manner leading to requirements for: repeatability; integrity against system malfunction and interference from other uses; information protection and source and destination authentication; facilities for encryption and key management.

Whenever open systems components fail, rendering their applications unavailable or unreliable, there is the need for dependable reports, to secure error reporting and recovery as well as failure diagnosis and detailed logging. Last but not least: there are requirements for monitoring and controlling costs, implying requisites for: accounting information; cost parameters; performance monitoring and audit trail.

The above requirements for OSI Management are supported through a number of management services. Each service provides a range of facilities that may be effected either by local operation or by the communication of information between open systems, or both. System management provides mechanisms for the monitoring, control, and coordination of all OSI resources within open systems.

To meet this very wide range of requirements, the nature of management must be considered. Management is manifested in a number of ways. Management is related to activities which control or monitor the use of resources. Within Open Systems, the resources can be those that provide data storage or processing capability, or can be those that provide a communications capability. It is the latter and the communications concerning their management that fall within the scope of OSI Management. Those data processing and data communications resources (whether OSI resources or not) that may be managed through the use of OSI Management are referred as Managed Objects. The management of OSI resources and their status across all layers of the OSI architecture is.achieved through a set of application processes residing in different open systems, which communicate with each other and play complementary roles in order to provide the management activities described above. Communication rules are defined by systems management protocols which are therefore, applications protocols.

OSI Management is accomplished by Systems management, (N)-layer management and (N)-layer operation.

Systems management provides mechanisms for the monitoring, control and coordination of all managed objects within open systems. Systems management communications concerning systems management functions of an open system are attained realized through the system management application-entity (SMAE).

(N)-layer management provides mechanisms for the monitoring, control and coordination of those managed objects used to accomplish communication activities within an (N)-layer.

FIGURE 1: OSI NETWORK MANAGEMENT ENVIRONMENT

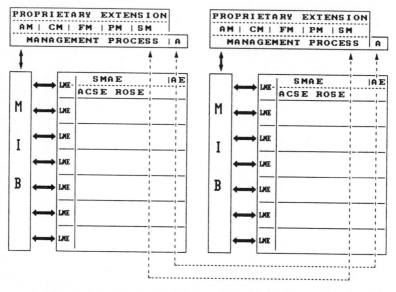

SMAE PROVIDES PROTOCOL FACILITIES FOR OSI MANAGEMENT
USES ROSE AS A REMOTE OPERACTIONS SERVICE
USES ACSE FOR ASSOCIATION CONTROL

(N)-layer operation provides the mechanisms for the monitoring and control of a single instance of communication.

Systems management is the preferred form of management information exchange and provides mechanisms for the exchange of information relating the managed objects.

Management processes, which support OSI Management, receive control information from people and/or software acting as a management process's local administrative agents and from remote systems through their SMAEs, (N)-layer management entities and (N)-entities. The management processes exert control directly upon managed objects in the same open system and upon managed objects in other systems by protocol exchanges through their SMAEs, (N)-layer management entities or (N)-entities. The flow of control from administrative agents to local management processes occurs entirely within the Local System Environment, and as such it remains outside the scope of OSI Management standardization.

The set of management data in an open system, available to the OSI environment, is called Management Information Base (MIB). The MIB is the conceptual repository in an open system for all information needed, regarding the reference model. This concept does not imply any form of storage for the information; its implementation is a matter of local concern and outside the scope of OSI standards.Data within the MIB is structured according to the requirements of the management processes which need to access it.

Although, in the OSI management model, the MIB has other uses (it includes data used by each layer management function and each protocol), for the purposes of MIS, the MIB can be considered as simply a definition of the information that is to be transferred by MIS exchanges. There are elements in the MIB that are common to more than one functional area of the MIS. For example, apart from the identity of a particular OSI resource, further common information is relevant to configuration management, to fault management and to accounting management. The MIB contains all information relevant to the operation of the OSI environment. This information can be categorized as follows:

—Event-type information: counter (errors, time-outs), etc.;

—Structured information: directory information base
      (application layer information, network layer information);

—Attribute type information: parameters (i.e. window size).

OSI communications concerning the system management functions are realized through a System Management Application Entity (SMAE), which consists of the System Management Service Element (SMASE), Common Management Information Service Element (CMISE), Remote Operation Service Element (ROSE) and Association Control Service Element (ACSE).

A management process may assume the roles of a managing process, an agent process or both. At least one management process will exist in each system that is involved in the transfer of information. Any management process will communicate with a remote management process for the purposes of transferring management information via the System Management Application Entity (SMAE) as showed in the figure 1.

The Common Management Information Service Element (CMISE), provides a generalized set of services for the transfer of management information and control. The Specific Management Information Service Element (SMISE), is defined in terms of the various types of MIS for which requirements have been identified (e.g. Accounting Management, Fault Management). The CMISE are:

M-INITIALIZE, M-TERMINATE and M-ABORT provide application
    association and termination;
M-EVENT-REPORT is used to report an event associated with
    management information to a peer CMISE-service-user;
M-GET is used to retrieve management information from a peer
    CMISE-service-user;
M-SET is used to request the modification of information values;
M-ACTION is used to request a peer CMISE-service-user to
    perform an action on a managed object;
M-CREATE is used by an invoking CMISE-service-user to request
    a peer to create a representation of a new managed object instance;
M-DELETE is used by an invoking CMISE-service-user to request
    a peer to delete a representation of a new managed object instance.

There are also specific service elements concerning each one of the main functions supported: accounting, performance, security, fault and configuration (Specific Management Functional Areas). For instance, the service element concerning fault management would be:

FM-ERROR-REPORTING: notify of a resource error in its
    management domain;
FM-GET-ERROR-COUNTERS and FM-ZERO-ERROR-COUNTERS allow
    accumulate error statistics reports;
FM-SET-THRESHOLD emits alarm signals, whenever a threshold is
    exceeded;

FM-INITIATE-TEST is a control function that requests from the system managing a resource to issue a command to have it tested, and, at the same time, requires a response from the addressed system, concerning its readiness to perform the test. The CMIS M-ACTION service is invoked to exchange this management information;

FM-TEST-REPORT is an unsynchronized operation associated to the request to invoke the test, because testing normally takes a significant amount of time and, therefore, should not be viewed as an atomic operation; other service elements therein related are: FM-TEST-STATUS, FM-TEST-ABORT, FM-TEST-SUSPEND and FM-TEST-RESUME;

FM-TRACE requests the management process in the destination system to test the station's operational status and its connecting links.

Although human beings are ultimately responsible for managing the OSI environment, responsibilities may be delegated to automated processes. Integrated test systems can be software-controlled, to effect the test under optimized strategy, as it will be described in the next section.

3. SUPPORT TO NETWORK MANAGEMENT

Integrated test systems are essential to support the network management activity. This activity, however, is usually carried out in a centralized manner, or at least on a hierarchical basis. This means that, in order to capture information about the state of the network, or to request that information, commands and responses must be sent throughout the network, implying on additional network costs associated to this overhead traffic. It is desirable to have support to effect the test in a optimized strategy, as proposed by Agre [1] whose paper describes an adaptive strategy designed to achieve specific objectives, such as reducing testing costs. An algorithm generates a fault diagnosis strategy in the form of trees. Each test is assumed to have a cost, called the weighting function, which represents some form of resource consumption (e.g. time or money). Data on test times, tests costs or node failure rates can be used by the algorithm to generate fault diagnosis trees, with specific objectives such as minimizing the time, cost, or number of tests required to isolate a fault.

Tests can be performed either collectively in one step or sequentially. Sequential testing is frequently more efficient as a fault may be inferred without requiring all the test results. Sequential decision problems have been studied in the context of decision tables, pattern recognition, and artificial intelligence. Most of these approaches rely on a static model of the system faults and their interaction. Recently, the application of artificial intelligence to the development of expert systems for fault diagnosis has been investigated

[2-3],[7-8]. A study was conduced by the author to this purpose, leading to a prototype implementation.

The expert system designed is oriented to OSI environment; figure 2 shows the steps taken to build it. As a first approach it was decided begin with the transport layer. This selection arose from the fact that the transport layer provides the most basic service independent of the kind of network used. Thus, there would be more portability for the solution, providing a way to manage the network service available to all end-systems in the network.

According figure 2, the first step involved the collection of relevant network syndromes. The problems occurring and being detectable by the transport layer can be relevant for one or more of the five classes of OSI management functions: fault performance, configuration, security and accounting. So they were grouped into different problem-causing categories: lack of resources, software bugs, unreliable sub-network and users.

Two examples in the lack of resourses category are the following:

PROBLEM 1: a transport connection can not be open
HOW IT IS DETECTED:
    T-disconnect.ind with cause Lack of local or remote resources of the
    TS (Transport Service) provider because of currentOpenConnections is equal
    maxOpenConnections
ACTION RECOMMENDED:
    Increment the Tide Mark unsucessfullOutConnections
    If the threshold is reached then generate an FM-ERROR-REPORTING
SUGGESTED CORRECTIVE ACTION:
    Consider to redefine maximum number of transport connections

FIGURE 2: STEPS TO BUILD THE EXPERT SYSTEM

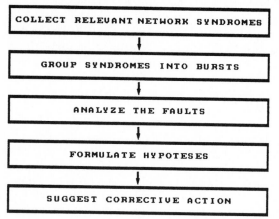

PROBLEM 2: a transport connection can not be open
HOW IT IS DETECTED:
    T-disconnect.ind with cause Lack of local or remote resources of the
    TS (Transport Service) provider because of N-disconnect.ind
ACTION RECOMMENDED:
    Increment the Tide Mark networkUnavailable
    If the threshold is reached then generate an alert
SUGGESTED CORRECTIVE ACTION:
    Issue a FM-GET-ERROR-COUNTERS to get the counter value
    limitOfNetworkConnectionsReached from the network layer
    If not 0 consider redefine/negotiate maximum number of network connections

This system is intended to help people involved with network management, most of them are really problem solvers. Excessive network downtime often happens because people responsible for network restoring simply cannot remember all the component's failure symptoms. They take wrong turns and waste time because they ignore important facts; ones fail to perform a simple test, or even overlook a warning light, signalizing what is wrong. In a layered protocol, the location of a protocol fault is difficult to determine. The fault may be due to a lower layer condition or to a parameter error at the tested protocol layer. The method for isolate the faults occurring in a layered protocol requires, to begin with, the identification of faults that can occur in that environment. Table 1 shows a summary of faults that can occur at each OSI layer.

Table 1: Faults X layer

	PHY	LINK	NET	TRANSP	SESSION	PRES	APPL
REJECTION	X	X	X	X	X	X	X
ABNORMAL DISC.	X	X	X	X	X	X	X
UNKNOWN ADDRESS			X	X	X		
SEQUENCE		X	X	X	X		
CONGESTION			X	X	X		
PROTOCOL VERSION		X		X	X	X	
SERVICE CLASS			X	X	X	X	
INVALID FORMAT		X	X	X	X	X	X
MESSAGE TOO LONG		X		X		X	
TRANSM. ERROR		X		X			
DENIED ACCESS			X	X	X		
UNREACH. ADDRESS		X	X	X	X		
PROTOCOL ERROR		X	X	X	X		

A way to improve the network management activity is to aggregate an automated support to deal with the M-EVENT-REPORTS (steps 3 and 4 in figure 2). The initial process would watch symptoms, discarding "false" ones (those that are mere consequences of a major cause) and filtering events reported. This phase may involve the use of M-GET service element, togather more information, from other possibly related open systems. A list of possible causes would be brought forth; additional observation and testing may be triggered to prove hypotheses and to improve trouble diagnose. FM-INITIATE-TEST and M-ACTION are used to direct a management process to perform a test on a resource to determine wheter it maintains service capability. Even the strategy used to decide which resource checked in the first place should be optimized.

The process of observation, hypothesis, and testing is repeated until the problem is solved Maybe additional information should be provided by the network human operator or by the maintenance staff. A facility to easy interaction with the system should be also provided (the user interface showed in figure 3).

The inference engine is the system component which controls the deductive process; it implements the most appropriate strategy or reasoning process for the OSI environment diagnosis. The knowledge base contains all of the relevant domain-specific information permitting the program to behave as an OSI specialized, intelligent problem-solver.

At the bottom level, the system must actually perform primitive actions and tests to realize its goals. These are performed by sending appropriate messages to the nearest management process. The performance of actions and tests is mediated through the MIB-Management Information Base, which represents the system's current beliefs about the world and by the nearest management process which by its turn interchanges commands and other information with other management processes. In this view, a test directly updates the data base with new facts as they become known.

FIGURE 3: NETWORK MANAGEMENT SUPPORT COMPONENTS

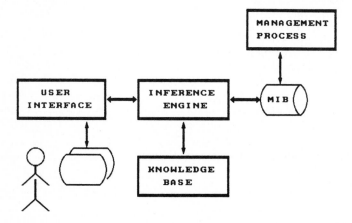

The system aim to minimize one of the biggest problems facing modern computer networks, the lack of a skilled labor force to deal with large network problem-solving situations. Solving the more serious problems requires that the operators:

a) monitorize the system and maintain a mental model of its state;
b) recognize problems by their symptomn;
c) obtain additional data on the symptoms causes;
d) diagnose genuine problems;
e) take appropriate steps to solve problems .

Steps a) to d) are easier to be automated. Although step e) could be automated, through network reconfiguration, human intervention is still needed to fix problems or to effect some tests that cannot be automatically controlled; sometimes parameters may not be directly examined. The feedback provided after problem-fixing must be also included in the knowledge base, to improve its capability to solve further problems or at least to indicate their solutions. In the beginning, the expert system contains very few rules and the majority of decisions will be human-operator determined. To do this the MIB will be searched in many different ways do retrieve meaningful information. So it was decided organize it as a SQL database. The database can be searched both by the expert system and by the human expert. New rules keep being formulated as new problems are being solved by the human expert. The greater the number of rules built into the system, the smaller will be the frequence of problems left to be handled by the human expert.

The initial knowledge base was built from the layer behavior description documents. The new rules and the confidence factors associated with each one of them are being derived from the observation of real open systems functioning.

4. CONCLUSIONS

The application of expert systems techniques to network management represents a promising approach to managing the increasing complexity and dynamics that characterize a computer network environment. The requirement for high availability and high performance computer networks has created a demand for fast, consistent, expert-quality response to operational problems. The expert systems techniques provide a basis for automating operations despite the complexity and the dynamics that characterize the computer network environment.

A major uncertainty in the ultimate success of application of expert systems to network management lies in the ability to deal with a very high number of events in real-time. But considering the on-going developments of computer architectures specially oriented to artificial intelligence applications, it is expected that this problem will be solved in a near future.

REFERENCES

[1] AGRE,J. A message-based fault diagnosis procedure. SIGCOM'86, Vermont, August 1986.

[2] MILIKEN,K et al, YES/MVS and the automation of operations for large computer complexes. IBM Systems Journal Vol. 25. No 2, 1986

[3] JOSEPH,C et alii. MAP Fault Management Expert System. Integrated Network Management I, IFIP, Boston, May -1989 4.ISO/IEC JTC1/SC21. Information Processing Systems -Open System Interconnection. System Management - Fault Management, April 1988.

[5] ISO/IEC JTC1/SWC21 Information Processing Systems - Open System Interconnection. Systems Management: Overview (First Enhanced Working Draft) April 1988

[6] ISO/IEC JTC1/SC21. Editors DRAFT of Information Processing Systems - Open System Interconnection. Management Information Protocol Specification - Part 2: Common Management Information Protocol, June 1988

[7] WALDES,P, LUSTGARTEN,J & STOLFO,S. Are maintenance expert systems practical now? Technical report CUCS-166-85, Columbia University, 1985.

[8] GOODMAN. Rodnei, et alii, Real Time Autonomous Expert Systems in Network Management Integrated Network Management I, IFIP, Boston, May -1989

Information Network and Data Communication, III
D. Khakhar and F. Eliassen (Editors)
Elsevier Science Publishers B.V. (North-Holland)
IFIP, 1990

SERVICE MANAGEMENT ARCHITECTURE

Janez Skubic
Ericsson Radio Systems AB

ABSTRACT

The services offered by telecom service providers are becoming more and more extensive and adaptable, while networks are being built up from a variety of heterogeneous systems.

Under these circumstances, the different services of the network cannot any longer be managed efficiently if they are managed separately from each other. There is a need for an overall service management plan that defines the service and network management solutions generically, for all types of services and systems.

This paper presents a Service Management Architecture which is such an overall plan for wireline and radio access telecom networks.

1. INTRODUCTION

The production of telecom services has come a long way: from manual, operator-assisted services to today's fully automatic call processing. Automation means that telecom services can now be generated in large volume and inexpensively, and are now generally available to and affordable for everyone.

In addition to basic telephony and computerized call processing, telecom providers offer a number of service management and network management services to their customers, for example handling of subscriptions, development and marketing of new services, customized management of private networks.

Service management and network management are at present rather labor-intensive. Providers are doing their best to satisfy their own internal service management needs, but are not yet in a position to generate these types of services in sufficiently large volume to be able to extend them to their customers in more than special cases.

One of the reasons for this relatively late attention to the automation of network management processes is the changing nature and complexity of service management. The various types of services are optimized for their particular function and are generally difficult to integrate. The network's resources consist of a large number of managed entities which are heterogeneous, which are constantly changing in quantity, mutual relationships and in their nature.

For these reasons it has been difficult to justify the large scale development of integrated network management systems. The situation is, however, changing. Service management and network management systems are becoming a necessity at the same time as developments in technology are beginning to offer the solutions.

This paper is a general statement of the problem that Service Management Architecture, SMA, is aimed at solving.

SMA is a structured plan for solutions in the areas of service management and network management. It is intended to make it easier to design network components to fit the service provider's overall service management objectives. SMA is consequently not a product but may be interpreted in terms of products: existing products and new products.

The method of deriving the service management solutions is described in section 5. The components of SMA - applications and their interfaces - are reviewed in section 6.

Service Management Architecture in its present form addresses the service management problems of public telecom networks.

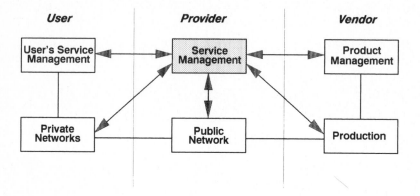

Figure 1. Service Management

An architecture needs to accommodate a wide variety of components so that the system, i.e. the network, can perform harmoniously within its environment. It is therefore obvious that the SMA concept favors standard components and standard interfaces; in particular the CCITT-TMN recommendations [1], the national TMN standards like the US ANSI T1M1 specifications [2][3] and the OSI communications and network management standards [4].

2. THE PRINCIPLES OF SERVICE MANAGEMENT ARCHITECTURE

Finding the balance between the division of the problem into parts and the integration of these parts constitutes the art of service management architecture.

The overall problem needs to be broken down into smaller parts to make it manageable. At the same time what is common to the different parts needs to be related so that the parts can function harmoniously together.

If service management problems could be solved independently of each other, one by one, an architecture would not be of much use. This was the case with the early networks. Nowadays, service management problems need to be solved interdependently.

The basic architectural principles of the SMA are: completeness, integration and uniformity.

Completeness - The architecture needs to fully address the problem to be solved. All factors that might influence the solutions need to be addressed. Service management architecture needs to address not only the provider's internal problems but also the provider's interfaces with customers and vendors.

Integration - Service management solutions should be integrated as far as possible, and the solutions need to complement each other.

Uniformity - Interfaces and environments should be general enough so that they can accommodate changes in the service and network configurations.

3. ARCHITECTURE AS A PROBLEM-SOLVING PROCESS

Service and network configurations will be simpler if we make use of generic solutions. This requires anticipation of new situations. And this is where the use of an architecture is appropriate. An architecture may be seen as a problem-solving method.

Service management problems have three levels of complexity:

Individual Service Management - Service management solutions are designed specifically for each service and resource type.

Integrated Service Management - The scope of service management is widening and service management solutions must be able to keep up with this development. These solutions need to cover several if not all different types of user, provider and vendor service management system.

Evolutionary Service Management - In real life, networks are constantly changing. New types of services and equipment are added continuously, and these need to be managed together with the existing ones.

The traditional two-stage problem-solving approach where a requirements specification states the problem and the design then follows directly from this specification, handles the first level of complexity quite adequately. However, this approach is at best laborious for deriving integrated and evolutionary management solutions.

SMA adds a new dimension to the problem-solving process by separating the statement of the problem from its solution and by separating the solution from its realization.

The SMA problem-solving approach consists generally of three steps: problem definition, solution to the problem and determination of the implementation structure.

A description of the SMA problem-solving approach follows:

Problem definition

The problem may be expressed in many different terms, for example in terms of the services the provider wants to carry out, capabilities, functions, information flow. The architecture concept must make it possible to address any type of problem in an organized manner.

As support for the classification of problems, SMA includes a Service Management Model (see section 4).

Solution to the problem

SMA defines the solution to a problem in terms of what the provider needs to know and do to generate the service. These solutions are represented in the model as management constituents, actors and nodes (see section 5).

Implementation structure

SMA does not seek to define how the solutions are to be implemented but rather how they need to be structured from the overall perspective. It ensures that the solutions will perform harmoniously once they are implemented in different products. SMA is not a one-system or one-product architecture.

The components of the SMA implementation structure are applications and their interfaces (see section 6).

These three steps are described in the next three sections.

4. THE SERVICE MANAGEMENT CONCEPT

Service Management is considered here as an extension of telecommunications network management. It includes all the activities of the service provider designed to produce and manage telecom services and the network's resources. This includes the management of subscriptions, handling of service requests, production and distribution of services, management of the network's resources.

All activities performed by provider are structured by the *Service Management Model.*

The service provider is here a public telecom company or a department in a corporation that produces and sells telecom services.

The Service Management Model builds on the following concepts:

-    A distinction between the concepts of user, provider and vendor. Users, providers and vendors work together and are considered as independent partners in their relationship.

-    A distinction between four service components: service development, service administration, service control and service production. Figure 2. A provider develops new services and offers them on the market. The customer then subscribes to these services. The provider receives and carries out service requests and delivers the services.

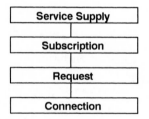

Figure 2. Service Model

-    A distinction between access, production and management activities. The model is intended to represent the cases in which the provider strictly separates the customer interface from the large scale production interface. In many cases it is advantageous to handle user specifics as close to the user's access to the network as possible. In a similar manner, management activities may be distinguished from the production activities to provide support for the management, using indicators as opposed to events.

See Figure 3 for an overview of the model.

Definition of actors in the management constituents

The concept of **actor** corresponds to the concept of entity. An actor is an entity but with an added dimension: it can perform a range of different roles relative to other entities. An actor is defined in terms of its operational environment, contents, services and language.

Example: An actor that is defined at an information collection point may specify what kinds of information need to be collected for various types of network exceptions.

Network management problems are seldom deterministic. The concept of actor helps in handling non-deterministic situations given that it makes it possible to represent not only the existing but also potential relationships.

Allocation of actors to nodes.

A service management solution is final when the actors are allocated to the nodes.

A **node** may be an existing network component, a new network component, a management system or an organization unit.

The amount of flexibility permissible in the allocation of actors into nodes will depend on the implementation of the node's system. Generally, the actors should be collocated or distributed in a network of nodes.

6. THE COMPONENTS OF SERVICE MANAGEMENT ARCHITECTURE

The components of SMA are service management applications and their interfaces (see Figure 6).

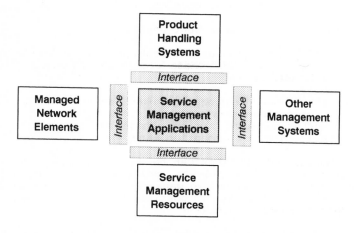

Figure 6. Service Management Architecture

Service Management Applications - are the application programs
and the data that implement management solutions as defined in
terms of the management constituents, actors and nodes.

Service Management Interfaces - are the interfaces between the
Service Management Applications.

6.1. SERVICE MANAGEMENT APPLICATIONS

The aim of SMA is to define management applications independent
of their implementation.

An application may be implemented differently at different stages
of technological development. It may be implemented differently
by different vendors. The purpose of the architecture is to make
it possible for these different implementations to function
together harmoniously.

Service Management Applications provide three types of services:
cooperation, production and coordination.

- cooperation services make it possible for the systems in
the network to work together.

- production services are the productive services
that the network and/or organization provide the user with.

- coordination services make it possible to manage the
production services.

Cooperation Services

Cooperation services make possible the interconnections between
management systems and network elements, work centers, operations
support systems, administrative systems (see
Figure 7).

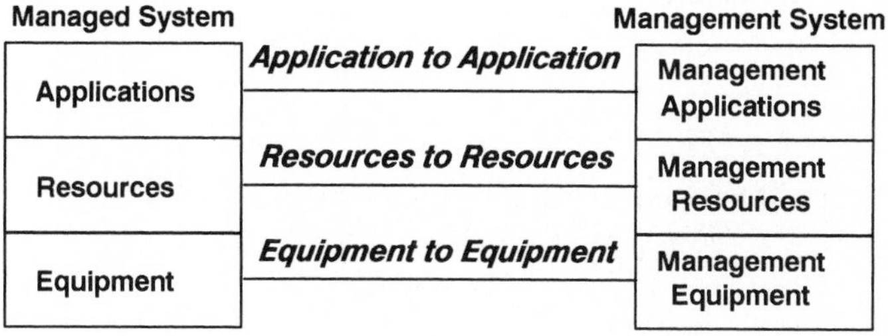

Managed System		Management System
Applications	*Application to Application*	Management Applications
Resources	*Resources to Resources*	Management Resources
Equipment	*Equipment to Equipment*	Management Equipment

Figure 7. Cooperation Service Types

Examples of cooperation services are: communications gateway
services, interface adaptation, message distribution, message
routing, protocol conversion, reformatting of information,

creation of views, presentation services.

The Service Management Applications that provide cooperation services are called **agents**.

An agent represents an external system taken into the service management system. Example: The agent that provides the interface between a human user and a management system is the presentation agent. The agents that provide the interfaces with network elements are the Network Element Agents.

Production Services

Production services are the real service management services. They are structured according to what part of the managed system they apply to: the application, resource or equipment management services.

Applications means here both application software and/or data. Resources means here the operating system, communications system, database management system, libraries of tools, general information. Equipment means here deliverables including the managed system hardware, software and documentation.

Accordingly, there are three types of the production services: Application management services, resource management services and equipment management services (see Figure 8).

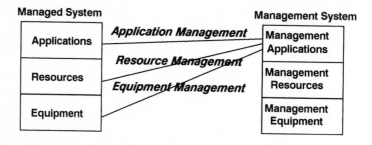

Figure 8. Service Management Service Types

Application Management Services - manage the managed system's applications. Application management is functionally structured into performance management (including accounting management), configuration management, consistency management (including fault and security management) and evolution management. These functional areas correspond generally to the management areas as outlined in the OSI standards. The evolution functional area includes the support for the addition of new types of application management capabilities.

Resource Management Services - manage the network resources.

Examples: management of databases, communications, operating systems.

Equipment Management Services - manage the network equipment. Examples: installation and testing of hardware and software, management of hardware and software configurations.

The applications that provide production services are called **servers**.

Coordination Services

Coordination services coordinate the service management applications in a service management network. Examples: allocation of service management responsibilities among the management systems, address management, mutual backup arrangements among the management systems.

The applications that provide coordination services are called **coordinators**.

6.2. SERVICE MANAGEMENT INTERFACES

Resource Interfaces

Resource interfaces define the environment in which service management applications are designed, managed and run.

Network Element Interfaces

Network element interfaces are the interfaces between the managed network elements, i.e. service production systems, and the management systems which host the service management applications.

Management Interfaces

Management interfaces are the interfaces between a service management system and other management systems. Management systems have a variety of denotations depending on their primary function. Examples: service control systems, resource management systems, operations support systems, work centers, administrative systems, user network management systems.

Product Handling Interfaces

Product handling interfaces are the interfaces between the service management system and the vendor's product handling and customer support systems.

7. SERVICE MANAGEMENT SYSTEMS

A service management system includes three types of applications: agents, servers and coordinators. Figure 9.

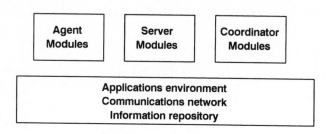

Figure 9. Management System Concept

Systems that are dedicated for service management are generically called service managers. A service manager works together with network elements, administrative systems, operations support systems, work centers, other service management systems, product handling and design support systems. Figure 10.

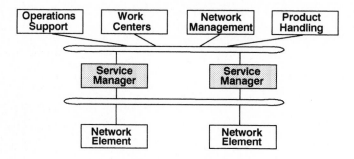

Figure 10. The Service Manager Concept

The aim is to make it easy for each service provider to set up the service management arrangements that best fit his particular circumstances and management style and at the same time give scope for evolving service management solutions as his situation changes with time.

8. CONCLUSION

Service Management Architecture provides a means of representing the service provider's overall problem. It provides an understanding of the service provider's overall service production, service control, service administration and service development. An overall perspective is necessary as the network components need to be able to cooperate closely with each other.

SMA is not intended to be a product nor is it an attempt to describe the network components completely. Its purpose is to define the roles of the components in relation to each other. The closer the cooperation between the components, the more comprehensive the representation of their roles in the SMA needs to be.

Thus SMA makes it possible to represent existing as well as new network components.

Even if the SMA in its current form is designed as a general architecture, it is primarily intended for application to fixed and the mobile access public networks.

REFERENCES

[1] CCITT Recommendation M.30, Principles for a Telecommunications Management Network

[2] T1M1, Principles and Functions, Architecture and Protocols for Interfaces Between Operations Systems and Network Elements (Draft)

[3] T1M1, Modelling Guidelines

[4] ISO DIS 7498/4, Information Processing Systems - Open Systems Interconnection - Basic Reference Model Part 4 - OSI Management Framework

Information Network and Data Communication, III
D. Khakhar and F. Eliassen (Editors)
Elsevier Science Publishers B.V. (North-Holland)
© IFIP, 1990

High Speed LANs and MANs - Protocols and Problems

Peter Davids, Peter Martini

Dept. of Computer Science (Informatik IV), Aachen University of Technology
Ahornstr. 55; D-5100 Aachen; West Germany
☎: +241/80-4522; FAX: +241/80-6295; e-mail: ...unido!rwthinf!martini

Abstract

Progress in optical component design allows ever increasing channel capacity for Local Area Networks (LANs). Now that we have become familiar with data rates in the range of 10 Mbit/s a new generation of computer networks offering raw transmission capacities in the 100 Mbit/s range has become commercially available. Upcoming standards for High Speed Local Area Networks (HSLANs) and Metropolitan Area Networks (MANs), prototypes and products commercially available make high speed networks operating at data rates exceeding 100 Mbit/s move into the focus of interest. In this paper we study fiber optic configurations for high speed networks. Furthermore, we describe the current status of standardization and analyze the most important medium access control protocols with respect to their performance.

I. Introduction

In the last decade, optical fiber has emerged as the most important medium for high speed communication systems. From bit rates in the range of only 6 - 30 Mbit/s, modulation bit rates of optical transmission systems have increased year by year. Today, the data rate of optical transmission systems installed in the field and carrying commercial service exceeds 1 Gbit/s. Research in fiber optic transmission systems has even shown that one optical fiber has a potential throughput of 4500 Gbit/s which may be achieved using frequency division multiplexing and coherent detection (see [1]).

Thus, what has been called 'High Speed Communication' not so many years ago must now be called 'Medium Speed Communication' or even 'Low Speed Communication'. Even today, many computer network users still have to live with lines providing no more than 9.6 kbit/s. However, each and everyone of us who has ever used a PC interconnected to a laserwriter, a fileserver and/or a mainframe computer by a Local Area Network such as Ethernet or Token Ring can no longer imagine that 9.6 kbit/s can be enough. The next step is already in front of us: High Speed Local Area Networks (HSLANs) and Metropolitan Area Networks (MANs) provide data rates in the range or even in excess of 100 Mbit/s. However, this is the data rate provided by the physical medium and is by far not the data rate provided to individual users.

At first sight, problems to be overcome in HSLANs and MANs appear to be exactly the same as the problems which have already been solved in LANs. A closer look shows that considerable protocol modifications or even new protocols are unavoidable if we want to exploit the data rate offered by the physical medium. Moreover, new topologies tailored to the requirements of new medium access control protocols have also been proposed. These configurations for fiber optic systems are studied in section III. After that, the most important protocols for high speed networks are discussed in section IV. In sections V. and VI. we study the performance of medium access protocols. But first of all, applications for HSLANs are discussed in section II.

II. Applications for High Speed Networks

The first application envisaged for HSLANs was a high bandwidth interconnection of storage and mainframe computers. However, as time progressed, other applications have moved into the focus of interest. Workstations with megabytes of memory and high resolution displays will revolutionize the way we generate, store, manipulate and use images. Moving these images between storage and workstation will require communication systems much more powerful than the LANs we use today. A totally different application are backbone networks interconnecting lower rate LANs. In the case of MANs, these systems may even operate over areas in excess of 50 km in diameter. Depending on the distances to be covered the following major applications for HSLANs may be distinguished:

The *Data Center Environment* is characterized by a relatively few number of stations, typically mainframe computers and peripheral equipment, where a high degree of reliability and fault tolerance is required.

In contrast to this, the *Office/Building Environment* is characterized by a relatively large number of stations (typically smaller computers, communications concentrators, workstations, and peripherals).

Finally, the *Campus Environment* is characterized by stations distributed across multiple buildings where links of up to several kilometers may be encountered. This application is typically used for trunk lines between office/building and/or data center environments.

One step further, we reach *Metropolitan Area Networks*. Future communication systems tailored to the requirements of this scenario will consist of numerous high speed subnetworks interconnected by high speed backbones.

III. Fiber Optic Configurations

From a technological point of view, fiber optic communication systems may easily be configured by unidirectional optical point-to-point-links between actively coupled stations. This approach prefers ring and star topologies. However, busoriented fiber optic Local Area Networks have also become feasible due to a new class of medium access protocols which, unlike the classical medium access protocols token bus and CSMA/CD, allows efficient bandwidth utilization.

A. Ring Networks

Ring Networks consist of a set of stations logically connected as a serial string of stations and transmission media to form a closed loop. Information is transmitted sequentially, as a stream of suitably encoded symbols from one active station to the next, where 'active' means that stations generally regenerate and repeat each symbol.

The most important standard for HSLANs which has been proposed by the ANSI committee X3T9.5 is based on a ring structure. Section IV.A. includes a description of this standard.

B. Star Structures

Optical star networks have been successfully implemented to bridge large geographical distances in CSMA/CD-LANs. Furthermore, physical star structures are proposed for broad-band ISDN (see e.g. [2]). One important reason is that security and privacy problems are much harder to solve in bus structures or ring networks. On the other hand, star structures are currently not within the scope of standardization activities for HSLANs or MANs.

C. Bus Structures

Most of the Local Area Networks which have been installed up to now use bus structures. However, the classical protocols CSMA/CD [3] and token bus [4] suffer from inefficient bandwidth utilization if data rate or geographic distance or even both are decisively increased. This is due to the fact that each transmission is followed by a gap of the order of the round trip delay. Moreover, in contrast to LANs the majority of fiber optic networks employs unidirectional transmission because it causes much less implementation problems.

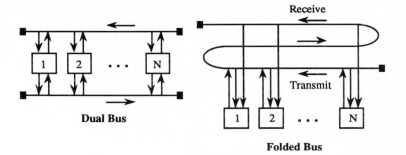

Fig. 1 Bus Structures

Some years ago, *'folded bus structure'* and *'dual bus structure '*(cf. Fig. 1) have been proposed (see e.g. [5]) to allow broadcast communication with unidirectional transmission. Several alternative bus structures have also been discussed. On the other hand, the dual bus structure is the only one which is proposed by a standardization committee: the IEEE 802.6 proposal for a Metropolitan Area Network standard called DQDB is based on this dual bus. This standard is described in section IV.B.

IV. Protocols

In this section, we consider two protocols which have been proposed by standardization committees. The protocol discussed in section IV.A. has been defined for fiber optic HSLANs. In contrast to this, the protocol presented in section IV.B. is tailored to the requirements of Metropolitan Area Networks. Nevertheless, it may also evolve as an interesting candidate for HSLANs.

A. FDDI

The Fiber Distributed Data Interface (FDDI) is a proposed new ANSI Standard (cf. [6] - [9]) for HSLANs. The FDDI fiber optic ring network provides a high bandwidth general purpose interconnection (100 megabit per second) among computers and peripheral equipment. It may be configured to support a sustained transfer rate of approximately 80 megabits (i.e. 10 megabytes) per second. However, FDDI may not meet the response time requirements of all unbuffered high speed devices.

FDDI establishes the connection among many stations distributed over distances of several kilometers in extent. Default values have been calculated on the basis of 1000 physical connections and a total fiber path length of 200 kilometers.

The FDDI consists of 4 standards which follow the layering of the OSI Reference Model (cf. Fig. 2).The PMD (Physical Layer Medium Dependent)-sublayer provides the digital baseband point-to-point communication between stations in the FDDI network. It provides all services necessary to transport a suitably coded digital bit stream from station to station. In contrast to this, the PHY (Physical Layer Protocol)-sublayer provides the connection between PMD and the Data Link Layer. The Medium Access Control (MAC) standard of FDDI is primarily concerned with the delivery of frames including their insertion, repetition, and removal. It controls the accessing of the medium and the generation and verification of frame check sequences to assure the proper delivery of valid data to the higher layers. The control necessary at the station level to manage the processes underway in the various FDDI layers is provided by the station management (SMT).

122

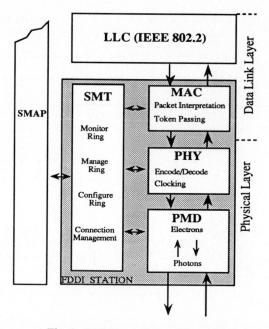

Fig. 2 FDDI Layer Block Diagram

In FDDI, access to the Physical medium (the ring) is controlled by passing a Token around the ring. The Token gives the downstream station (receiving relative to the station passing the Token) the opportunity to transmit a frame or a sequence of frames. If a station wants to transmit, it strips the Token from the ring. After the captured Token is completely received, the station shall begin transmitting its eligible queued frames. Each Frame starts with a Preamble which is at least 64 bit long. This preamble is followed by a starting delimiter (8 bit), Frame Control (8 bit), Destination Address (16 bit or 48 bit) and Source Address (16 bit or 48 bit). The length of the information field is variable, but is limited by the maximum frame length which is 4500 byte. This payload field is followed by a Frame Check Sequence (32 bit), End Delimiter (4 bit), and a Frame Status field ($\geq$ 12 bit) used for indicating errors or correct reception. After transmission, the station issues a new Token for use by a downstream station.

FDDI supports two major classes of service, namely 'synchronous' (guaranteed bandwidth and response time) and 'asynchronous' (dynamic bandwidth sharing). The synchronous class of service is used for those applications whose bandwidth and response time limits are predictable in advance, permitting them to be allocated (via Station Management). Traffic generated by applications whose bandwidth requirements are less predictable (i.e. bursty or potentially unlimited) is transmitted as asynchronous traffic. The same holds for applications whose response time requirements are less critical. Asynchronous bandwidth is instantaneously allocated from the pool of remaining ring bandwidths that are unallocated, unused, or both.

Within each station, the MAC transmitter maintains a Token Rotation Timer (TRT) to control ring scheduling for asynchronous traffic. This timer is reset each time a token arrives before TRT reaches the 'operative Target Token Rotation Time' (T_OPR) which is negotiated during ring initialization via a 'Claim Token process'. FDDI guarantees an average TRT (or average synchronous response time) not greater than T_OPR, and a maximum TRT not greater than twice T_OPR.

Synchronous Transmission: Synchronous Frames may be transmitted whenever the station captures a token. In order to allow this kind of operation, each station has a known allocation of synchronous bandwidth which is allocated by the station management. It should be noted that the support for synchronous transmission is optional, and is not required for interoperability.

Asynchronous Transmission: Whenever an 'early' token is captured, i.e., a token arriving before TRT reaches T_OPR, the current value of TRT is saved in an asynchronous Token-Holding Timer (THT), and TRT is reset to time the next token rotation. THT is enabled (running) during asynchronous transmission and the difference between its current value and the target value (T_OPR) reflects the remaining asynchronous bandwidth available to this station.

The Medium Access Protocol described up to now supports fair access at a frame granularity. However, multiple levels of asynchronous priority may optionally be distinguished. For each implemented priority level, a threshold value is established, forming a set of threshold values. A Token may only be captured for transmission of a frame of priority i if the current TRT is larger than the associated priority threshold. Furthermore, the token may no longer be used for transmitting frames of a specific class if the THT reaches the threshold of this particular class.

Almost since the first proposal, FDDI has been criticized because it does not support telephony and other isochronous services. Meanwhile, a compromise has been reached resulting in the proposal called 'FDDI-II'. FDDI-II adds a circuit-switched service to the packet service of the basic FDDI by inserting a 'Hybrid Ring Control' (HRC) between Medium Access Control and Physical Layer. HRC multiplexes data between the packet MAC and the isochronous MACs (I-MACs). Details about the allocation of isochronous bandwidth may be found in [10].

B. DQDB

The Distributed Queue Dual Bus (DQDB, cf. [11]) Metropolitan Area Network (MAN) is a new standard proposed by the IEEE 802.6 Working Group on Metropolitan Area Networks (MANs). DQDB (originally known as 'QPSX' for 'Queued Packet and Synchronous Exchange') defines a Dual Bus subnetwork with a shared medium physical layer of two unidirectional buses, an arbitrated media access control sublayer based on Distributed Queueing; and a pre-arbitrated media access control sublayer for the support of isochronous services. The standard allows for bridges to interconnect two or more Dual Bus subnetworks to form a Metropolitan Area Network operating over areas in excess of 50 kilometers in diameter.

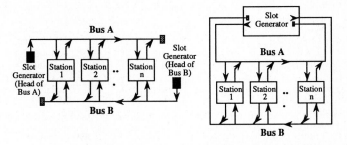

Open Dual Bus Topology   Looped Dual Bus Topology

Fig. 3 Bus Topologies for DQDB

DQDB subnetworks consist of a pair of contra flowing unidirectional buses which can operate either as open dual bus topology or as looped dual bus topology, cf. Fig. 3. In both topologies, nodes are attached to each bus via a write connection and a read tap placed upstream of the write connection. They observe the data passing on a bus, but never remove it and only alter it when permitted by the access protocol described below. Both buses are operated synchronously within the MAC sublayer using fixed length slots. These slots are generated by the nodes at the head of each bus and flow downstream past each node, before being discarded at the end of the bus. Each slot contains an access control field which is used to control the writing of segments into a slot and the reading of segments from occupied, or busy, slots. It should be noted that the medium access control (MAC) protocol and protocol data unit formats contained in the DQDB standard allow subnetworks of different data rates to operate in the same manner.

Protocol Data Units

The slot structure (cf. Fig. 4) is independently generated for each unidirectional bus by the slot generator at the head of that bus.

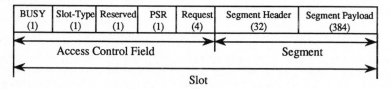

Fig. 4 Slot Format (length in bits)

Each slot consists of an Access Control Field and a 'segment', where a segment is nothing but a protocol data unit transferred between peer entities. The Access Control Field (ACF) is used to control the reading of a segment from a slot and the writing of segments into slots. The first bit of the ACF indicates whether the slot contains data (BUSY = 1) or the slot is available (BUSY = 0). In DQDB, there are two types of slots called 'queued-arbitrated' (Slot-Type = 0, used to transfer asynchronous segments) and 'pre-arbitrated' (Slot-Type = 1, carrying isochronous-sample segments), respectively. Access to these slots is controlled by strategies discussed below. This section also shows the meaning of the request bits. Finally, each slot contains a segment consisting of a segment header (not discussed in this paper) and a segment 'payload' which is 48 bytes long.

Slot Access

Details of the pre-arbitrated slot access mentioned above are not relevant for the study presented in this paper. Therefore, we focus on access to the queued-arbitrated slots which are used to transfer asynchronous segments. However, in some scenarios we assume a certain percentage of pre-arbitrated slots.

Access to queued-arbitrated slots is controlled by a function called 'Distributed Queue' which allows the formation and operation of a queue of asynchronous segments which is distributed across the subnetworks. In order to make this distributed queue perform as a centralized queue, each station maintains a dedicated counter for each of the contra flowing unidirectional buses (cf. Fig. 5).

Operation of the counters requires operations on both the busy and request bits contained in each slot. In the following, we consider the access to bus A (the operation of queue formation on bus B is a mirror image of this case).

Nodes with no asynchronous segments queued to send on bus A count the number of nodes downstream on bus A which have registered requests at the node for access to bus A. However, the node only counts the requests which have not yet been satisfied. Each such request which is detected on bus B causes the request counter to be incremented by one. In contrast to this, each empty slot passing on bus A causes the request counter to be decremented by one (provided it is not zero).

Any node wishing to send an asynchronous segment on bus A sends a request for itself on bus B. It must then transfer the current value of the request counter (RC) into a 'countdown counter' (CD), cf. Fig. 5.

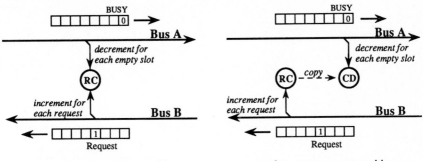

no asynchronous segments waiting   asynchronous segments waiting

Fig. 5 Counter operation for Bus A

The countdown counter indicates the number of requests for access to bus A which have to be satisfied before the segment at the node can be sent, and is decremented by one for each empty slot which passes on bus A. In this state the request counter continues to register requests for access to bus A which are received on bus B. When the countdown counter reaches zero, the asynchronous segment is written into the next empty slot which passes on bus A. If this transmission is to be followed by another transmission by the same node then the node has to send another request and the procedure described above starts again.

It should be noted that the DQDB standard defines four levels of priority. However, a study of how these levels may be used is not within the scope of this paper.

V. Performance Analysis of FDDI

FDDI may be modelled as a multiqueue system with single cyclic server where one server has to serve customers waiting in several different queues, cf. Fig. 6. In this system, the server polls a queue as to whether or not there is a customers waiting to be served. After finishing service at the queue, or if there are no customers waiting in the queue, the server switches to the next queue in cyclic order.

In FDDI, the cycle time of the server is controlled by the timed token protocol described above. The performance of FDDI is heavily affected by the choice of the operational Target Token Rotation Time (T_OPR). This is extensively studied by Dykeman and Bux in [12]. Several interesting results of this analysis - which does not take into consideration synchronous transmissions - are discussed in the following.

The rotation time of the token cannot be smaller than the ring latency T_L which is the sum of propagation delay in the fiber and station latencies. Choosing T_OPR = T_L means that no asynchronous data may be transmitted. In contrast to this, for T_OPR = ∞ each station capturing the token is allowed to transmit all the frames which are ready for transmission. Obviously, the maximum throughput may be achieved for T_OPR = ∞. In this case, a heavily loaded station may capture the token once and keep on transmitting frames without ever passing the token to its successor in the physical ring. Thus, protocol overhead due to token passing may be completely eliminated.

Of course, there may be applications requiring guaranteed response time which can only be achieved by small T_OPR. Then, we are faced with a tradeoff between small response time (i.e. guaranteed medium access within a certain time budget) and throughput.

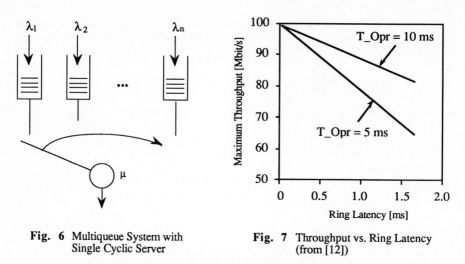

Fig. 6 Multiqueue System with Single Cyclic Server

Fig. 7 Throughput vs. Ring Latency (from [12])

The impacts of T_OPR and ring latency on the maximum throughput are studied in Fig. 7. Bux and Dykeman assumed 1.6 kbyte frame size, 5.085 µs/km propagation delay and 0.6 µs station latency. The number of stations is varied from 10 to 1000 and the fiber length is varied from 1 km to 200 km resulting in a ring latency from 0.011 ms to 1.62 ms. Fig. 7 illustrates that the impact of the ring latency is heavily affected by the operational Target Token Rotation Time T_OPR. This had to be expected since larger T_OPR means that more data may be transmitted during each token rotation.

It should be noted that the impact of frame size on the maximum throughput may be ignored since the transmission of MAC-overhead is included in the calculation of throughput. However, slightly better/worse results for larger/smaller frames are due to the rule that frame transmissions are not interrupted because of Token Holding Timer expiration.

Up to now we have studied the throughput assuming one priority level. In this case, each station has fair access to the common transmission channel. Results change decisively if we assume multiple priority levels. Now, there is no guaranteed throughput for low priority transmissions, i.e. transmissions associated with a smaller token holding time threshold. Instead, saturated senders belonging to the highest priority level monopolize the full channel bandwidth, i.e. tokens may never be used except for highest priority transmissions.

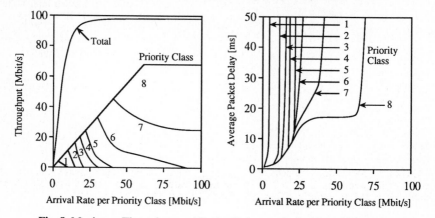

Fig. 8 Maximum Throughput and Packet Delay vs. Arrival Rate (from [12])

The simulation results presented in Fig. 8 show the maximum throughput vs. the arrival rate per priority level. Eight different priority levels have been represented in the simulation model by eight different active stations, each trying to transmit frames at a station specific priority level. The token holding time thresholds are as follows:

Level 8: 100 ms   Level 7: 76.5 ms   Level 6: 56.2 ms   Level 5: 39.0 ms
Level 4: 25.0 ms   Level 3: 14.0 ms   Level 2: 6.2 ms   Level 1: 1.5 ms

The ring latency has been assumed as 1.0236 ms and frame size has been assumed as 1.6 kbytes. In contrast to Fig. 7 we do not assume saturated senders but exponentially distributed interarrival times with identical arrival rates of frames at each station.

The figure shows how increasing throughput of high level transmissions makes low level throughput decrease. In this example only the priority levels 7 and 8 have guaranteed throughput. Of course, throughput for a given priority level is not only determined by the token holding time threshold but also by ring latency, by the arrival rate of frames belonging to higher priority levels, and by the number of stations transmitting higher priority frames.

Figure 8 also includes results with respect to average frame transmission delays. For arrival rates between 30 Mbit/s and 60 Mbit/s the average delay for frames of priority level 8 is independent of the arrival rate! In this region frames with the largest transmission window benefit from the throughput reduction of other priority levels.

VI. Performance Analysis of DQDB

A. Delay Analysis

Since DQDB is a rather new protocol, there are only a few papers available dealing with the performance of this system. In [13] Newman and Hullet presented a rather crude model of DQDB. The performance comparison included in [13] shows smaller packet delays for DQDB when compared to Token Passing or CSMA/CD. Similar results have been published in [14].

Our delay analysis is based on simulation using the ATLAS tool (Analysis Tool for Local Area Network Simulation) which has been developed at our institute, [15].

In our simulation, the model of each station comprises one transmit buffer, one countdown counter and one request counter for each bus. Due to memory capacity limitations, buffer size has been restricted to 100 packets which has been enough except for very heavy load. Flow control mechanisms and retransmission procedures have not yet been implemented. Pre-arbitrated traffic may be included but is not taken into consideration in our delay analysis.

For our analysis, we assume mutually independent and statistically identical arrival processes at each DQDB station. Packets arrive with exponentially distributed interpacket times with mean value according to the generated load chosen. From [16] we adopt the probability density function of information field length with mean value 40.85 byte. Additionally, each packet contains 35 bytes internet overhead. Of course, these packets are subject to the segmentation process. Destinations are assumed to be uniformly distributed.

To achieve statistical significance the duration of simulations has been set to 100 seconds of real system time which means the generation of 10^6 to 10^7 packets. The simulation model and its implementation has been validated by setting appropriate checkpoints in several trace runs and by a comparison to the results presented in [14] and [17].

We assumed 25 km medium length, 25 nodes (spaced equidistantly along the medium) and 100 Mbit/s total data rate, i.e. 50 Mbit/s on each bus. Fig. 9 shows the average packet delay (waiting time for medium access + transmission time) obtained for station 13 (located in the middle) and results obtained for station 1 (located next to the slot generator, cf. Fig. 3). The load generated by each station has been varied from 0.1 Mbit/s to 2 Mbit/s.

Obviously, packet delays depend on the geographic location within the network (intervals of confidence have been 2 % to 3 % of the mean values). Similar results have also been published in [14] for a totally different load model and 100 km medium length.

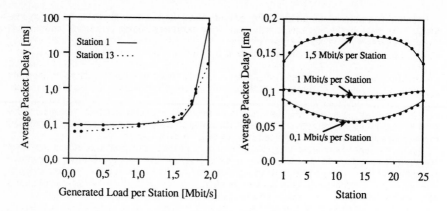

Fig. 9 Average Packet Delay

To get a more detailed insight into the correlation of geographic location and packet delay, Fig. 9 also shows the results obtained for each station where we chose 0.1 Mbit/s, 1 Mbit/s and 1,5 Mbit/s generated load per station, respectively. The reason for the different results is as follows: For light load, the probability that both buses are simultaneously busy is very small. Therefore, the successor of a customer already waiting for service of Bus A has a good chance to find Bus B idle. Stations located in the middle benefit greatly from this effect because their load is assumed to be balanced between the servers. In contrast to this, all packets generated by stations located next to the slot generator are destined to the same bus.

Of course, system performance is nothing but an answer to a dedicated load. Therefore, results would differ from the curves shown in Fig. 9 if different arrival processes would be assumed. However, for light load DQDB has to be expected to prove as a fair medium access protocol (all transfer times are very small). For this scenario, asymmetries in access delays are not significant since the customer of a communication system generally does not become aware of delays in the order of milliseconds.

B. Throughput Analysis

For heavy load, downstream stations do not have a chance to get a free slot unless they make upstream stations know that they request service by this specific bus. However, it takes L_{Ai}/V (distance L_{Ai} divided by the signal velocity V) to make all upstream stations know that station i wants to access bus A, cf. Fig. 10. It takes the same time for the free slot to reach the station.

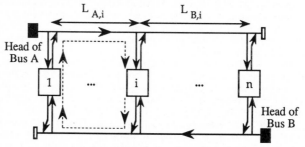

Fig. 10 Propagation Delays in DQDB

In the following, we study the impact of propagation delays by assuming the worst case of a heavily loaded system, namely a system with saturated senders. In this case, each transmission is followed by a new reservation.

For saturated senders, it may easily be shown that the station-specific throughput achieved strongly depends on the order in which stations start transmitting segments, cf. [18]. Since we are interested in the impact of propagation delays we choose a scenario where we observed the most decisive impact of this parameter. This is a scenario where upstream stations are initially active. In this case, downstream stations may transmit a request at once but have to wait until the request reaches the slot generator via the reverse bus and the free slot travels all the way down the bus. Furthermore, the distributed queue protocol makes the station refrain from accessing the medium until all requests transmitted earlier have been satisfied.

Figure 11 shows the impact of medium length on the throughput achieved by 5 saturated senders for a scenario where we assumed a data rate of 50 Mbit/s per bus. Furthermore, we assumed the stations to be spaced equidistantly on the bus with station 1 and station n operating as slot generators. The symbols show simulation results, the lines connect values obtained analytically. Details about the analysis are included in [19] and [20].

For 100 km medium length, station 1 may use bus A almost exclusively. This effect is decisively reduced for smaller distances. It should be noted that station 2 to 4 obtain almost equal shares of the remaining bandwidth. Of course, station 5 does not transmit to bus A at all.

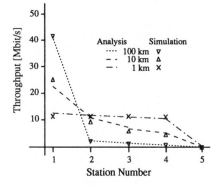

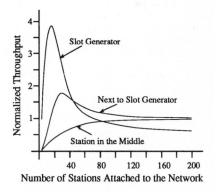

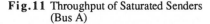

Fig.11 Throughput of Saturated Senders (Bus A)

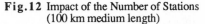

Fig.12 Impact of the Number of Stations (100 km medium length)

With only 4 stations transmitting to one bus, waiting times for medium access are small. For that reason, throughput is strongly affected by reservation delays. The situation is different for more stations requiring access to the common bus. This effect is studied in Fig. 12 where we show the total throughput (bus A and bus B) normalized to the throughput in the case of fair bandwidth sharing, i.e. normalized to (2 • 50 Mbit/s)/n.

The figure compares the throughput of a station located in the middle to the throughput of the station next to the slot generator and the throughput of a station operating as slot generator. Again, we assume uniform distribution of stations along the bus.

For 100 km bus length and a small number of stations attached to the network, throughput is heavily affected by the station's geographic location. With 3 stations attached to each bus, DQDB yields unfair bandwidth sharing. The situation gets even worse if more stations are added. The reason is as follows: Throughput of the slot generators decreases slightly with more stations attached to the network. On the other hand, stations attached far away from the slot generators do not really have a chance to capture a fair part of the capacity. Since the throughput shown in figure 12 is normalized to the throughput for fair bandwidth sharing (this throughput decreases for increasing n), the normalized throughput increases decisively.

Of course, waiting times in the distributed queue increase with an increasing number of stations. This effect finally yields fair bandwidth sharing of each bus which means unfair treatment for the slot generators which transmit to one bus only. Therefore, the normalized throughput of slot generators approaches 0.5 for n → ∞. It should be noted that this is fair in the case of a looped dual bus topology where station 1 and station n are identical. Of course, the extension of the region of unfair treatment depends heavily on the medium length and the data rate. The larger the propagation delays when compared to the slot transmission time, the larger the region of unfair treatment.

Up to now, we have not taken into consideration the impact of pre-arbitrated slots. Since the reservation scheme for this traffic class is still out of the scope of the DQDB proposal, we have to make some assumptions with respect to the operation of the headend stations which have to mark slots as queued-arbitrated or pre-arbitrated.

In our simulation, the type of each generated slot is controlled by a Bernoulli random variable, i.e. each generated slot is marked as queued-arbitrated with probability p and marked as pre-arbitrated with probability 1 - p. The results discussed up to now are based on the choice p = 1. Now, by varying the parameter p we study the effect of slots which can carry requests but are not available for the transfer of asynchronous segments.

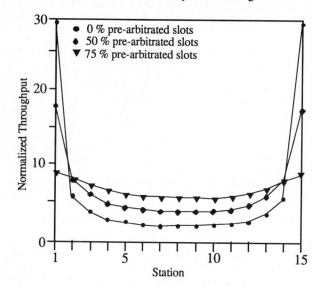

Fig. 13 Impact of pre-arbitrated slots

Fig. 13 shows the results for a scenario with 100 km medium length and 15 saturated senders equidistantly spaced on the bus. With no slots marked as pre-arbitrated the throughput obtained by the two slot generators is larger than the sum of the throughputs of all other stations. In this case, the slot generator achieves more than 60 percent of the capacity of 'its' bus.

If half of the slots generated are pre-arbitrated, the throughput of the each slot generator is reduced to about 18 %. If only 25 % of all generated slots are available for asynchronous transmission, the station-specific throughput varies between six and eight percent. In this case, bandwidth sharing may be called fair although the slot generators are still somewhat preferred.

VII. CONCLUSION

The 1980's saw optical fiber emerging as the most important medium for future communication systems. Today, FDDI based products operating at 100 Mbit/s are commercially available and additional vendors will follow soon. FDDI based communication systems are tailored to the requirements of private network owners (companies, universities, government agencies, ...) looking for a communication system which provides a high bandwidth interconnection among computers and peripheral equipment. In contrast to this, DQDB has mainly been designed for public network providers. On the other hand, MAN installations may also be private: a single large company may lease private lines to connect several sites within a metropolitan area. This type of MAN is nothing but a very large LAN. However, dedicated cables will be too expensive for the majority of customers.

When faced with the choice between FDDI and DQDB, the user has to keep in mind that these standards have been tailored to the requirements of different applications: The FDDI based networks which are commercially available today surely meet the requirements imposed by 'traditional' LAN applications. On the other hand, the latency is not low enough for a true multimedia LAN. Furthermore, in basic FDDI we are faced with a tradeoff between small response time (i.e. guaranteed medium access within a certain time budget) and throughput. This makes DQDB networks a much better choice for applications where support of voice and other fixed-rate services is essential. On the other hand, dividing even the largest files into short segments and reassembling the segments at the destinations results in an increasing network load due to a massive amount of overhead. Therefore, the user has to make up his mind about his specific requirements.

Neither standardization bodies nor manufacturers may be blamed for misapplication of standards. On the other hand, misapplication of standards can be expected. And - according to [21] - 'one can make book that the misapplication will not be the fault of the user, but will rather be laid at the foot of the designer or the standard itself'. As an analogy, Cargill mentions a person who buys an economy car and expects it to perform as if it were a Porsche. When performance is disappointing and the inevitable accident occurs, it always is the fault of the designer of the car or the car itself, and not the driver of the car.

To overcome the problem of throughput degradation in applications with large fiber length and small response time requirements, FDDI-II has been defined as an upward compatible extension of FDDI which provides the packet transport used by FDDI and most LANs as well as an isochronous transport similar to that provided by public switched networks. However, up to now FDDI-II based products are not yet available. Furthermore, interconnecting an FDDI-II network to ATM-based B-ISDN is by far not as easy as bridging DQDB-based networks to B-ISDN.

When comparing FDDI and DQDB from a fairness point of view it may be stated that FDDI yields fair medium access for any given medium length. In contrast to this, the fairness discussion for saturated senders has shown that DQDB is unfair in subnetworks inter-connecting few stations and covering large distances. This scenario shows the limits for backbone networks interconnecting few stations scattered over large areas. For this special application, DQDB is questionable.

Of course, studying performance characteristics for saturated senders may be criticized as an analysis for 'hypothetical conditions which just do not happen' as James F. Mollenauer who is the chairman of the IEEE 802.6 working group put it in [22]. On the other hand, the ability to guarantee a given throughput/delay performance is one of the essentials in public networks where users may demand constant quality of service (regardless of the network load).

A way to reduce asymmetries in bandwidth sharing is to reduce the percentage of slots available for asynchronous traffic. With an increasing percentage of pre-arbitrated slots, the capability to transfer network control information remains unchanged. In contrast to this, the number of queued-arbitrated slots which are in transit between adjacent stations is reduced. Section VI.B. shows that a large amount of isochronous traffic reduces unfairness due to geographical disadvantages. A similar effect is reached by making the stations not to try to operate at full network utilization. This approach which is suggested in [17] has been accepted by the DQDB working group during the meeting in Montreal by the end of September 1989.

132

Up to now we have restricted our discussion to protocols proposed by standardization bodies. Their activities show a trend towards increasing data rates and increasing geographic distances which is also reflected by a great variety of projects. A discussion of all these communication systems is far beyond the scope of this paper.

Future will show whether these are right who call FDDI 'the Ethernet of the future'. Whether it is FDDI or DQDB or something else, high speed communication systems for local and metropolitan areas may only reach a high number of installations if prices drop decisively and new applications requiring higher data rates than in conventional LANs become widely accepted.

References

[1]   B.S. Glance et al., 'Densely Spaced FDM Coherent Star Network With Optical Signals Confined to Equally Spaced Frequencies', *IEEE J. Lightwave Techn.*, Vol. 6, No. 11, Nov. 1988, pp. 1770 - 1781
[2]   G.H. Domann, 'B-ISDN', *IEEE J. Lightwave Techn.*, Vol. 6, No. 11, Nov. 1988, pp. 1720 - 1727
[3]   ANSI/IEEE Std. 802.3-1985, ISO Draft International Standard 8802/3, Carrier Sense Multiple Access with Collision Detection (CSMA/CD)
[4]   ANSI/IEEE Std. 802.4-1985, ISO Draft International Standard 8802/4, Token-Passing Bus Access Method and Physical Layer Specifications
[5]   F.A. Tobagi, 'Fiber Optic Configurations for Local Area Networks', in *'Computer Networking and Performance Evaluation'*, T. Hasegawa et al., (Eds.), North-Holland 1986, pp. 163 - 172
[6]   FDDI Token Ring Media Access Control, American National Standard for Information Systems, X3.139-1987
[7]   FDDI Physical Layer Protocol (PHY), Draft Proposed American National Standard, X3T9/85-39, X3T9.5/83-15, Rev. 15, September 1987
[8]   FDDI Physical Layer Medium Dependent (PMD), Draft Proposed American National Standard, X3T9/86-71, X3T9.5/84-48, Rev. 7.3, May 1988
[9]   FDDI Station Management, American National Standard for Information Systems, X3T9/85 - X3T9.5/84-49, Aug. 1988
[10] M. Teener, R. Gvozdanovic, 'FDDI-II Operation and Architectures', Proc. of the *14th Conf. on Local Comp. Networks*, IEEE Computer Society Press, 1989, pp. 49 - 61
[11] Proposed Standard: DQDB Metropolitan Area Network, P.802.6_/D9, Unapproved Draft - Published for Comment Only, IEEE, August 7, 1989
[12] D. Dykeman, W. Bux., 'Analysis and Tuning of the FDDI Media Access Control Protocol', *IEEE Journal on Selected Areas in Communications*, Vol. 6, No. 6, July 1988, pp. 997 - 1010
[13] R.M. Newman, J.L. Hullet, 'Distributed Queueing: A Fast and Efficient Packet Access Protocol for QPSX', in *New Communication Services: A Challenge to Computer Technology*, P. Kühn (Ed.), North-Holland 1986, pp. 294 - 299
[14] M.N. Huber et al., 'QPSX and FDDI-II Performance Study of High Speed LAN's', Proc. of *EFOC/LAN-88*, pp. 316 - 321
[15] P. Davids, 'ATLAS - Reference Manual, Version 2.1', Lehrstuhl Informatik IV, Technical University of Aachen, 1989, (in German)
[16] P. Martini, T. Welzel, 'LAN interconnection by token rings: A performance analysis', Proc. of *EFOC/LAN '87*, pp. 281 - 286
[17] E. L. Hahne et al., 'Improving the Fairness of Distributed-Queue-Dual-Bus Networks', submitted to *IEEE INFOCOM '90*
[18] J.W. Wong, 'Throughput of DQDB Networks under Heavy Load', *IBM Research Report*, RZ 1813 (#65107), 1989
[19] P. Martini, 'Designing High Speed Controllers for High Speed Local Area Networks', Proc. of *GLOBECOM '89*, Dallas, IEEE, 1989, pp. 5.4.1. - 5.4.5.
[20] P. Martini, 'Fairness Issues of the DQDB Protocol', Proc. of the *14th Annual Conference On Local Computer Networks*, IEEE Computer Society Press, 1989, pp. 160 - 170
[21] C.F. Cargill, 'Standards and the Local Computing Network: Future Directions', Proc. of the *14th Annual Conference On Local Computer Networks*, IEEE Computer Society Press, 1989, pp. 9 - 11
[22] J.F. Mollenauer, 'Standards for Metropolitan Area Networks', *IEEE Communications Magazine*, Vol. 26, No. 4, April 1988, pp. 15 - 19

Information Network and Data Communication, III
D. Khakhar and F. Eliassen (Editors)
Elsevier Science Publishers B.V. (North-Holland)
 IFIP, 1990

FLEXIBLE TWO-WIRE LEASED-LINE TRANSMISSION SYSTEM

Steinar Tveit

Ericsson Telecom AS
Billingstad, Norway

The importance of DataCommunications in the framework of public and
private telecommunication is becoming ever more evident.

This paper discusses the role of leased-line services in the ISDN era, and
describes a system developed by Ericsson for a service concept in digital
environments. This system could form an integrated part of a PTT leased-line
service, or it could form the infrastructure of a corporate network utilizing the
digital transport network offered by the PTTs.

INTRODUCTION

During the seventies, the standards for dedicated switched data networks were developed.
Circuit and/or packet switched networks (X.21 and X.25 respectively) became a mandatory
part of the PTT services, are also playing an important role in corporate network
environments.
In the eighties, the focus was on the concepts for service and network integration. Today,
on the threshold of the nineties, ISDN has been adopted by PTTs worldwide as the
universal service of the future. It is the first version of ISDN that we see in service today.
B-ISDNs are evolving, together with corporate networks, such as WANs and MANs,
providing for new markets and services.
In spite of the ever increasing pace of development within the telecommunications sector,
a question that often comes to mind is; what happened to the simple modem-to-modem
based line service that was the origin of data communication services? Surprisingly
enough, and out of proportion compared with the efforts and resources put into switched
data networks, the major growth of data communication is still taking place in the leased-
line and telephone dial-up services.

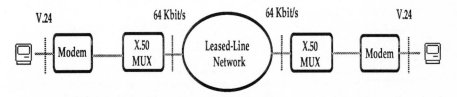

FIGURE 1. Simple modem connection in a leased-line network

By definition, a leased-line service offers a (semi)permanent connection in a network between two network terminal endpoints. Traditionally, customers select a modem with characteristics conforming to their installed equipment, e.g. terminals and terminal controllers. Additional terminals require additional modems. At a break-even point in cost, a number of low-speed modems are replaced with a higher speed modem or a PCM interface. In addition, a customer multiplexer or equivalent is required, supporting the appropriate interfaces.

This situation, in fact, describes one of the driving forces behind ISDN; the idea of standardizing user interfaces (S-interface), thereby allowing a number of terminals to access the PTT network over a single pair of wires. The result of these efforts is, as we know, the ISDN 2B+D structured subscriber channel, providing up to 8 terminal interfaces to the S-bus.

The digital transport networks of the PTTs are, in the low end, standardized at 64 Kbit/s and 2.048 Mbit/s. For data communication purposes, low speed channels are multiplexed into a 64 Kbit/s channel.

Up to today, multiplexing schemes according to CCITT Recommendations X.50 and X.51 have been dominating in the PTT market. These recommmendations were introduced in the mid-seventies and were designed to meet circuit switched data networks (X.21) requirements.

In corporate networks, in addition to X.50 and X.51, a number of statistical and TDM-multiplexers have found their markets. Typical to these is that they are based on propietary protocols and multiplexing schemes, limiting the usage to "closed" networks.

Facing todays needs X.50 and X.51 suffer from:

- *No standard for coding of 19.2 Kbit/s.*
  Considering all applications and terminals running at this speed, a solution for the 19.2 Kbit/s bit-rate has to be offered.

- *Low utilization of bandwidth.*
  The overhead in X.50 and X.51 is 16 Kbit/s, allowing a net data rate of 48 Kbit/s, or 75% utilization. Considering the overhead of an end-to-end protocol, utilization is too low.

- *No standard for coding of 8, 16, 32, 48 and 56 Kbit/s.*
  ISDN defines submultiplexing schemes of n x 8 Kbit/s, also used in coding of voice compression solutions. In addition, in the existing market, equipment and applications running at 48 Kbit/s and 56 Kbit/s are installed. Hence, to cater for coming (ISDN) and existing user interfaces, additional used rates must be introduced.

- *Complex multiplex structure.*
  In addition to the overhead already mentioned, the multiplexing structures are very complicated, leading to expensive network solutions.

- *Operation and maintenance form are integrated part of the multiplexing structure.*
  This dependency is not necessarily a conceptional drawback to these recommendations. However, considering the ongoing standardization work

aiming for common O&M interfaces for all telecommunication equipment, modifications have to be made.

The leased line services must also be upgraded to cater for applications requiring user rates between 64 Kbit/s and 2.048 Mbit/s.

In other words, an n x 64 Kbit access, with n in the range of 1 to 31, is required for purposes such as:

- Connections between PABX`s at different locations
- Transmission of files
- Transmission of graphics
- Imaging

A LEASED LINE SERVICE IN THE ISDN ERA

In general, we do not question the potential of ISDN with related services. However, in the transition period from old to new technology, there is a need to bridge the two eras.

For several data communication applications within an ISDN, the following drawbacks can be envisaged:

- For existing terminals and other equipment, adapters to the ISDN S-interface are required.
  For single, low-speed terminals, adaptations to communication to the D-channel could provide a reasonable quality of service.
  For a multi-terminal subscribers (the typical leased-line user), however, the D-channel will not provide sufficent throughput and bandwidth. On the other hand, the usage of B-channels will result in a low bandwidth utilization. The latter solution could also lead to prohibitive charging for low-speeed applications.

- Traditional polling systems in data network applications are not suited for ISDN, mainly because of charging principles and load on switching resources in the network.

- Call set-up times in ISDN are, at least in the first phase, what we typically find in digital telephone exchanges, that is 1-2 seconds. A number of applications require call set-up times in the magnitude of 100 ms.

To summarize: until the communication equipment industry has fully adopted ISDN recommendations, and until the characteristics of ISDN have come closer to meeting the true requirements of a number of data communication applications, there is room for an upgraded leased-line service; a service taking advantage of the digital infrastructure of the PTT transport network.

FLEXNETWORK

ERICSSON's Solution For Leased-Line Networks

Ericcson has developed an access network, based upon

- Recent standards for multiplexing schemes and rate adaption (X.58 and V.110)
- ISDN technology on 2 wire transmission
- Integrated modem and multiplexing functions
- General n x 64 Kbit/s access
- Recent standards for operation and maintenance (TMN - Telecommunication Management Networks).

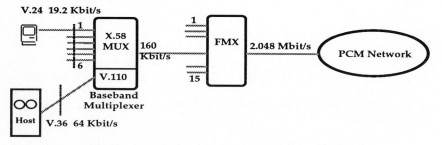

FIGURE 2.   Network access elements in the FlexNetwork

Subscriber Equipment and Interfaces

Baseband Multiplexer (BM)

The user access to the FlexNetwork is based upon the characteristics of the ISDN basic access, i.e. the standard transmission rate is 160 Kbit/s.As a leased-line service requires no D-channel signalling, the full 160 Kbit/s bitstream of the ISDN 2B+D structure in a FlexNetwork carries the following information:

B1   64 Kbit/s information channel
B2   64 Kbit/s information channel
C   8 Kkbit/s for operation and maintenance
D   16 Kbit/s, not used
A   8 Kbit/s, alignment

B-Channels

"B1" is submultiplexed   according to CCITT Recommendation X.58. This provides subrates of 1.2, 2.4, 4.8, 9.6 and 19.2 Kbit/s.
"B2" is processed according to CCITT Recommendation V.110 to achieve 64, 56 or 48 Kbit/s.

The Baseband Multiplexer provides 7 different interfaces to the customer:

- Up to six V.28/V.24 interfaces for any combination of bit rates up to 19.2 Kbit/s
- One V.35/V.36 interface for 64, 56 or 48 Kbit/s

The multiplex schemes allow for simultaneous transmission on all 7 interfaces. By means of plug-in units the following options may be used:

V.13 - simulated carrier
V.14 - asynchronous coding
V.36 - scrambling / descrambling

C- Channel

In general all the functions in a BM are remotely controlled via the control channel (C-channel).

The following functions are implemented:

- Transmission quality control in both directions
- Supervision of frame synchronization in the BM
- Loopsettings in the B-channels
- Configuration of bit-rates for the sub-channels in use in the two B-channels.

As an option, loopsettings (local and remote) can also be activated according to CCITT Recommendation V.54.

Baseband Multiplexer N x 64 Kbit/s (BM 4)

The BM is a baseband multiplexer with a line speed of 288 Kbit/s with a capacity of 256 Kbit/s trnasparent data. This allows for up to 4 B-channels. However, the B-channels can be configured to either 64, 128 or 256 Kkbit.

The BM 4 has four ports with V.11 electrical interfaces. In addition to the n x 64 Kbit/s user rates, 48 and 56 Kbit/s (V.110 rate adaption) are also supported.

V.13 simulated carrier
V.36 scrambling / descrambling and
V.54 loopsetting

are available by means of plug in-units.

138

Transmission (Modems)

The modems in a BM have a 160 Kbit/s or 288 Kbit/s transmission system. This transmission system is a biphase-coded 2-wire echocanceller system. The range is equal to 40 dB cable attenuation. Cable diameters may be mixed.

The range of the modems are as follows:

	160 Kbit/s	**288 Kbit/s**
0.4 mm cable	4.2 km	3.5 km
0.5 mm cable	6.0 km	5.0 km
0.6 mm cable	7.0 km	5.5 km

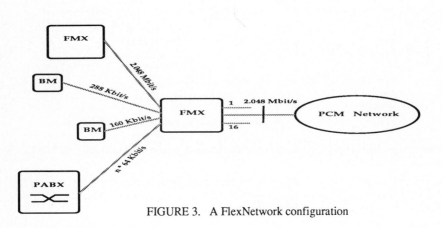

FIGURE 3. A FlexNetwork configuration

Multiplexers (FMX)

In the network hierarchy all BMs (160 Kbit/s and 288 Kbit/s) are connected to a flexible 2.048 Mbit/s multiplexer (FMX).

The multiplexer can be configured depending on

- Size of the network
- Whether the multiplexer is located in private or PTT premises
- Whether a cross-connect function is needed or not
- Selection of Baseband Multiplexers.

Basic Unit

The basic unit of the multiplexer is a 19" inch rack system with either a 48 V DC or a 230 V AC power supply. A 2.048 Mbit/s interface card and a CPU card for the O&M system are included. The backplane of the magazine has a bus system where each line card may be allocated to specific time slots in the 2.048 Mbit/s bitstream via O&M commands. The magazine has a total capacity of 10 linecards different types.

The O&M module includes the following functions:

- Supervision of 2.048 Mbit/s line
- Supervision of subscriber line
- Internal supervision of multiplexer
- Test facilities
- Configuration of multiplexer, baseband multiplexer (V.110 and X.58)

A standardized Q.2 interface according to the new G. TMN recommendations is used with a 4-wire RS485 interface at the physical layer. The ISO 7809 (NRM) protocol is employed at the link layer.

Line Cards

LT-160 - a modem card corresponding to a BM at the customer´s side
LT-288 - a modem card corresponding to a BM 4 at the customer´s side
LT-2048 - a line card for 2.048 Mbit/s

The LT-2048 line card has a standard G.703/G.704 interface. The line card can be used for insertion of time slots from a 2.048 Mbit/s system. The actual number of time slots inserted can be configured from 1 to 31.

LT - V.11 - a Line Card with a V.11 Interface

This linecard has a V.24/V.11 interface for a n x 64 Kbit/s connection to the customer. Three physical ports are available with selectable user rates , n = 1, 2, 4 or 6.

FMX with Cross-Connect, TSD 64

The Time Slot Distributor 64 K (TSD 64) is a software controlled timeslot distributor switch. It is a non-blocking system for up to 512 64 Kbit/s time slots. With the TSD 64 functionality the FMX can be equipped with up to sixteen 2.048 Mbit/s connections to the network (please see also figure 3). TSD 64 is able to crossconnect single 64 Kbit/s data channels and n x 64 Kbit/s data.
The product is implemented according to the ETSI/TM3 draft recommendation (Nov. 89).

The TSD 64 also provides a cross-connect system with the capability of switching

140

subchannels. As a consequence subchannels within a 64 kbit/s timeslot can be routed to different destinations.

NETWORK MAINTENANCE

All transmission and multiplexer equipment is remotely controlled. In the Baseband Multiplexer all configuration, loop-settings, transmission, quality supervision and alarms are controlled from the FMX via the C-channel of the subscriber line.

The 2.048 Mbit/s multiplexer is connected to a maintenance center via a G.TMN standardized Q.2 interface.

This concept provides for a very smooth and efficient operation of the network. Whenever a baseband modem is installed, establishment of additional connections through the network is simply performed by O&M commands. No strapping of modems or other hardware related actions are required.

The O&M system is designed to be run on either:

- a personal computer (PC)
- a server connected to a LAN
- a fault tolerant computer

The solution selected depends on the actual market requirements.
The main functions of the network management system are:

- Fault management
- Configuration management
- Performance management
- Accounting
- Security (access)

CONCLUSION

Leased-line services as part of the PTT offers will still play an important role in the years to come. Efforts have been put into standardization work to cater for new user requirements and to ensure higher efficiency and easy operation of the service.
Based on the new recommendations, Ericsson has developed a leased-line system with ISDN transmission technology and standard operation and maintenance interfaces as key elements. This system enhances, in a cost-effective manner, the functionality and capacity of the leased-line service.

Information Network and Data Communication, III
D. Khakhar and F. Eliassen (Editors)
Elsevier Science Publishers B.V. (North-Holland)
© IFIP, 1990

141

ATM - THE TARGET SOLUTION

RUNE SKOW

Alcatel STK Research Centre
Oslo, Norway

The demands for more information and higher throughput imposes a new set of requirements on the future network services. ATM (Asynchronous Transfer Mode) is a service-independent bearer, applicable for all categories of user services. Within CCITT considerable advances have been made towards the specifications of a set of universal recommendations for Broadband ISDN, based upon ATM.

The RACE program is a European collaboration in research and development for integrated broadband communication. Several RACE projects are engaged in the studies of ATM-related topics.

1 Introduction

At Alcatel STK, Business Communications Systems for the next decade are being planned. The next generation of private exchanges will be capable of switching highly mixed traffic. The services will range from voice communications to high quality video and high speed data, thus integrating the services offered by today's ISDN and telephone networks with LANs, and also allowing better performance and new services.

Such highly integrated communication systems are made possible through a new switching and transmission concept called ATM - (Asynchronous Transfer Mode). This technology is still in its definition phase. CCITT, ETSI and other standardization bodies are at present working on the standards for ATM. Common research projects, such as the European RACE program, acts as a knowledge base for this standardization work.

This paper intends to give an introduction and an overview of ATM. As ATM will be the target transfer mode for the future integrated broadband networks, realized through Broadband ISDN, some important fundamentals of B-ISDN will also be presented.

2 Communications Evolution

Communication is one of the most fundamental needs of man. The need for communication is evolving steadily, as we move towards the so-called Information Society.

The ways the information from the originator to the recipient is conveyed will become more sophisticated, and allow more and different kinds of information to be transported.

The advanced methods of today facilitate the generation and distribution of information. As more information is distributed, new services and media are developed and taken into use.

Together with better and less costly information processing, new services give rise to new opportunities, which in turn increase the availability of information. In this way it seems that there is no upper limit to the amount of information required to be transported and made available, neither for professional use nor for pleasure.

2.1 Broadband ISDN is Coming

The increasing demands for communication services are pushing for new and effective means for the transport of information. ISDN (Integrated Services Digital Network) is introduced (so far with rather limited availability), providing the users with 2 x 64 + 16 kbit/s (Basic Access). Thus, ISDN represents a great step ahead towards more capacity and functionality. But will this be adequate, even for the nearest future ?

The answer is quite clear. Today several different communication networks are installed at the user's premises. These are networks tailored to specific services. ISDN gives the promise of true service integration. The Narrow Band ISDN (NB-ISDN) will surely increase the quality of today's services. However, to handle enhanced and new services one must await the introduction of Broadband ISDN (B-ISDN).

The B-ISDN will provide high bandwidth (approximately 150 Mbit/s), which opens up for new possibilities for the interconnection of Local Area Networks (LAN), high speed data transfer, digital video and new video services.

At present (source: RACE, GSLB PN), the upper limit for POTS ("Plain Old Telephone System") is reached. The penetration of POTS has now started to level off, while integrated narrowband access (NB-ISDN) is increasing slowly. For TV distribution, cable distribution systems are emerging. In some European countries already more than 70% of the receivers are connected through CATV (Cable Television). The number of CA-TV subscribers is expected to increase for a long period still.

While NB-ISDN access and CATV systems are reaching a higher number of subscribers, the development and standardization of B-ISDN is progressing rapidly. Broadband experimental networks are already operating in

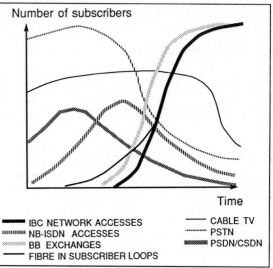

Figure 1 Penetration of Communication

some areas, and several projects are evolving. The RACE program will demonstrate broadband networks as basis for B-ISDN in 1993. Shortly after this a limited range of B-ISDN access equipment is expected to be available. It is predicted that (source: Ovum) 7% of the traffic in public carriers will be for broadband services. Further, the report predicts that by the year 2000, about 16 percent of all business sites in France, Germany, Great Britain and USA will have integrated broadband access.

When investing into a new, integrated broadband communications system, one must be absolutely certain that this new system will match the foreseen demands. A major challenge the designers are facing is the fact that one has rather limited experience with broadband services.

Asynchronous Transfer Mode is a transfer mode designed without a particular service in mind, and is therefore service independent. ATM is well suited for transfer at low (several kbit/s) as well as high (100 Mbit/s) data rates. A central feature of ATM is its flexibility as regards the allocation of bandwidth for a given service. The result is a much improved efficiency, thus allowing a better utilization of the available network resources. These are the main reasons why ATM is chosen as the transport vehicle for B-ISDN.

3 What is ATM?

3.1 Basic Switching Techniques

Different switching and transmission modes are known. Circuit Switching (e.g. as used in POTS) and Packet Switching (e.g. X.25) are the two main classes of digital switching techniques. These two switching techniques have rather distinct characteristics. Circuit Switching allocates a fixed bandwidth, and is characterized by a fixed, low delay. However, Packet Switching will in general use a dynamic (i.e. time-variable) bandwidth allocation scheme,

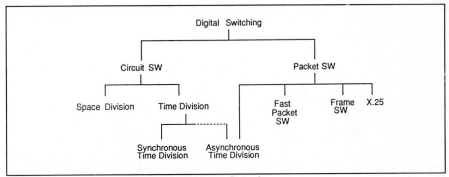

Figure 2   Digital Switching Techniques, Genealogy

producing variable delays. Various solutions in between exist, combining these two categories and their pros and cons. (see Figure 2). With variable bandwidth and virtual connections, the transmission equipment can be utilized to a much higher degree.

Virtual Connections and Virtual Channels are described in section 3.7 "Connections in ATM".

3.2 The ATM Concept

ATM has its basis in packet switching, but it does also feature some elements of circuit switching - the connection oriented mode. The basic idea of ATM is *simplified connection-oriented high speed packet switching*.

To ensure high throughput, some "simplifications" have been introduced.

· Connection-Oriented Mode

When a connection is established (at call setup), the route through the network is determined. All consecutive cells of the same call will follow the same logical path, called Virtual Circuit. The necessary resources, like link bandwidth etc. are reserved, and tables with header information for the identification and routing of cells are established for the whole session.

As all cells will follow the same route, the transmitted cell sequence will be maintained end-to-end across the network. This reduces the overall complexity, which is important considering the very high bitrates involved.

· No Link-By-Link Error Control

As the transmission media have become more reliable, it is estimated that transmission errors will be of the order of 10^{-8}. On basis of this, the checking and correction of transmission errors will introduce more overhead and a higher loading of the network. Retransmissions initiated from a higher protocol layer will be likely for those services requiring completely error-free transmissions.

· No Link-By-Link Flow Control

Due to the high capacity of transmission and packet processing, in combination with bandwidth allocation functions, no flow control will be required at the link level.

ATM is a refinement of the techniques known from Fast Packet Switching, which in turn is derived from Packet Switching.

3.3 Asynchronous vs. Synchronous Transfer Mode

Asynchronous transfer is referred to as ATM, and STM is referred to as synchronous transfer mode.

As regards asynchronous principles; two terms are often confused and used interchangeably. However, their definitions are in fact quite distinct. These terms are the two acronyms ATM and ATD respectively.

· ATM

ATM, Asynchronous Transfer Mode is the name of a *transfer mode* for transporting data by means of cells (or packets) of a fixed length, on a relatively high speed connection. The cell stream from the information source will usually be asynchronous, in the sense that the time between two consecutive cells is only dependent on the information rate of the source. The cell is composed of an information field carrying the user data, and a header used for routing and switching.

· ATD

ATD, Asynchronous Time Division is the name of a *multiplexing technique* which makes ATM possible. The continuous bit stream is organized into time slots capable of transporting cells for ATM.

· STM

Synchronous Transfer Mode is in many ways an opposite to ATM. In STM, consecutive timeslots for one specific connection will be equally distributed in time along the transmission medium. For the cases when the source has no relevant information to transmit, then "dummy information" will be inserted into the associated slot, thus wasting resources which otherwise could have been used by other users.

3.4 The ATM Cell

The ATM Cell is standardized to a format of 53 bytes, after one year of intense discussions between US, Japan and the European delegates of CCITT. The cell consists of two main parts, the

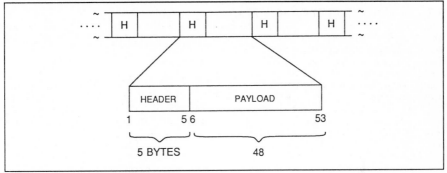

Figure 3   The ATM Cell

Header and the Payload respectively.

° **The ATM Header**

The prime role of the ATM header is to identify cells belonging to the various virtual channels of the ATM connections. The header has 5 octets, and is slightly different at the UNI (User Network Interface) and the NNI (Network Node Interface). The differences are related to the Virtual Path Identifier (VPI) and the Generic Flow Control (GFC), as shown in fig. 4 & 5.

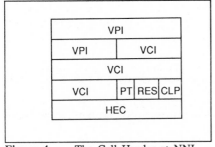

Figure 4   The Cell Header at NNI

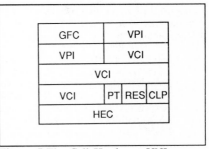

Figure 5 The Cell Header at UNI

The most important part of the header is the routing field (VPI/VCI). The VCI (Virtual Channel Identifier) is 16 bits long, while the VPI is 12 bits long at NNI and 8 bits at UNI. The GFC of 4 bits length is for use within the CPN, for access contol of a shared medium. The exact use of the GFC is not yet formalized in the standards. The Payload Type field (PT) is 2 bits long. For user data it will have the binary content 00. Other uses of the PT is for further study. The Cell Loss Priority (CLP) field is one bit long. The CLP indicates whether particular network functions (buffer overflow control etc.) are authorized to discard the cell, or if the cell is given priority. For error control (detection and correction), an 8 bit field is reserved. The error control applies for the header only. In addition to the fields mentioned, 1 bit is reserved for functions not yet specified (RES).

• The ATM Payload
The ATM payload is 48 bytes long. The payload is not processed by layers below the ATM Adaptation Layer (AAL), see fig. 6. This means that a possible error control will be service specific, and handled either in the AAL or above.

3.5 ATM Protocol Reference Model

As shown in Figure 6, the ATM protocol is divided into different layers. So far only the lower layers are considered with respect to standardization. The lower layers for ATM are called the Physical Layer (PL), the ATM layer and the ATM Adaptation Layer (AAL) respectively.

The exact mapping to the OSI reference model is not quite clear, but functionally the AAL will form part of the OSI layer 2, the Data Link Layer.

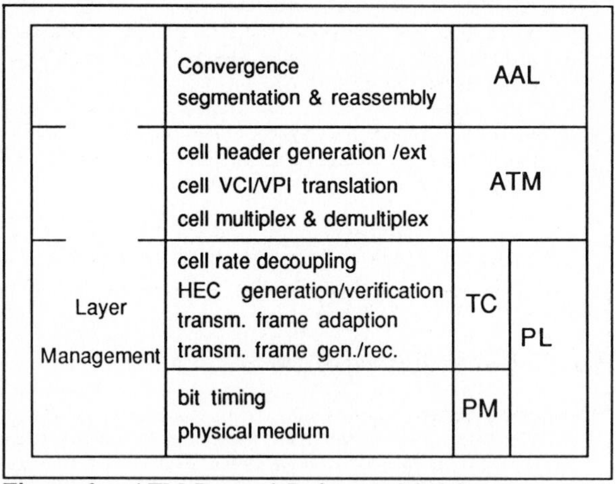

	Convergence segmentation & reassembly	AAL	
	cell header generation /ext cell VCI/VPI translation cell multiplex & demultiplex	ATM	
Layer Management	cell rate decoupling HEC generation/verification transm. frame adaption transm. frame gen./rec.	TC	PL
	bit timing physical medium	PM	

Figure 6   ATM Protocol Reference Model

• The Physical Layer (PL)
The PL is divided into the Transmission Convergence (TC) and the Physical Medium (PM) sublayers respectively.

The TC sublayer receives service-associated cells from the ATM-Layer above. The cell rate decoupling functions will insert "idle" (dummy) cells to establish the nominal gross bitrate of the cell stream.

Cell delineation is performed by verifying that the Header Error Check (HEC) - byte matches the four previous bytes of the header.

The PM sublayer deals with functions like line coding to obtain synchronization at the bit level.

• The ATM-Layer
The ATM-Layer performs functions on a cell basis. This includes header generation/-extraction, cell multiplexing/demultiplexing and VCI/VPI translation.

• The ATM Adaptation Layer (AAL)
The AAL is divided into different classes, in order to handle the different service classes. The layer above the AAL-Layer will handle frames or continuous bit streams that are all service specific. The information on the service specific format will be segmented and packed into ATM cells - and reassembled on return.

All layers above the AAL-Layer are service specific and not ATM specific. But still there are some aspects of ATM that might have some influence upon the service - e.g. the very high transfer rates involved and the probability of cell loss.

As regards the PL layer, there are two options for transmission and synchronization. These are as follows:

• **Pure ATM**

> Here the bit stream contains "active" ATM cells in sequence, with idle cells interleaved to maintain the continuity of the bit stream. In principle, the link could be loaded up to 100% with active ATM cells and no overhead.

• **Framed ATM**

> A periodic transmission-related frame contains the ATM cells. There will be some overhead related to the frame itself. This overhead can also include data fields used for maintenance information.

> SDH - the new Synchronous Digital Hierarchy (CCITT rec. G.707, G.708, G.709), is the most likely candidate for framed ATM. SDH is based on containers ("large cells"), carrying a payload of 149.760 Mbit/s.

> The Line bit rate will be either 155.52 or 622.08 Mbit/s for both options. As maintenance cells and other overhead are included in the SDH transmission scheme, the net bit transfer rate is limited to 149.760 Mbit/s.

3.6 B-ISDN Reference Model

The B-ISDN network will gradually be supported by the Teleadministrations worldwide. At

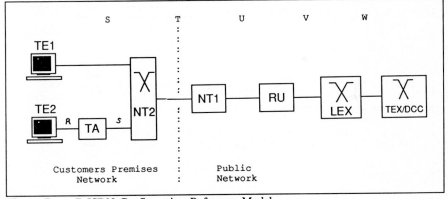

Figure 7 B-ISDN Configuration Reference Model

present there is a high activity for the standardization of B-ISDN. Through ETSI the European countries are trying to reach a common European position, which is also considered by CCITT, aiming for a universal standard.

The functional grouping and interfaces are discussed with basis on the reference model. This model is similar to the one known from NB-ISDN, see Figure 7. The reference points indicated are:

S - located between the terminal and the NT2
T - located between the NT2 and NT1 (UNI)
U - located between the NT1 and RU   (RU = Remote Unit)
V - located between the RU and LEX (NNI)
W - located between the LEX and TEX (NNI)

The V and W reference points are still subject to discussions within CCITT, and they do not have their counterpart in the NB-ISDN reference model.

The responsibility of the network administration extends up to the User Network Interface (UNI) at the T - reference point.

The complete configuration shown in fig. 7 is not required for all applications. The NT2 might be omitted if only one terminal is to be connected to the UNI, for the case where the interfaces are matching (S = T, at 155.52 Mbit/s).

3.7   Connections in ATM

In an ATM network the nodes are interconnected by means of high capacity links. These links are capable of handling a great number of simultaneous virtual connections.

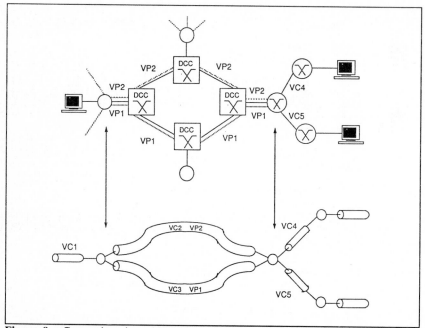

Figure 8   Connections in   ATM Network.

ATM is basicly connection oriented. At present, work is being done to also define a method for the support of connectionless services in ATM networks.

In the CPN; the Customer Premises Network, the links will typically have a bandwidth of 155.52 Mbit/s, and in some cases even 622.08 Mbit/s might be foreseen.

In Figure 8, Virtual Circuits, Virtual Channels, and Virtual Paths are indicated.

* **Virtual Circuit:**
>An end-to-end connection through the entire network. A Virtual Circuit consists of a concatenation of one or more Virtual Channels.

* **Virtual Channel:**
>A virtual connection between two adjacent nodes in the network.

* **Virtual Path:**
>A Virtual Path is used to simplify the cell handling and switching in the public network. A Virtual Path will be common for a number of Virtual Channels. The cell header contains a VPI field. On basis of this field the cell is routed through the network, according to a pre-defined path. By using VPI routing no header switching (like VCI translation) is necessary. A virtual path can be seen as a "link" between two nodes performing VCI switching.

Signalling and call handling procedures are required prior to the set up of ATM connections.

The call handling procedures are based on the framework of NB-ISDN. The lower layers of the protocols are specific to ATM. At layers 2 and 3, the modified and enhanced CCITT's ISDN recommendations I.441 and I.451 can be applied.

Signalling messages will be transported in dedicated Signalling Virtual Circuits (SVC).

4 Services and Service Integration

Through ATM and the integration of services made possible by B-ISDN, the concepts of communications will change dramatically. New services will be introduced. Some services that already exist today, but only available at a very limited scale, will enjoy a wider spread.

The bitrate of 155.52 Mbit/s might seem tremendous at first glance. However, when considering the bandwidth required for the transfer of e.g. live video signals, this bitrate will only accommodate a limited number of channels, even with the use of signal compression techniques. Similarly, the exchange of large data files between computers and LANs requires high bitrates.

The various user groups will have different service demands. The services will in turn differ as regards the type of communication, type of information and quality classes. This fact will influence the bandwidth requirements. The type of service might also have impact on the implementation of the distribution system, e.g. like the network topology for the case of direct broadcasting.

Some services will be provided locally, i.e. within the CPN. Other services will be provided by the public network, or by external service-providers via the public network.

The quality of service specified will influence the amount of bandwidth required, but evolving coding techniques may improve the quality-to-bandwidth ratio. Standard TV quality will be in the range of 10 - 34 Mbit/s using new coding algorithms. Studio quality or HDTV is foreseen at 60 - 140 Mbit/s.

CCITT has defined two main categories of communication services. These are "interactive" and "distributive" services respectively. The interactive services can be further partitioned into conversational, retrieval and messaging / mailing services. For distributive services it is distinguished between services with or without individual presentation control. The applied types of communications will have impact on the signalling as well as on the topology of both the CPN and the public network.

4.1 User Requirements

One important aspect is that the broadband network must be "future proof". This is ensured through the ATM principle. The number of channels is virtually unlimited, and the channel bandwidth can be used in a dynamic fashion. This makes ATM-based networks service independent, thus constituting a general transport network for the whole range of services irrespective of their individual characteristics.

Table I below gives examples of the bandwidth requirements of some typical user services.

Table I   Indication of bandwidth requirements for services

Service:	Bandwidth estimates
- Telephony	12 - 64 kbit/s
- Voice mail	12 - 32 kbit/s
- Document (text) mail	10 - 80 kbit/s
- Video telephone	10 - 34 Mbit/s
- Video surveillance	2 Mbit/s
- File transfer	.1 - 10 Mbit/s
- Audio broadcast and Audio retrieval	1 - 2 Mbit/s
- Video Broadcast and Video retrieval	10 - 34 Mbit/s
- High Definition TV (HDTV)	60 -140 Mbit/s

For residential users, distribution services like audio and video entertainment is of importance, besides voice and video communication.

For business users, conversational services will be the most important ones in addition to CAD/CAM and LAN-to-LAN data communication. Conversational services do also include facilities for video conferencing.

High quality document and picture transfer (like "enhanced faximile") are assumed to be very popular. Also interactive video for learning purposes might become commonplace.

For business users it can be concluded that the demand for high speed data communication might exceed the demand for (high quality) video services.

To satisfy the service demands of business users, interface bitrates of the order of 600 Mbit/s at the UNI are suggested. 150 Mbit/s might also be adequate, unless high definition video services are required.

5 The RACE Program

RACE stands for "Research and Development in Advanced Communication technologies in Europe".

The RACE program focuses on Integrated Broadband Communications (IBC). In this program technology as well as terminals and services for IBC are studied and developed.

The RACE Definition Phase was set up in 1985, and concluded that there was a potential for collaboration between network operators, service providers, industry and research centres in Europe. In 1987/88 the EEC commission gave its "go" for the RACE Main Phase (RMP). The RMP is three-fold. Part I covers systems development and implementation. Part II deals with R & D for broadband communications technology. Part III involves the functional integration and pilot projects for applications.

The main objectives of the RACE program are to promote the European telecommunications industry, to enable European network operators to compete under the best possible conditions, to make new services available at a cost and within a time frame at least as favourable as elsewhere - through common research and development in Europe.

Through this work several countries in Europe will be able to provide commercial broadband services from around 1995.

In total there are about 85 different projects, in which about 2000 European experts are collaborating. Among these projects, the following ones are relevant to the development of ATM and B-ISDN standards:

R1011:	Business CPN
R1022:	Technology for ATD
R1035:	CPN
R1044:	User Network Interface (UNI)

6 Standardization Work

With the emerging demand for broadband services, the Integrated Services Digital Network (ISDN) will evolve towards a broadband ISDN. The technology for implementing such broadband networks is already available, creating a need for standardization.

In international standardization bodies, recommendations and standards for the future B-ISDN are now being drafted. There is full agreement that B-ISDN shall be based on the ATM concept. Circuit-switched STM based networks however, are seen as interim solutions only.

The present standardization work is mainly concerned with the description of the ATM protocol reference model, including the characteristics of the UNI and NNI. Besides, specifications are developed for the broadband services, functional architecture and network aspects of B-ISDN.

6.1 Relevant Standardization Bodies

In the development of an ATM-based communications system, many different standards have to be considered. These are not just limited to communication-oriented standards, but also to the operational, environmental and mechanical aspects etc. This paper focuses mainly on new standards related to broadband communication. The most relevant bodies for standardization are listed below:

- CCITT: Worldwide body organized under ITU. B-ISDN aspects are mainly studied in SG XVIII/WP8. A set of new recommendations on broadband are now being drafted, which will be included in the I-series (ISDN).

- ETSI: European body. Broadband studies in ETSI are organized in a dedicated group called NA5 (formerly CEPT NA5 (GSLB)). A working party is dedicated for the specifications of Metropolitan Area Networks (MAN).

- ECMA: European body of mainly computer and data equipment manufacturers. A dedicated group for communication aspects is TC32: "Communications, Networks and System interconnection".

- ANSI: American body. Sub-committees dealing with broadband issues are mainly:
         T1S1 - Services, architecture and signalling
         T1X1 - Digital hierarchy and synchronization
         X3T9 - Optical LANs etc.

- IEEE: American body. An important committee in this context is IEEE 802, which is concerned with the standardization of LANs. Within 802 there are at present 10 Working Parties, e.g. 802.6 (MAN) and 802.7 (BBTA - Broadband Technical Advisory Group).

The activity on broadband aspects, particularly ATM issues, is very high at present, especially within CCITT SG XVIII/WP8, ETSI NA5 and ANSI T1S1.

Research programs and field trials are important in providing input to the standardization process. In the broadband area the European RACE and ESPRIT programs are particularly important, with many contributions to the mentioned standardization bodies.

6.2 Relevant Specifications

Broadband ISDN

Most current broadband recommendations from CCITT exist only as drafts. Some of the most important ones are:

I.121   Broadband Aspects of ISDN
I.150   B-ISDN ATM Functional Characteristics
I.311   B-ISDN Network Aspects
I.321   B-ISDN Protocol Reference Model
I.327   B-ISDN Functional Architecture
I.361   ATM Layer Specifications
I.363   ATM Adaptation Layer Specifications
I.413   B-ISDN UNI
I.432   B-ISDN UNI Physical Layer Specifications

LAN/MAN standards

Interworking with LAN/MANs will be of importance. Of particular relevance is the IEEE 802.6 MAN standard, sometimes also referred to as DQDB. A MAN can be seen as a pre B-ISDN network, in the sense that it is designed to cope with the prevailing urgent demand for connectionless broadband communication. In order to ensure compatibility with the B-ISDN equipment to be introduced 4-5 years later, the relevant standardization bodies (ETSI, CCITT) aim towards the highest possible degree of commonality between the two sets of specifications.

Synchronous Digital Hierarchy

A new transmission hierarchy usually referred to as SDH (Synchronous Digital Hierarchy) has been standardized by CCITT. The current recommendations (G.707, 708, 709) specify the transmission frame at the NNI for bit rates at 155.52 Mbit/s and 622.08 Mbit/s. Higher bit rates at 1.2, 1.8 and 2.4 Gbit/s are for further study.

SDH can be used for the transport of ATM cells. At the CCITT SG XVIII/WP8 meeting in June - 89, it was agreed that SDH can be applied at the UNI (T-interface) as an option.

7 Conclusions

As new services and demands for information exchange are increasing rapidly, communication networks are lagging behind in matching the imposed requirements. Existing networks were designed to support specific services, making a given network optimized for its particular range of services only. However, when new services are introduced, the network will no longer be suited to handle the new services efficiently.

Networks based on the ATM principles will provide the ultimate in flexibility. Any service and any mix of services will in principle be possible. This flexibility is the reason why ATM networks often are referred to as being "future safe".

By applying a dynamic and statistical bandwidth allocation scheme, the utilization of the resources in an ATM based network will be much improved over the present system solutions.

This is reflected in the following conclusion expressed in CCITT's recommendation I.121:

"ATM is the target transfer mode for B-ISDN".

Information Network and Data Communication, III
D. Khakhar and F. Eliassen (Editors)
Elsevier Science Publishers B.V. (North-Holland)
© IFIP, 1990

THE FUNCTIONALITY OF THE ATM ADAPTATION LAYER

Augusto CASACA and Mário NUNES

INESC
Rua Alves Redol, 9
1000 Lisboa
Portugal

The basic characteristics of the ATM based B-ISDN are
introduced, followed by an explanation of the
respective Protocol Reference Model. In this model the
ATM Adaptation Layer provides the necessary functions,
which are not provided at the ATM layer to support the
service of the higher layers. The functionality of the
ATM Adaptation Layer is then analysed, considering the
support that the ATM Adaptation Layer has to provide
to Constant Bit Rate and Variable Bit Rate services.

1. THE ATM BASED B-ISDN

An Integrated Services Digital Network (ISDN) is a digital
communication network in which the same switches and paths
are used to establish connection for the different services.

The first ISDN to be defined was the Narrowband-ISDN (N-ISDN)
in which the user can access the network through a basic
interface 2B+D (2 x 64 Kbit/s + 16 Kbit/s) or a primary
interface 30B + D (30 x 64 Kbit/s + 64 Kbit/s) [1].

The Broadband - ISDN (B-ISDN) is an extension of the N-ISDN
concept, with capabilities to cover broadband aspects, namely
the provision of channels to carry high bandwidth services,
which may require speeds up to 155 Mbit/s for the user
access. The future B-ISDN will be characterized not only by
its capability to support high bandwidth services, but also
by its flexibility to adapt to a wide range of constant and
variable bit rates of the information sources.

Examples of services that will take full advantage of a B-
ISDN communication infrastructure are high speed file
transfer, high quality audio and high quality video, namely
HDTV.

The transfer mode recommended by the CCITT for the B-ISDN is
the Asynchronous Transfer Mode (ATM) [2]. ATM is a packet
oriented transfer mode, using an asynchronous time division

156

multiplexing technique based on fixed size blocks, called cells.

ATM has the flexibility of the packet transfer mode and the simplicity of the circuit transfer mode based on a synchronous time division multiplexing technique. The structure of synchronous networks in what respects the fixed dimension of the information block carried in each time slot is kept in ATM, however, each block (cell) will contain an explicit identification of the destination channel, in opposition to the synchronous networks, where the channel identification is based on the position of the slot in the multiplex frame [3].

An ATM cell consists of a header and an information field which are respectively 5 byte and 48 byte long, as shown in Fig. 1.

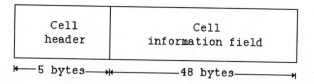

FIGURE 1 - The ATM cell format

The main role of the header is to identify the cells belonging to the same virtual channel on a multiplexed link, and therefore it is used to route the complete cell through the network. The cell header is protected against bit errors.

ATM does not impose a fixed rate of transmission to each source of information, which will send a cell to the ATM link as soon as it has enough information to fill a cell and there is an empty slot available. This means that the ATM network structure does not need to change, even if the rates of transmission for some services decrease in the future, due to the evolution of codec technology.

2.   ATM REFERENCE CONFIGURATION AND PROTOCOL ARCHITECTURE

The definition of user-network interface standards is very important to permit the development of B-ISDN terminals and private B-ISDN switching equipment to be connected to the ATM network.

Towards this aim the CCITT has defined a reference configuration for the ATM based Customer Premises Network (CPN), which defines the user access to the network. The reference configuration is shown in Fig. 2 and it is similar to the one that had already been established for the N-ISDN.

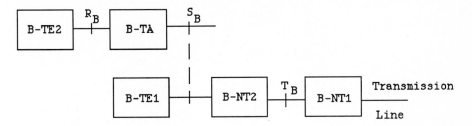

FIGURE 2 - Reference configuration for the B-ISDN CPN

The reference configuration consists of functional groupings and reference points. A functional grouping is a set of functions which may be needed in a user access to the B-ISDN. The five blocks in the figure represent the functional groupings in this configuration. A reference point is a conceptual point dividing functional groupings. In a specific implementation, a reference point corresponds to a physical interface between equipments. In this configuration, the reference points R_B, S_B and T_B are identified.

The Terminal equipment may have a cell formatted output, in which case it is ATM compatible (B-TE1), or it is non-ATM compatible (B-TE2). In the latter case a Terminal Adaptor (B-TA) is required to convert the specific characteristics of each type of terminal to the ATM network.

The Network Termination 2 (B-NT2) corresponds to user equipments, such as private switching units or local area networks. The Network Termination 1 (B-NT1) is required for transmission purposes, such as line termination and timing.

The user-network interface is defined at T_B. Two bit rates are possible at T_B : 155 Mbit/s and 622 Mbit/s. The characteristics of the interface at S_B are not completely defined yet, but it can be assumed that in a first phase it will work at 155 Mbit/s.

The ATM based B-ISDN has a protocol architecture that can be described in a Protocol Reference Model (PRM), which follows the principles of layered communication. The PRM is shown in Fig. 3.

There are three planes in this model : user, control and management. The user plane is concerned with the user information flow transfer. The control plane handles the call control information, dealing with the signalling aspects of the network. The management plane performs management functions and provides coordination between all the planes.

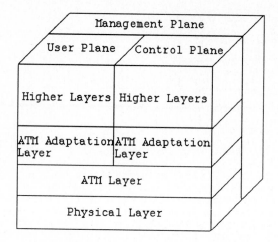

FIGURE 3 - B-ISDN ATM Protocol Reference Model

This PRM is not completed yet, but the functions of the two lowest layers are already well defined. The Physical layer essentially deals with the physical medium, bit timing, transmission frame adaptation and cell delineation. The ATM layer is independent of the physical medium and has the functions of cell multiplexing/demultiplexing, virtual channel identification and cell header generation/extraction.

The ATM Adaptation Layer (AAL) is presently under study, and it provides additional functions above the ATM layer to guarantee the quality of service required by the different services and not provided directly by the ATM network. It is therefore dependent on the service.

In the user plane the AAL is terminated in the B-TA or in the B-TE1. In the control plane the AAL is terminated in the B-TA or B-TE1, as well as in the B-NT2 and in the Network Exchange Termination.

There are two different classes of services that the AAL has to support from the higher layer in the user plane : Constant Bit Rate (CBR) and Variable Bit Rate (VBR) services. CBR services are characterized by the generation of a bitstream at a constant bit rate based on the source timing. Examples of CBR services are telephony, high quality audio and video. VBR services are characterized by the generation of bursty data. Examples of VBR services are packet oriented data and packet video. In the control plane the AAL has to support signalling, which has the characteristics of a VBR service.

The study of the functions of the AAL to support these two classes of services is done in the next two sections.

3. AAL FUNCTIONS FOR CBR SERVICES

For the support of CBR services the AAL has to map constant
length information units from the higher layer to the ATM
cell information field and vice versa.

This mapping process is better described with the help of
Fig. 4.

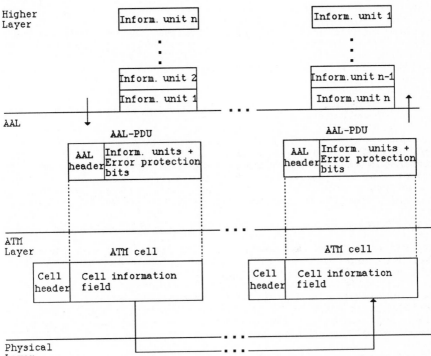

FIGURE 4 - AAL mapping functions for CBR services

At the sending side the AAL collects constant length
information units coming from the higher layer, adds error
protection bits to each information unit and appends the AAL
header to form the AAL-PDU which is passed to the ATM layer
to fill the cell information field. At the receiving side the
inverse process takes place. The ATM layer passes the cell
information field to the AAL, which then reconstitutes the
respective information units and passes them to the higher
layer.

The full implementation of the AAL for CBR services has, however, some more requirements that are not fully shown in this figure. The specific AAL requirements depend on the type of CBR service to be supported. Here, the AAL requirements for the most common CBR services, i.e, high quality audio, video and telephony will be examined in detail.

3.1 - High quality audio and video

The AAL functions for high quality audio and video are similar. The implementation of some of these functions may however be different, due mainly to the distinct requirements for error protection of each service. The AAL functions are now analysed by considering first the functions in the sending direction and then the ones in the receiving direction.

3.1.1 - Sending direction

i)   The AAL receives constant length information units from the higher layer. In the case of audio the information unit is an audio sample, and in the case of video it can be a video line. For example, in audio it can be assumed that 16 bit samples are generated from each stereophonic channel of sources such as a PCM tuner, Compact Disc player or Digital audio tape.

ii) Each of the information units must then be protected against the occurrence of bit errors in the network, although the bit error rate in a B-ISDN is expected to be very low. This is achieved by adding to every information unit a number of extra bits for forward error correction purposes. Different forward error correction codes are expected to be used for audio and video, due to the different characteristics of each service.

As an example, for high quality audio, assuming that the information unit corresponds to a 16 bit audio sample, a Hamming code that adds 6 error correcting bits to each sample may be used, which permits the correction of 1 error and the detection of 2 errors.

iii) Cell losses may occur in the ATM network due to buffer overflow in the network switches. Cells may also be misdelivered because of cell header errors that could not be corrected. The phenomenum of cell loss will occur more frequently than the misdelivery of cells and it is expected that the ratio of lost and misdelivered cells to cells correctly delivered is better than 10^{-7}. Although cell loss is a low probability event, special protection mechanisms must be considered in high quality audio and video transmission as the occurence of a cell loss is more disturbing for the quality of these services than the occurence of single bit errors [4].

The use of forward error correction for each information unit is not enough to allow the recovery of a cell loss at the receiving side, as it only permits to recover a small number of errors. However, by using a bit interleaving mechanism together with forward error correction a cell loss is completely recovered.

In the bit interleaving mechanism, consecutive [information unit + error correction bits] are written into the successive columns of a bit interleaving matrix as shown in Fig. 5. The number of columns of the matrix is 376, corresponding to 47 bytes and the number of lines is equal to the length of the information unit plus the forward error correction bits. In the given example of audio, the matrix has the dimension (22 x 376). After the matrix is complete, it is read line by line. Each line is 47 byte long and the extra byte consisting of a cell sequence number is added as an AAL header to complete the AAL-PDU. By numbering in sequence the cells read from the bit interleaving matrix it is possible to detect a cell loss or a cell out of order at the receiving side.

By using the bit interleaving mechanism, if a cell is lost, only 1 bit from each information unit will be lost and therefore by means of forward error correction the correct value of the information unit can be recovered at the receiving side.

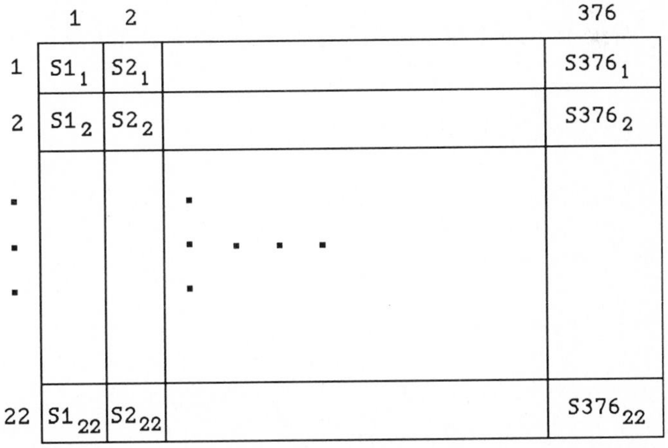

	1	2		376
1	$S1_1$	$S2_1$		$S376_1$
2	$S1_2$	$S2_2$		$S376_2$
.		.		
.		. . . .		
.		.		
22	$S1_{22}$	$S2_{22}$		$S376_{22}$

Si_j - bit j of sample i

FIGURE 5 - Example of bit interleaving matrix for high quality audio transmission

162

3.1.2 - Receiving direction

i)   After receiving an AAL-PDU from the ATM layer, the AAL checks the cell sequence number and has to take the necessary actions in case there is a cell loss or a cell misdelivered. If a cell is missing, the lost cell information field is replaced by one with a predefined contents. If a misdelivered cell is detected, the respective AAL-PDU is dropped.

ii) The AAL-PDUs without the sequence number are then consecutively written in the successive lines of a matrix with the same dimension as the matrix at the sending side. After the matrix is complete, it is read column by column to obtain the consecutive information units plus the forward error correction bits. This process is the inverse of the bit interleaving mechanism executed at the sending side.

iii) The forward error correction for each information unit then takes place. In the case there has been a cell loss, only 1 bit of the inserted cell with predefined contents is present in the information unit, due to the bit interleaving; therefore the original value of the information unit can be recovered.

iv)   To guarantee that the information units are sent to the receiver at the correct clock frequency, it is necessary that for   CBR   services,   the   AAL   performs   end   to   end synchronization. This is a requirement in an ATM network due to the packetization process and cell delay variation. One possible method to achieve this synchronization in high quality audio and video is to use an adaptive strategy. In this method, the frequency of the clock at the receiving side is adjusted according to the filling level of the receiving data buffer. The long term average read out frequencies at the sending and receiving side will be identical.

3.2 - Telephony

The transmission of voice has less stringent requirements than the transmission of high quality audio and video, therefore the AAL functionality is simplified in this case.

3.2.1 - Sending direction

The AAL receives 1 byte long voice samples from the higher layer and collects 47 consecutive samples, which together with a Sequence Number (SN) will form the AAL-PDU for telephony, as shown in Fig. 6.

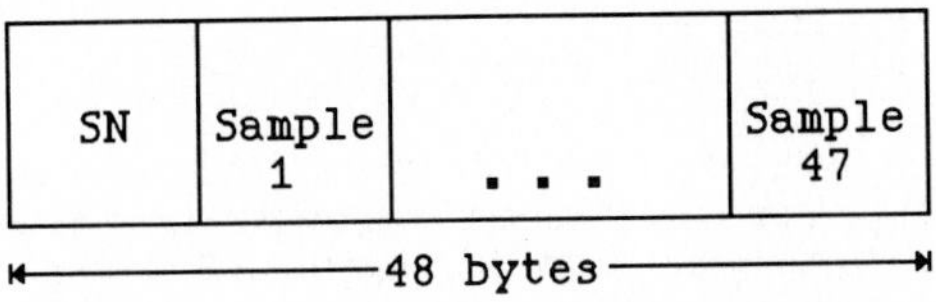

SN	Sample 1	. . .	Sample 47

|◄─────────────── 48 bytes ───────────────►|

FIGURE 6 - AAL-PDU for telephony

No forward error correction mechanism is provided, as telephony may tolerate bit errors without impairing significantly the quality of service.

If the total end to end delay involved in a telephony connection is too large, then to avoid the use of echo cancellers it is necessary to fill the cell information field only partially to reduce the delay. In this case, to avoid the need of a specific field in the AAL-PDU to indicate the number of valid bytes in the cell information field, this number can be defined at call set-up.

3.2.2 - Receiving direction

At the receiving end, the AAL must start by checking the cell sequence number and perform the same corrective actions that were indicated for high quality audio and video. Of course, if there is a cell loss in this case, the dummy data inserted to replace the lost cell will appear at the receiver, as there is no cell loss recovery mechanism.

After being checked, the sequence number is dropped and the remaining part of the AAL-PDU is disassembled to reconstitute the original voice samples.

In telephony, end to end synchronization has also to be made, but in this case the most appropriate method will be a slipping strategy. In this strategy the synchronization is based on a timing reference at the receiving side, meaning that the receiving data buffer is read out with the frequency of this timing reference. Cell slips, due to frequency deviations between the clocks at the sending and receiving sides may be reduced by the provision of high accuracy clocks [5].

4.   AAL FUNCTIONS FOR VBR SERVICES

In general terms the AAL supports VBR services by mapping variable length information units from the higher layer to the ATM cell information field and vice-versa.

Two types of VBR services with different requirements and consequently with different AAL functions can be identified :

i) services without a time relation between source and destination; ii) services with a time relation between source and destination.

An example of the first type of service is packet data at the user and control planes, and examples of the second type are VBR audio and video services in the user plane.

4.1 - VBR services without timing relation

The functions associated with AAL for this type of VBR services are better described by referring to Fig. 7.

In the sending direction the AAL receives a PDU from the higher layer, which is the Data Link Layer (DLL) in the case of packet data. The AAL has to segment the DLL-PDU in order to form a number of AAL-PDUs, in which each of them will fit into a cell information field. The number of generated AAL-PDUs depends on the length of the DLL-PDU.

Although there are still some open issues in the definition of the AAL-PDU, one possible solution is shown in Fig. 8.

In this case the AAL-PDU consists of a segment, segment header and segment trailer.

The segment contains information from the DLL-PDU. In the case of the DLL-PDU being smaller than the segment length there will be a single segment, and dummy data has to be inserted to complete the segment. The insertion of dummy data has also to be done in the last segment, unless the length of the DLL-PDU is a multiple of the segment length.

The segment header has two fields : Sequence Number (SN) and Segment Type (ST). The SN is used to detect lost or misdelivered cells at the receiving end, as it was described for CBR services. The ST identifies if the segment is either the first, continuation, last or single segment.

The segment trailer has also two fields : Length Indicator (LI) and Cyclic Redundancy Check (CRC). The LI indicates the number of valid data bytes contained in the segment. The CRC covers the complete AAL-PDU and is used for detection/correction of bit errors. The inclusion of this CRC field in the AAL-PDU may be avoided, in case it is decided to do the bit error control only at the DLL [6].

Every AAL-PDU is then passed to the ATM layer, where the cell header is appended, and sent to the network.

At the receiving end, the cell header is dropped at the ATM layer, and the cell information field is passed into the AAL. After receiving all the cell information fields of the same DLL-PDU, the AAL reassembles the DLL-PDU, by a process that is the inverse of segmentation. In case a misdelivered cell is detected it is dropped at the AAL, and in case there is a cell loss, this error is indicated to the higher layer.

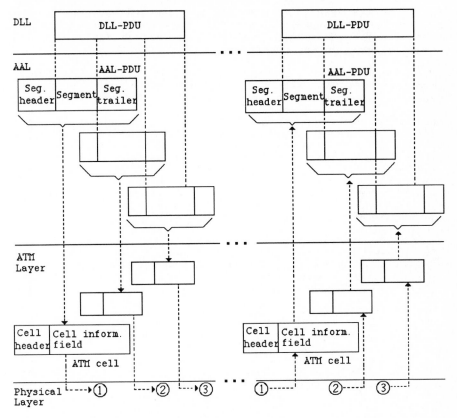

FIGURE 7 - AAL mapping functions for VBR services
(packet data)

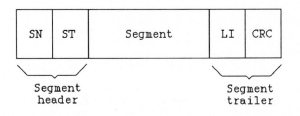

FIGURE 8 - AAL-PDU structure for packet data

4.2 - VBR services with timing relation

The functions associated with the AAL for VBR services with a time relation between source and destination are in broad terms similar to the AAL functions for packet data, plus the source clock recovery mechanism.

A VBR audio or video information unit coming from the higher layer to the AAL follows a segmentation and reassembly process identical to the one described for packet data.

As to what concerns the AAL-PDU format, although it is still also an open issue, it might have a format similar to the one in Fig. 8, but in which the ST field would also indicate the type of information contained in the segment (e.g. timing information or signal component), besides the usual indication of being the first, continuation, last or single segment. The field with the error protection bits, should in this case provide a Forward Error Correction code, covering all the AAL-PDU because in audio and video, no retransmission of information is required in case of error.

The source clock recovery may be assured by means of the insertion of periodic time stamps, in which the sender writes an explicit time indication in the cell information field, or by the use of synchronization cells.

5.   CONCLUSIONS

The AAL is a layer which exists in the ATM Protocol Reference Model to provide the quality of service required by the user services and not provided directly at the ATM layer.

The required functionality of the AAL for the CBR and VBR classes of services was analysed. From that analysis it can be concluded that the AAL functionality is service dependent. However, it is desirable to define a kernel of common functions which can be applied to all the services in the same class. This would lead to a subdivision of the AAL into two sublayers for each class of service. The lower sublayer would group the common functions and would be unique for all the services in the class. The higher sublayer would deal with the specific aspects of each service and therefore would be service dependent. This is a matter that requires further study.

The AAL functionality, together with the definition of the respective protocol and of the communication primitives with the ATM layer and the higher layer is presently being studied in the standardization bodies, namely the CCITT, in order to have a first set of recommendations on this issue, still in 1990.

REFERENCES

[1] CCITT I.400-Series Recommendations, Geneva, 1988.

[2] CCITT Recommendation I.121, Broadband Aspects of ISDN, Geneva 1988.

[3] J. P. Coudreuse, Prélude ou la naissance d'une technique de transfert de l'information, L'Echo des Recherches n. 126, 4 trimestre 1986.

[4] U. Assmus, H. Hessenmuller, Terminal adaptor for CBO video signals in the ATM based B-ISDN, RACE 1022 Workshop, Paris, October 1989.

[5] RACE 1022 - Deliverable 203, Report on specification of Terminal Adaptors, December 1988.

[6] B. Pauwels, M. de Prycker and M. de Somer, Some aspects of network functions in an ATM based Broadband CPN, NA5 Seminar on SPN, Nuremberg, November 1987.

Information Network and Data Communication, III
D. Khakhar and F. Eliassen (Editors)
Elsevier Science Publishers B.V. (North-Holland)
© IFIP, 1990

IS THE SUBSCRIBER PART OF B-ISDN BEING STANDARDIZED FOR B-ISDN?

Magnar Sunde

ELAB-RUNIT, SINTEF
Trondheim, Norway

ABSTRACT

Asynchronous Transfer Mode, ATM, is proposed for B-ISDN, Broadband ISDN, by CCITT, the international standardization organization for telecommunication networks. The Subscriber Premises Network, SPN are however supposed to be connected via point-to-point solutions which do not utilize all advantages of ATM.

This paper proposes one possible point-to-multipoint solution on the user-network interface which does not complicate the proposed point-to-point interface mechanisms. On the contrary, point-to-multipoint solutions pave the way for the proper utilization of the ATM principle in a bus concept.

1. INTRODUCTION

ISDN is being introduced, however, the speed of developments have meant that some of its basic concepts are already old fashioned. Since digital speech coding was supposed to need 64 kbit/s, this was chosen as the fundamental rate for ISDN connections. Multiples of 64 kbit/s channels will be offered, and parts of the network can use lower rate links for some services, but the system is rather rigid.

B-ISDN, Broadband-ISDN, the next generation's public network, is now in a phase where the fundamental principles are outlined. But even in this early phase, important advantages of new technology seem to be disregarded.

2. ASYNCHRONOUS TRANSFER MODE, THE COMING TRANSFER MODE

The ISDN mode is called circuit switching, because there is a "circuit" between the participants for the duration of each session. The participants are synchronized, they know exactly when and how information is supposed to arrive.

Asynchronous Transfer Mode, ATM, is the B-ISDN alternative to
circuit switching. Information is sent in packets called
cells, which are only sent when there is information to be
included in the cells. CCITT´s proposed ATM cell format on
the user-network interface is shown in Figure 1 [3].

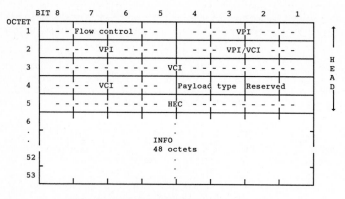

VPI - Virtual Path Identifier
VCI - Virtual Connection Identifier
HEC - Header Error Correction

Figure 1. CCITT´s proposed ATM cell format.

The information sources of Broadband ISDN are likely to
generate traffic in bursts. ATM is designed to prevent a huge
capacity being required through the network for the length of
each session.

However, it is more complicated to receive information when
the arrival time is unknown, and the cells need an address
field which must be analyzed in every node.

The ATM concept establishes virtual connections through the
network, permitting short channel numbers to be used between
the nodes. The cells have a standard length to simplify
buffers, thereby avoiding the length indicator requirement.

Work is being done to define capacity allocation procedures
and find appropriate police functions. These functions are to
prevent a subscriber using more capacity than that allocated
to a particular session.

3. WHY ATM IS CHOSEN FOR THE BROADBAND ISDN

In spite of its complexity, ATM has been chosen in the
Broadband ISDN because of its good utilization of
transmission capacity.

The public network cannot have a large enough capacity to
allow all subscribers to send a burst at the same time.
However, since there is a large number of contemporary

connections, statistically the bursts will not arrive
simultaneously. Thus all subscribers can send bursts when
appropriate as long as the traffic pattern is in accordance
with the capacity allocated for the session.

4. THE SUBSCRIBER PREMISES NETWORK, THE EXPENSIVE PART

The public network represent a huge investment, demanding
effective solutions, but the Subscriber Premises Network is
not less important.

As companies reorganize or install new equipment, the demands
for the Subscriber Premises Network often change. Rewiring
and replacing old equipment might be the result.

This is expensive and much has been done to wire buildings
better. ATM might be a tool for improved and less expensive
Subscriber Premises Networks, because resources can be shared
in a dynamic way.

5. IS THE SUBSCRIBERS NETWORK BEING MADE FOR ATM?

ATM is useful in networks where several applications can
share a limited switching or transmission resource because
they all do not need these resources at the same time.

The standardization organizations recommend a Network
Termination unit number 2, NT2, with interfaces to terminals
and to the public B-ISDN as shown in Figure 2. NT1, Network
Termination unit number 1, is placed within the subscriber´s
property to convert between the non standard U-interface and
the T_B-interface. The S_B - and T_B-interfaces are both
recommended as point-to-point interfaces. A point-to-
multipoint solution was considered favorable by many people,
but no means of agreement was seen on a common access
mechanism. S_B and T_B are recommended in the first phase with
the same transfer rates.

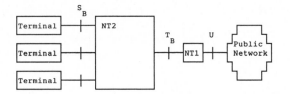

Figure 2. The Subscriber Premises Network.

The advantages of the ATM principle are used on the T_B-
interface where traffic from many terminals is dynamically
multiplexed into one channel, making it convenient to fit the
subscribers traffic into the B-ISDN. The chosen solutions,

however, give no advantages in the Subscriber Premises Network.

The subscriber must install one cable between the NT2 and every terminal. This cable and the endpoints of the S_B-interface, must fulfill high transmission demands because of the possible length. Furthermore, it is difficult to connect new terminals to this star configuration. ATM gives no advantages on such a long point-to-point interface.

As every NT2 inlet is equipped with the same capacity as the outlets, this means in theory, that the NT2 must be able to switch a full capacity cell stream from every inlet at the same time. Therefore the ATM principle cannot be used to reduce the size of the NT2.

The switching mechanism in an NT2 is far more complicated with ATM than it would have been with circuit switching. The head of every cell must be analyzed to decide the destination and the NT2 may receive more cells with the same destination than the destination's link is capable of transferring. This requires huge buffers in the NT2 or flow control between the NT2 and the terminals.

ATM gives the terminals the capacity they need, when they need it and transmission capacity is saved in the public network, but the price is paid by the subscribers who require a very sophisticated NT2.

6. ONE POSSIBLE SUBSCRIBER NETWORK OPTIMIZED FOR ATM

The standardization organizations know that a point-to-multipoint solution is often advantageous in the Subscriber Premises Network. Therefore an adapter solution is recommended, but the transmission demands of the S_B-interface are still made for star configurations with long cables. There will also be an interfacing problem between the network's internal protocols and the T_B-interface.

This paper proposes a T_B-interface which may be used as a point-to-point interface. It is, however, constructed to be used in a point-to-multipoint bus solution with very little extra effort. The bus solution is shown in Figure 3.

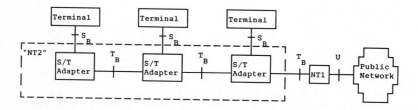

Figure 3. Adapters and terminals along the T_B-bus.

The main difference between this solution and CCITT's adapter solution is that the T_B-interface protocol is here constructed in a way that also makes it usable as an internal bus interface. No conversion is therefore needed. Next, the S_B-interface is short, this means low transmission demands.

The standard S_B-interface should not be more than 10 meters, the length of the cable between the wall outlet and the terminal. This length yields an electrical interface which is cheap and simple.

The T_B-interface should also be electrical. Even this interface will not include long transmission lengths as it connects the terminal adapters and the Network Termination unit number 1, NT1, which is placed on the subscriber's property. If an optical interface is used between the NT1 and the public network, only one conversion is needed. This will be situated in the NT1.

6.1 The ATM layer of the T_B-interface

CCITT's cell head on the user-network interface contains four bits for flow control.

On the T_B-interface one busy-bit should be set by the originator of a cell to make it easy for the receiver to decide whether the cell is used or not. The three remaining bits should be set to zero by the public network. They may be used by the subscriber's access mechanism.

Those who want a centralized NT2 can ignore the four bits and use the point-to-point T_B-interface solution.

6.2 The ATM layer of the S_B-interface

Towards the terminal, the cell head should contain two busy-bits indicating whether there is capacity in each of the two bus directions. A centralized NT2 may use the busy-bits so that one of the two busy-bits actually indicates congestion on the T_B-interface while the other one indicates internal congestion between terminals.

6.3 S_B/T_B adapters along the bus

Adapters may be mounted in the wall outlets along the T_B-interface which is now a double electric bus as shown in Figure 4. Each adapter must forward cells to the the next adapter on the bus in both directions.

The "standard" point-to-point T_B-interface protocol may be used, except that the adapters must look at the busy-bit to see if a cell can be used by the terminal to send information or not. When a cell is being used, the adapter must set the busy-bit. A buffer with three cell capacity is needed to

delay the cell flow through the adapters. During this time
the busy bit is analyzed, the proper busy-bit is set on the
S_B-interface and a cell is possibly received from the
terminal. The cells from the terminals are placed in a buffer
which can contain one cell. This buffer is needed, because
the cells on the two busses are not synchronized with the S_B-
interface.

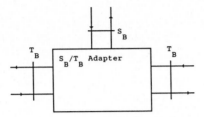

Figure 4. S_B/T_B adapter.

Simple adapters will send all cells received on the bus from
the public network to the terminal via the S_B-interface.
Cells from the terminal may only be sent on the bus towards
the public network. This solution does not limit the
possibility of sending and receiving cells to/from the public
network and it is cheap, but there will be no internal
sessions.

The next step is to let the adapters only pick cells with the
correct address, which corresponds to the Virtual Path
Identifier of the cell head, from both busses. Internal
sessions are then possible as far as the capacity is not
occupied by external cells. The VPI number may be strapped in
the adapters and will be included in every cell sent to the
terminal on the S_B-interface to inform the terminal of its
own VPI number. The terminals inform other terminals and the
public network about their VPI through the signalling
messages when sessions are established. Thus all cells on the
bus contain a VPI identifying the receiver.

The adapters may be further sophisticated to the extent the
subscriber wishes:
- VPI may be automatically distributed among the adapters.
  One of the adapters may initiate or control the
  distribution.
- Cells which are received by the right adapter may be reused
  to improve the capacity on the bus.
- There may be an advanced access mechanism like DQDB, IEEE
  802.6's Distributed Queue Dual Bus [2],
- Cells from the terminal may be buffered in the adapter to
  avoid the delay of bus cells through the adapter, and
  other improvements,

but they are not necessary and may only be installed by those
subscribers who need them to gain extra capacity for internal
sessions.

This gives an S_B-interface on the terminal cable and standard
terminals that can be connected and disconnected when the
subscriber´s network is running as long as the adapters are
already there.

Those who want a star configuration with a long S_B-interface,
may use the adapters just like amplifiers to get an S_B-
interface longer than 10 meters.

6.4 Switching

The switching is done by the adapters along the bus. This
switching range from the simple distribution of external
cells done by simple adapters to adapters with advanced
access mechanisms. Advanced adapters receive and send on the
busses in both directions on the basis of the address
included in the cells, the Virtual Path Identifier.

Cells from the terminals are sent on the correct bus by the
adapter depending on whether the included address, Virtual
Path Identifier, is higher or lower than the address of the
terminal generating the cell.

6.5 Signalling

External sessions are established by use of a "setup"-message
in a cell sent to the public network. In the public network,
the inquired capacity is evaluated and the message is
forwarded or a disconnection message is returned. Internal
"setups" are returned from the public network with the bus
address set to "broadcast". The terminal(s) with the correct
capabilities may then respond by sending a message directly
to the initiating terminal whose VPI was indicated in the
first message.

Those subscribers who have a lot of internal traffic may
include a master terminal as number one on the bus. This
terminal will receive the first "setup"-message and only send
it out on the bus with the broadcast address if there is
enough capacity for the new session in the subscriber´s
network. The initiating terminal´s bus address which was
included in the "setup"-message is replaced by the master
terminal´s bus address to make all signalling messages pass
through the master terminal. The master terminal will then
have a complete overview of the ongoing sessions. Ordinary
information cells will be sent directly between the
communicating terminals.

7. CONCLUSIONS

ATM offers numerous flexible solutions in the Subscriber
Premises Network, but the advantages are not being utilized
by the standards that are internationally proposed today. One
of the main reasons is that it seems impossible to find one
common access mechanism for a point-to-multipoint solution
between the public network and the terminals. This problem
should, however, not <u>prevent</u> the use of <u>any</u> access mechanisms
which could allow terminals to be connected directly along
the T_B-interface cable using cheap, simple adapters.

If the public network includes one busy-bit and leaves three
bits "blank" in the head of ATM cells sent on the T_B-
interface, then subscribers can use the T_B-interface directly
as a bus solution. The bus may be simple and cheap for small
subscribers, but can be extended by advanced adapters as
demand grows.

When the number of terminals increase, new adapters can be
plugged in along the bus instead of drawing out a new cable
from a centralized NT2. In the worst case, the centralized
NT2 has no spare outlets for a new terminal.

The S_B-interface may be simple with a reach like a terminal
cable, i.e. about 10 meters, far less than in CCITT´s
proposed point-to-point solution. The adapters along the bus
can be simpler than one centralized NT2, but the capacity for
internal sessions is limited by the transmission capacity on
the bus, i.e. the transmission rate on the T_B-interface, and
the access mechanism used on the bus.

The cables on the S_B- and T_B-interface should be electrical,
because the transmission lengths are short, making expensive
optical links redundant.

The result will be a flexible Subscriber Premises Network.
The subscriber can include as many functions as wanted into
the network. The potential range spans from a cheap bus with
only external sessions to a bus with a very sophisticated
access mechanism and many internal sessions, or even a star
configuration with a centralized NT2.

REFERENCES

[1]   CCITT COM XVIII, Part C of the report of the Seoul
      meeting, February 1988.

[2]   R.M. Newman, Z.L.Budrikis and J.L.Hullet, "The QPSX
      Man", IEEE Comm. Mag., vol 26, no.4, pp.20-28, April
      1988.

[3]   CCITT SG XVIII, TD 14-E, Meeting report of sub-working
      party 8/1 ATM, Geneva 19-30 June 1989.

[4]   Hermansen, Jensen, Morland, Riksaasen, Sunde and Tøndel,
      ELAB-RUNIT report STF44 F89022, TILBRED-LINJE
      abonnenttilknytning til bredbåndsnett, Trondheim,
      Norway, Feb. 1989.

Information Network and Data Communication, III
D. Khakhar and F. Eliassen (Editors)
Elsevier Science Publishers B.V. (North-Holland)
© IFIP, 1990

Metropolitan Area Network - Concepts, Architecture and Evolution towards B-ISDN

Øyvind Liberg

Alcatel STK Research Centre
Oslo, Norway

1. Background

It is recognized that there exists an immediate demand for multi-megabit communication over long distances. This demand is rapidly increasing, and hence addresses cost-effective methods to meet these demands. The most important example is probably the interlinking of Local Area Networks (LAN), without having to trade interconnectability with loss of performance. Other prominent examples are the linking of mainframe computers, remote file servers, virtual disk systems and rapid transfer of high quality images, like medical X-ray pictures, maps etc.

The N-ISDN concept, although adept at covering a whole range of services, is much inadequate when it comes to the transfer of large amounts of data within short time intervals. N-ISDN does hence not represent a satisfactory solution to the examples above.

The evolving ATM-based B-ISDN concept is expected to handle all foreseen combinations of high and low speed traffic, even well into the next century. However, ATM is still in the process of being specified; a process that will last at least until the end of 1991. This technology requires a range of new network and system elements to be developed. The first B-ISDN trial networks are expected to be operative around 1993. This is longer than most large business and public sector customers can afford to wait, because the need for broadband communications is already pressing. In countries with unregulated telecommunications markets (e.g. in USA) there is the potential "threat" from broadband networks (perhaps non-standardized) provided by non-public network operators. This will certainly lessen the pressure as regards the immediate demand for transport capability, but might at the same time slow the introduction of a standardized network like the B-ISDN. Besides, there might be interworking problems with some of the proprietary systems.

One may ask why not use leased, (semi)-permanent lines instead, like one or more 2 Mb/s lines, as required. Such a solution will certainly be adequate for a great part of the applications. However, the cost of line hire will turn out to be extremely high in most cases, except for those few where the required transmission capacity is relatively constant, and matching the rated transfer capacity of the line. The majority of applications will probably show a very peaky pattern, with long intervals with little or no data transfer between peaks. For these applications it is obvious that a system providing transfer on demand is more attractive, and hence rules out leased lines as a viable solution in the general case.

What is required is then a communications system with an inherent element of flexibility, in the sense that the access to the network is under the control of the individual subscribers. It does not have to feature a comprehensive set of service interfaces, as most of these are already taken care of by the several co-existing networks (X.25, telephone, telex etc). The predominant application is LAN interconnection. The ability to perform independent switching between various services (as e.g. those represented by a multimedia terminal) is of course an attractive feature, but does not represent any matter of urgency.

Not surprising, all such considerations eventually boil down to the question of overall cost and cost effectiveness. Considering the limited time perspective of perhaps only 3-4 years, the required system must be very cost effective, indeed. If not so, it cannot possibly become a viable alternative to leased lines when it comes to the overall economy.

Cost effectiveness is, amongst other things, associated with the economy of sharing between several users. A suitable candidate for a system solution is therefore one based on a shared medium, as opposed to a system where each subscriber has his own access line to a switching node. Realizing that the traffic as represented by LANs is highly asynchronous, shared media protocols are very powerful vehicles for such bursty traffic patterns. The time in between each such data burst is then available to other users.

Some protocols have the potential to carry hybrid traffic; that is a combination of both asynchronous and isochronous traffic. The latter eliminates the need for dedicated subscriber access lines for isochronous traffic, and as such represents another cost reducing aspect.

Regardless of what has been said about the potential cost effectiveness; there is little chance that a pre B-ISDN system will gain any impetus, unless it can clearly substantiate a lifespan that extends much beyond the moment B-ISDN is introduced. The reasons for this are several. For a start there is always the reluctance to introduce yet another system, with the inherent problems of interworking with present as well as future systems. The danger of causing delays to the take-off of B-ISDN has already been mentioned. Regardless of the use of cost-effective concepts and methods; the investments are going to be very large in any case. The questions of reuse and the potential for integration with the B-ISDN system are therefore well founded.

The Metropolitan Area Network (MAN) is a system concept that addresses the problems presented above. It is based on a shared medium architecture, using a connectionless protocol. Besides giving an introduction to network architecture and concepts, it is the purpose of this paper to focus on the "life after B-ISDN" aspects of Metropolitan Area Networks.

2. The MAN Concept

A Metropolitan Area Network provides the solution to the immediate need for wide area multi-megabit data transfer. In general, it is a digital communications network of high capacity, providing distributed switching between its access nodes for a range of services. By virtue of its traffic handling capacity and its geographical coverage, it has the capability to function as a backbone network for other networks, like LANs.

The MAN is based on a shared medium subnetwork, which consists of a pair of unidirectional buses and a number of access points (nodes) attached along these. The subnetwork operates up to broadband rates (of the order of Mb/s), and covers an area up to at least 50 km in diameter. A number of such subnetworks may be interconnected to provide network services over a wide area (WAN). In principle, a MAN-based broadband network may cover the entire country, and even cross national borders.

The connectionless transport of asynchronous data between LANs is identified as by far the most important service. Plans exist for the simultaneous transport of isochronous signals originating from voice, audio and video-based services.

The scope of the services and the potential for nationwide coverage position the MAN concept in the province of the public network service provider. However, the MAN concept has also got potential for large, private networks.

The detailed specifications of MAN are still in the course of preparation. It is the European Telecommunications Standards Institute - Network Aspects sub-technical committee #5 (ETSI NA5) that is the prime standardization body in the development of a MAN standard in Europe. ETSI intends to have the MAN standard completed by the end of this year (1990).

It is the Medium Access Control (MAC) protocol which has received most attention as regards the on-going standardization work. Recently, ETSI decided to adopt the MAC protocol, as defined by the working committee 802.6 of the Institute of Electrical & Electronics Engineers (IEEE). This standard is perhaps better known as the Distributed Queue Dual Bus (DQDB) protocol. The potential of this protocol was soon realized by those involved in the development of the MAN standard. This lead to a broader scope for the DQDB protocol, with a view to its use as basis for a MAN.

The extensive work done by the U.S. research institute Bell Communications Research (Bellcore) on their Switched Multi- megabit Data Service (SMDS) concept, has to a large extent been the platform for the definition of the MAN system.

3. The DQDB MAN Standard

A thorough description of the DQDB MAN standard is beyond the scope of this paper. However, the widespread interest in the MAN concept is largely due to the very clever and efficient procedure employed for the access to the shared medium. This Medium Access Control (MAC) protocol is an essential part of the MAN standard. According to the IEEE 802. LAN standards, the MAC sublayer is the part of the data link lower layer that supports network topology-dependent functions (e.g. those associated with a shared medium in this case). It uses the services of the Physical layer below to provide connectionless services to the Logical Link Control (LLC) sublayer above.

The functions of the MAC layer include the following:

- Initial MAC Protocol Data Unit (IMPDU) generation, fig. 1.
  It includes MAC addressing and error checking.

- Packet segmentation & reassembly. This process is also illustrated in fig. 1.
  The details here are important for the future harmonization with ATM and B-ISDN.

- Distributed Queue Dual Bus (DQDB) access control.

- Network configuration control. This features a selfhealing mechanism for the communication on the subnetwork in case of a physical break of the transmission medium.

The MAC layer may be regarded as a functional subset to the DQDB layer. Besides the MAC connectionless services, the functions of the DQDB layer do also support services based on a connection-oriented transfer mode for both isochronous traffic (e.g. voice signals) and asynchronous traffic (e.g. signalling). In a MAN context, these connection-oriented services are considered less important than the connectionless services, but might be supported at a later stage.

Of all the MAC layer functions, that of the DQDB access control has received most attention. This is reflected in the fact that the acronym DQDB has given its name to the entire MAN standard.

The DQDB protocol provides distributed access for the fixed length data segments called Derived MAC PDU (DMPDU) of fig. 1. The data segments to be transmitted are arranged according to a queuing scheme. Each of the nodes downstream keep a record of the number of vacant timeslots they must allow to pass until any one is allowed to access a slot. In this way there is no chance of nodes accessing the bus simultaneously. Hence, there is no such thing as data collision on the bus. This ensures an efficient utilization of transmission capacity, since no slots are wasted on retransmissions of corrupted data. This applies even at traffic loads near 100%. Such efficiency is in contrast to most other protocols, which show a sharp decline in performance even at moderate traffic.

The access mechanism is suitable for implementation in hardware, and hence ensures a very high speed of operation.

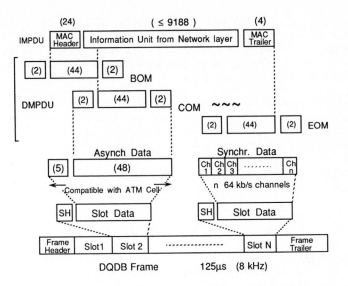

Fig. 1. Segmentation & DQDB Frame Structure

Fig. 2 illustrates the queuing principle. The system features two uni-directional buses, one for each direction. On each bus there are two access control bits, called "Busy" (B) and "Request" (R). The R-bits flow in the opposite direction of the transmitted data. An identical, but independent arrangement exists for the other direction. The B-bit indicates whether the slot is occupied by data, and hence not available for use by another node.

When a node has a segment for transmission, e.g. on the A-bus, it will issue an R-bit on the reverse bus (B). This bit will inform all the upstream nodes (i.e. against the flow of bus A) that an additional data segment from a node downstream has been queued for access. Each node keeps a record of the number of segments queued by the nodes downstream from itself by counting the R-bits as they pass on the reverse bus. Each R-bit passing causes a Request Counter (RC) to increment by one. It will decrement by one each time an unoccupied slot passes on the other bus. This is so, because the empty segment that passes the node is allocated a segment from a node further down the bus. With these two simple counting actions the RCs keep accurate record of the number of segments queued for transmission by all the nodes downstream.

Suppose a node has prepared a segment to be transmitted. It then loads the current value of the RC onto a second counter called the Countdown Counter (CC). At the same time the RC is reset, and an R-bit associated with this particular segment is issued. The segment is now placed in its appropriate position in the queuing system.

The CC value is decremented by one for each empty slot that passes. This means that a node downstream will use it for its own segment. Then there will be one less ahead in the queue, hence decrementing the CC. The node that queued can access the bus and load its data segment into the first unoccupied slot appearing after the CC has reached zero. This action ensures a first-in first-out sequence for access.

This scheme provides a mechanism for access priority. Each level of priority has its own set of counter pairs and access control bits. Hence there will be separate distributed queues for each level of priority. The DQDB protocol allows up to four such levels. In a practical system data for signalling and network control will be allocated a higher level of priority than ordinary traffic.

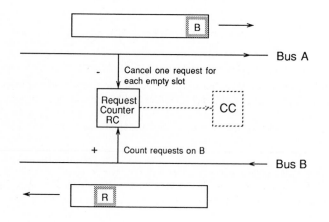

Fig. 2.   Distributed Queue - Principles

4. MAN Architecture

The following description and terminology of the MAN architecture is taken from the Alcatel MAN. First consider the definition and description of some of the fundamental "building blocks" of a MAN, see fig. 3.

In this context, a subnetwork may be defined as a dual bus network with two or more access points (nodes) attached to it. Each bus is uni-directional. The physical transmission medium of the bus is most likely an optical fibre. This figure shows three examples of possible subnetwork configurations. The way these nodes are arranged along the buses, together with the way the transmission medium is spread out, give rise to subnetworks of different properties.

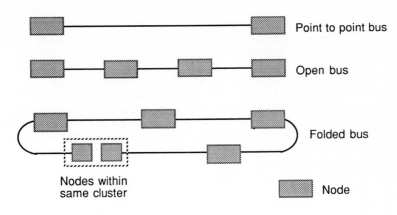

Fig. 3. Subnetwork Configurations

The point-to-point subnetwork has nodes attached to its end points only. This fact does that the access protocol, as employed by the nodes, does become virtually independent upon the length of the bus (i.e. the distance between the two end-nodes). This property is made use of for the interconnection of widely spaced subnetworks.

The open bus topology is identical to the one above, but with the addition of access nodes positioned in between the end nodes. This fact puts an upper limit to its overall length. A typical figure is 150 km end-to-end.

The looped bus topology is identical to that of the open bus. However, the bus is folded back on itself, so that the end nodes become co-located. When folded as a circle, this corresponds to a subnetwork diameter of approximately 50 km. Note that there is a significant difference between a folded bus and a loop. A loop is closed, whereas there is no signal flow between the end nodes of a folded bus, although its end nodes are co-located. A folded bus has the potential of self-healing.

"Shared medium" means that all the nodes within a subnetwork use the same physical path as the transport vehicle of their signals. Switching is performed in each node. This is accomplished by the fact that each node analyzes the node address associated with a given amount of data. If it finds that the address agrees with its own address, it reads the associated data. Otherwise, the information is just ignored, and it flows past the node without being processed in any way. And so it continues until the final destination is reached. Since switching functions are associated with each and every node along the subnetwork, this is referred to as "distributed switching".

186

The bitrate associated with a subnetwork is very high. The first Alcatel MAN systems will feature transmission interfaces of 34 Mb/s and 140 Mb/s (for the American market 45 Mb/s versions will be developed).

Fig. 4 shows a network composed of subnetworks. Three subnetworks (labelled SN1-3) are shown, all of the folded type. These subnetworks are interconnected via Routers (R). SN-1 and SN-2 are co-located at a particular point, as shown. However, SN-1 and SN-3 are some distance apart. They are interconnected by means of another subnetwork, in this case of the point-to-point type. As already mentioned, this subnetwork topology has the potential to connect nodes almost irrespective of distances.

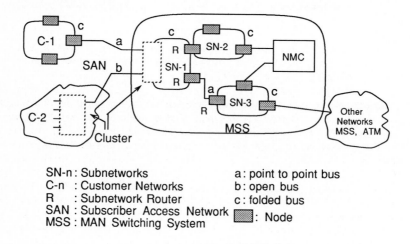

SN-n : Subnetworks   a : point to point bus
C-n   : Customer Networks   b : open bus
R   : Subnetwork Router   c : folded bus
SAN : Subscriber Access Network   ■ : Node
MSS : MAN Switching System

Fig. 4.   MAN - Network Architecture

Communications between these interconnected subnetworks follow much the same basic principles for switching as described above for a separate subnetwork. In principle, a router performs much the same functions as any other node, although some of its functions are somewhat more complicated. When it reads an address that is associated with another subnetwork, the router will do the necessary actions to have this amount of data sent across to the relevant subnetwork. The transfer of information across a number of subnetworks enables large, meshed network structures to be formed.

A system of interconnected subnetworks forming a natural group by virtue of its geographical coverage or otherwise, is referred to as a MAN Switching System (MSS). Although each of its constituent subnetworks may be limited in expanse, an MSS may cover a vast area. The individual subnetworks may not be dimensioned for the same bitrates, as the chosen bitrates will be governed by the traffic load in each case. In a practical system, it is likely that the transmission capacity will be the limiting factor as regards the overall size of the MSS. However, through the use of a meshed network topology this limitation may be alleviated.

Interconnection of separate MSSs is possible by means of Inter-MSS routers. As opposed to the routers employed within the same MSS, an inter-MSS router terminates the layer 3 protocols as well, making routing independent within each MSS.

A number of nodes may be grouped in a cluster to allow common resources (both hardware and software modules) to be shared. Examples of shared hardware modules are the transmission interfaces to the dual bus, power supplies and equipment for configuration control and maintenance.

An MSS is associated with a Network Management Centre (NMC). This centre contains the equipment to allow the network provider to perform tasks related to operation, maintenance, administration, charging, configuration and provisioning functions.

Consider the leftmost part of fig. 4. Here there are two groups of customer premises networks, labelled C-1 and C-2. They are both connected to SN-1 over a Subscriber Access Network (SAN), which is basicly just another subnetwork.

Consider the details of the C-2 customer equipment. This is shown in fig. 5. Through the use of application adapters (AA), various types of LANs and customer equipment may be connected. This particular example shows a host computer, an Ethernet, a Token Ring net and a PABX. By adapting to a common interface denoted Application Adapter Interface (AAI), identical Subnetwork Interface Modules (SIM) can be employed.

A number of these SIM modules share a common equipment module, labelled CE. The cluster of CE and SIM modules is referred to as a Customer Gateway (CGW). This cluster is connected to the MSS over a Subscriber Access Network (SAN), which may be configured as either of the subnetworks of fig. 3.

Note that communication between e.g. the local LANs is possible. In this case the signals are switched in the SIM modules, and no data flows across the SAN to the MSS. Charging is not performed. However, when data is carried across the SAN to the MSS, then the charging functions of the MSS are invoked, because the MSS is not a part of the customer equipment.

Consider the other dashed box featured in fig. 4. The content of this (with some additions) is shown in fig. 6. Again for the sake of sharing common modules, a number of adjacent nodes belonging to the same subnetwork may be grouped together. This group is referred to as an Edge Gateway Cluster. Each SAN is terminated in an Edge Access Unit (E). The cluster may also accommodate access units for routers (R) and; if relevant also one or more inter-MSS routers. Switching is performed in each node. Switching between adjacent nodes within the same cluster is hence possible.

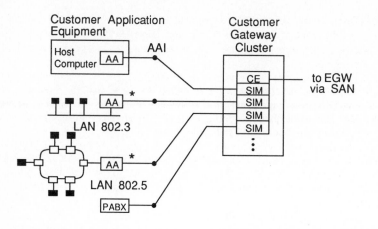

Customer Application Equipment

Customer Gateway Cluster

AA : Application Adapter
AAI : AA Interface
* May be located in cluster or remotely

CE : Common Equipment Module
SIM : Subnetwork Interface Module
SAN : Subscriber Access Network

Fig. 5. Public Networks - Customer Equipment

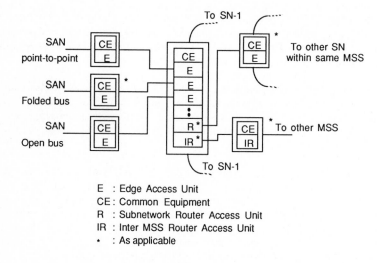

E : Edge Access Unit
CE: Common Equipment
R : Subnetwork Router Access Unit
IR : Inter MSS Router Access Unit
* : As applicable

Fig. 6. Edge Gateway Cluster

5. B-ISDN

The B-ISDN is the target broadband network. Its deployment is probably 4-5 years behind that of the MAN. However, MAN is not intended as a competitor to B-ISDN, although some have expressed concern about a possible delay in the deployment of B-ISDN if MAN relieves the most pressing demand for broadband communications. This is certainly debatable, since it is very likely that an early introduction of MAN will result in a stimulated interest in broadband-based services.

It is beyond the scope of this paper to go into the details of B-ISDN. Only a summary is given here to allow a comparison with MAN.

The CCITT I.121 recommendation defines the basic principles. B-ISDN is a high-speed packet-switched network concept, based on an Asynchronous Transfer Mode (ATM). The basic idea of ATM [1] is to allow the best possible utilization of the network capacity, while at the same time supporting an unrestricted mix of services. This is so, because each node represents a load to the network only whenever it has something to transmit. In this way services of even widely different peak bitrates can be handled by the same network.

The information from the individual services is arranged into cells, which then in turn are multiplexed to form a cell stream. All the cells are of fixed lengths, and are composed of a 5 bytes long header and an information field of 48 bytes. The header contains a pair of labels, called Virtual Channel Identifier (VCI) and Virtual Path Identifier (VPI) respectively. By means of these the cells can be routed individually to their respective service destinations. The VCIs and VPIs are allocated through a call set-up procedure, and remain unchanged for the entire duration of the call. ATM is hence basicly a connection-oriented technique, as opposed to MAN which at least in the first phase is based on a connectionless protocol. However, plans exist also for a connectionless ATM service.

Consider the B-ISDN reference architecture in fig. 7a. This is a functional model, which identifies four reference points R_B, S_B, T_B and U_B. Of these only the S_B and T_B reference points will be subject to standardization. These two interfaces will support all B-ISDN services. The "T_B" interface is also referred to as the User Network Interface (UNI), because this represents the borderline between the customer premises equipment (CPE) and that administered by the network provider.

The functions represented by the Network Termination 2 (NT2) may not be required for smaller systems, in which cases the S_B and T_B interfaces will coincide. However, this does not imply complete identity between these two interfaces.

There may or may not be a direct correspondence between this reference model and the actual physical modules it represents. Thus, the NT2 may be realized using a shared medium configuration. Such a distributed NT2 is therefore in agreement with the scheme applied for MAN.

6. Evolution of MAN towards B-ISDN

As mentioned initially, the impact of the MAN concept is largely governed by its ability to become integrated with the future B-ISDN. Mainly, this merging is two-fold. First there is the merging with B-ISDN technology, like ATM switches. Then, since the preferred interface for subscriber access in B-ISDN will be the UNI reference point, there is also a question of harmonization at the subscriber interfaces.

With both the MAN and the B-ISDN standards being in the process of development, the standardization bodies have the best position possible to arrive at a set of harmonized standards. And indeed, such an alignment is deliberately sought by those involved. But it is still too early to say to what extent this effort will be successful.

Consider again the timeslot structure shown in the lower half of fig. 1. The length of a DQDB segment header corresponds to the header of an ATM cell. Similarly, there is full match in the lengths of their payloads. This means that MAN equipment can be used for the transport of ATM cells. Such transport will be transparent in the sense that nothing is added to or removed from the ATM cells. This does at least ensure a role for existing MAN equipment for the transfer of cells between nodes.

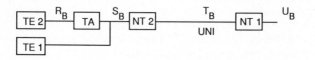

Fig. 7a. B-ISDN Reference Architecture

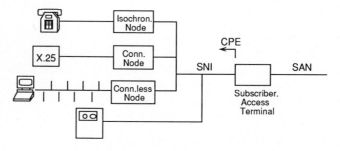

Fig. 7b. MAN Reference Architecture

However, this is only one side of the interworking scheme between DQDB MAN and   B-ISDN, because identical cell sizes alone do not ensure compatibility between services and functionality in general. Full compatibility is, amongst other things, governed by the internal structure of the headers/- trailers through the protocol layers.

Of particular importance is to establish full alignment between the two systems as regards the asynchronous connection-oriented bearer services (like ATM). The connection-oriented bearer function is defined as the prime transport mode of ATM.

With a (near) complete correspondence at all layers, the future scenario of fig. 8 can be foreseen. Here ATM switches are employed at three levels; that is within a MAN subnetwork (1), between subnetworks (2), and also between two or more MSSs (3). Of these, the interconnection of MSSs will probably be the first application of ATM switches in a MAN scenario. A switch for this particular application needs only support switching of entire trunk lines, i.e. no facilities for switching between the individual channels. The lines can be set up on a permanent basis. Hence this represents a somewhat simpler switching fabric than that required with the function of channel switching included.

It is anticipated that this first-generation of ATM switches will be available shortly after the first commercial MAN systems are in operative service (1992-93). The introduction of "fully fledged" ATM switches (i.e. those performing combined VCI/VPI switching), as represented by (1) in the figure, will probably take place around 1995-96.

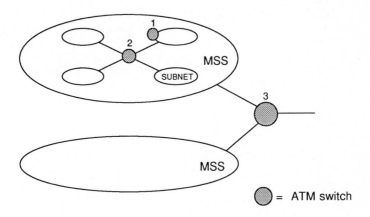

Fig. 8. MAN Extension by ATM Switches

Now consider the evolution of the subscriber interfaces. Consider fig. 7b. When considered together, the nodes shown can be seen as representing the combined functions of Terminal Adapters (TA) and NT2 in the B-ISDN model. The LAN that is being interfaced corresponds to the R_B reference point. Further, if non-compatible with B-ISDN, a LAN terminal corresponds to a TE2-type of equipment. When the TA function is an integral part of the terminal, then it is of the TE1-type.

Since the reference architecture of MAN does not feature an explicit functional entity like the NT2, the Subscriber Network Interface (SNI) and the UNI interfaces appear to be rather different. The SNI can be regarded as a distributed interface, unlike the UNI which is modelled as point-to-point. These might at first seem like two incompatible reference points. However, when recalling the MAN cluster of fig. 5, it is clear that such an architecture is indeed compatible with the functions of an NT2. The CGW cluster performs multiplexing functions between the traffic from all its access nodes onto a single SNI interface. Switching of traffic between the local nodes is also supported, without having to go via the SAN and an external exchange for this. The ensuing concentration of traffic makes better use of the high capacity of the SAN, since a single terminal on its own is unlikely to require such a high bitrate.

On the contrary, the SNI can also be seen as a distributed interface by regarding the different types of nodes as being the nodes of a MAN subnetwork, either of the "open bus" or "folded" type. Hence, the use of the DQDB protocol at the SNI interface gives a very flexible system topology, catering for a distributed as well as a single-point connection across to the SAN.

The termination unit located in between the SAN and the CPE corresponds to the NT1. This unit, as well as the attached subscriber access line, are owned and maintained by the network provider.

To summarize; when viewed in the perspective of time, the future use of existing MSS equipment might be that of an overlay network for subscriber access. Concentrated traffic to and from the MSS networks might then be transported by a B-ISDN collection network to ATM switches. The extent to which this will become a reality without resorting to complicated adapter modules, is determined by the ensuing commonality between the evolving MAN and B-ISDN standards.

References:

1. "ATM: The Target Solution", INDC-90.

Information Network and Data Communication, III
D. Khakhar and F. Eliassen (Editors)
Elsevier Science Publishers B.V. (North-Holland)
IFIP, 1990

ACHIEVING THE INTELLIGENT NETWORK OBJECTIVES OF
THE 1990'S BY INTEGRATING HETEROGENEOUS SYSTEMS

Harold A. Anderson, Jr.

IBM Corporation
Route 100
Somers, NY 10589
USA

ABSTRACT

The Intelligent Network concept has broadened to include all
aspects of managing telecommunications services and resources.
This has resulted in a requirement to integrate a telecommunications enterprise's Systems Network Architecture (SNA) based
business information system, Signalling System Number 7 (SS#7)
based service control system and Telecommunications Management
Network (TMN) based network management system into a distributed
system which presents a single system's image to all users. We
review SNA, SS#7 and TMN in terms of their supporting the distributed processing requirements of the Intelligent Network and
the telecommunications plans for the 1990's that will drive the
Intelligent Network requirements. We conclude with a discussion
of approaches to developing the Intelligent Network distributed
system.

1. INTRODUCTION

Over the past thirty five years telecommunications enterprises around
the world have made major investments in their business information system, (circuit-switched) service control system and network management
system. The results have been dramatic: new services and greatly improved "plain old telephone service" (POTS), major productivity improvements and significant reductions in network operations cost.

Today, telecommunications planners see even more promising opportunities in the 1990's to offer new services and improve the management and
control of their business because of the computer and and communications
technology advances expected during this decade. But to really capitalize
on the full potential of these advances will require a distributed system
that supports all the major applications needed to run the business at
the operations control level. The telecommunications planners' challenge

is that each of the three major application systems has its applications and data distributed over a separate computer network that is evolving to meet its own distributed systems requirements. Typically, a Systems Network Architecture (SNA) network supports the business information system (BIS). A Signalling System Number 7 (SS#7) network supports the (circuit-switched) service control system (SCS). And a Telecommunications Management Network (TMN) supports the network management system (NMS). Thus, work has recently begun in the telecommunications industry, and in particular in CCITT Study Groups XI and XVIII to architect and model a distributed system we refer to as THE INTELLIGENT NETWORK DISTRIBUTED SYSTEM, that integrates the operations of the BIS, SCS, and NMS and facilitates data sharing and distributed processing (1).

A distributed system represents the next logical progression of computer networking. It not only masks the network's physical implementation and topology but also the very existence of a network from all system users. Transparent distributed processing is the hallmark of a distributed system. Therefore we will review the separately evolving communication services supporting the distributed processing requirements of BIS, SCS and NMS and then the telecommunications network plans for the 1990's that are causing the distributed systems requirement for the IN. We conclude with a discussion of three approaches to developing the IN distributed system.

2. SNA DISTRIBUTED PROCESSING

The business information system of a typical telecommunications enterprise can be characterized as a large SNA network connecting thousands of end-users at terminals or workstations to many transaction processing systems and batch processing systems. Very large databases are distributed across the network and are shared by high-end application systems (Figure 1).

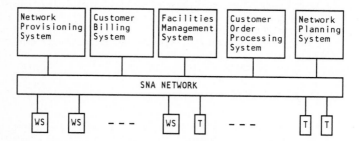

Figure 1. SNA-based Business Information System

Entrusting the conduct of business to the use of a computer network has resulted in SNA products having extensive network management facilities. The general purpose nature of a SNA network has required support for many types of data links: data channels, leased lines, switched lines, X.25 connections, token-ring LANs, etc.. SNA permits mesh connected networks, employs static routes and has sophisticated flow control algorithms. Contingent on some preplanning, network resource definitions may be added, deleted or updated. Different SNA networks can be interconnected via gateways which allow only authorized end-users in one SNA network to access resources in another SNA network (20,21). The communications services of SNA involving the path control and session layers have been relatively stable over the past several years, the emphasis has been on the specification of the application programming interface for program to program communication suitable for distributed processing with emphasis on distributed resource management.

ADVANCED PROGRAM TO PROGRAM COMMUNICATION (APPC) is the SNA communication services supporting distributed processing. APPC is based on the concept of a conversation which is the temporary dedicated use of a session for a particular purpose. When that purpose has been achieved the conversation ends, and the session may be used for other purposes. It is documented by specifying an application program interface (API) and the underlying communication protocols that support a conversation. Up until APPC, SNA architects focused on specifying SNA structure and SNA message formats and protocols and not API's. Specifying API's is a precursor to architecting a distributed system (6,12).

SNA networking has reached a level of maturity where distributed processing support has become extensive. Multiple transactions can be in progress between two applications. Presentation intensive computing (graphics, windows, etc.) has resulted in SNA presentation services being off-loaded to workstations. The multi-window presentation capability of workstations has led to concurrent access to several applications. Ease of use requirements have fostered transparent transaction routing capability. Distributed file management, distributed database management, client/server applications on IBM systems are based on transaction management services of SNA; i.e. APPC.

In the future, SNA will increase its support for peer to peer networking to take advantage of the capabilities of the intelligent devices being attached to SNA networks (23). Device intelligence will be exploited to allow for the dynamic building and updating of network directories and network topology databases, thereby greatly simplifying network installation planning.

3. SS#7 DISTRIBUTED PROCESSING

SS#7 is the ANSI and CCITT standard for the special-purpose common channel signalling network used to control circuit-switched services (Figure 2). Control is accomplished with the exchange of datagrams over an SS#7 network between call processing applications associated with the telephone switches setting up a call connection (14,15,19). SS#7 is a prerequisite for network-wide ISDN services. An SS#7 network is engineered to achieve high reliability by employing redundant hardware, duplexed equipment, and duplexed lines. A nondisruptive route switching mechanism is used to switch traffic off of one route to an alternate route when there is a problem. If a serious malfunction occurs datagrams may be discarded because of the premise that the end-user will hang-up if there is a problem making a call and simply try again.

SS#7 standards have been evolving to meet broadening application requirements.   The first application envisioned was basic telephony which led to the specification of the protocols needed to provide POTS and ISDN services and supported by the Telephone User Part and ISDN User Part, respectively.   The success of 800 Number Service and Credit Card Calling proved the value of attaching computers to an SS#7 network.   An asynchronous communication protocol is used between a telephone switch's call processing application and the remote computer's application which allows several requests to be outstanding and results to be returned in any order.

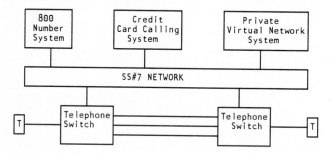

Figure 2.   SS#7 Service Control System

Today, SS#7 standards have evolved to support the client/server transaction model based on the remote operations services of X.410.   The component is called Transactions Capabilities Application Part (TCAP) (3).   TCAP enables two applications to have a complex dialogue consisting of remote operation requests and returned results.   The introduction of the client/server transaction model and the invocation of computer processing during the setup of a telephone call to analyze information about the the caller and called parties marks the beginning of distributed processing support in SS#7.   In addition, there is an emerging requirement for distributed data management in circuit-switched service control (9). Thus, SS#7's datagram services had to be augmented by including OSI-based connection-oriented network services in SS#7 standards.   These services consist of four grades of connection-oriented services.

Originally SS#7's network control and network management facilities were rudimentary.   The general consensus was that SS#7 was a special-purpose network installed in a controlled environment where changes were infrequent and always carefully preplanned.   However, SS#7 networks have reached the point where multi-vendor equipment and different SS#7 networks need to be interconnected.   This has resulted in Bellcore specifying an SS#7 gateway function for use in the USA.   In addition, SS#7 standards have been extended to include directory services to locate application subsystems, a control point facility to control application subsystems and perform load balancing and comprehensive OSI-based network management services; e.g., Operations, Maintenance and Administration Part.

At the current time we can conclude that SS#7 standards address computer networking requirements more than distributed processing requirements. Communication services for managing distributed resources have not been completely addressed.

4. TMN DISTRIBUTED PROCESSING

Every type of network element in a telecommunications network is managed by a corresponding operations support system (OSS). A telecommunications enterprise may employ more than sixty different OSS types and have hundreds of systems installed. Extensive work is under way in the CCITT to have the next generation of OSS's form a Telecommunication Management Network that is based on LAN's, X.25 and OSI layers 4 to 7 communication services tailored for network management (17). This includes OSI support for file transfer, remote operations, electronic-mail, transaction processing and directory services. Thus, we can conjecture that having the advantage of starting after SNA, OSI and SS#7, TMN architects understand right from the outset that distributed processing must be supported.

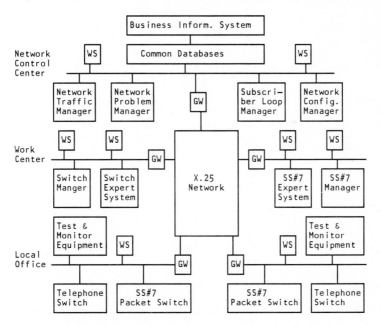

Figure 3. TMN—based Network Management System

One objective of TMN is to interconnect the OSS's into a hierarchically distributed system we referred to as the NMS (Figure 3). However, some of the older generations of telecommunications equipment and facilities will remain installed for many years along with their corresponding OSS's because of their long depreciation times. This is euphemistically referred to as the "embedded base" and will limit the degree of system integration possible.

The OSS hierarchy of NMS has three levels (10). At the lowest level are network elements located in a local office along with their associated intelligent testing and monitoring devices and craftsmen's' workstations. All collocated equipment are interconnected via a LAN. A LAN gateway is used to communicate over an X.25-based network to OSS's in the middle level of the hierarchy. The middle-level OSS's are referred to as network element managers. A network element manager manages one type of network element. Network element managers are located at work centers. A work center may contain several types of network element managers, special expert systems and workstations all interconnected via a LAN. A work center LAN gateway is used to communicate over the X.25-based network with the local offices' LAN gateways and the network control center's LAN gateway. The OSS's at the highest level of the hierarchy are referred to as network managers and are located at the network control center. A network manger has a network-wide view of some aspect of network management: traffic management, network configuration, etc.. The network managers have a need to share data among themselves as well as with the business information system.

Today, the telecommunications industry is at the stage of architecting TMN and planning the integration of OSS's into a hierarchically distributed system. Standards proposals go beyond communication protocols and cover the range of distributed services; directories, relational databases, programming interfaces, etc.. There is much synergism occurring between the development of TMN standards and OSI network management standards (4,13). The later now embraces the object-oriented paradigm of software engineering. No longer is the focus solely on defining message types, formats and protocols. It also includes defining classes of network objects and the operations to be performed on each class. We can conclude that the TMN architecture is comprehensive and will influence all telecommunications equipment developed during the 1990's.

5. TELECOMMUNICATIONS NETWORK PLANS FOR THE 1990's

The SNA-based BIS, SS#7-based SCS and TMN-based NMS discussed above are being greatly influenced by the telecommunications network plans of the 1990's. We will review the most significant ones.

Foremost, is the digitalization of the telecommunications network which was planned back in the 1960's and will be completed early next century. The Integrated Services Digital Network (ISDN) was conceived as a consequence of digitalization and initially emphasized integrated digital transmission rather than integrated services. Provisioning of ISDN has resulted in extensive coordinated modifications to the BIS, SCS, and NMS. New integrated voice/data applications are being planned for ISDN to provide enhanced telephony services (11). The success of ISDN will depend in part on the speed of development and provisioning of these services, their cost and how well the three systems can be interworked.

The emerging plans for an all fiber-optic network has resulted in the specification of a new family of intelligent transmission equipment based on the ANSI Synchronous Optical Network (SONET) standard or comparable CCITT Synchronous Digital Hierarchy (SDH) standard (2). Multi-vendor intelligent SONET equipment will be interconnected via dual fiber-optic rings which will allow the network to survive major component failures. SONET's distributed control philosophy emphasizes extensive self-monitoring, automatic failure recovery, rapid network reconfiguration and customization of transmission services at the network termination inter-face. With this much intelligence in the form of microprocessors, soft-ware and data distributed among SONET equipment there is a requirement to protect network control from unauthorized access, software bugs and computer "viruses". Especially since a telecommunications enterprise's operations staff and those of its customers will be allowed to share network management responsibility. A SONET-based transport network will make it feasible to offer multi-media communication services and video services to the home or business. In the USA, several field trials are already underway to understand all aspects of providing video services in the home including supporting real-time menu-driven program se-lection, previewing video clips, service customization, credit authori-zation and billing.

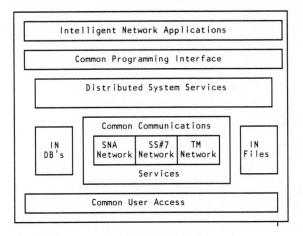

Figure 4. Intelligent Network Distributed System

Plans are afoot to evolve today's mobile communications system into the Personal Mobile Communications system that will allow a subscriber using a portable phone, computer or fax device to have access to any service he has subscribed to from any network access point (independent of geographic location). To accomplish this will require the sharing of customer, billing and service information across a telecommunications network (5).

The objectives of IN are to enable a telecommunications enterprise to quickly create new services, get them rapidly installed and in use, to share network management responsibility with customers, and to greatly reduce network operations costs (1,7,8,22). The initial focus of IN was on transaction processing and distributed data management for the SCS (9). However, the telecommunications plans for the '90's have caused the the IN concept to become more inclusive and now it is recognized that to achieve the IN objectives requires the interworking of the BIS, SCS and NMS. Ideally, the goal is to integrate these three heterogeneous systems into a "seamless" distributed system that provides a single system's image to every type of system user (Figure 4). This presents us with a major problem to solve. Each of the three system's communications services are different and are at a different stage of development in supporting distributed processing. It will be important for SNA, SS#7, and TMN application-layer communication services to converge as much as possible. In addition, a seamless distributed system requires addressing standardization of the application development environment and application platform which includes programming interface, user access, database management, file management, etc..

6. INTELLIGENT NETWORK DISTRIBUTED SYSTEM

There are various approaches to integrating the BIS, SCS and NMS into a distributed system. All of them depend on sophisticated directory services to locate distributed service providers and resources. We can not go into detail about the directory other than to point out it will play a critical role in the IN distributed system. We will describe in general terms three system integration approaches to developing the IN distributed system.

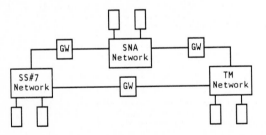

Figure 5. Gateway Approach to Implementing the IN Distributed System

The gateway approach involves developing a gateway for each network pair (Figure 5). The gateways would have to be more than transport network gateways and perform upper-layer communication protocol conversion and manage all cross-system communications entailing remote service requests, distributed data manipulation, data transfer, problem notifications and error recovery. A major drawback of the gateway approach is that each distributed system is still separate and unique in all aspects of program development and systems management. Regardless of the drawbacks of gateways in not achieving a single system's image it is probably the best way for interworking the "embedded base" with the IN distributed system. Prototype object-oriented database management systems have been successfully used to provide a uniform interface for accessing heterogeneous database management systems. In the next few years the related exploratory work based on the object-oriented paradigm, AI programming techniques, expert systems and database management should be synthesized into a high-performance knowledgebase system technology. This leads us to conjecture that the embedded base will be interworked with the IN distributed system using a gateway based on a knowledgebase system capable of automated reasoning about how to perform distributed processing with systems in the embedded base.

The common function approach to interworking distributed systems is based on identifying the most widely used services in distributed systems and making them common across different system types (Figure 6). This can be done by taking a facility from one system type and adapting it to run on the other system types. This approach is being taken by IBM to interwork Systems Application Architecture (SAA) systems and AIX systems. The common facilities span programming languages, window-based presentation services, communications, network management, SQL database management and distributed file management. This approach makes some aspects of application program development and end-user system interaction compatible across heterogeneous distributed systems. It may be the most practical way to start developing the IN distributed system.

Applications	SQL DB Manager		SQL DB Manager	Applications
Common Presentation Services	Common Communications Services		Common Communications Services	Common Presentation Services
Local Oper. System	Distributed File Manager		Distributed File Manager	Local Oper. System

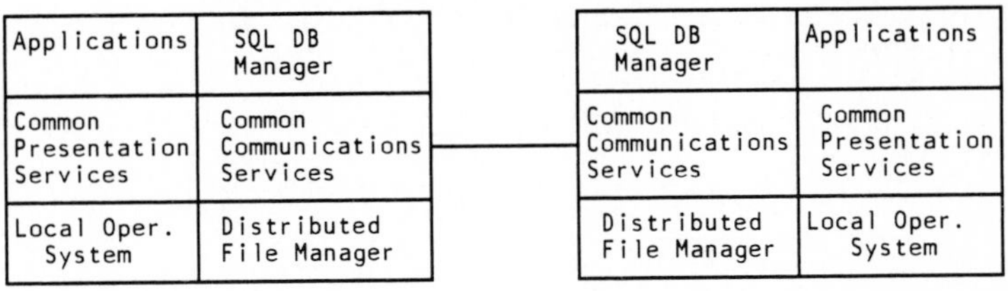

Figure 6. Common Function Approach to Implementing the IN Distributed System

The single systems image approach to developing an IN distributed system is ambitious. It requires an architecture to guide its long term development. The objective is for programmers, operators, and end-users to perceive the system as a single homogenous system. IBM's SAA is an example of what is required. SAA is an architecture for a distributed system that communicates over SNA and OSI and consists of heterogeneous systems which include ESA/370, AS/400 and PS/2 and their corresponding operating systems (16,18,24). The architecture defines the distributed system services required to AUGMENT THE EXISTING LOCAL OPERATING SYSTEM (Figure 7). so that the existence of heterogeneous systems, their geographical dispersion and underlying networks are masked from everyone. The comprehensive distributed system services that have to be specified in detail include:

*   The Common Programming Interface which standardizes how an applications requests either a service or resource.

*   The Common System Services which are the generic set of services typically required by application from an operating system.

* The Distributed Resource Managers which encompass transaction management, database management, file management, etc. and control both local and remote service request processing or remotely.
* The Common Communications Services which mask computer network differences and presents a generic set of standard services to the Distributed Resource Managers, applications, or Interconnected System Manager
* The Directory Services which locate where a service is to be performed
* The Interconnected System Management Services which unifies the management and operations control of heterogeneous systems especially insuring abnormal conditions are handled consistently across all systems.
* The Common User Access which manages the dialog between the end users and the system insuring a consistent system appearance.

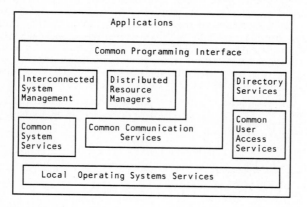

Figure 7.   SAA-based Approach to Implementing the IN Distributed System

SAA can be viewed as the specification of a layer or shell of distributed services that is added to a local operating system so it can participate as a component of a distributed system.   SAA is a good framework for understanding the totality of what has to be considered and specified in developing the IN distributed system by integrating heterogeneous systems.   More than programming interfaces and managing distributed databases and files have to be standardized.   The growing importance of distributed systems standardization is attested to by ISO and CCITT standards committees having both initiated projects with goals similar to SAA, the Open Distributed Processing project and the Communications Framework for Distributed Applications project, respectively.

7. CONCLUSIONS

From the perspective of computer networking, the Intelligent Network of the 1990's is a plan for developing a distributed system that integrates the separately evolving business information system, (circuit-switched) service control system and network management system of a telecommunications enterprise. Data sharing, distributed transaction processing and location transparency are of paramount importance in developing the INTEGRATED APPLICATIONS of the Intelligent Network.

Integrating heterogeneous systems that are functionally enriched is technically challenging. It will take years to accomplish and that is why it is important to have a distributed system's architecture guiding the conversion and migration to the Intelligent Network distributed system. IBM's SAA is a realistic example of what is involved in standardizing distributed processing. The distributed systems architecture will have to specify programming interfaces, directory services, distributed resource managers' capabilities, user access standards, common communication services, consistent treatment of errors, etc.. A preferred way to get started is to address the simpler system interworking issues dealing with common programming facilities, common communications capabilities, file and database sharing and common presentation services. In addition, the techniques for interfacing the IN distributed system to the "embedded base" that will be around for years will have to be dealt with. Applying the object-oriented programming and database technologies to this problem appears very promising.

ACKNOWLEDGEMENTS

Brian Bennett, Joseph Cox, Robert Sawyer and Peter Willen of IBM contributed to the synthesis of information and to the formulation of the concepts presented in this paper.

REFERENCES

1. J. J. Appel and M. J. Polosky, "Pacific Bell's Network System's Concept of the 90's", IEEE Journal of Selected Areas in Communications, Vol. 6, No. 4, May, 1988, pp. 627-632.

2. R. Ballart and Y. Ching, "SONET: Now Its the Standard Optical Network", IEEC Communications Magazine, Vol.27, No. 3, March, 1989, pp. 8-15.

3. CCITT Study Group XI,"Report R33 - Draft Recommendation Q.771 to Q.774 Transaction Capabilities", Geneva, Nov. 3 to 14, 1986.

4. CCITT Recommendation M.30: Principles for a Telecommunications Management Network

5. D. C. Cox, "Portable Digital Radio Communications, An Approach to Tetherless Access", IEEE Communications Magazine, Vol.27, No. 7, July, 1989, pp. 30-40.

6. J. P. Gray, et al, "Advanced Program to Program Communication in SNA", IBM Systems Journal, Vol. 22, No.4, 1983, pp. 298-318.

7. R. J. Hass and R. B. Robrock, "The Intelligent Network of the Future", Globecom '86, 1986, pp. 1311-1315.

8. R. J. Hass and R. W. Humes, "Intelligent Network/2: A Network Architecture Concept for the 1990's", International Switching Symposium 1987 Proceedings, Vol.4, March 1987, pp. 944-951.

9. C. S. Head, "Intelligent Network: A Distributed System", IEEE Communications Magazine, Vol.26, No. 12, Dec., 1988, pp. 16-20.

10. K. Hoshizawa, "Network Operations in the INS Age", Japanese Telecommunications Review, April, 1987, pp. 6-16

11. F. C. Iffland, et al, "ISDN Applications: Their Identification and Development", IEEE Network, Vol. 3, No. 5, Sept., 1989, pp. 6-11.

12. Introduction to APPC, IBM , IBM Form GG24-1584, 1986.

13. OSI/Network Management Forum Architecture, Issue 1, January, 1990.

14. Specifications of Signalling System No. 7 Recommendations Q.701-Q.714 (Study Group XI), CCITT Red Book, Vol. VI.7, Oct. 1984

15. Specifications of Signalling System No. 7 Recommendations Q.721-Q.795 (Study Group XI), CCITT Red Book, Vol. VI.8, Oct. 1984

16. SAA Overview, IBM , IBM Form GC26-4341, 1988.

17. V. Sahin, "Telecommunications Management Network (TMN) Architecture and Interworking Design", IEEE Journal of Selected Areas in Communications, Vol. 6, No. 4, May, 1988, pp. 685-696.

18. J. P. Sanders, et al, "A Communications Interface for Systems Application Architecture", IEEE Journal of Selected Areas In Communications, Vol. 7, No. 7, Sept. 1989, pp. 1073-1081.

19. G. G. Schlanger, "An Overview of Signalling System No. 7", IEEE Journal on Selected Areas in Communications, Vol. SAC-4, No.3, May 1986, pp. 360-365.

20. Systems Network Architecture Concepts and Products IBM , IBM Form GA-27-3136, 1986.

21. Systems Network Architecture Technical Overview, IBM , IBM Form GC-30-3073, 1986.

22. C. R. Scherer and T. A. Murray, "Management of the Intelligent Network", IEEE Communications Magazine, Vol. 26, No. 12, Dec., 1988, pp. 21-24.

23. R. J. Sundstrom, et al, "SNA: Current Requirements and Direction", IBM Systems Journal, Vol. 26, No.1, 1987, pp. 13-36.

24. E. F. Wheeler and A. G. Ganek, "Introduction To Systems Applications Architecture", IBM Systems Journal, Vol. 27, No.3, 1988, pp. 250-263.

Information Network and Data Communication, III
D. Khakhar and F. Eliassen (Editors)
Elsevier Science Publishers B.V. (North-Holland)
© IFIP, 1990

HYPATIA

- proposed concepts to cure information overflow in electronic information delivery systems

Kolbjørn Henrik Aambø and Terje Bakka

USE, Postbox 1059, University of Oslo,

N-0316 OSLO, Norway

Abstract

A proposed solution to the general problem of information overflow is described by a integrated hypermedia system, HYPATIA [Hypatia]. HYPATIA structures information objects by such characteristic hypermedia techniques as inter-object links, graphical traversing and free text search. A model of the inter object links is given as English text and in the graphical data modeling language NIAM.

1 Introduction

One autumn Monday morning in the last year of the eighties Mrs. Y. arrives early the Laboratory for Mouse Tail Sciences . In the paper mail she finds a stack of magazines, a few business letters and some handwritten comments about the latest findings on tumour in mouse tails, done by her colleagues during her vacation. There is also a big pile of documents stacked in the mailbox, for the practical reason that this is the only place orderly enough to prevent documents from disappearing. She is reluctant to log on to the computer, knowing that her one week vacation has caused a pile-up of unread electronic mail entries. Normally, she will cut out interesting entries and insert them into a free text search facility to ease the retrieval of interesting opinions of other scientists. Today the possible amount of new information seems too overwhelming.

The world of electronic information delivery systems can be divided into the two categories, mail systems and conferencing systems, which are in some ways fundamentally different from each other.

Electronic Mail systems are based on the send-to-an-address-and-forget-it metaphor, more or less an emulation of paper mail. Most electronic communication between two people is done by electronic mail. This is specially true if information is exchanged between two computer installations. Examples of standards and defacto-standards for such systems are e.g. Unix-mail, X.400 and IBM Proffs.

Conferencing systems are harder to describe in everyday metaphors. A common metaphor for conferencing systems is the *bulletin board*. Several systems exist for conferencing; such systems are General Electric GENIE, Compuserve and PortaCOM [PortaCOM]. The GENIE system also include a free text search system, but a poor browsing system. The best browsing system is probably Apple-Link which is a GENIE branch service for Apple Computer, Inc.

Information received and mailed by information delivery system is in most cases stored in ad-hoc store-and-retrieve systems which are hardly standardized at all. In our opinion the most lacking functionality in current state-of-the-art information delivery systems, is the inability to simultaneously search for information in any mail, conference and archive-systems given a certain number of key words and phrases. To find information in present systems, the store-and-retrieve systems of several different systems have to be searched. To solve these problems, a common storage, browsing and information retrieval system for *both* mail and conferencing systems should be implemented. An implication of present systems is lack of standards which pose a considerable load on the user by demanding fluency in several separate systems for mail and conferencing.

The main goal of this paper is to describe a common framework for a system to integrate storage, information retrieval, browsing, conferencing, mail, and archiving. An implication of such a system is a single user interface for a complete information delivery system.

To solve the information overflow problem in information delivery systems we propose to create a structure that links together information objects which are associated with each other. Another complimentary technique to solve the same problem is to make all information available through a free text search system. We would prefer a system that can deal with both inter-object links and free text search. We would also prefer the system to combine traditional store and forward conferencing with the X.400 and X.500 Mail and Directory systems through a *uniform interface metaphor*. This metaphor should be able to present information about how different information object are *related to each other*. There should also be a way to display the relations between objects based on their attributes or *contents* such as theme, time-line (moment of publishing), specific words, or author. This should be done by specifying filter scripts executable by the free text search system.

This article presents how information objects should be related to each other in order to make a uniform interface metaphor possible.

2 How to integrate mail and conferencing by a common storage, retrieval and archiving system

Current conferencing systems are used to exchange small messages, typically a few screen-fulls long. Most (but not all) small texts are statements or comments on others statements. We find a rising demand for systems that can exchange vast multimedia documents containing text, graphics and sound, and even animation sequences, video etc. Conferencing systems supports message exchange between people that can not be present at the same place and at the same time. Most conferencing and mail systems have very limited abilities to retrieve old entries conserning a specific subject. A browser to make overviews of discussions is also lacking.

We are convinced that these problems should be solved by a integrated system for Archive, Mail and Conferencing. A system that can integrate archive, mail and conferencing systems, and at the same time make information easily available for browsing and retrieval is in many ways similar to what many refer to as a Hypermedia system.

2.1 Hypermedia - a navigation method

The term hypermedia embeds characteristic techniques such as: *Inter-object Links*, *Navigation by Graphical Traversing* and *Free Text Search*. These terms are essential in hypermedia systems and will thus be discussed.

2.1.1 Inter-object links

One of the pioneers in the field of computing, Vannevar Bush, had the idea of letting an automaton deal with the management of the sets of associative links. According to Ted Nelson (who also coined the term *Hypertext*), the automaton should do the repetitive work of e.g. finding the page given in an index, fast access to referenced documents and quoting phrases elsewhere in the document or docuvers[1] given a link to them [Hypertext]. The methods have later been generalized to cover more than text only; other media such as graphics and sound have been introduced and the term hypermedia has gained acceptance [HyperMedia]. The introduction of new media (in addition to text) has made the possibility for alternative ways to manage immense storage and navigate in them even more important.

Nelson's opinion is that hypertext imposes *no physical structure* on the document; it may consist of chunks of text and links between them. When the text is viewed on the screen, an asterisk (or another symbol) in the text indicates a possible jump to somewhere unknown by the user. To avoid getting lost, the address of the previous location is saved on a stack every time a jump is performed. By a popping operation on a stack the user can return to the previous location if she wants to.

A *hyperdocument* can be viewed as a database with a number of items, interconnected by interactively- and manually-made links. Hypermedia systems make it possible to navigate using these links. You can have as many links as you wish, pointing to and from each node in the document. Since links are so vital, the user's ability to create them easily is essential. Each item in the hyperdocument corresponds one-to-one to a potential view on the display. The item or node has a unique name to identify it by reference.

A view of the node can contain a link icon (e.g. an asterisk). A link icon indicates where a jump to follow a link to another object may be performed. When we follow a link, visual effects can be added, to enable us to tell what kind of transitions are done; for instance, by simulating the turning of pages in a book. The transitions must be performed well to make the visual effects seem realistic.

2.1.2 Navigation by graphical traversing (browsing)

Another way to navigate in the hypermedia documents is to have an overview of the link-web of the hyperdocument, or part of it, displayed on the screen. The problem of making global maps to ease navigation has not been solved generally, but solutions exist for special purposes.

If we compare inter-object links with a web, say of streets, we can easily agree that it is of no practical importance to us to know where a street take us if our destination is not on this particular street. What we need to know is how the streets are linked to make transportation from one place to another possible. A good overview of the streets is a map. What we need is a "street map" for inter-object links.

---

[1] Ted Nelsons term for a vast collection of documents

2.1.3 Free text search

In traditional database design, data modulation techniques structure the information in to objects and object attributes. In a hyperdocument link structures may be static if made beforehand by the creator of the hyperdocument, or dynamic if a reader is able to make his own inter-object links. The decisions made about the links in a hypermedia system, and the organization of object attributes, is made by a few people on the basis of what *system constructors* consider essential to the problem at hand. The *user* of the database or hypermedia system may however have a different view of the world, and may find the author's choices inappropriate. This problem may be seen as one of the major causes for what has been called user disorientation in large systems.

One solution to user disorientation in hypermedia systems is query/search systems, notably Free Text Search. In a typical free text search system, text attributes are inverted on all words except for explicitly defined stop words. To invert a object, index of all occurring words in all text attributes of all information objects is made, then a table of pointers to all objects containing every single word. Searching is done with a search language. Retrieval time is *independent* of the size of the object collection. The performance of such systems is such that several objects may be retrieved during a split second from a Giga-byte collection of text attributes. Queries involving heavily truncated words may be more time consuming, since the operation is more dependent on the size of the index. Normal queries with Boolean expressions containing about 30 terms take approximately 1-5 seconds in a system like Search in Free Text [SiFT].

Documents that satisfy the query might be stacked with the most relevant documents on top. Degree of relevance in documents can be determined by the number of Boolean terms satisfied in the query. Documents with all Boolean terms satisfied are considered the *most* relevant, the ones with only one Boolean term satisfied the *least* relevant.

The disadvantages of free text search are the inverting time and storage space consumption. Inverting time in modern systems is done *incrementally*, and is often independent of the size of the document collection already inverted. The space consumption is from 1.5 to 4 times the size of the original text attributes.

Functionality in hypermedia systems is improved by offering a free text search facility. We can then navigate without being dependent on the links declared in the hyperdocument.

The state of art in free text search or information retrieval [Salton] is currently implemented in systems like: Basis from Batelle, BRS/Search by BRS, SiFT by the Norwegian Government Computer Centre, STAIRS by IBM, STATUS 2, and TRIP by PARALOG AB.

3 HYPATIA, a Mail, Archive and Conferencing concept

In this chapter we will give the conceptual model for an internal structure of a mail, archive and conferencing system from a inter-object link point of view. The part of the conceptual model that will be described is the part which gives most information about the different object types in relation to each other. The structure will be presented both as English text (in bold) and as NIAM -diagrams [NIAM].

3.1 How to read NIAM diagrams

In NIAM diagrams two different *roles* are in use, the *one-many* (1:n) *role* and the *one-one*

(1:1) *role*:

One-one :　　　　　　　　　　　One-Many :

In addition there are several *restrictions*; The *Always* restriction is *unary* i.e. its interpretation is to state that one particular role must always be satisfied. The combination of a

one-one role and an *always restriction* is expressed such: 　　　　　　　　 but may in some applications be more understandable written as: ──────▸ to signifying a *SubClass* pointing to a *SuperClass*. Some times it is required that one instance of a class exist before the other object may be put into existence. For example, a Person that is the mother of a Child must *exist in advance* to give birth to a child. To express such a relation we use a *Before-after restriction*:

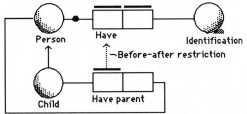

The final element that needs explanation in NIAM is a way to describe *many-to-many* (n:m) relationship. An example of a (n:m) relationship is membership in an organization. A person can be a member of several organizations, and an organization has several person (as members). We express such relations with an *object diagram*:

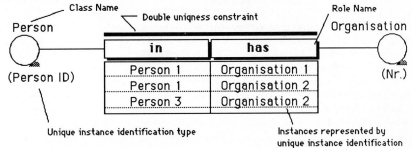

An object diagram is later expressed as part of the web of roles and classes called the NIAM diagram. In NIAM, n:m relations are the source for new classes, with unique class names. In the example above we may call the n:m relationship a *membership*. The n:m relationship between instances of the classes *person* and *organization* is expressed as the new class *membership* in the following way:

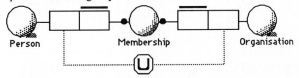

The ⓤ -restriction express that the combination of a *person* and an *organization* is a *combined unique* constellation - one particular person may not be a member of one particular organization more than once at any time, which is reasonable.

3.2 A description of a conferencing system

3.2.1 The Entry that represent the message

An *Entry* may be a *Comment* to another Entry

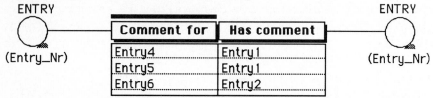

An entry that represent a statement from a person may be a comment to only one other entry. Seen from the other point of view, one entry can be commented by several other entries. This is a one-to-many relation between an entry and the entries that comment it.

An entry is only the *representative* of a persons statement. The statement itself is a object associated with an entry. We may use the terminology of the Japanese TRON project and say that an entry is the *Virtual object type* and the document is the *Real object type* [TRON].

An *Entry* may have a *Document* as its content.

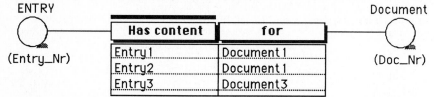

An entry can be a representative for only one statement represented by a (multimedia) *Document*. A document can be referred to by several Entries. We say it is a many-one relative between the (virtual object type) entry and the (real object type) document.

An entry represents a statement from one specific *User*. An entry may have a user as an *Author*.

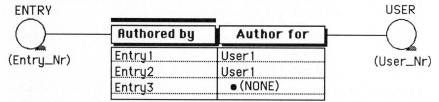

This means that an entry can be traced back to the author that is responsible for posting the entry and its (possible) multimedia *document*. In the case of anonymous authoring the *User_Nr* is given a appropriate *NONE* (•) value.

The entries that have been discussed until now, are for *in-house communication only*. This means that the entries are typically store forward conferencing objects. In addition we have the two sub-classes of the object-type *entry* that are for communication with the world outside the conferencing system. Formal information exchange with other organizations are often done by mail. We have two types; incoming and outgoing mail:

An Out_Entry is a subclass of entry

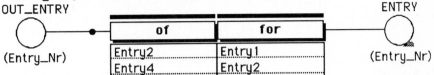

An *Out_Entry* is associated with information that is *sent* out of the system by (electronic) mail. If the message is not storeable on a computer we can store information about the message in a information field in the (virtual) *Out_Entry* object.

An *In_Entry* is a subclass of *entry*.

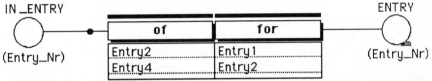

An *In_Entry* is associated with information that is *received* by the system via (electronic) mail. If the message is not storeable on a computer we can store information about the message in a information field in the (virtual) *In_entry* object.

An *Out_Entry* may be written for an *In_Entry*.

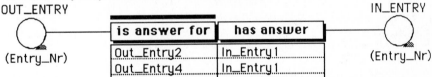

In cases where an *In_Entry* *must* be answered, we register an *Out_Entry* as the answer for that *In_Entry*.

An entry may be protected by a (entry) *Protection*

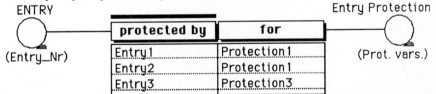

How protection for entries should be done is described below in the sub-section *«What to do with the entry»*. The protection should give the author rights to alter the entry and its document. Protection can also regulate other peoples access to read and possibly alter the entry and its document. A default entry protection is always associated with the conference. However, an author can choose a different protection for his entry. The authors freedom to choosing a different protection should be limited in some way by the conference default protection.

The concept of *Out_Entry*, *In_Entry*, *Out_Entries* written as an answer for *In_Entry*, and protection of entries are concepts taken from NOARK (Norwegian Archive system), [NOARK]. We have seen the *written for* concept as a *specialization* of the earlier mentioned comment concept. We find this a natural way of seeing things, since an *Out_Entry* in a way, is some sort of comment to the corresponding *In_Entry*.

3.2.2 An entrys relation to the rest of us

PortaCom has demonstrated the usefulness of categorizing entries according to subject matter. To be part of a discussion on a specific subject, the user must be a member of the conference containing this particular discussion. We will formalize the meaning of this through NIAM diagrams .

3.2.3 The Discussion

An entry can be associated with several *Conferences*. One conference may have several entries associated with it.
An n:m (many-to-many) relation between an entry and a conference is named a *Discussion*.

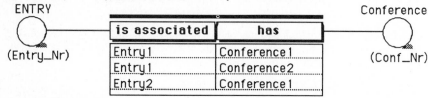

The practical implication of the discussion construct is that a series of entries can be associated with several conferences (see Public conference below). This is done by letting the user have access to the discussion through membership in one or more conferences.

3.2.4 The Membership

A *User* can be associated with several conferences. A conference may have several users.
We name the n:m relation between user and conference a *Membership*.

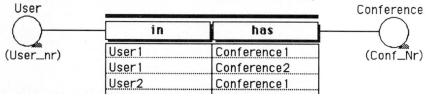

A membership is given as the concatenation of the reference of the user and the reference of the conference. But how do we become a member? For some applications it is practical to let the users themselves do the actions to be a member. For other applications it is more «secure» to let some kind of super-member of the conference registering new members. How a membership should start and which properties a membership should have depends on the *protection of the conference.*

3.2.4 How to protect conferences for different applications.

A conference is *always* protected by a *Protection*.

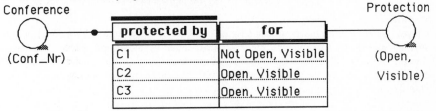

Conference   Protection

protected by	for
C1	Not Open, Visible
C2	Open, Visible
C3	Open, Visible

(Conf_Nr)   (Open, Visible)

The protection of a conference is done by combining the Boolean variables *Open* and *Visible* in the following way:

Open   A person can enlist as a member.

Not open   A person must be *registered* as a member by an organizer.

Visible   A conference can be made visible by making name, (E-mail) address, description, members, etc. available in an electronic directory system. Members, and in some conferences also, none-members can publish information. Publishing is made dependent on variables internal to the conference. (See *What to do with entries...* below)

Not visible implies that the existence of the conference should not be available to the general public through an electronic directory system. Information about the conference may only be available to members. Only members can publish. This class of conferences is made to prevent leakage of information by information exchange with entities external to the conference.

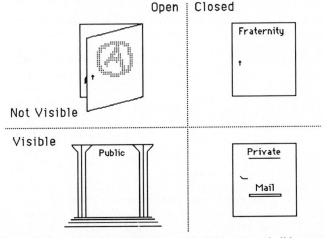

By combining the two Boolean variables open and visible we can build several metaphors for conferencing. We divide the metaphors into four classes according to combinations of open and visible. Conferences that are *Visible* are visible in a directory system:

Public (Open, Visible)
Open implies that any person can ask for a membership and get one. The only thing that can prevent a person from being a member is the organizers blocking of the person's name due to improper behaviour. Public conferences have the unique ability to exchange information with other public conferences by information sharing through the discussion mechanism.

Private (Closed, Visible)
Closed implies that membership can only be obtained by active action from the organizer. Private conferences can exchange information with other visible conferences by information copies. Information copies are special objects that share many of the properties of conventional mail objects. The conference system register information copies as *Out_Entries*. *Out_Entries* have a special header with a unique entry number. The receiver of an *Out_Entry* can reply by returning an information copy containing this unique entry number as some kind of Ticket number. When the conferencing system receive information objects with Ticket numbers, they will automatically be routed to the appropriate discussion and registered as an *In_Entry* to the corresponding *Out_Entry*.

Both private and public conferences are visible in directory systems. In conferences that are *not visible* and either open or closed, are maintained in the *anarchy* and *fraternity* respectively. At the same time they have the property of not being visible in directory systems. Conferences that are *Not Visible* are invisible in a directory system:

Anarchy (Open, Not Visible)
Open implies that everybody joining a conference without an organizer are personally responsible for what happens in the conference.

Fraternity (Closed, Not Visible)
A fraternity have some similar functionality as a Masonry or a development group. A fraternity conference is made to make none-disclosed information available to a well defined group and prevent leakage of information.

We have considered applying a *depth* concept to constrict the different members' ability know each others' identity.

In the different conference classes we have only talked about *authoring* - the ability to make statements and comments on others statements. To make such statements available for other members, the statements have to be *published*. In particular conferences we want everybody to be *both* an author and a publisher. In other conferences which may be more newspaper-like, we want *moderated* publishing where only *organizers* are able to publish.

3.2.5 What to do with the entries - a scheme for default entry protection in particular conferences

A conference always has a default entry Protection.

Conference	has default	for	Entry Protection
(Conf_Nr)			(Prot. vars.)
	Conference 1	Protection1	
	Conference 2	Protection1	
	Conference 3	Protection3	

Example of proposed default entry protection for the four conference classes:

	Author	Organizer	Member	Nonmembers
Authoring :		☒	☒	☐
Publishing :	☒	☐	☐	☐
Read Unpublished :	☒	☐	☐	☐
Read Published :	☒	☒	☒	☐
Delete :	☒	☒	☒	☐

Fraternity

	Author	Organizer	Member	Nonmembers
Authoring :		☒	☒	☐
Publishing :	☒	☐	☐	☐
Read Unpublished :	☒	☐	☐	☐
Read Published :	☒	☒	☒	☐
Delete :	☒	☒	☐	☐

Private Mail

	Author	Organizer	Member	Nonmembers
Authoring :		☒	☒	☐
Publishing :	☒	☒	☒	☒
Read Unpublished :	☒	☐	☐	☐
Read Published :	☒	☒	☒	☐
Delete :	☒	☒	☐	☐

Public

	Author	Organizer	Member	Nonmembers
Authoring :		☒	☒	☐
Publishing :	☒	☒	☒	☒
Read Unpublished :	☒	☐	☐	☐
Read Published :	☒	☒	☒	☒
Delete :	☒	☒	☐	☐

An author is a member of a conference who has made a statement either as an initial statement or as a comment to another statement. When an entry is made it is not visible to other members until it is published.

An entry can be published by an author or by a *nonmember* in a visible conferences that allows it (this is done by sending an *In_Entry* to the conference). Publishing can be allowed by other members than the author if they are given the ability to read unpublished entries.

The inverse function of publish is delete. If allowed, this can be used to «censure» unwanted entries. In particular, it can be used to let an organizer remove statements that are regarded as unethical according to one country's laws or for downright demonstration of power... When members other than the author delete an entry it is only removed as published (it is «unpublished»). When an author deletes it, the associated document is suppressed or possibly removed entirely.

We have considered two types of nonmembers: anonymous members and members with a unique name, real or pseudonymous. Anonymous authors are impossible because of the problem of identification: which anonymous person owns which entry. For this reason anonymous publishing is possible in visible conferences only.

3.3 The structure of object types in the HYPATIA system

When we combine the binary relations given above we obtain a graph of binary relations as shown below.

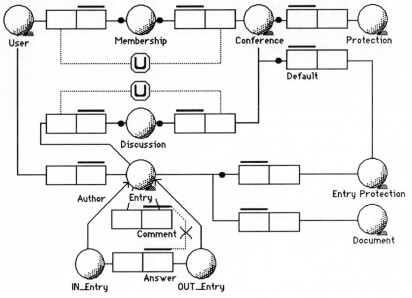

3.4 An example of objects (instances) in the system

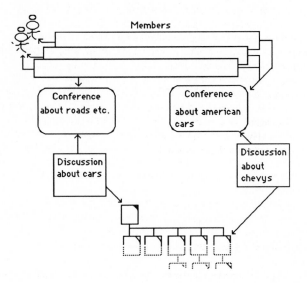

The figure above show a discussion of cars in a conference about Roads etc. One of the comments diversify in the direction of talking about Chevy cars which the author of that entry also found relevant for a conference about American cars. He signifies this by letting a discussion associated with the American car conference point to a *sub-tree* in the discussion of cars in the conference about Roads etc. This is also an explanation of why we call a web of entries commenting each other a *discussion tree*.

3.5 Communication outside HYPATIA

By connecting HYPATIA to a Electronic Mail server which follows the X.400 recommendation from CCITT[2], documents may be exchanged between a conference in HYPATIA and nonmembers of the conference outside the HYPATIA-system. In HYPATIA this communication is administered by means of the *In_Entries* and *Out_Entries* (see section 3.2.1 above). Communication between a conference in HYPATIA and nonmembers outside HYPATIA by means of X.400 can only take place if both the conference and the nonmember(s) have X.400-addresses. Additionally the conference must be Visible (section 3.2.4).

The conferences and its associated information (e.g. the X.400-address) should be registered in a X.500 Directory system. By using the X.500 Directory Services nonmembers may get information about conferences in HYPATIA. The X.500 Directory, specified by CCITT, is a service which offer communication-related information about persons, organizations, services etc.

4 Final remarks

We have described concepts of a mail, archive and conferencing system by English text and NIAM diagrams. What remains to be seen is how well our model will fit practical applications such as electronic magazines. Another aspect to be dealt with in a practical system, is how to make an appropriate interface metaphor for information browsing. We have done some work on this matter but space prevent a presentation in this paper.

Further work should also deal with the problem of constructing more general inter-object links such as transclutions[3], which add the ability to refer to part of other documents. Another interesting subject is the ability to make comments by annotation. An elegant way to annotate, is to position transclutions in the text to be commented. The method of inter-object links described in this text is indeed *independent* of the actual (multimedia) document. The transclution addresses the case of positioning in such a document. Transclutions applied on texts is described in [Hypertext]. Our work will be continued by an animation prototype that can reveal the pros and cons of our concepts.

---

[2] CCITT: The International Telegraph and Telephone Consultative Committee.

[3] Transclution is Ted Nelsons term for interdocument-links which can reference a given *amount* of text.

218

5 References

[Hypatia] **Kolbjørn H. Aambø and Ingvil Hovig**: "The term HYPERMEDIA & a thought-experiment HYPATIA" (Proceedings of the EUTECO'88 on Researche into Networks and Distributed Applications, Vienna, Austria, 1988. NORTH HOLLAND, 1988)

[PortaCom] **B.N.Meeks**: "An overview of conferencing systems." (Byte December 1985, pp. 169-184)

[Hypertext] **Theodor Holm Nelson**: "Computer LIB / Dream Machines", (the distributors 1989). "Including As We May Think" by Vannevar Bush.

[HyperMedia] **Jeff Conklin**: "Hypermedia: An Introduction and Survey.", (IEEE COMPUTER September 1987).

[SiFT] "SiFT, Searching in Free Text a text retrieval system, USER GUIDE 2and edition." (Norwegian Government Computer Centre, 1987).

[Salton] **Salton/ McGill**: "Introduction to modern information retrieval." (McGraw-Hill Book Company, 1983).

[NIAM] **G.M.Nijssen, - T.A.Halpin,** : "Conceptual Schema and Relational Database Design - A Fact Oriented Approach." (PRENTICE HALL 1989).

[TRON] **Ken Sakamura** (Ed.): "TRON Project 1987, Open-Architecture Computer Systems." (Springer-Verlag 1987).

[NOARK] **Statens rasjonaliseringsdirektorat**: "NORSK ARKIVSYSTEM - Standard for EDB-jounalføring i statsforvaltningen -Kravs-pesifikasjon" (Aschehoug/ Statens rasjonaliseringsdirektorat 1984).

Information Network and Data Communication, III
D. Khakhar and F. Eliassen (Editors)
Elsevier Science Publishers B.V. (North-Holland)
IFIP, 1990

X.400 MIGRATION STRATEGIES

Dr George W Wells
ICL Network Systems
Six Hills House
London Road
Stevenage, Herts
SG1 1YB
UK

ABSTRACT

The adoption of the CCITT X.400 series of recommendations
will lead to a global electronic message handling system to
which all other messaging systems can be connected and
interoperated. The range of currently available messaging
systems, many of which are incompatible, is vast and includes
at the extremes proprietary office systems and the postal
services.

To integrate these messaging systems and services is a major
undertaking however the strategy is simple. Each end user
system with messaging capability to be included will need
some X.400 functionality and each administrations will need
to provide an X.400 Message Transfer Service.

Migration strategies can be adopted which provide a basic
service expandable in both capacity and functionality. The
X.400 recommendations and their implementation agreements now
being put in place favour a progressive approach, earlier
implementations being compatible with later versions and the
administration networks expanding by adding nodes (message
transfer agents) as traffic increases. These administration
networks will access other message handling services such as
telex and fax, and accept private networks as well as
individuals as subscribers.

1.   INTRODUCTION

Proprietary electronic mail systems were first introduced by
Dialcom (USA) in the early 1970s. These systems were
primarily used to provide a service to subscibers but it soon
became apparent that unless subscribers with a community
interest joined a service together or joined many services
there was a high probability that the number of messages
exchanged would remain low. While service operators were
attempting to achieve critical mass those communities that
naturally existed, such as companies, were installing
internal electronic mail systems, often using existing

mainframes and terminals. The E-Mail supplier in this case was the mainframe supplier. It is not surprising then that modern office systems which have message preparation and management among their major facilities are supplied by IT companies, not telecommunication companies.

The common need to pass messages from one of these proprietary systems to another led to the creation of an international standard for message handling, the CCITT X.400 series of recommendations (reference 1). The concept is simple, anyone wishing to send a message beyond their domain uses a recommended submission procedure and accepts incoming messages which also use one of the recommended procedures. There are several procedures or protocols covered by these recommendations.

This paper is concerned with the introduction of the services and protocols defined in the X.400 series of recommendations.

Introduction should in each case be to a plan which implements a migration strategy, the objective of which is to ensure that an extant message handling system can interoperate with other messaging systems so creating a single coherent universal telecommunication system for messages.

The types of extant message handling systems (MHS) considered here are,

> company MHSs which can be from several vendors and interworked only with difficulty

> public service MHSs, usually from a single vendor, and only in the recent past connected to other similar systems

> other MHSs, some global, which are not X.400 based, eg. the world telex service.

The rate of introduction is constrained by the availability of commercial X.400 conformant MHSs. This factor perhaps has the most influence on the practicality of any migration strategy schedule and will be considered first.

2.   PROFILES

The recommendations do not address the problem of implementation, for this detailed agreements are needed which remove the many options. Without these agreements and adherence to them systems designed to conform to the recommendations will not interoperate with other systems also thought to be conformant. Conformance to one of the agreed profiles therefore is essential if interoperability is to be achieved.

These agreements may be ISO/IEC JTC1 International

Standardisation Profiles (2), European Functional Standards such as ENV 41202 (3), or the Stable Implementation.

Agreements published by the National Institute of Standards and Technology (NIST, formerly NBS) (4).

To be useful all functional standards have to be compatible, although some can differ by including non essential options.

To date functional standards have been produced after the ratification of the recommendations to which they relate. To shorten the overall timescale work on functional standards will now be undertaken in parallel with work on the recommendations. Some suppliers have developed systems, either singly or in cooperation with others, by anticipating the final version of a functional standard, that is by adopting a convergence strategy, which has proved both difficult and costly.

3. RATIFICATION CYCLE

The functional standards relate to the underlying recommendations which are ratified by the CCITT at its Plenary Assembly held every four years. The first X.400 standard was ratified in 1984 and revised again in 1988. Work is now progressing on the 1992 revisions.

There is a requirement that functional standards relating to later versions of the recommendations should accommodate earlier versions.

The four year cycle can prove too long in practice and leading companies have been known to risk the purchase of convergent systems even though these may later prove to be non-convergent and no better than proprietary systems. To reduce the incidence of this occurence the CCITT have introduced a new approval procedure for acceptance between the Plenary Assemblies.

4. OPTIONS

Functional standards have the minimum number of options. They are not featureless, just that when an option is adopted it is often then made mandatory.

Despite this some options are allowed and there are also many unspecified system attributes. One of the best examples perhaps is performance, measured as message throughput or availability. Domain management, cost of system support, will be other significant differences among otherwise conformant systems.

5. MIGRATION STRATEGIES

Given the dynamic nature of these network application standards their introduction requires a migration strategy which could cover several years. Some suppliers understand this need and have a staged development programme, undertaking to provide a series of software systems over several years on a hardware platform until the final system delivered conforms to the stipulated stable standard.
Fortunately there is a generic strategy which can be used which satisfies most migration needs. It is based on the observation that when the X.400 functional units are arranged as a string the protocols linking them will be either implicitly or explicitly implemented depending on which functional units are to be coresident.

For example, when all units are collocated with the user an intelligent message handling system results typical of a private network connecting many sites served by office systems. This grouping of functional units is suitable as the first phase in the introduction of X.400 to a proprietary multivendor company MHS.

In contrast when none of the functional units are located with the user the network resembles that of an E-Mail service provider and is also a suitable first step to X.400 interoperability.

To understand this generic strategy better it is necessary to introduce the functional units and their linking protocols.

5.1 Generic Strategy

The figure below shows a string of functional units typical of those employed in an X.400 message handling system.

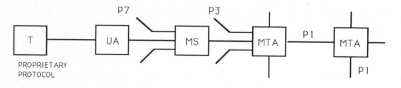

Figure 1

T, User's terminal
UA, User Agent. Handles all the protocols for interaction with the rest of the message handling system.
    MS, Message Store. Used for storing messages and selective retrieval.
    MTA, Message Transfer Agent. Used to transfer messages on a store and forward basis. A node of a Message Transfer System.
    P7, the protocol used when the UA is remote from the MS.

P3, used for the submission and receipt of messages to and from the adjacent MTA.

P1, used to transfer messages between MTAs.

No protocol is defined between the terminal (T) and its unique UA.

In the X.400 1984 recommendations no MS existed and a UA was connected directly to the MTA using the P3 protocol. In practice but not widely recognised at the time the functions of the MS were often located with the UA. When this was not so or the UA/MS switched off messages which could not be delivered by the adjacent (serving) MTA were returned to sender; the MTA has storage for message queues but not for subscribers.

With this information the following arrangements are possible;

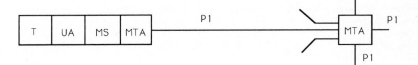

Figure 2

In figure 2 the strategy is to implement P1 only. The office system on the left has all the X.400 functions but none of the intervening protocols. It is a proprietary system changed only to support P1.

The MTA on the right may be a telecommunications centre of a private domain or the adjacent MTA of the public administration domain.

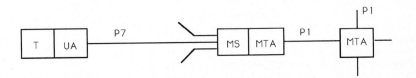

Figure 3

In this arrangement 2 protocols are implemented having separated the UA from the MS. The UA is then said to be remote (RUA). If it is also shared it can be designed to support many terminals although each T must have its own (virtual) UA.

In figure 4 the remote UA is moved along the string to the right. The (dumb) terminal is now connected to its (shared) UA by a nonstandard protocol. Such a proprietary message submission and delivery procedure exists in all extant E-Mail services.

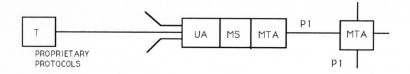

Figure 4

The proprietary protocol is usually chosen to make access to the (now local) UA by a public switched network simply and inexpensively.

With all the X.400 functional units on the right only the P1 protocol is again needed.

5.2 Company MH Systems

Companies often find themselves with message preparation and management systems from several suppliers which are not designed to interoperate. The problem can be solved by forming for each vendor's equipment a domain of interoperating systems and linking these to other vendor domains by gateways. This could involve designing a gateway for every conceivable pair of vendors. The X.400 solution however is to have each single vendor's domain so formed equipped with MTA functionality and linked to other non compatible domains, both within the company and without, using the P1 protocol.

With this arrangement the end user systems remain proprietary except for their support of the P1 protocol. Proprietary office (end user) systems provide choice and being application oriented generally use one of the Open operating systems.

5.3 Public Service MH Systems

These are centralised systems with subscribers using a wide range of terminals connected through one of the public switched networks. The addition of MTA functionality supporting P1 enables these systems to interwork with others similarly equipped by connecting to an administration domain of MTA nodes. The administrations's strategy is to start with a small number of nodes and add to them as traffic increases.

The next stage would be to separate out the MS functionality enabling remote UAs to be supported using the P7 protocol. This move also enables shared UAs to be distributed as concentrators to reduce communication costs.

Centralised service systems need extremely high availability. This can justify the use of fault/disaster-tolerant configurations.

Non-X.400 MH Systems

There are many message handling services, most of which do not interoperate electronically. Such services include,

        postal service
        telex
        facsimile   telematic services
        teletex
        videotex

and private networks such as SWIFT using their own community protocols.

With the advent of the X.400 based MH Services these other services can be made to interoperate, transferring messages freely between services through the X.400 MHS by using Access Units (AU). This bilateral arrangement then requires the design of an Access Unit for each non-X.400 MH service.

With so few X.400 MHS terminals in the public domain most administration message traffic is being handled as telex and fax so these are the first AUs required.

6.   CONCLUSIONS

A great deal of effort is being expended to produce agreed functional specifications. Governments, PTTs, and many institutions worldwide are encouraging the use of Open systems to achieve interoperability between different vendors' systems, giving wider choice, and consequently reduced costs.

Organisations operating in a competitive environment are seeking to achieve uniqueness at low cost by adopting Open systems early and/or using them as platforms for their own applications.

In conclusion one can safely predict that like the ubiquitous postal and telephone services the X.400 based MH service will span the globe and in a decade be available to all.

Information Network and Data Communication, III
D. Khakhar and F. Eliassen (Editors)
Elsevier Science Publishers B.V. (North-Holland)
IFIP, 1990

Two Routing Strategy Ideas for land-based mobile PR-Nets

Channing Jones, Toni Anwar

Department of Computer Science (Informatik IV)

Technical University of Aachen

West Germany

Abstract :

A system of communication between cars includes the benefit of direct and fast reaction to changing situations in traffic. A simple and effective strategy for spreading messages is necessary. In this paper two broadcast routing strategies are introduced to solve this problem : one using global coordinates and the other direction oriented.

1. Introduction

Integration of a mobile radio network for a better road traffic is a challenge we are faced with today. There are some projects in Europe, U.S.A or in Japan for regulating road traffic [PROM-87, VPRH-87], which are based on a mobile radio network. For this system, one requires some strategies to route the information sent by stations in a crowded city area, due to the shadowing of signals by buildings, trees or other objects. This paper handles two routing strategies for different conditions.

2. Global Coordinate Strategy

This Routing Strategy requires the global position of a car in a roadnetworld, which could be stored as a map in a disc.

a. Hardware Components

The basis for this system would be a micro processor, with a mass data storage medium such as a CD-ROM disc and an output device such as an LCD-Screen together with a loudspeaker for speech. This system would be similar to ones already developed by BOSCH such as the EVA-System [NePS-83, NeZe-86, DoFS-88, Pete-89]. This uses navigation feedback with a stored map and measures internally distance and angle traversed by the vehicle. In addition one could supplement the system by adding an electronic compass.

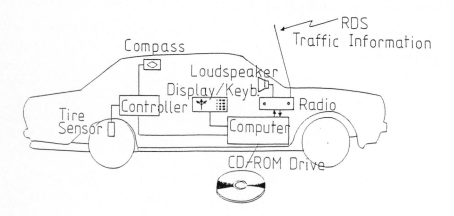

Fig. 1 A car with its onboard-computer

b. Software Components

A navigation feedback system needs detailed knowledge of the local roadnetwork it is traveling through. To cover a sufficiently large area using as little storage space as possible, a compact but informative data storage system is needed. For this purpose we propose a two-dimensional cartesian coordinate system with the ordinate axis pointing northwards. Each location inside the region covered by this system would be identifiable by two integral numbers x,y. The smallest identifiable location would then be one square meter. Since the hardware component system has an exactness no greater than 10 m, the proposed minimum distance of 1 m is sufficient. The region covered by a coordinate using two 16-bit integer number is a square with a side length of approx. 65 km. This area is sufficiently large enough to cover even the largest of cities in West-Germany.

A **road network** would be coded as follows :
- Each road intersection is stored as a vector (x,y) with x,y being the global coordinates of the intersection midpoint.

- Following this vector is a list of other vectors (or crossing points) to which that vector is directly connected in a straight line.

- In addition to just the coordinates of the connecting vectors, information should be stored pertaining to traffic rules and flow :

1 byte	: medium speed on connecting road
1 flag	: obstruction ? (y/n) on connecting road
1 byte	: obstruction id (points to element of a list)
1 flag	: one-way street ? (y/n)
1 flag	: 1 = one-way street in direction of travel

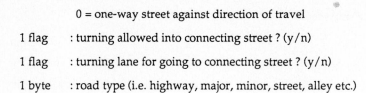

        0 = one-way street against direction of travel

1 flag   : turning allowed into connecting street ? (y/n)

1 flag   : turning lane for going to connecting street ? (y/n)

1 byte   : road type (i.e. highway, major, minor, street, alley etc.)

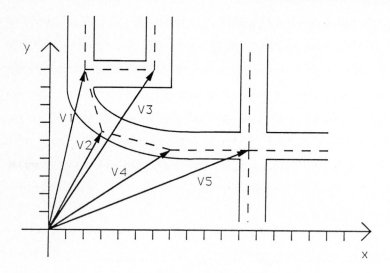

Fig. 2 An example of road network vectors

List of connecting vectors :
V1 : (V2,V3)
V2 : (V1,V4)
V3 : (V1)
V4 : (V2,V5)
V5 : (V4)

- Each **intersection** could also have the following information stored :

1 flag   : traffic light

1 flag   : yield + list of directions

1 flag   : stop + list of directions

- A **curving road** would be described by a number of points, so that straight lines connected between them would approximate the curve. The points would be placed at distances of a 30° angle turn following the curve of the road. These vectors would use a flag to identify them as no true intersections.

There may be more information storage to complete the knowledge of traffic rules and flow, but for the purposes of this communication routing strategy only **the road network topology with global coordinates, possible construction and accident sites, current location and traveling direction of the vehicle and planned route of travel** are necessary. All other parts of data are not examined in detail.

- A **planned route of travel** would simply consist of a stack of vectors with the top element being taken away when its intersection is traversed. The last vector contains the coordinates of a destination point.

The following shows a rough estimate of the amount of memory needed to map a large city such as Hamburg :
- number of road network knots per square km : ~ 100
- total amount of knots over an area of 753 km^2 (Hamburg) : 75300
- average number of bytes needed per knot : ~ 13
The resulting amount of memory needed is about 1 MB

c. Broadcast Routing Strategy

In the following examples a broadcast is necessary for stations to receive important information :

- A construction site has been recently set up on a road blocking one or both lanes of traffic.

- A recent accident has happened resulting in local traffic slowdown and
  congestion.

In the first example workers would set up a short range traffic beacon which
periodically sends out a message of the situation.

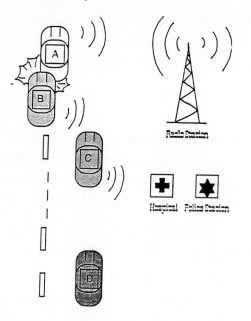

Fig. 3 Traffic accident and the necessary communications

In the second example passing cars (for example car C) or persons stopping by
and the accident victims (for example cars A and B) would either send out a
message from their car or would activate a nearby traffic beacon. These could be
built into the many emergency phones already in existence (e.g. along the
autobahns in West-Germany).

After the arrival of police or an ambulance, these people could also set up a
traffic beacon.

After a car receives the message the computer determines whether it is relevant or not. This is determined by the following criteria :

The message is relevant if the message has **not** already been previously received **and** :
- The site lies on the planned route of travel
- Or, if there is no planned route of travel then if the site lies within a certain range (e.g. 1 km inside a city, 5 km outside of city) and the current direction of travel.

The beacon lies within a certain range and an angle projected from the direction of travel. Optimal values for distance and angle can be found empirically or statistically (like in the project **LISB**, West-Berlin [Tomk.89]).

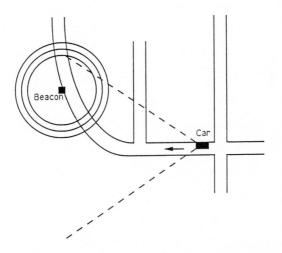

Fig. 4 Comunication between a car and a beacon

If the message is relevant the computer stores it and warns the driver of the new situation, in order to possibly calculate a new route, and also transmits the message.

If the message is not relevant then the message is destroyed and not transmitted.

3. Direction and Time Oriented Routing Strategy

Hard- and software components of this strategy are similar to those introduced in previous chapters. If there is no computer stored mapping, then a compass is necessary. Also, a real time clock is needed.

In one of the situations described in the previous chapter, a transmitted message needs not contain the coordinates of the site but instead the time of message initiation travelling direction of the vehicle which transmitted the message, and information pertaining to the positions of the cars & site along the road. The latter positions can be obtained by the placement of traffic beacons acting as **milestones** along the length of the road. These would emit messages containing a whole number X, with this being the X-th kilometer along the road. After passing at least two beacons a car computer would know if it were traveling in the direction of rising or falling X-values.

Routing Strategy

A car determines a message as relevant using this strategy in the following cases:

- If the vehicle is traveling **towards** the site and a certain time limit (e.g. 5 minutes) since the initiation of the message has not been reached yet.

In order to determine whether or not a vehicle is traveling towards the site the following parameters are needed :
- The kilometer number to which the site is closest
- Whether the vehicle is traveling in the direction of falling or rising kilometer numbers and the kilometer number of the vehicle.

Thus if the kilometer number of the site is lower than the one of the vehicle and the vehicle is going in the direction of falling kilometer number, then the vehicle is going towards the site, or if the kilometer number of the site is greater than that of the vehicle and the vehicle is going in the direction of rising kilometer number then it is also going towards the site.

4. Analysis

Both routing strategies do not need any routing tables to store the positions of nearby stations, and therefore the stations do not need to always send their changed position, so the stations could send more information in an information frame. Another advantage of this strategy is, that the stations do not need to reserve some of their data storing system to store the routing table, and therefore can store more important information. The network will be less loaded, because a receiving station would only spread a message if it is relevant enough for the area within its transmission range.

5. Summary

In this paper we presented two routing strategy ideas for land-based mobile PR-Nets. The first one uses global coordinates of the car-site (for example using the

236

EVA-System) and the second one uses the direction of the transmitting car and the receiving car, to determine whether the message is relevant enough to keep and spread again. These strategies do not need any routing tables to store the positions of the nearby stations, and therefore the stations do not need to always send their changed position. Another advantage of these strategies is, the stations do not need to reserve some of their data-storing system to store routing table. With the developed hardware, which is already in existence, one will be able to use these strategies in the near future.

6. References

BaEp-81   D. J. Baker, A. Ephremides: The architectural organiza-
           tion of a mobile radio network; IEEE Trans. on Comm.,
           Vol. COM-29, No. 11, 1981.

BrWa-89a   V. Brass, B. Walke : Aktualisierung stationslokaler
           Routing-Information in einem mobilen, dezentral organi-
           sierten multi-hop Paketfunk-Netz; Kommunikation in ver-
           teilten Systemen, Stuttgart, Informatik Fachberichte 205,
           S. 294 - 308, 1989.

ChFr-85   I. Chlamtac, W. R. Franta: A Multiaccess Protocol for
           Multihop Radio Networks; IEEE Trans. on Comm., Vol.
           COM-33, No. 10, 1985.

ChKu-85   I. Chlamtac, S. Kutten: On Broadcasting in Radio Networks
           - Problem Analysis and Protocol Design; IEEE Trans. on
           Comm., Vol. COM-33, No. 12, 1985.

DoFS-88   H. Dodel, W. Fogy, A. Stiller: Derzeititge und zukünftige
           weltweite Ortung und Navigation für alle Verkehrsarten;
           ntz Bd. 41, 1988, Heft 6, S. 320 - 342.

DuVo-89   R. Duckeck, R. Vollmer: TMC-Das Verkehrsfunksystem von
           morgen. Bosch Manuskript 1989.

EfFl-86   W. Effelsberg, A. Fleischmann: Das ISO-Referenzmodell für
           offene Systeme und seine sieben Schichten; Informatik
           Spektrum, Band 9, Nr. 5, 1986.

FuMz-83   A. Fuchs, M. Mackert, G. Ziegler: EVA - Netzabbildung und
           Routensuche für ein fahzeugautonomes Ortungs- und Naviga-
           tionssystem, Blaupunkt-Sonderdruck aus "Nachrichtentech-
           nische Zeitschrift", Bd. 36, Heft 4, S. 214-218, 1983.

Garc-86   J. J. Garcia-Luna-Aceves: Analysis of Routing-Table
          Update Activity in Multihop Packet-Radio Networks; Proc.
          of the ICCC'86, P. Kühn (ed.), Elsevier Science
          Publishers B. V. (North-Holland), 1986.

HoLi-85   T. C. Hou, V. O. K. Li: Routing Strategies of Multihop
          Packet Radio Networks with a more realistic Packet Recep-
          tion Probability; Proc. of the INFOCOM'85, pp. 303, 1985.

HoLi-86   T. C. Hou, V. O. K. Li: Transmission Range Control in
          Multihop Packet Radio Networks; IEEE Transactions on
          Communications, Vol. COM-34, No. 1, January 1986.

KlSi-87   L. Kleinrock, J. A. Silvester: Spatial Reuse in Multihop
          Packet Radio Networks; Proc. of the IEEE, Vol. 75, No. 1,
          1987.

Lee-82   W. C. Y. Lee: Mobile Communications Engineering; McGraw-
          Hill Book Company, ISBN 0-07-037039-7, 1982.

NePS-83   P. Neukirchner, O. Pilsak, D. Schlögl: EVA - Ortungs- und
          Navigationssystem für Landfahrzeuge; Blaupunkt Sonder-
          druck aus "Nachrichtentechnische Zeitschrift", Bd. 36,
          1983, Heft 4, S. 214 - 218.

NeZe-86   P. Neukirchner, W. Zechnall: EVA - ein autarkes Ortungs-
          und Navigationssystem für Landfahrzeuge; Bosch Technische
          Berichte 8, 1986, S. 7 - 14.

Pete-89   Peters: Elektronischer Lotse geht nun an Bord; FAZ,
          9.5.1989, Technik und Motor, S. T4.

PROM-87   : PROMETHEUS - General Introduction; 2nd PROMETHEUS -
          Symposium, Brussel, 30. Nov. - 1. Dez., 1987.

Span-87   O. Spaniol: Mobilfunknetze, Vorlesung im SS87, RWTH
          Aachen, Lehrstuhl für Informatik IV.

Span-89   O. Spaniol: Datenkommunikation I, Vorlesung im WS88/89,
          RWTH Aachen, Lehrstuhl für Informatik IV.

Tane-88   A. S. Tanenbaum: Computer Networks (2nd ed.); Prentice-
          Hall International Editions, ISBN 0-13-166836-6, 1988.

Tomk-89   R. von Tomkewitsch: LISB (Leit- und Informationssystem
          Berlin); Münchner Kreis, 17. - 18.4.1989, München.

VPRH-87   C. Voy, F. Panik, D. Reister, L. Ham: PROMETHEUS, ein
          europäisches Forschungsprojekt zur Gestaltung des
          Straßenverkehrs der Zukunft; Automobil-Industrie, Heft 2,1987.

Information Network and Data Communication, III
D. Khakhar and F. Eliassen (Editors)
Elsevier Science Publishers B.V. (North-Holland)
© IFIP, 1990

239

MOBITEX - A SYSTEM FOR MOBILE DATA COMMUNICATION

Michael Larsen
Swedish Telecom Radio,
SWEDEN

The MOBITEX system developed in Sweden, Scandinavia, is designed for the new generation of public mobile networks for data communications.

The announcement about MOBITEX was made in December year 1988 by Cantel, the Canadian national cellular telephone service provider, and by Ram Broadcast in USA, last summer. The intention to build a national public mobile data network was significant for two reasons.
For one thing, this was a strong indicator that mobile data is set to become another major growth area in telecommunications, following on the heels of cellular mobile telephony.

The second notable aspect of Cantel's and RAM Broadcast's announcement was that it chose as the basis of its planned mobile data network a new system standard, MOBITEX.

MOBITEX is a new mobile data communication system standard designed for use in nationwide public networks. It is designed for dispatch type data traffic, enabling fleets of vehicles to send and receive data, text and voice messages to and from a control center or each other. MOBITEX is attracting strong interest from communications network operators in many countries.

New Mobile Data Demands

The technology of present generation mobil telephony is designed for voice traffic where communication is always one-to-one, and call holding times are relatively long.

It is possible to use the mobile telephone network for data traffic, with personal computers and even fax machines sending and receiving text and data. But there is an important and growing need for data communications for which a cellular mobile telephone network is not well suited - dispatch type traffic typical of taxi firms, transport companies and emergency services.

Until now, this type of organization has generally used private mobile
radio (PMR) to link all the mobiles to the central controller. Typical
messages in this kind of situation are very short. There is often a
need to make broadcast messages that are aimed at every mobile in a
group or on a network.

A cellular mobile telephone network is not an efficient way of sending
very short messages, since the call set-up times for each message are
quite long. And there is no way of sending broadcast messages over a
cellular mobile telephone network.

With the growing use of computer systems, many of these
organizationsare actively looking at ways of integrating their in-house
information systems with fleet control. When this happens, the messages
transmitted over the network will be data and text, rather than voice,
meaning the duration of the messages will become even shorter.

What is needed to hendle this new type of mobile communication traffic
is a network concept that permits the same freedom of movement as a
cellular mobile telephone network, but which is optimized for data and
text traffic rather than voice.

Open System Standard

Swedish Telecom have chosen to use an open standard for the radio
interface in the MOBITEX system.

Until now, all mobile data communications systems available on the
market have been based on proprietary radio protocols which give users
no freedom of choice since they can buy terminals only from the network
operator.

With an open system standard, other manufacturers will be able to make
terminals for a MOBITEX network using the published technical
specification. This will give users considerable freedom of choice;
opening up the terminal market to any manufacturer will introduce
competition and consequently benefit users through lower prices.

An other part is that the use of open standards could quickly establish
the MOBITEX system as a standard in many countries.

A MOBITEX network has a cellular structure, rather like a mobile
telephone network. There are radio base stations that provide access
into the network for the mobile units. These are connected through a
hierarchy of digital exchanges.
The radio base stations provide regional or national coverage, and like
a mobile telephone network they allow users to travel throughout the
area served by the network, sending and receiving messages.

Functionally, however, there is a fundamental difference, in that the
MOBITEX system uses a data packet transmission system. For the very
short duration messages typical of data networks, this permits
efficient use of the network and of the radio spectrum.

MOBITEX Network

The use of packet data transmission through the network provides
another important network feature that is not possible with a mobile
telephone network: a message electronic mailbox.

The message electronic mailbox ensures that the message always gets
through to its destination. If a mobile unit is out of radio contact
for some reason, for example because it is passing through a road
tunnel, then any messages destined for it can be stored within the
network for re-transmission later.

Another function that the mobile data network will provide is a
broadcast or group call message to all mobile units, or predetermined
groups of mobiles.

There is a voice communication option on a mobile data service, but it
is expected that in many countries the speech option will not be
offered at all, or will be set at a very high tariff, to be used for
priority and emergency calls only.

Complementary Networks

The architecture of a MOBITEX network is similar to that of a cellular
network. But from the network operator's viewpoint, there are some
major differences. Cellular mobile telephony is optimized for mainly
voice communications; MOBITEX is optimized primarily for data.

MOBITEX can handle broadcast traffic to all or groups of mobiles; a
cellular mobiletelephone cannot.

One of the most important differences between MOBITEX and cellular
mobile telephony is the far more efficient use MOBITEX makes of
available radio spectrum due to the packet switching and transmission
technique. Where a mobile telephone system can typically handle 20 to
25 subscribers per channel, the MOBITEX data system can handle up to
1,000 per channel.

MOBITEX is not seen as a competitor for cellular mobile telephony.
Rather it is complementary. It is likely that the two types of networks
will remain as separate networks, since it is not possible to optimize
one and the same mobile network for both voice and data traffic.

Terminals

The MOBITEX terminals that are fitted in the vehicles or remote
locations will range in complexity from a simple keypad with a few keys
that are used to send pre-arranged codes to a full alphanumeric keypad
and display that permits full text communication, or even a laptop
personal computer.

Additional equipment such as an integral hardcopy printer, visual display, taxi meters or various sensors such as distance meters for automatic data transmission, can be connected.

Vehicles can be equipped with an emergency message button that uses the public data network. This will initiate a plain language text message that automatically over-rides any other data transmission or reception in progress. The message received by the dispatch terminal consists of a standard text relating to an emergency call, plus specific information (for example on the position of the mobile terminal).

The fixed terminal can be a simple data terminal that is used only for data communications to the mobile units, or it can be a multi-purpose terminal also used as part of a company's general computing and communications systems.

Typical MOBITEX Users

Typical users of the new mobile data services are expected to be private and public sector organizations such as police, warehousing and transport companies, utilities, taxi and mini-cab firms and sales organizations.

These will in the main be organizations that are at present users of private mobile radio for traffic dispatch purposes. In addition, some organizations for whom PMR has not been a satisfactory solution will take advantage of mobile data networks; service and maintenance organizations with teams of field staff are good example.

The first MOBITEX public mobile data network to enter commercial service is in Sweden, operated by Televerket, the Swedish PTT. Towards the end of 1988, the MOBITEX mobile data network covered Sweden's major cities and roads.

Experience in Sweden has shown the productivity gains that can be achieved by automating the direction of taxis to customers, using computers linked by radio to data terminals in the taxis. A central computer can automatically select the nearest available taxi to the customer and transmit instructions via the mobile data network to the cab concerned. The driver simply presses an acknowledgment button. An integral priner gives the driver a hard copy confirmation of the next pickup point.

Such applications minimize empty runs by 20-30 percent. The system also helps to coordinate traffic where journeys are paidfor by the state, such as hospital traffic.

MOBITEX has also helped to bring costs down; by requiring fewer people in the office to give orders. Manual dispatching requires one minute per customer, since the operator must write down the order, the number of people, the address and the phone number. Data dispatching requires only seven seconds per order, allowing eight to ten times more customers to be handled per minute.

Several Swedish cab companies have already implemented the use of
MOBITEX, and more are on the verge of doing so. A cab company of 93
vehicles in Örebro began using the service in march, 1988. A cab
company in Västerås comprising of 103 cabs, just began their use in
January, 1989. A cab company in Halmstad has signed contracts to begin
use in 1990.

With MOBITEX, mobile police are able to access directly various
computer databases, such as vehicle registration numbers. The group
call facility enables broadcast messages to be transmitted to all or
groups of vehicles from the control center, and permits broadcast
messages to be sent, for example, to police force vehicles only, or to
police and fire brigades, thus serving a coordinating function in the
case of emergencies and serious accidents.

A special MOBITEX service that is currently being developed for
ambulance use is a means of transmitting patient information from the
ambulance to a doctor. This information includes vital information such
as average hearbeat over the latest 30 seconds. With this information,
the doctor on the receiving end of the information is able to assist
the paramedics with treatment of the patient in the ambulance.

Several distribution companies have shown an interest in a MOBITEX
application with which drivers can register deliveries in situ, receive
warehouse information and achieve more rapid invoicing. Mölndals Lbc,
just outside Gothenburg, has started with MOBITEX. They have found that
they will achieve a quicker invoicing. The pay-off-time will be less
than one year. And postal authorities are looking for an application in
which a vehicle can be given as efficient directions as possible in
order to enable an increase in volume capacity.

With the use of MOBITEX, transport company drivers are able to inform
the controllers of their location and status and receive directions.
Local wholesaleor retail delivery vehicles can notify the warehouse of
what has been sold, so that replacements are ready and waiting when the
van returns to the base.

On-site mechanical handling vehicles such as fork lift trucks can be
directed in automated warehousing systems, and drivers can have direct
access to the main computer from their trucks with MOBITEX.

It is not just the service industries that make use of mobile data. In
August, 1988, and 1989 at a PLM golf tournament, MOBITEX was used at
each of the 18 holes. When a pay was made, the MOBITEX operator was
able to transmit the golfer number and his number of strokes via
MOBITEX to tournament headquarters. This provided a constantly accurate
compilation of tournament information and statistics at all times.
IBM transmitted the results from the world championships in
orienteering last summer. It became quite a success for the public who
followed the games.

THE STRUCTURE OF THE GSM SYSTEM

The GSM system can be regarded as a system that is still in the development stage. Within the project, considerable testing activity is in progress concerning the system's basic functions.
These tests will certainly give rise to modifications, but there is no reason to suppose that they will have a radical effect on the general direction of the GSM concept.

The most important difference between NMT (Nordic Mobile Telephone) and the GSM system is that the latter system is based on digital technology and the philosophy of the ISDN network, while the analog NMT system is basically a telephone service plain and simple.

Network Structure

The structure of the GSM network (see Fig 1) resembles somewhat that of existing analog cellular systems, which is not surprising since the most important functions are the same in both cases. The MSC represents the frontier between the fixed public network and the mobile network.

In GSM, there are a number of additional functions. The most prominent of these is the possibility of international roaming.
This requires that the position of the mobile unit within the network be registrered and communicated between the HLR (Home Location Register) and the VLR (Visited Location Register) nodes in the GSM system. In this way, it is possible to call a mobile unit anywhere in Europe where there is radio coverage.

User Interface

The fact that the channel structure of ISDN is reflected in GSM means that the ISDN network's jack and plug function can also be carried over. A large number of terminal types have been defined for GSM of which some (i.e. those of Type MT 1) offer the same user configuration as for the ISDN network. However, it should be noted that the similarity is not total. The GSM configuration S offers a configuration **functionally** identical with the ISDN network. In other words, terminals designed for the fixed ISDN network can be connected to a GSM MT 1 terminal, but the transfer of information in GSM will be slower. For ordinary speech communication, this has no importance. But for data communication, there will be a difference apparant to the user.

With regard to the man-machine interface, this is essentially the same as for fixed telecommunication. However, two differences should be observed:

- The mobile telephone system has its own area code, which means that ths area code must always be transmitted from the mobile unit.

- Within the mobile telephone system, so-called preseizure dialling is used. This means that the destination number must be dialled in its entirety before the telephone receiver is lifted or a "send" function is activated.

Services

In this section, a number of GSM characteristics are presented which are of interest when comparing GSM with its analog predecessor.

Speech quality:

GSM uses digital speech signals. The speech quality is more independent of propagation conditions. The user will experience a stable and relatively high speech quality.

GSM's speech coding has a build-in delay of about 90 millisecond. Normally, when the connection does not introduce any further delays, this is not apparent to the user. However, if the connection includes a satellite link, for example, then the total delay is increased and the speech quality will degrade.

DTMF, voice band data:

The speech coding used in GSM differs fundamentally from traditional wave form coding, such as PCM and delta modulation. It is heavily optimised for transmission of human speech, and the ability to transmit simple tone signals is limited. The GSM system's speech coder can handle DTMF when conditions are good, but this function is not completely reliable. Instead, a special arrangement is required for transmitting DTMF tone signals and voice band data.

The GSM system supports DTMF signalling from a mobile unit to the base station. This is achieved using builtin functions for detecting dialling key signals. The equivalent DTMF signal is transmitted as a data signal and then converted to ordinary DTMF before it is transmitted further in the fixed network.

In other direction, from base stationto mobile unit, the network must detect the fact that a DTMF is being sent at a given moment in time, this in order that the exchange can convert the signal to a data signal that can be transmitted through the mobile D channel. No such function has been specified, and for this reason, DTMF signals cannot be directed to mobile units, at least for the time being.

Transparent data:

The speed of the GSM system's B channels is, as mentioned above, lower than in the ISDN network. The highest speed that is available for users is 9.6 kbit/s. Higher speeds can only be achieved by connecting more channels and multiplexing in the subscriber's equipment. Such a solution has been discussed, especially in connection with mobile PABX units. However, no such specification exists, and it is unlikely that equipment with this function will be developed within the first years of operation.

Security Functions:

The GSM system offers a number of security functions which deserve a special mention. The GSM system has been provided with these functions because a radiobased telephone system does not provide the physical protection that can be found in fixed, cable-based systems. Because of the rapidly increasing availability of mobile terminals and other similar equipment which is capable of giving illegal access to the network, it has beed deemed important to provide GSM with powerful security mechanisms.

Authentication is a function that provides a secure identification or the subscriber. This function prevents illegal use of another subscriber's number, and thus guarantees that the correct subscriber is charged.

Encryption of information. All user information (speech and data) is transmitted in encrypted form over the GSM network. This encryption system is extremely resistant.

Supplementary Services:

There are a number of supplementary services available within the GSM system. In most cases, these are identical in content and handling with those available within the fixed telephone network. Over and above these, there are a number of functions that have been specified which are directly concerned with mobility.

Costs

In the long rum, mobile units for the GSM system are expected to be cheaper than analog stations. This is partly because digital technology is more suitable for intergration circuit, and partly because production volumes will be large and many manufacturers will be involved.

As regards network costs, the structure of the GSM system is much more complicated than that of an analog system. In addition, the GSM system requires more advanced O & M and administrative support systems. This would seem to indicate a higher user cost with GSM than with NMT. To some extent, this is balanced by the increased base station capacity in the GSM system.

Facts about GSM

Frequency band	890–915 MHz, 935–960 MHz
Multiple access	Narrow band TDMA
Bit rate/carrier	270 kbit/s
Channels/carrier	8 (later 16)
No. of carriers	altogether 124 duplex carrier waves in the band
Frame length	4.6 ms
Bit rate/channel	22.8 kbit/s (gross bit rate)
Modulation	GMSK
Speech coder	RPE–LPC with voice
Activity	activity detector
Speed, speech coder	13.8 kbit/s (later approx. 6.9 kbit/s)

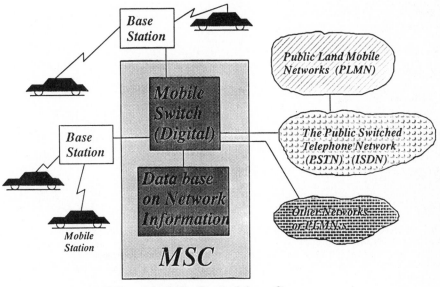

MSC = Mobile Switching Centre

Figure 1. The Structure of GSM Network.

Information Network and Data Communication, III
D. Khakhar and F. Eliassen (Editors)
Elsevier Science Publishers B.V. (North-Holland)
IFIP, 1990

Directory Services for Mobile Communication

Kai Jakobs, Frank Reichert
Technical University of Aachen
Informatik IV (Dept. of Computer Science)
Ahornstr. 55, D-51 Aachen, West Germany
Tel.: +49-241-80-4521; Fax: +49-241-80-6295
Telex: 08327804 thac d; e-mail: ..unido!rwthinf!jakobs

Abstract

This paper discusses prospective benefits of the directory service for users of mobile communication systems. A classification of mobile users is given, their specific requirements are identified. These requirements are matched against the directory's functionality, major technical problems are pointed out. Finally, we propose some necessary enhancements and modifications. The directory service as such is shortly reviewed with particular emphasis on authentication services.

1. Some Introductory Remarks and Overview

The paper is intended to show that a much broader community of users may benefit from directory services as it had been assumed. Originally intended to act mainly as a service provider for the Message Handling System (MHS), the directory now also appears useful eg. for the community of mobile radio users.

First of all we will describe the envisaged environemnt. We will also introduce a rough classification of mobile users. These different classes of users call for different types of services.

Subsequently we will review the mobile user's requirements for an information service like the directory. Needs typical for the respective user class are pointed out.

Thus, the second main part of the paper discusses problems related to use of the directory in a mobile environment. These problems include association of directory user agents with directory system agents, problems of distributed authentication as well as required additional contents of the directory information tree. It should be noted that the directory may eg. serve for authentication purposes in a very general way, so that every user (including of course mobile users as well) wishing to use any service requiring for authentication will have to use the directory.

250

In a "normal" non-mobile environment a directory user agent will usually be associated with one particular DSA. This is obviously impossible with mobile communication. In addition to the general problem of distributed operations one of the most important aspects in this context will be authentication of a user to a DSA other than his home DSA.

Another aspect particularly interesting for a mobile user will be the contents of the DIT. Currently, this contents is mostly limited to information more or less directly related to communication tasks. However, this will have to be enhanced towards more general information as well as very particular information typically required by mobile users. We will identify areas of information that will have to be included and discuss impacts of this inclusion on the DIT. These impacts include for example additional object classes and attribute types, respectively.

Finally, we will also discuss technical problems, i.e. requirements currently not being covered by the directory. This includes eg. naming and replication of data.

For those who are not familiar with the directory standard the annex will shortly review the directory's basic functionality. In particular, we will discuss authentication basics being of special relevance for mobile communication.

2. Mobile Users and the Directory
Within this section we will discuss some relevant properties of the mobile environment, introduce a rough classification of mobile users and analyze requirements typical for the respective classes of users.

2.1. The Mobile Environment

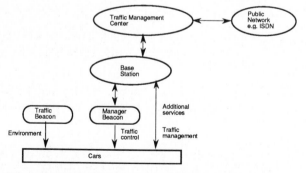

Fig. 1: Hierarchical Network Topology for
Mobile Communication (according to [Kre 89])

Some characteristics of the mobile environment will have consequences for this very particular type of directory user. This is for example due to limitations in bandwidth: Since the communication channel will also be used for voice and continuous traffic, it will not always be available for data transmission. Therefore, time may increase drastically to obtain the required information.

Have a look at the mobile communication environment depicted in Fig. 1. A mobile user accesses the appropriate *Base Station* (BS), which in turn connects him to the *Traffic Management Center* (TMC) responsible. It appears meaningful to integrate DSAs at TMC level; since it is very likely that TMCs will mostly be located close to conurbations, this placement would be useful for non-mobile communication as well. However, to avoid unnecessary long distances between user and DSA, it may be useful to store at least those copies of data which are of only regional relevance in base stations as well.

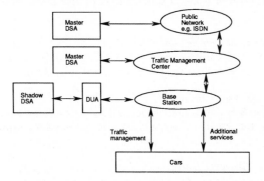

Fig. 2: Location of DUAs and DSAs in the mobile communication system

Another question concerns location of the directory user agent, DUA. You may think of three possible options:

- DUA functionality is provided by the user.
  This presupposes that the user for instance owns his private computing power. Although this may be true for most business travellers, it may not be assumed for the driver.

- DUA integrated in a TMC.
  This approach shows similar benefits than does integration in base stations. However, since the number of TMCs will be relatively small, this may easily become a bottleneck.

- DUA is integrated in a base station.
  This alternative should be preferred since it guarantees access for both classes of users independent of their respective equipment. Additionally, it may be possible for the owner of a private DUA to access the directory directly (i.e. via a TMC).

Fig. 2 shows possible location of the directory's elements in relation to those types of network nodes typical for the mobile network.

Another aspect important for the mobile user will be replication of information. Since the current standard does not provide f r this functionality, this topic will be discussed in sect. 4.

2.2. Classes of Mobile Users

As far as requirements and necessities are concerned, you cannot speak of the mobile user as such. There is a broad variety of different demands depending on the particular mobile environment. Therefore, some classification is essential.

Before discussing his requirements it is necessary to specify what the term "mobile user" means for us although this might be intuitively clear. We will distinguish two classes of users with each class imposing different demands:

- The "Driver"
  As the name indicates, driver refers to the "pure" road traffic environment. Typically, a user of this class will be someone on a trip requiring information closely related to travelling aspects.

- The "Business Traveller"
  With this name we indicate a user currently on a business trip. Typical elements of this user's environment are the car, the laptop and some kind of network access unit; keyword: the mobile office.

Of course, these two classes of users may not be said to be completely disjunctive. Nevertheless, this classification exhibits the basic differences between them.

2.3. Mobile User's Requirements

Requirements on the directory imposed by mobile users are twofold as well. They may be subdivided into:

- General requirements
  They are common to "normal" users and to mobile users rather than specific for mobile users. Due to the similarity of the business traveller's demands with common office requirements, we will associate these requirements with the business traveller.

- Special requirements
  These demands are typical for mobile users. They may as a first approach be associated with the driver's demands, that is, these requirements focus on classes of information typically needed in a traffic environment.

Thus, the two classifications introduced may be reduced to one. Demands of the business traveller category are well understood. They may for instance include access to message handling services and, of course, access to an information service like the directory, since information available for him locally are naturally limited. Note that access to the directory will also be required for message handling applications. These demands will include:

- Independence from internal network details.
  Nobody is willing first to learn details on eg. gateways or network topology in order to be able to address his partner correctly.

- User-friendly naming
  That is naming based on normal knowledge one usually possesses, lets say from a business card, rather than names like today´s "maier%-vax1.UUCP%germany.CSNET@ csnet-relay.ARPA" which is much more a nice memory training exercise than it is an easy-to-remember name.

- General assistance
  This includes assistance for example in case a user name is not known correctly. On the other hand, this includes a service similar to the *Yellow Pages*. After introduction of yellow pages in the telephone network utilization of the network rose drastically. This very mere fact indicates importance of a service like this.

- Additional information services
  Such services may for instance include information on a recipient's user agent's telecommunication capabilities.

Of course this list does not claim for completeness, but it gives an impression about the kind of services usually to be required from the directory. Note that these requirements are not necessarily typical for a mobile user, but they are of major concern for him as well.

In addition to these demands the driver shows to have some more extensive, dedicated claims. His interests are to a large extent different from those identified for the business traveller. This becomes easily understandable when comparing the different environments of the two classes.

As stated above, the drivers major needs for information concern aspects related to the traffic situation. These requirements turn out to be twofold:

- (usually short lived) information from his surrounding area, eg. on traffic jams.

- long lasting information, take route planning or sights as examples.

Whilst the first will usually be provided elsewhere, the latter is a typical application of the directory. Thus, it is this additional information that constitutes the driver's demands on the directory.

There is one crucial common point::the need for secure communication. This includes data integrity, data confidentiality and authentication services. In addition, services like eg. billing and accounting are based on authentication as well. This is of special importance since the mobile user will have access to wide area networks like ISDN. This implies strong authentication, possibly in conjunction with well-defined access control capabilities.

3. Meeting the Demands

To be in line with the lists of requirements given above, we will first discuss if and/or how the business traveller's demands are met by the current (1988) directory standard.

3.1. The Business Traveller

When designing the directory it has always been one of the main intentions to relief the user from network internal details (which may be especially valuable for packet radio networks). This is achieved by assigning a name to every user (i.e. object). In contrast to network addresses which may change quite often and unpredictably these names are intended to be long lived (cf. Annex A.2).

It has been mentioned above that a name is assigned to every user. The directory standard calls those names user-friendly. Although this is not quite true yet, compared to network addresses which may be up to 40(!) digits long present directory names really are a considerable improvement.

As we know from the telephone network, things like phone books, yellow pages and telephone inquiries are essential. Thus, it is obvious that equivalences are required in data networks as well. The directory's general mapping functions provide these services (actually, that is exactly what the inquiry does: mapping a given name onto a network address - the phone number). By providing *List* and *Search* operations as well as *Filter* mechanisms the directory allows its users to retrieve specific information - the yellow pages service.

Data stored in entries associated with the network's users comprises a great variety of information, ranging for instance from details on postal delivery and telecommunication capabilities up to information on his business or research interests. In fact, almost all information a user wants to store in his entry may be found.

3.2. The Driver

As outlined above, the driver needs specific types of information currently not provided by the directory. Thus, it will be helpful to introduce new object classes and additional attribute types.

Information of the directory is kept in entries, each entry being associated with exactly one real-world object. Within the entry, information is stored as attributes (cf.Annex A.1.). Entries holding the same attribute types, i.e. the same type of information, form an object class. Currently, object classes as well as attribute types specified by the standard are more or less closely related to communication aspects. More "customary" information, as it is needed by the driver, is currently not intended to be provided by the directory.

However, provision of such information would be a minor problem. Every administrative authority is allowed to define new, appropriate attribute types. Additionally, the current standard permits creation of so-called *Unregistered Object Classes* (UOC). Those object classes are supposed to be locally administered and to be of local significance only (local in this context again means one management domain). A UOC may comprise any information, in particular it may comprise newly defined attribute types. Current standardization bodies' recommendations even go one step further suggesting entries which may belong to more than one object class. As far as provision of additional information is concerned, both approaches, the UOC as well as *Multiple Object Classes*, show the same benefits. Nonetheless, the latter appears to be preferable since provision only of registered object classes does not alter the outwardly appearance of the directory [ISO 89]. To be more precise, UOCs, which may be added to the DIT at any level (not only at leaf level), would alter the DIT structure and the thus valid name form accordingly.

3.3. Authentication
The directory standard includes an *Authentication Framework*, describing concepts for provision of secure communication. The framework distinguished between simple and strong authentication, respectively. Let us consider simple authentication first.

As already pointed out in the standard [ISO 88], "..simple authentication is primarily intended for local use only, i.e. for peer entity authentication between one DUA and one DSA.." It is also stated that the password is valid only within the user's home domain. No procedures are specified how to authenticate at another DSA using this password. It follows immediately that simple authentication may not be applied in a mobile environment, where the user will frequently be attached to DSAs others than his home-DSA.

Employing strong authentication, the mobile user has to face the problem how to authenticate himself to a non-home DSA. This "distributed authentication" may work as follows:

- User A connects to the non-home DSA X, enciphering the message with his secret key.

- Given that X belongs to a different domain than the user's home-DSA Y, X tries to obtain A's public key from Y. In doing so, X traverses a certification path to reach the common point of trust, cf.Annex A.2.

- The result is returned to X from the point of common trust and may be conveyed to A.

Of course, the same mechanism may be applied for bilateral authentication of two communication partners A and B.

4. Technical Problems
Within this chapter we will discuss technical problems rising from use of the directory in mobile communication, i.e. demands not met by the current standard. Anyway, most of these deficiencies are subject to standardization work.

4.1. Naming

The first thing to be considered concerns the naming problem. Since to a certain extent the name is the user's interface to the network, this calls for a degree of user-friendliness as high as possible. It has, however, been realized by now that considerable additional efforts will have made to enhance the directory's naming capabilities (cf. eg. [Jak 89b], [Neu 89]).

A Name (taking the author as a guinea pig) might look like this

Attempt A:
```
{C=DE, O=Techn. Univ. of Aachen, OU=Computer Science, OP=Kai Jakobs}
```

This is, of course, a nice, easy-to-remember name - for English speaking people. The German attempt may look quite different:

Attempt B:
```
{C=DE, O=RWTH Aachen, OU=Lehrstuhl Informatik IV, OP=Kai Jakobs}
```

However, another German might also try this:

Attempt C:
```
{C=DE, O=RWTH Aachen, OU=Math.-Nat. Fak., OU=Fachgruppe Informatik,
OU=Lehrstuhl Informatik IV, OP=Kai Jakobs}
```

You see the problems:

- Different mother tongues of users may lead to different attempts in naming objects (attempt A).

- The DIT is not exactly tree shaped (cf. Fig. A6). Thus, it is possible that some name parts may occur more than once in a DN. Trouble is preprogrammed (attempts B+C).

In terms of the directory, the first means that different attribute values are guessed by a user rather than a different name form. The directory provides an Alias mechanism intended to meet precisely this problem (cf. Annex A.1). However, making extensive use of aliasing may easily inflate the DIT with additional alias entries thus decreasing speed of search and increasing management and update problems, respectively. A differnt solution to this problem would be permitting *Multiple Distinguished Values*. Currently, just one distinguished value is permitted (cf. Fig. A3).

The latter problem is much harder to settle. Possible solutions have been discussed and it is very likely that the relevant parts of the standard will undergo considerable changes in the near future. In particular, the DS will provide the user with schema information. That is, the user may learn the DIT structure of the requested entry's home domain (as a result he may for instance be appropriately prompted by the system). However, management and distribution of schema information is one of the hottest topics of today's discussion in the standardization bodies.

Although the dilemma described above is not specific to mobile environment but is a general problem of the directory, its consequences are particular unpleasant for mobile users who will very often need the information faster than a common user does.

4.2. Replication of Information

It has been mentioned above (cf. sect. 2.1.) that directory system agents (DSAs) should be integrated in traffic management centers (TMCs). Referring to the network topology introduced in [Kre 89], there will be about one hundred TMCs (however, this number depends on the bit rate available between the TMCs and on the range of services to be provided). This number of DSAs should be sufficient to guarantee short response times. Nonetheless it would be helpful especially for the mobile user to replicate some part of the information. This will be of special value for the "driver-data" which will usually be of rather local relevance. Thus, this replicated data should be stored at base station (BS) level (cf. fig. 2, this does of course not mean that every BS will necessarily have to act as a DSA). Replication of selected data at BS level offers the mobile user a number of attractive features:

- Very short response times
  Since there will usually not be very many queries at a time and since the amount of data to be stored will be relatively small requested information will be very soon available.

- Less bandwidth required
  A high percentage of queries (especially those initiated by "drivers") may be satisfied locally.

- Better access to the whole system
  This is due to better accessability of a DSA.

- Lower transmission costs
  Since a considerable amount of data will be stored locally (i.e. in the same cell the user is located) the number of distributed DS operations may be reduced significantly.

Taking all these advantages into consideration inclusion of computing power into a number of base stations to provide for DSA capabilities seems very desirable. This holds even despite the fact that BSs were originally supposed to be as simple as possible.

With the current directory standard replication of information is allowed but not supported; replication is said to relay on bilateral agreements. In particular, the list of topics to be discussed includes:

- Definition of the replication model
- Specification of additional services and protocol elements
- Consistency requirements
- Management and administration problems

258

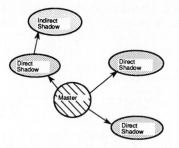

Fig. 3: Model of data replication

A standard document on information replication is supposed to be approved by 1992.

5. Conclusions and Some Final Remarks

The directory is intended to serve all users of all data communication systems. Of course, that means it will also have to serve mobile users. This is of particular significance since on one hand side the "mobile office" will play an important role in the near future and on the other hand communication requirements in the road traffic environment are on the rise as well.

We have addressed requirements imposed on the directory by mobile users. A rough classification of two different types of users has been introduced together with each type's specific requirements on the directory. Although in general directory services provide for considerable support of mobile users as well, we have to face restraints pertinent to mobile communication. These problems are mainly due to time constraints which may conflict with possibly time consuming distributed operations. The effect of extensive time consumption may also be observed in conjunction with data replication. Replication of data will considerably reduce communication time as well as communication costs. Additionally, naming problems, rising from the not exactly tree-shaped directory information tree may have greater influence on mobile users than they already have on normal users, anyway.

Standardization of the directory is still continuing. The naming problem has been realized by standardization bodies; we are optimistic that solutions will be found. The same holds for replication.

The driver's demands on the directory are generally much easier to meet. His problem mainly focusses on additional types of information currently not provided by the directory. Thus, his requirements can easily be fulfilled by simply introducing new object classes and new attribute types, respectively. Both is partly supported today and may be expected to be provided by future versions of the standard.

For the "Driver" user class we also have to face some problems originating from aspects of data protection. This is of particular relevance for the

envisaged road traffic environment, take the possibility to keep a watch on
every driver's travels as an example.

To sum everything up, you can say that the directory's services will make all
mobile user's communication life a little more comfortable.

6. References

[Bau 89]: Bauer, R., Pfundstein, M.:
Realization of a Distributed Data Base in the European Mobile Radio
Telephone System
Proc. Communication in distributed systems, Stuttgart, Springer
Verlag 1989

[Her 89]: Herda, S., Kowalski, B.:
Sicherheitsverfahren in Verteilten Systemen
Tutorial Communication in distributed systems, Stuttgart, 1989

[Hui 88]: Huitema, C.:
The X.500 Directory Service
Computer Networks and ISDN Systems, Vol. 16, pp. 161-6, 1988

[ISO 88]: International Standards Organization
ISO IS 9594, Information Processing Systems - Open Systems
Interconnection - The Directory Part 1 - 8, 1988

[ISO 89]: International Standards Organization
ISO SC21 N3569, On issues of the working document on the
directory schema, Oslo 1989

[Jak 89a]: Jakobs, K.:
ISO's Directory Proposal - Evolution, Current Status and Future
Problems
Canadian Journal of Information Sciences, vol. 14, No. 1, 1989

[Jak 89b]: Jakobs, K.:
ISO's Directory Proposal - Does It Require Enhancement?
to be published in Proc. 9th Int. Conf. on Remote Data Processing
DPD '89, Karlovy Vary 1989

[Kre 89]: Kremer, W. et al.:
Entwurf einer Netzwerktopologie für ein Mobilfunknetz zur
Unterstützung des öffentlichen Straßenverkehrs (in German)
Proc. Communication in distributed systems, Stuttgart, Springer
Verlag 1989

[Mit 89]: Mitchell, C. et al.:
CCITT/ISO Standards for Secure Message Handling IEEE Journal on
Selected Areas in Communications, Vol.7, No.4, May 1989

[Neu 89]: Neufeld, G.W.:
Descriptive Names in X.500
Proc. SIGCOMM '89, ACM Press 1989

Annex: The Directory Service - A (Very) Short Survey

This section is intended to provide a very condensed overview of the subject. It is only supposed to introduce the topic to the reader. Those who have a deeper interest in the directory's functionality should eg. read [Hui 88] or [Jak 89a] or should refer to the original standard [ISO 88].

A.1 Overall Functionality

The directory service provides a uniform naming scheme for and information about a network's resources (including e.g. hosts, processes, devices and human users). In terms of the DS, these resources usually are referred to as *Objects*. A non-ambiguous name is assigned to every object. In general, a DS has to provide three types of service:

- mapping name --> information
  For example, an object's name may be mapped on its network address.

- mapping name --> set of names
  A set of objects is identified by one single name.

- mapping information --> set of names
  This service establishes a "Yellow Pages" function.

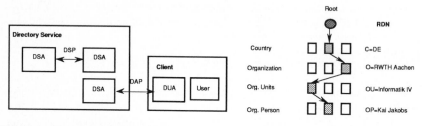

Fig.A1: The Directory Model
DAP = Directory Access Protocol
DSP = Directory System Protocol

Fig.A2: Example of a Distinguished Name

Usually, the DS is described as a - highly distributed - Client-Server System. This may be characterized by a typically small number of hosts (the servers, the *Directoty System Agents* (DSA)) providing callable services to the other hosts of the system (the clients, the *Directory User Agents* (DUA)).

```
Name::=
    CHOICE {      -- only possible solution for now --
        RDN Sequence}
RDNSequence::= SEQUENCE OF RelativeDistinguishedName
DistinguishedName::= RDNSequence
RelativeDistinguishedName::= SET OF AttributeValueAssertion
AttributeValueAssertion::= SEQUENCE {Attribute Type, Attribute Value}
```

Fig.A3: ASN.1 definition of "Name"

Every object is represented by an *Entry*, all the totality of entries forms the *Directory Information Base* (DIB). An object's name and the information stored in an entry are composed of *Attributes*. An attribute is a tuple <AttributeType, AttributeValue>.

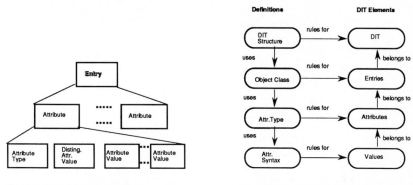

Fig.A4: Basic Model of an Entry   **Fig.A5**: The Directory Schema

A name is assigned to every object. This name is called *Relative Distinguished Name* (RDN). Every RDN is non-ambiguous relative to its immediate superior. The sequence of RDNs of an object plus those of its superiors forms the *Distinguished Name* (DN) of this object. The DN is globally unambiguous. The directory also provides for one kind of alternative names, called *Aliases*.

Relation between objects in a network is usually hierarchical. Thus, the DIB will be structured in a tree-shaped way. This tree is called *Directory Informatio Tree* (DIT). Information about objects is stored in the DIT. Every DSA holds data about a subset of objects and has Knowledge about objects known by other DSAs (to provide for distributed operations).

The directory's *Schema* specifies the structure of the DIT, defines *Object Classes* (eg. Country, Organization), attribute types (eg. country name or telephone number) and attribute syntaxes (eg. printable string or numeric string) permitted. The schema is composed from a number of subschema each valid within one particular management domain.

The attribute type indicates the class of information given by that attribute. An object class definition specifies a set of mandatory and optional attributes for an entry of a given class.

From an organizational point of view, the DS is hierarchically subdivided into subdomains, each of which is administered and managed by an *Administrative Authority* which assigns names and specifies subschemas.

Note that functionality of the ISO directory is based on the overall assumption that information stored will be long-lived. Highly transient data, as for instance on traffic conditions, has to be provided by a different, though to some extent directory-like service which may be called a "GSM-directory" [Bau 89]. In the subsequent sections we will limit ourselves to the "ISO-directory"

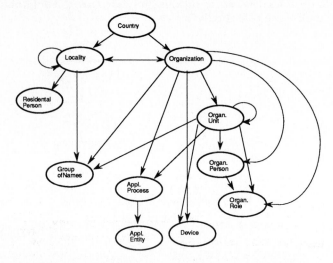

Fig.A6: Suggested Structure of the Directory Information Tree (DIT)

A.2 Authentication Services

This chapter cannot discuss problems of cryptosystems and authentication in detail (cf. eg. [Her 89] or [Mit 89]). However, some basics should be shortly addressed.The directory provides for two levels of authentication:

- simple authentication
  based on a user's distinguished name and a password

- strong authentication
  employing public key cryptosystems

Simple authentication is primarily intended for local use, i.e. authentication for example between a DUA and its home DSA. An elementary way to achieve simple authentication is depicted in Fig. A7.

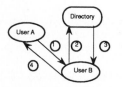

Fig.A7: Simple Authentication   **Fig.A8**: A Sample Certification Path

Initiator A sends his distinguished name and password to recipient B. B contacts the directory, where the password is matched against the one stored as the entry's *UserPassword* attribute value. The DS informs B about the credential's validity, this information may then also be conveyed to A. Of course, this procedure should not be regarded as a basis of secure communication [ISO 88].

Strong authentication makes use of properties of *Public Key Cryptosystems* (PKCS). With PKCSs, every user holds a public key to encipher data and a secret key for deciphering. The names of the respective keys already indicate their major characteristic: the public key may be announced to everyone in the system, whilst the secret key is only known to its owner - this is the most vital condition. It is obvious that this scheme can only work if it is impossible to derive the secret key from the public key.

Whereas every PKCS may be used to submit secret information, an additional property is required to apply the system useful for authentication purposes as well - the reversing of encipherment and decipherment. This property is called *Permutability*. With a PKCS being permutable the secret key may be used to encipher a message. Thus, since the secret key is only known to one particular user, this user's identity may be verified by deciphering the message using the public key.

Public keys are created and assigned by a *Certification Authority* (CA). The CA must be trusted by at least one user. The user's public key is then stored in his entry as an attribute of type *UserCertificate*. Besides the public key this attribute holds some additional parameters, eg. validity of the key. Thus, in case user A requires secure communication with user B, A first has to obtain B's public key. It is, however, essential for A to obtain the key from some entity he trusts (and, of course, in which B trusts as well). This entity is called a *Point of Common Trust*. Since A and B may be situated in different *Security Domains* (a security domain may, but needs not, be identical to a management domain), this may require A to traverse a *Certification Path,* i.e. an ordered sequence of certificates, to reach this point and to obtain B's public key, cf. Fig. A8.

Information Network and Data Communication, III
D. Khakhar and F. Eliassen (Editors)
Elsevier Science Publishers B.V. (North-Holland)
© IFIP, 1990

ARCHITECTURAL ELEMENTS OF A VAN SERVICE

Tom SKOVGAARD and Jens T. RASMUSSEN *)

danNet a/s
Birkerød, Denmark

This paper discusses some key elements of the service
and the architecture of non-interactive value added
networking. The paper identifies essetial
characteristics of services such as electronic mail,
file transfer and EDI in a heterogeneous value added
network (VAN) environment. Furthermore some
architectural elements of the supporting scenario for
these services are described.

1. INTRODUCTION

1.1. The scope

The scope of this paper is non-interactive (store-and-forward)
communication between computers. The paper brings forward some
significant architectural and technical aspects concerning the
exchange of information between heterogeneous computer systems
in a value added network environment.

1.2. Non-interactive information exchange

The specific type of information exchange considered in the
paper is the non-interactive, often referred to as store-and-
forward oriented information exchange. The paper defines the
typical services related to non-interactive computer
communication, basically electronic mail, Electronic Data
Interchange (EDI) and file transfer.

A definition of non-interactive communication, or electronic
mail, is given in [1]:

'Electronic mail is the store-and-forward transport of
electronic objects, across a heterogeneous environment,
among people, among people and applications, and among
applications',

with the supplementary comments, that what distinguishes
electronic mail from other technologies is its store-and-
forward delivery in a non-intrusive nature, and that 'an
electronic mail system does not commit to transport an object
from the source to the recipient instantaneously or even within
a few seconds'.

In [2] the definition given by the Electronic Mail Association

(EMA) is quoted:

> 'Electronic mail is the generic name for non-interactive communication of text, data, image or voice messages between a sender and designated recipients by systems utilizing telecommunications links'.

Electronic mail services, the normal term for non-interactive information exchange, are normally used for file transfers (the transfer of binary data files of any structure), Electronic Data Interchange (EDI, the exchange of business data between administrative computer applications, for example in the EDIFACT format [3]) as well as for electronic messaging between human beings.

1.3. Integrating electronic mail systems

The integration of different store-and-forward oriented services and systems in a Value Added Network (VAN) scenario, implies the integration of more or less incompatible services as well as incompatible systems and communications protocols. Examples of such an integration are given in [4]. Figure 1 illustrates a non-interactive communications scenario.

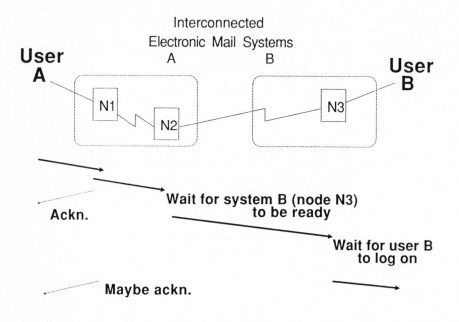

FIGURE 1
Interconnected electronic mail systems A and B

Elements of a VAN, integrating different electronic mail systems, concern communications functions, addressing, document conversion etc. In the following sections these aspects are described in more detail.

2. SERVICE CHARACTERISTICS

2.1. Elements of electronic mail services

The integration of different non-interactive communications systems and services, in a VAN environment, has the purpose to provide full functionality to the users, as far as possible. However, todays many different electronic mail systems have incompatible services and service characteristics. When interconnecting different electronic mail services in a VAN, only a subset of the service elements will be available to users of different systems.

The common element of all electronic mail services are basically 'to transfer a text' (an unstructured text). Users of different electronic mail services will, besides this basic facility, have access to a range of different service elements, which are valid as long as the scope is limited to each users own homogeneous environment. Such service elements are for example the reply function, acknowledge receipt, carbon copy, attach file, mailinglist, forward mail, etc.

2.2. Incompatibilities between electronic mail services

Thus, a user (A), attached to an electronic mail system with gateways to other electronic mail systems or VANS, are faced with the problem, that creating and sending an electronic message (mail, file or EDI-message) to another user (B) involves answering questions like:

- do replies work
- how are invalid recipients reported back
- what is the maximum document size supported
- is the 'carbon copy' facility supported
- is the mailing list facility supported
- what kind of document conversion is involved
- etc.

The international CCITT recommendation, [5], defines a set of service elements for an electronic mail service. However, compared to existing electronic mail services, X.400 is neither close to a superset nor to a subset of these. This is illustrated in figure 2.

From the user point of view, a non-interactive information service provides the capability for transfer of structured information from one user to another, across some underlying infrastructure. This infrastructure, which may comprise computer centres, VAN service providers etc., affects directly as well as indirectly the service characteristics of such a service. And indeed, it should, since the non-interactive information services often depend directly on advanced features within this infrastructure.

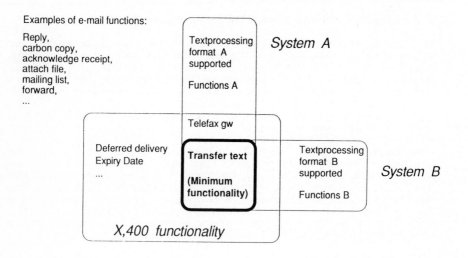

FIGURE 2
Incompatibilities and differences in functionality
between electronic mail services.

Within a homogeneous system, a non-interactive information service may be structured and defined according to a single specification, for example the X.400 set of recommendations from CCITT. However, when non-interactive information services are to be interconnected across heterogeneous systems, through gateways, international services or VAN services, even the basic characteristics of the service may be affected. Such a scenario is illustrated in figure 3.

2.3. Service matrices

In a heterogeneous electronic mail scenario, as illustrated in figure 3, the services can be described by means of a number of 'service matrices', one for each service aspect. A complete description of the services in such a scenario will imply a significant number of such matrices, corresponding to the service aspects.

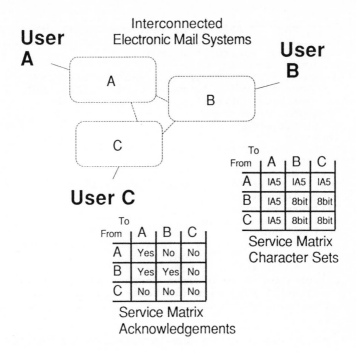

FIGURE 3
Integrated systems and related service matrices

The complexity of integrating different, more or less incompatible electronic mail services in a VAN scenario is significant. The order of this complexity will be evident, when the concept of service matrices are matched with the list of basic service aspects in the following section.

2.4. Service aspects of electronic mail services

A complete list of service aspects of non-interactive communications is not given in the litterature. Fragments can be found in [1], [2], [5] and [6]. In the table below, we have compiled an comprehensive list. This list comprises the basic categories of service elements, which should be considered in relation with the integration of non-interactive information exchange. Even for other types of services and value added networking, many of these categories are relevant.

Information Network and Data Communication, III
D. Khakhar and F. Eliassen (Editors)
Elsevier Science Publishers B.V. (North-Holland)
© IFIP, 1990

AN ISDN APPLICATION FOR PERSONAL COMPUTER COMMUNICATION

Teruhiro KUBOTA, Hiromiki MORIYAMA

Network Systems Development Center,
NTT
Tokyo, Japan

Abstract

An ISDN-PC communication protocol based on an OSI reference
model is proposed. A method to implement the ISDN-PC communication protocol, using a PC-board with an embedded microprocessor,
is described. Since the PC-board can deal with protocol
processing of layers 1 to 7, it can reduce the PC-CPU load and
provide application programs with a common interface to OSI
communication functions. As applications of ISDN-PC
communication, PC-to-facsimile delivery and multimedia messaging
through a Message Handling System are described.

1. INTRODUCTION

NTT began a commercial Integrated Services Digital Network (ISDN)
service in April 1988, offering a 2B+D (192 kb/s line rate) circuit-
switched service. Since that time, a 23B+D (1,544 Mb/s line rate)
circuit switched service was started in 1989.

ISDN provides high speed, high quality, digital communication for
various applications of which personal computer (PC) communication is
one of the most attractive. This paper describes PC communication
over an ISDN in terms of communication protocols and possible
application.

2. PURPOSE OF USING ISDN FOR PERSONAL COMPUTER COMMUNICATION

The number of PCs used for PC communication is increasing, especially in business. PC communication services, based on MHS (Message
Handling Systems), are becoming available. These PC communications now
use Public Switched Telephone Networks (PSTNs) as access lines to PC
communication centers. To communicate over PSTNs, PCs use modems such
as Microcom Networking Protocol (MNP) modems, and 4800 b/s half-duplex
Japanese Unified Standard for Telecommunication (JUST) adapters in
Japan.

As ISDN becomes widely available as access lines for PC communications, business PC communication users will gradually migrate to
ISDN from PSTN. PC communications over ISDN have the following
advantages compared to those over PSTN.

1) The 64 Kb/s circuit or packet-switched B-channel mode enables

higher speed communication. This feature is suitable for large volume data and image transmission. The high speed reduces holding time and the charge can be reduced proportionately, in the case of circuit switching.

2) ISDN has a lower error rate than PSTN, thus reducing data error and the need for retransmission, thereby increasing communication speed.

About ten million PCs are currently in use in Japan. So, there are millions of potential subscribers for ISDN-PC communication. Thus, PC communication is important for the enhancement of the ISDN network.

3. ISDN-PC COMMUNICATION PROTOCOL

Standardization of the ISDN-PC communication protocol is important for connectivity. This communication protocol has to contain not only the ISDN protocols but also higher layer protocols. As the ISDN-PC communication protocol is based on OSI, application protocols (for example, MHS and FTAM) can be stacked on it. These application protocols enable communication between PCs and between a PC and a host.

In May 1987, the Telecommunication Technology Committee (TTC) formulated national ISDN protocol standards for Japan, conforming to the CCITT recommendation I series. These standards deal with protocol layers 1 to 3. To standarize higher layer protocols of ISDN-PC communication, NTT has made a proposal to the TTC. Standardization of the ISDN-PC communication protocol is now proceeding.

The proposed ISDN-PC communication protocol has a structure using the following four types, as shown in Fig. 1.

-Type (A) : the common profile for various services (MHS, DIR, FTAM, etc.) conforming to the OSI protocol.

-Type (B) : the profile for X.410 MHS.

-Type (C) : the profile for the 1988 normal mode MHS to support the Message Transfer Protocol (P1).

-Type (D) : the profile for JUST-PC application.

Type (A) is used for center-to-end communication, and types (B) and (C) for center-to-center communication. Type (D) is added for the JUST-PC application.

The protocols in layers 4 to 7 conform to the international CCITT recommendation X.200 series (1988 version). Types (A) and (C) have normal operation modes, and type (B) has the operation mode of the X.410 (1984 version) specified in X.227.

The protocols in layers 1 to 4 are based on the TTC functional standard JT-T.90 for interconnection among ISDN-G4 facsimiles.

Any set of higher profiles (layers 5 to 7) in this structure can be freely stacked on any of the lower profiles (layers 1 to 4).

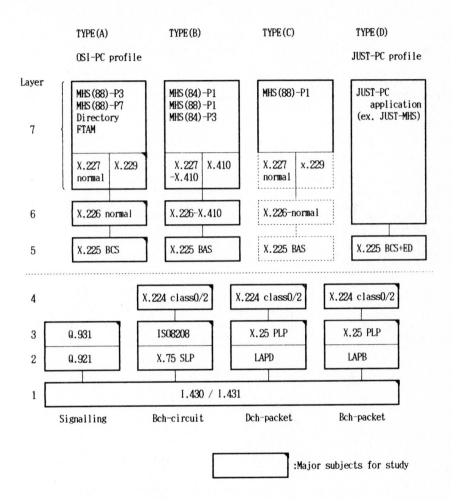

FIGURE 1   Proposed ISDN-PC communication protocol structure

4. AN ISDN-PC COMMUNICATION PROTOCOL IMPLEMENTATION METHOD

Realization of high-speed data transmission is one of the key factors in implementation of the ISDN-PC protocol. PCs access a PC communication center for two possible kinds of communications: conversation or file transfer. For example, the 9.6 Kb/s D-channel packet is used for conversation, and the 64 Kb/s B-channel circuit or packet is used for file transfer. In each case, the PC communication speed is faster than PC communication over PSTN. A front-processer (for example, a board or an adapter) is necessary to terminate the ISDN interface.

In addition, an ISDN-PC has to process the communication protocol which contains higher layer (up to eventually 7) protocols. The processing of the ISDN-PC communication protocol imposes a heavy load on the PC-CPU, if it has to process each of the OSI higher layers. A way to reduce this processing load is to place the processing of, for example layers 4 to 7, on a PC board. Protocol processing of layers 1 to 7 can be done by a PC-board with an embedded microprocesser (as shown in Fig. 2) or adapter. According to this architecture, the PC-CPU is free to deal with application services only.

It is required that the interface between an application program and a PC board be a universal interface. The universal interface means that an application program doesn't have to know about the internal structure of the board or the communication protocol. This interface provides an access-method to the OSI protocols and ISDN transmission mode. Thus, application programs (such as MHS and FTAM) on the PC can use the ISDN-PC communication protocol via this universal interface.

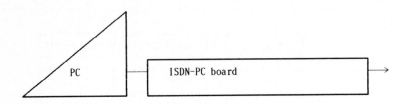

(1) ISDN-PC system configuration

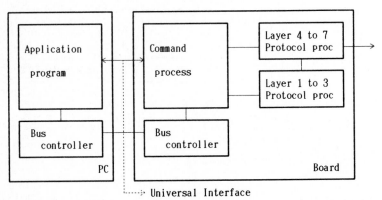

(2) ISDN-PC software construction

FIGURE 2 (1/2)   Configuration of ISDN-PC system

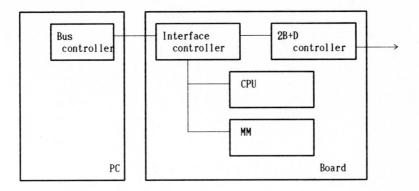

(3) ISDN-PC hardware construction

FIGURE 2 (2/2)   Configuration of ISDN-PC system

5. APPLICATION OF ISDN PC COMMUNICATION

5.1. PC-to-Facsimile Delivery

PC-to-facsimile terminal delivery is an attractive service for an ISDN-PC communication terminal. Media conversion from text mail to a facsimile image enables mail delivery from the PC to a facsimile terminal and increases the range of communications.

The facsimile conversion can be expanded to deal not only with text mail but also wordprocessor documents which have specific control codes. To convert a wordprocessor document into the image for a facsimile terminal, the originator has to specify the type of document. A protocol element has to be added to the submit-envelope in order to specify the type of document.

The network configuration with facsimile conversion facility is shown in Fig. 3. Facsimile conversion facilities are remote from the PC communication center, so that delivery from a facsimile conversion facility to a facsimile terminal is done by a local call in ISDN or PSTN. For PC-facsimile communication, an ISDN-PC accesses the PC communication center via ISDN, while a PC connected to PSTN accesses the PC service center via PSTN. The PC sends the text mail, with an indication showing PC-to-facsimile delivery, to the PC communication center. The center then sends it to a facsimile conversion facility, which sends a converted image to the G4 facsimile in the ISDN or G3 facsimile in the PSTN.

5.2. Multimedia Messaging

It is important that facsimile conversion be able to deal with both text and image in the same mail. As an application of ISDN-PC communication, text and facsimile image can be sent in the same mail.

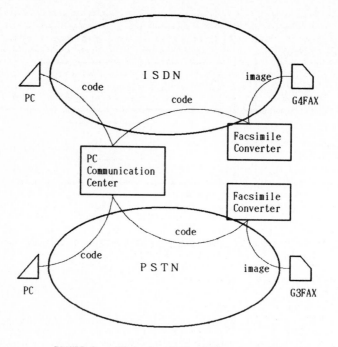

FIGURE 3   PC-to-Facsimile delivery service

As shown in Fig. 4, one ISDN channel is used for ISDN-PC communication and the other channel is used for G4 facsimile terminal communication. Using an codec, a G3 facsimile terminal can be used

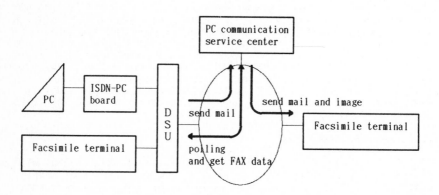

FIGURE 4   Multimedia messaging service

instead of a G4 facsimile terminal. One way to submit mail and images
is as follows. First, text mail is submitted to the PC communication
center. This mail has an indication showing a facsimile image waiting
to be sent. Seeing this indication, PC communication service center
make a polling and gets the facsimile image from the facsimile
terminal. The text mail is delivered to a mailbox or PC-terminal, or
the combined converted image of text mail and facsimile image is sent
to facsimile terminal.

6. CONCLUSION

    PC communication over ISDN is attractive for both networks and PC
communication users. In this paper, the PC communication protocol
over ISDN based on OSI was proposed. An implementation method of the
this communication protocol, using a PC-board with an embedded
microprocessor, was also described. This PC-board processes one to
seven layers of ISDN-PC protocol to reduce the CPU load, and provides
a universal interface to application programs on the PC. Finally, as
applications of ISDN-PC communication protocol, PC-to-facsimile
delivery and multimedia messaging were also described.

REFERENCES

[1] CCITT SG VII : Recommendations on Message Handling systems;
X.400 etc., 1984
[2] Japanese Unified Standard for Telecommunication - Personal Computer; Notification No. 971 of the Ministry of Posts and Telecommunications, 1984
[3] Japanese Unified Standard for Telecommunication - Message Handling Systems; Notification No. 887 of the Ministry of Posts and Telecommunications, 1987
[4] T.Nakayama, M.Nomura: "Developments of MHS in NTT - Connection
of Personal Computers to MHS -", Proc of ICCC' 86, pp.61-66, 1986
[5] A.Iwabuchi, Y.Shimazu, M.Nomura, T.Itoh: "Message Communication
Network Services for Personal Computers", Proc of ICCC '86, pp.248-253,
1986
[6] T.Soga, S.Fujiwara, T.Kawahara: "NTT-PCN : Development and
Operation", Proc of ICCC '88, pp.533-537, 1988
[7] K.Hibino, T.Soga, M.Uchida: "Personal Computer Communication
Network System over ISDN", Proc of PTC'90, pp.436-440, 1990

Information Network and Data Communication, III
D. Khakhar and F. Eliassen (Editors)
Elsevier Science Publishers B.V. (North-Holland)
© IFIP, 1990

MULTICOPY ARQ ERROR CONTROL TECHNIQUES FOR MULTIPOINT SATELLITE LINKS

Ulrich Quernheim and Stephan Jacobs

Institute Informatik IV, RWTH Aachen,
Ahornstr. 55, D-5100 Aachen, West Germany
Phone +49-241-804523
FAX +49-241-806295

The number of satellite networks with many terminals and in parallel
the number of point-to-multipoint data distribution applications
using such nets will increase rapidly. Transmission errors may be
met by FEC or ARQ techniques. A main aspect of ARQ error control
in point-to-multipoint communication is the buffering of the
acknowledgements. In this paper we discuss two buffering strategies
combined with go-back-N and selective repeat ARQ protocols and
with multicopy techniques. Throughput evaluation shows the
advantage of acknowledgement buffering and of multicopy protocols
over single copy protocols. Throughput and optimal number of
copies are computed partly analytically and partly by simulation.

1. INTRODUCTION

Satellite networks have a number of advantages, for instance flexibility and
simple broadcast facilities for the distribution of identical information.
Transmission protocols must take into account the special features of satellite
links (e.g. long distance for geostationary satellites, 2*35,800 km or 0.27 s).
Data transmission via satellite links is affected by errors, e.g. caused by rain
fading. Due to the expected lack of free frequencies (today: 4/6 GHz, 12/14
GHz) and other reasons (antenna gain etc.), higher frequencies will be used in
future satellite systems (e.g. 20/30 GHz). These frequencies involve stronger
fading effects.

To ensure a relatively reliable transmission an FEC (forward error correction)
or ARQ (automatic repeat request) error control technique may be applied to
the satellite link. Reliability includes correct, in-sequence transmission without
loss or duplication of data. In this paper we restrict to ARQ protocols, because
FEC cannot guarantee error free data transmission. The bit stream to be

transmitted is subdivided into frames, which are subsequently numbered and contain control information and redundant bits for transmission error detection. There are three main categories of ARQ techniques, stop-and-wait, go-back-N, and selective repeat. Over satellite links with their large propagation delay stop-and-wait protocols are inefficient because after sending a frame the link is idle until the sender receives a positive or negative acknowledgement (ACK/NACK) from the receiver station. In contrast to this frames are transmitted continuously with go-back-N and selective repeat techniques, respectively. If a frame is negatively acknowledged by a receiver (or if a timeout occurs) the sender restarts transmission beginning with that frame using a go-back-N protocol. All N frames sent between the erroneous one and its retransmission are ignored by the receiver. The sender needs a buffer of size N+1 frames (corresponding to one round trip delay) for those frames which may be rejected and retransmitted. The receiver, however, only needs a buffer for one frame. Using a selective repeat protocol, only the rejected frames are retransmitted. Since a receiver station must rearrange frames which are out of sequence, it needs a buffer for at least N+1 frames.

The broadcast property of satellite channels simplifies distribution of identical information to multiple receivers; all stations in the beam coverage zone may receive the satellite signal. An increasing number of satellite networks with many small terminals will be established (e.g. VSAT-nets), thus broadcast (data) transmission will increase considerably, too. With point-to-multipoint communication error control by an ARQ protocol is more complicated than with point-to-point transmission; some stations may receive a frame correctly, whereas other stations may reject the same frame. If p_u (p_d) is the probability that a frame is transmitted correctly from the sender to the satellite (from the satellite to a receiver, assuming that p_d is independent and the same for all receivers), then the probability that a frame is correctly received by a station (K stations) comes to $p = p_u * p_d$ ($p_u * p_d^K$). Therefore, the throughput decreases if the number of stations increases. Thus, sometimes (high error rates, many receivers) it may be favourable to transmit more than one copy of a frame subsequently. Many variants of the basic ARQ protocols for point-to-point communication have been studied, cf. [9] and [14]. In [7], [12], and [13] ARQ protocols for point-to-point satellite communication and in [1], [4], [18] multicopy protocols are discussed. Numerous protocols for multipoint communication have been analyzed, cf. [2], [3], [6], [8], [15], [17]. In [6] Gopal, Jaffe compare single copy go-back-N protocols, and in [17] Wang, Silvester suggest multicopy stop-and-wait and go-back-N protocols for multipoint communication, which use the outcomes of previous transmissions of a frame in different extent.

We compare three multipoint multicopy variants of go-back-N and selective repeat, respectively, which differ in their ability to buffer and use the acknowledgements of previous transmissions of a frame not being accepted by all receivers. The GBN_0 (SR_0) protocol does not store the ACKs, whereas the GBN_all (SR_all) and GBN_all* (SR_all*) protocols do (for GBN_0 and GBN_all cf. [6] and [17] in the single copy and multicopy case). The multicopy protocols are adaptive in the way that the number of copies of a frame sent subsequently depends on the number of receivers, the round trip delay, and the frame error rates. The number of copies is optimized partly analytically and partly by simulation. Additionally, in the GBN_all* (SR_all*) protocol the number of copies in a retransmission depends on the number of stations having rejected that frame and may be different from that in the first transmission.

2. POINT-TO-MULTIPOINT ARQ PROTOCOLS

2.1 Environment

The scenario considered here comprises one sender and K receivers interconnected via a broadcast satellite channel (one uplink and K downlinks); an ARQ protocol is used. Each frame transmitted by the sender is received nearly simultaneously by all K receivers, which are assumed to sense the channel continuously. Acknowledgements are transmitted to the sender via a suitable return channel (possibly a terrestrial channel). We describe the three go-back-N protocols and the differences of the corresponding selective repeat protocols. An example of the respective performances is given in figures 1 to 4. The sender uses a list of expected acknowledgements (LEA) for those frames which have already been transmitted, but have not yet been accepted by all receivers.

2.2 Go-Back-N Protocols

The three multicopy go-back-N protocols differ in the ability of the sender to remember acknowledgements of copies not yet accepted by all receivers and in the number of copies of a frame sent subsequently. The receiver operations are identical for the three protocols. The receiver first checks the FCS to determine whether or not the frame has been received correctly, and returns an ACK or a NACK, respectively, containing the frame number. If this frame number is the one expected by the receiver, it accepts the frame, which is delivered to the upper layers of the protocol hierarchy. If the predecessor of the frame has not yet been accepted or if the frame has already been accepted by the station earlier it will be discarded. Even if the frame is not expected, it is necessary to send an ACK to prevent deadlocks using the GBN_0 protocol described below. The sender transmits frames and expects ACKs/NACKs continuously. After sending m copies of a frame the associated time-out-counter is set; m is chosen optimally, its value depends on K, N, and the frame error rates. The protocols differ in the way how the outcomes of previous transmissions of a frame are used, cf. [6], [17]:

GBN_0: The sender receives the ACKs/NACKs for the *m* copies of a frame sent subsequently. If not all stations have accepted the frame at the same time (at least one of the *m* copies), the sender retransmits this and all subsequent frames. The retransmission of a frame is handled by the sender in the same way as the first transmission; the sender does not remember the outcomes of the first transmission of *m* copies when he checks the acknowledgements for the retransmission. So it is possible that all stations have received the frame correctly (in the first or second transmission), but the sender starts a third transmission of *m* copies.

Two conditions have to be fulfilled so that ACKs are accepted: Because of go-back-N all predecessors must have been received correctly, and because of the "0"-protocol all ACKs have to be received by the sender at the same time.

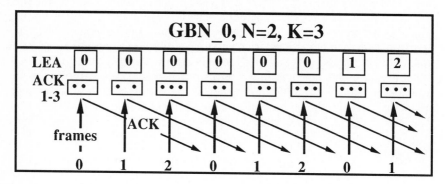

Fig.1: Performance of GBN_0

GBN_all: The LEA contains entries for every receiver, whether a particular station has accepted a frame or not. An ACK will only be registered, if the ACKs of this receiver for all previous frames have already been registered. So it does not matter, if a retransmitted frame is not received correctly by a station, which received this frame correctly the first time. If all receivers have acknowledged a frame, this frame can be discarded, the associated time-out-counter can be stopped and the ACKs of the next frame will be expected. LEA contains entries not only for every receiver but also for all expected frames.

Now only one condition must be fulfilled so that ACKs are accepted: All predecessors of the respective frame have to be received error free and acknowledged by all receiving stations.

GBN-all*: Here the number *m'* of copies during a retransmission of a frame depends on the number *K'* of those stations not having accepted this frame

instead of K. For m' the optimal value of m for K' receivers in GBN_all is chosen.
In the single receiver case (point-to-point) the protocols coincide.

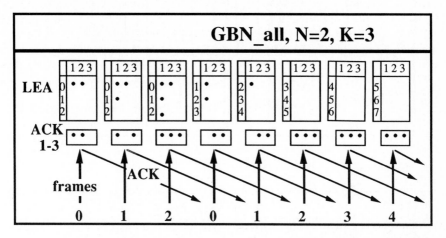

Fig.2: Performance of GBN_all

2.3 Selective Repeat Protocols

In the case of selective repeat all receivers have buffers to store frames which are out of order. Frames are accepted even if their predecessors were not error free (exception: buffer overflow). So the sender may accept an ACK even if its predecessor was a NACK. Therefore, only erroneous or lost frames have to be retransmitted, but not all successors. Again we consider three protocols differing in the way how ACKs are used.

SR_0: The sender receives the ACKs/NACKs for the m copies of a frame sent subsequently. If not all stations have accepted the frame at the same time (at least one of the m copies), the sender retransmits this frame, but not the subsequent frames. The retransmission of a frame is handled by the sender in the same way as the first transmission; the sender does not remember the outcomes of the first transmission of m copies when he checks the acknowledgements for the retransmission. So it is possible that the sender starts a third transmission of m copies, although all stations have received the frame correctly in the first or second transmission .
One condition must be fulfilled so that ACKs are accepted: Because of the "0"-protocol the ACKs of all stations have to be received by the sender at the same time.

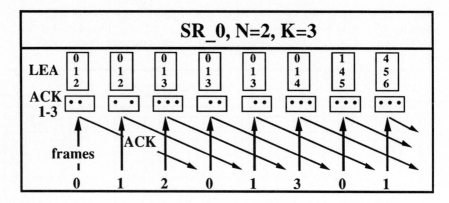

Fig.3: Performance of SR_0

SR_all: The LEA contains entries for every receiver, whether a particular station has accepted a frame or not. So it does not matter, if a retransmitted frame is not received correctly by a station, which has received this frame correctly in the first transmission. If all receivers have acknowledged a frame, the copy of this frame can be discarded, and the associated time-out-counter can be stopped. The LEA contains entries not only for every receiver but also for all expected frames.

There is no condition relative to predecessors or ACKs of other stations which has to be fulfilled so that ACKs are accepted.

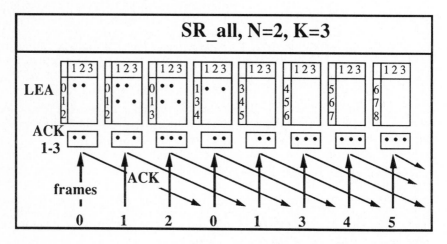

Fig.4: Performance of SR_all

SR-all*: Here the number m' of copies during a retransmission of a frame depends on the number K' of those stations not having accepted this frame instead of K. For m' the optimal value of m for K' receivers in SR_all is chosen.

In the single receiver case (point-to-point) the protocols coincide again.

The protocols can be classified by the conditions which have to be fulfilled to accept ACKs (fig. 5).

	ACK at the same time	error free predecessor
GBN_0	**X**	**X**
GBN_all		**X**
SR_0	**X**	
SR_all		

Fig.5: Classification of protocols

2.4 Implementation Aspects

An important problem of multipoint ARQ protocols is the scheduling of acknowledgements of many receivers; for every frame acknowledgements of all receivers have to be transmitted separately to the sender. But without reducing throughput considerably, receivers may send an acknowledgement for a sequence of frames (e.g. 10 or 100), respectively, so that the round trip delay is increased correspondingly. There might be an additional alert channel for urgent negative acknowledgements.

3. THROUGHPUT COMPARISON

We compare throughput of the protocols in satellite networks with a round trip delay of about 0.54 s. The throughput T of a protocol (as function of the frame error rates and the number of receivers) comes to

$$T = \frac{\text{number of frames transmitted successfully to all receivers}}{\text{total number of transmitted copies of frames}}.$$

We make the following assumptions:
- Uplink and downlink errors are randomly distributed with frame error rates b_u and b_d. Uplink errors affect all receiving stations (which are assumed to have equal properties), whereas a downlink error affects the corresponding station only; b_d is equal for all stations. The downlink error processes are independent, because most fading effects are local.
- The transmission of acknowledgements over a return channel is error free.
- The sender is saturated; there are always frames waiting for transmission.

Throughput of the GBN_0, SR_0(infinite buffers), and SR_all/SR_all*(infinite buffers) protocols is computed analytically. For performance evaluation of GBN_all, GBN_all*, SR_0, SR_all and SR_all* (finite buffers) simulation has been used.

3.1 Throughput Analysis

Let $p_{m,K}$ be the probability that a single frame transmitted m times subsequently (a station accepts, if it receives one error free copy) is accepted by all K receivers, then

$$p_{m,K} = \sum_{i=0}^{m} \binom{m}{i} b_u^{m-i} (1-b_u)^i (1-b_d^i)^K .$$

GBN_0: If m copies of a frame are sent subsequently, the frame is accepted by all receivers with probability $p_{m,K}$; if the frame is not accepted and must be repeated later, the following N copies of other frames are also lost. Thus, throughput may be computed as

$$T_{GBN\_0} = \max_m \left(\frac{p_{m,K}}{m + (1-p_{m,K}) N} \right) .$$

GBN_all, GBN_all*: The actual system state may be expressed by the K-tupel $(n_1,...,n_K)$, where n_i indicates the number of those frames accepted by receiver i which have not yet been accepted by all receivers, $0 \leq n_i \leq [(N + 1) / m]$. As the receivers have identical properties, we may assume $n_1 \leq ... \leq n_K$. Due to the huge number of states exact analytical evaluation of the throughput seems to be impracticable, thus we have used simulations. For single copy GBN_all Gopal, Jaffe [6] have proposed and validated an approximation model. Unfortunately, it cannot easily be extended to the multicopy case.

SR_0(infinite buffers): If we assume infinite buffers at the receiver, throughput is equal to the probability that a frame sent in m (m optimal) subsequent copies is accepted by all receivers,

$$T_{SR\_0(\infty b)} = \max_m \left(P_{m,K} / m \right).$$

SR_all, SR_all* (infinite buffers): Here the outcomes of previous transmissions are considered. As we assume infinite buffers, frames may be buffered at a receiver for an arbitrary time. So it is unfavourable to transmit copies of a frame which might be unnecessary. Therefore, throughput is maximized, if $m=1$ is chosen, and comes to (cf. [17] for $b_u = 0$)

$$T_{SR\_all(\infty b)} = T_{SR\_all*(\infty b)}$$

$$= 1 / \sum_{m=1}^{\infty} m \; Pr \begin{pmatrix} \text{a frame is accepted by all K receivers} \\ \text{exactly after transmission of m copies} \end{pmatrix}$$

$$= 1 / \sum_{m=0}^{\infty} Pr \begin{pmatrix} \text{a frame is not accepted by all K receivers} \\ \text{after transmission of m copies} \end{pmatrix}$$

$$= 1 / \sum_{m=0}^{\infty} (1 - P_{m,K}).$$

Throughput of SR_all(infinite buffers) is an upper bound for the throughput of all realistic (finite buffers) ARQ protocols.

SR_0, SR_all, SR_all* (finite buffers): To take into account finite buffers at the receivers simulations are used for the performance evaluation of these protocols.

3.2 Simulation

The simulation program for the point-to-multipoint scenario is written in QNAP2 language, cf. [10], [11], and [16]. QNAP2 (Queueing Network Analysis Package) is a program package developed by INRIA (Institut National de Recherche en Informatique et en Automatique) and Bull for evaluation of queueing networks based on the principles of parallel processes. In QNAP2 simulated networks consist of stations and related queues where customers (frames, packets) are served and routed through, according to predefined transition rules.

Our simulation program comprises the following queues:
sending-queue -
> holding copies of the frame for the LEA, copying the actual frame due to the repeat parameter and defining the transition rules to the satellite,

source-queue -
> always creating new frames if the sending-queue is empty,

LEA-queue -
> a passive queue (list), filled by the sending-queue and controlled by the timer-queue,

timer-queue -
> managing the LEA according to the described protocols using procedures to test, copy and clear the frames in the list,

satellite-queue -
> FIFO-queue, generating a propagation delay of 270 ms,

receiving-queue -
> consisting of a random generator which decides, whether a frame is lost or not.

Most of the simulation time is needed to handle discrete time events. Therefore, it is advantageous to combine some "small" events into one "large" if possible. Thus in the simulation the K receiving stations are united to one receiving-queue and hence the K frames sent from the satellite to the receivers are also merged. Accordingly, the satellite sends only one frame, which contains entries for each of the K simulated stations. Moreover, the frame includes a frame number and two time variables showing how much time has passed by since the first transmission of the frame (evaluating the mean delay) and the last one (detection of time-outs). As there is no difference between complete lost and partial disturbance of a frame no frame checking sequence (FCS) is used.

The duration of a simulation run was chosen to 20 s with a transmission rate of 1,000 frames/s, that means 20.000 frames were sent and additional 600 frames were generated to reach a stastionary behaviour. One simulation, consisting of 10 or 20 simulation runs, consumed between 10 and 25 hours CPU-time on a CELERITY 1260 D processor.To calculate confidence intervalls we used batch means algorithm, cf. [5], always computed for a confidence level of 95%. Evaluating the performance of a system by simulation always leads to the problem of validation and verfication. Simulations with simple parameters ($m=1$, $K=1$), that means single copy point-to-point go-back-N and selective repeat, lead to the same results as performance analysis which is possible in those cases.

4 RESULTS

Using simulation and analysis we evaluated the performance of five protocols (GBN-0, GBN-all, GBN_all*, SR_0, SR_all) varying the parameter m, that is the number of copies, and choosing the optimal value for it. Results presented in fig. 6 to 10 base on a transmission rate of 1,000 frames/s. Due to the propagation delay of a satellite link (geostationary orbit) N=540 is chosen.

GBN_0 (analysis): In the case of high frame error rates (e.g. b_u, $b_d \geq 0.03$) throughput may be increased by transmitting a sequence of copies instead of a single one. Assuming $b_u = b_d = 0.03$ m_should be 4 for more than 15 stations and 3, if there are less (fig. 6).

GBN_all, GBN_all (simulation):* The optimal number of copies is nearly the same as above. If the satellite network comprises many receivers GBN_all, GBN_all* lead to a better throughput than GBN_0 (fig. 7: $b_u = b_d = 0.03$, fig. 9: $b_u = b_d = 0.1$) Throughput results of GBN_all vs. b_u, b_d ($b_u = b_d$) are presented in fig. 10.

SR_0, SR_all with infinite buffer (analysis): The SR_all protocol with infinite buffers and $m = 1$ leads to the best throughput using an ARQ protocol. If only a few ($K<5$) receivers are listening, throughput of the SR_0 protocol does not differ significantly from the throughput of the SR_all protocol. But with increasing number of stations K, throughput decreases rapidly. So it is better to choose two copies (if $K>20$) transmitted subsequently (fig. 8).
SR_all (simulation): The optimal values of m are 1 ($K \leq 5$) and 2 ($K>5$), cf. fig. 7.

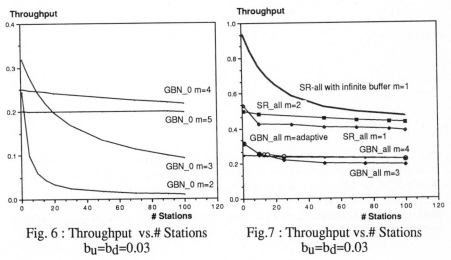

Fig. 6 : Throughput vs.# Stations
$b_u = b_d = 0.03$

Fig.7 : Throughput vs.# Stations
$b_u = b_d = 0.03$

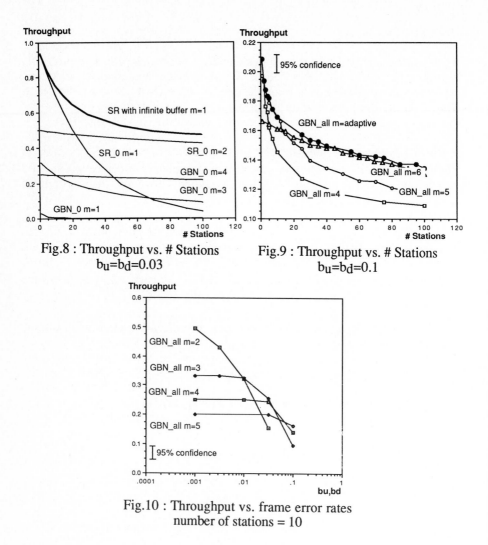

Fig.8 : Throughput vs. # Stations
$b_u=b_d=0.03$

Fig.9 : Throughput vs. # Stations
$b_u=b_d=0.1$

Fig.10 : Throughput vs. frame error rates
number of stations = 10

5. CONCLUSION

We have discussed some multicopy go-back-N and selective repeat protocols for multipoint satellite communication. Throughput evaluations show that for relatively high frame error rates (e.g. during fading periods or caused by small antennas) buffering ACKs increases throughput considerably. Moreover multicopy protocols may perform much better than single copy protocols. The optimal number of copies sent subsequently depends on the number of stations, the frame error rate, and the chosen protocol. The importance of buffering

ACKs and of multicopy transmission increases with the number of receivers. Due to the large round trip delay in satellite networks the advantages of multicopy transmission and ACK buffering are particularly evident. Thus, during fading periods a satellite channel may continue data transmission even though throughput decreases, whereas the link breaks down if a single copy protocol is used.

Furthermore we want to evaluate the performance of multipoint ARQ protocols considering inhomogeneous receivers and burst errors which are typical of satellite links.

REFERENCES

[1]   H. Bruneel, M. Moeneclaey, "On the Throughput Performance of some Continuous ARQ Strategies with Repeated Transmissions", IEEE Trans. Commun., pp. 244-249, March 1986.
[2]   S. B. Calo, M. C. Easton, "A Broadcast Protocol for File Transfers to Multiple Sites", IEEE Trans. Commun., p. 1701-1706, 1981.
[3]   S. R. Chandran, S. Lin, "A Selective-Repeat ARQ Scheme for Point-to-Multipoint Communications and Its Throughput Analysis", Proc. ACM SIGCOM Conference, pp. 292-301, Stowe, VT, August 1986.
[4]   Y. Chang, C. Leung, "On Weldon's ARQ Strategy", IEEE Trans. Commun., pp. 297-300, March 1984.
[5]   G. Fishman, "Principles of Discrete Event Simulation", J. Wiley & Sons, New York, 1978.
[6]   I. S. Gopal, J. M. Jaffe, "Point-to-Multipoint Communication over Broadcast Links", IEEE Trans. Commun., vol. COM-32, pp. 1034-1044, September 1984.
[7]   M. Hübner, F.Sausen, O.Spaniol, "Evaluation of Application-Oriented Satellite Link Protocols", Proceedings IFIP TC International Conference on Inform. Network and Data Comm., Ronneby Brunn, Sweden, May 1986.
[8]   K. Mase, T. Takenaka, H. Yamamoto, M. Shinohara, "Go-Back-N ARQ Schemes for Point-to-Multipoint Satellite Communications", IEEE Trans. Commun., vol COM-31, pp. 583-590, April 1983.
[9]   J. M. Morris, "On another Go-Back-N ARQ Technique for High Error Rate Conditions", IEEE Trans. Commun., vol. COM-26, pp. 187-189, 1978.
[10] D. Potier, "New Users' Introduction to QNAP2", INRIA Rapports Techniques No. 40, October 1984.
[11] "QNAP2 Reference Manaual, version V03", INRIA and Bull, May 1984.
[12] U. Quernheim, "Satellite Communication Protocols - a Performance Comparison Considering On-Board Processing", Proc. EUROCON'88,

We have demonstrated crucial substeps of the meta-communication methodology and will demonstrate a commercially available complete system in the near future.

Each of the steps in the meta-communication methodology is under continuing investigation. On the topmost level we would like to provide a user-friendly way of specifying constraints that represent the knowledge of a meta-communicating entity. This could be accomplished by a knowledge-based system that automatically constructs these constraints from formalized application requirements and environment constraints. A possible approach to this problem is given in [6]. On the level of combining constraints further research is needed to clarify the relationship: composition function $\longleftrightarrow$ predicates. Also, both the abstract and the executable specification language of Archetype have only partially defined interfaces to surrounding environments. These and other issues are subject of currently ongoing research.

In summary, we believe that future communications systems will be based on automatic meta-communication. We have demonstrated the feasibility of the meta-communication approach through our methodology and through implementations.

REFERENCES

[1]   Bjorner D., Jones C. B. *Formal specification & software development.* Prentice-Hall International, 1982.

[2]   Bochmann G. V., Sunshine C. A. A survey of formal methods. In *Computer Network Architecture and Protocols*, Plenum Press, 1982, 561-579.

[3]   Conry S., Distributed artificial intelligence in communications systems. Proceedings *IEEE Expert Systems in Government Symposium*, 1986.

[4]   Green P. Protocol conversion. *IEEE Transactions on Communications.* March 1986.

[5]   Groenback I. Conversion between TCP and ISO protocols as a method of achieving interoperability between data communications systems. *Journal of Selected Areas in Communications.* March 1986.

[6]   Hayward N., Meandzija B. Deriving protocol architecture specifications from formalized network application service requirements and environment constraints. SMU-CSE, 87-CSE-3, (January 87).

[7]   Lam S. Protocol conversion -- correctness problems. *Proceedings ACM SIGCOMM Symposium on Communications Architectures and Protocols.* August 1986.

[8]   Meandzija B. Archetype: a unified method for the design and implementation of protocol architectures. *IEEE Transactions on Software Engineering*, Vol. 14, No. 6, June 1988.

[9]   Meandzija B., Ho W. P.-C. Towards truly open systems. *Proceedings IFIP International Symposium on Protocol Specification, Testing, and Verification* (Eds. H. Rudin, C. West), (May 1987). North-Holland, 1987.

[10]   Meandzija B.: Design and automated generation of protocol architectures Using Archetype. *Proceedings 7-th International Conference on Distributed Computing Systems.* September 1987.

[11]   Meandzija B., Ho W. P.-C., Banerjee S. Distributed Design through Step-
         wise Refinement. *Proceedings IFIP Symposium on Protocol
         Specification, Testing, and Verification* (Eds. S. Aggarwal, K. Sabnani).
         North-Holland, 1988.
[12]   Meandzija B., Westcott J. (Eds.). Integrated Network Management, I.
         *Proceedings IFIP Symposium on Integrated Network Management.
         North-Holland, 1989.*
[13]   *Radigan J., Meandzija B. Y.A.N.C. (Yet Another Network Compiler).
         Second International Symposium on Interoperable Information Systems.*
         November 1988.

Information Network and Data Communication, III
D. Khakhar and F. Eliassen (Editors)
Elsevier Science Publishers B.V. (North-Holland)
© IFIP, 1990

DISTRIBUTED APPLICATION DEVELOPMENT:
PROBLEMS AND SOLUTIONS

Alexander SCHILL

University of Karlsruhe, Institute of Telematics
Am Zirkel 2, D-7500 Karlsruhe 1, W. Germany

In the distributed systems area, great advances have been achieved during the last decade. Especially in the area of communication networks and protocols, a rapid technological deployment has taken place. From the application point of view, a growing demand for distributed programming can be observed. Important example areas are computer-integrated manufacturing and office automation.

The paper gives a survey of the distributed application support area, especially focussing on distributed programming and configuration techniques, on the use of object-oriented techniques, and on development support. Several existing approaches are classified and compared to each other. Important communication approaches covered by the paper are extended message passing and remote procedure call facilities as well as new distributed object-oriented interaction mechanisms. Important distributed configuration management issues include placement and structure support for distributed applications, dynamic configuration change support, and associated configuration languages. Finally, as an integration effort, the architecture of an object-oriented environment for distributed application development support is outlined.

1. INTRODUCTION

In the distributed systems area, great advances have been achieved during the last decade. Especially in the area of communication networks and transport-oriented communication protocols, a rapid technological deployment has taken place. On top of these transport protocols, several higher-level communication facilities have been developed. Examples are basic message passing [26,30], remote procedure call [6] and object-oriented communication mechanisms [5]. These facilities are either offered by a distributed or network operating system or are fully integrated into a distributed programming language. This way, higher-level communication mechanisms are provided for the development of distributed applications [25]. Design, test, installation and administration of distributed applications are best supported by integrated language and tool approaches. Examples are design and configuration languages, animation tools, distributed debuggers, and distributed loaders. From the application point of view, a growing demand for distributed programming can be observed. Important example areas are computer-integrated manufacturing and office automation. Major goals to be achieved by distribution facilities in these areas are the decentralization of functions and data to increase the locality of an application, the interconnection of previously separated application programs, the shared use of distributed and expensive resources, increased reliability and load balancing [28].

The paper gives a survey of the distributed application support area, especially focussing on distributed programming and configuration techniques, on the use of object-oriented techniques and on development support. Several existing approaches are classified and compared to each other. Details are both derived from foreign system developments as well as from own experiences with distributed systems. As an integration effort, the architecture of an object-oriented environment for distributed application development support is outlined. Section 2 introduces major terms and definitions concerning distributed applications and systems, identifies basic requirements and presents the structure of an integrated model, language and tool approach as an architectural solution. Section 3 discusses and compares existing mechanisms for distributed programming. In section 4, mechanisms for distributed configuration management are described and classified. In section 5, the discussed facts and experiences are integrated resulting in a development support environment for distributed applications. Section 6 concludes with an outlook to future work.

2. DISTRIBUTED SYSTEMS AND APPLICATIONS

2.1. Overview and Definitions

A *distributed system* consists of a number of physical nodes, of their physical interconnections (e.g. local area networks) including intermediate gateways, and of the higher-level communication facilities used on top of the physical interconnections. Current trends in the distributed systems area can be characterized by the following features: *Size:* The size of distributed systems is increasing significantly from tens of nodes up to thousands of nodes. For the near future, networks with millions of nodes are projected. *Communication speed:* The physical communication speed of current networks is growing from about 10 Mbit/s up to 100-1000 Mbit/s. Therefore, gateways and communication protocols tend to become a bottleneck rather than physical communication links. *Degree of decentralization:* With their growing size, distributed systems become more and more decentralized. The nodes of a distributed system are often managed independently and usually only parts of an overall distributed system are operating at a time. *Communication facilities:* The communication facilities offered to the application develeeper are providing more and more higher-level interfaces to the basic transport-oriented communication services. This trend is important as a significant degree of distribution transparency in the area of distributed application development can be achieved this way (cf. section 3).

A *distributed application* is an application program consisting of several cooperating components running on different physical nodes [25]. The cooperation is realized by the use of distributed system communication mechanisms. To enable intercomponent communication, logical interconnections (i.e. more or less complex intercomponent references) can be established between them [18,1]. Distributed applications can be characterized by the following features [23]: *Complexity:* Typical distributed applications consist of a large number of cooperating components and interconnections resulting in a complex overall structure. Explicit facilities for structure management are required to manage this complexity during application development and maintenance (cf. section 4). *Irregularity:* The application topology with its interconnection and comunication structure is often relatively irregular and therefore difficult to understand and to analyze. For this reason, extensive development tool support is necessary (cf. sections 2.4 and 5). *Intensive communication and coarse-grained parallelism:* In general, the different components of a distributed application are communicating intensively. Therefore, efficient communication mechanisms are essential (cf. section 3). In addition, a distributed application exhibits a large degree of coarse-grained parallelism due to asynchronous communication facilities and due to independent operation of its different components. Both features make the analysis of the overall control flow much more difficult than it is in centralized sequential applications. *Dynamic changes:* Due to the relatively large size of current and future distributed applications, independent dynamic modifications of parts of a distributed application are a prerequisite for an adequate flexibility. Typical modifications, for example, are the creation and deletion of application components and of their logical interconnections.

2.2. Mapping of Distributed Applications to Distributed Systems

As obvious, a distributed application has to be mapped to an underlying distributed system. This mapping is performed by allocating the application components to the underlying physical nodes. An example of interconnected application components mapped to the nodes of a local area network is shown in figure 1.

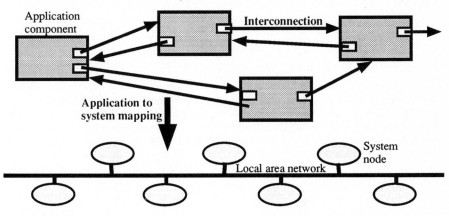

Figure 1: Distributed application mapped to an underlying distributed system

The mapping task can be explained and classified in closer detail by the following criteria:

Elements of allocation: The kind and grain of the allocated elements can vary in different approaches. Examples are the mapping of operating system processes to physical nodes in more conventional approaches like *Conic* [18] or the mapping of application objects to logical nodes in current distributed object-oriented approaches like *Emerald* [5]. Logical nodes are represented by operating system processes, in general.

Allocation technique: The allocation can either be performed *explicitly* or *implicitly*. In the first case, an application component and the system node it should be allocated to are named explicitly. In the second case, the allocation is performed by the system via a specific policy based on additional semantic information, e.g. concerning resource requirements [28].

Allocation control: In the case of implicit allocation, the semantic information used to control the allocation can be further classified into different categories. Each category consists of *system information*, i.e. facts about the underlying system characteristics, and *application conditions*, i.e. conditions to be satisfied by an appropriate application structure and allocation.

Resources: This category describes resource requirements of application components. These requirements have to be mapped to the actual resources provided by underlying system nodes which are used for allocation.

Dependability: This category is concerned with specific issues resulting from dependability requirements. Examples are the replication of application components or the allocation to a specific class of dependable nodes.

Collocation: This category describes the common allocation of different application components to an arbitrary node, e.g. to reduce remote communication.

Structure: This category is used to specify special requirements concerning application structure, e.g. the declaration of mandatory interobject references.

Explicit restrictions: With explicit placement restrictions, special charateristics of heterogeneous distributed systems can be expressed [28]. In such a case, the allocation of system-dependent components must be restricted to specific nodes satisfying their system requirements. By introducing additional explicit *allocation preferences* (i.e. optional hints leading allocation decisions instead of direct naming of one single node), the difference between explicit and implicit allocation becomes seamless.

Allocation time: The allocation can either only be performed at application startup time based on a-priori allocation information (*static allocation*) or can also be changed dynamically during application execution (*dynamic allocation*) [22]. By dynamic allocation facilities, reactions on changing environment conditions are enabled; this way, specific requirements, e.g. concerning dependability in the case of system failures can be satisfied.

Allocation independency: In the case of dynamic allocation, the degree of allocation independency is given by the feasibiliy of allocation changes without respect to component interconnections and communication. If a specific component interconnection implies the allocation of the related components onto a common node, no allocation independency is given [18] at all.

2.3. Basic Requirements Concerning Distributed Application Support

From the above discussion, a number of basic requirements concerning distributed application support can be derived:

Communication support: The intensive communication between the components of a distributed application should be supported by efficient and easy-to-use communication mechanisms.

Structure support: Adequate structuring mechanisms should be available in order to manage the complexity of a distributed application. Important requirements are hierarchical abstraction facilities, typing of components, and typing and explicit specification and management of component interconnections.

Allocation support: An explicit specification of the allocation of application components to system nodes should be possible. Where appropriate, this should be extended by implicit allocation facilities based on application-dependent information and associated conditions.

Change support: Dynamic changes of the structure and of the allocation of application components should be enabled. This is especially important for very large distributed applications and systems of the near future.

Flexible degree of distribution transparency: To facilitate application development, a high degree of distribution transparency concerning allocation and communication is desirable. However, to increase the efficiency of an application or to take specific informal, application-dependent requirements into consideration, distribution transparency should be reducible, e.g. by the provision of explicit allocation facilities as mentioned above.

Computer-aided development and tool support: Distributed application development should be computer-assisted even in its early phases. During detailed design, all information which is related to distribution aspects should be represented explicitly rather than be hidden in implementation code. This way, the use of distributed application development tools, e.g. of animation or distributed debugging tools [23] is enabled.

2.4. Model, Language and Tool Support

The basic requirements discussed above can best be satisfied by an integrated *model, language* and *tool* approach. Specific requirements concerning such an approach are described by presenting a basic structure of these three areas.

2.4.1. Models

Basic models important for distributed applications can be divided into structural ones (application and system model) and computational ones (basic model of computation and model of communication):

Structural models:
The structural *application model* comprises the various kinds of application components and their interconnections. Important representants are the process-oriented model with typed operating system process modules [18] and the object-oriented model with typed configured objects (i.e. encapsulations of data and operations) as basic elements of an application [5,28]. The structural *system model* comprises the kinds of system components, i.e. logical and/or physical nodes and node types (cf. section 2.2). In addition, the basic system communication facilities are part of it. An appropriate basic communication facility is port-based message passing with messages of arbitrary and unlimited length [11].

Computational models:
The *basic model of computation* is representing the distribution-independent parts of the basic computation of an application. Basic facilities are procedures and functions and their invocations or object-oriented computation mechanisms [32]. In addition, concurrency support by lightweight processes is part of this model. The *model of communication* comprises the mechanisms for communication between application components offered to the application developer. Examples are direct message passing between operating system processes like in the *V System* [9], port-based message passing like in *CHORUS* [4], remote procedure call [6] and distributed object-oriented invocation like in *Emerald* or *Distributed Smalltalk* [5,3].
Full distribution transparency is achieved by a fully-integrated model of computation and communication. For this reason, we are focussing on the object-oriented model of computation and communication (cf. section 3) and are augmenting it by an associated structural model based on an distributed configuration management approach (cf. section 4).

2.4.2. Languages

The models discussed above should be reflected by two major languages:

Configuration language: This language is used to describe structural and coarse-grained allocation aspects [18]. That is, its task is to handle distributed programming-in-the-large. It can be divided into an *initial configuration notation* to specify the initial structure of an application and a *dynamic change notation* to specify dynamic changes of the application structure if supported. To improve understandability and traceability, both notations should be declarative rather than procedural. This is possible due to the purely structural rather than computational elements they are specifying.
Distributed programming language: A distributed programming language is used to specify the computation and the communication aspects [25]. The communication facilities can

either be integrated into the language as separate language elements or be provided as an attached library. The first solution enables improved compile-time checks of semantic restrictions concerning communication and should therefore be preferred.

Specific, model-dependent problems like mobility of application components in distributed object-oriented approaches can be handled by both of these languages depending on the grain of the components. In general, all coarse-grained problems requiring explicit control by management components at runtime should be treated by the configuration language. Although both languages should be separated conceptually for improved clarity, they should be integrated internally to prevent redundancy of information. This can be achieved by an automatic transformation of the elements of the configuration language into related elements of the distributed programming language [28]. Alternatively, both languages can be integrated into a single powerful language [23]. This seems to be the best solution for a new standalone approach but is hardly feasible when using existing configuration and distributed programming languages.

2.4.3. Tools

Based on the languages discussed above, appropriate tool support should be provided. Besides a general classification into tools for application development and tools for application runtime management, a further distinction into different categories can be made [28]:

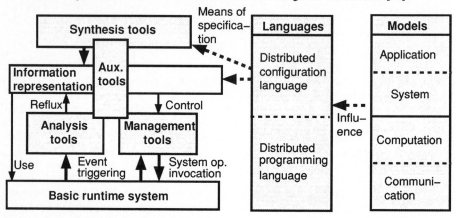

Figure 2: Integration of models, languages and tools for distributed applications

Management tools are using semantic information about the application and are exploiting this to manage structural and computational aspects. Examples are an object mobility control manager (deciding about adequate object migrations in distributed object-oriented systems), an initial configuration manager (creating the initial application structure), or a configuration change manager (performing dynamic structural changes). *Analysis tools* are observing an application and are generating additional semantic information about it. Examples are distributed monitor systems, e.g. to generate communication statistics, distributed debuggers, and animation tools. *Synthesis tools* are used to create and modify an application interactively. Examples are textual or graphical editors (possibly syntax-directed), and compilers and interpreters for the configuration and distributed programming languages. *Auxiliary tools* are used to integrate tools of the other categories and to import foreign tools not oriented towards distribution aspects. Examples are command interface shells and tool interface adaptation facilities.

The integration of models, languages and tools is outlined in fig. 2. The presented models influence basic design decisions concerning the configuration and the distributed programming languages [23]. These languages are the means to specify a distributed application using synthesis tools and auxiliary tools; this specification is translated into an internal representation. Management tools control the application execution which is performed by a basic runtime system. The management actions are based on this information and are realized via system operations. They are triggered by problem-specific application events provided by the runtime system [27]. Similarly, event-triggered analysis tools enable a reflux of evaluated data into the information representation. Examples of integrated tool approaches conforming to the given classification are found in [28] and are also mentioned in section 5.2. In the following sections, existing mechanisms for distributed programming and distributed configuration management are described and classified. Then the architecture and prototype of an integrated support approach for distributed applications using these mechanisms is presented.

3. MECHANISMS FOR DISTRIBUTED PROGRAMMING

3.1. Overview

The major issue of distributed programming approaches is to provide support for remote communication. In addition, basic synchronization primitives are required. From the system point of view, basic existing mechanisms for distributed programming can be divided into *operating system approaches* and *language approaches* [22]. From the technical point of view, they can be divided into *message passing, remote procedure call* and *object-oriented mechanisms*. Each of the three paradigms can both be provided at operating system level as well as at programming language level.

The operating system approach usually does not support type checking of communication interfaces between two partners and does not provide typed messages. This makes the development and maintenance of distributed applications more difficult. Moreover, no sufficient degree of distribution transparency can be provided by the system due to the lack of semantic information about the exchanged data. However, the operating system approach is more flexible concerning system extension and concerning the use of heterogeneous programming languages. The programming language approach provides explicit language elements for distributed programming. Examples are *send / receive* primitives, transparent remote procedure invocations, and transparent remote object invocations. Therefore, application development is facilitated; however, due to the frequent use of one single language, system extensions in heterogeneous environments are more difficult [5]. In the following, however, we are focussing on the language approach due to its higher level of distribution abstraction.

3.2. Message Passing Approach

Message-oriented communication facilities are based on primitives to exchange messages (ideally of unlimited length) between operating system processes [18]. Specific characteristics and options of this paradigm are described below in relation to [25,11]:

Direct / indirect communication: Direct message communication is based on an explicit naming of communication partners (i.e. processes) while indirect communication is based on intermediate ports serving as message queues. The major advantages of indirect communication are the ability for n:m addressing and the ease of change of logical interconnections. In addition, fault-tolerance can be achieved by a client/server-approach [29] based on indirect communication with two or more servers serving one port.

Return / reply facilities: Basic message passing is unidirectional. Extensions of this simple paradigm enable the direct return of a response from the recipient to the sender. Moreover, extended client/server approaches enable an additional final reply from the client (i.e. the sender) to the server (i.e. the previous recipient). This way, three-way handshake protocols can be implemented easily.

Transfer of remote references: Some extensions of basic message passing mechanisms enable the transfer of references to remote data structures within a message. This way, a client can provide controlled access to its private data to a server without the need to generate a copy.

Data translation: While the transmitted data are transparent to most message passing mechanisms, some extensions support explicit data translation between heterogeneous representations. For that, data descriptions have to be provided, e.g. based on standards like ASN.1 [15]. In language-oriented approaches, data layout descriptions can even be generated by the compiler. These facilities enable open systems communication between heterogeneous computers.

3.3. Remote Procedure Call Approach

The *remote procedure call (RPC)* in its basic form is defined as the synchronous transfer of control and data between different parts of an application program partitioned into disjoint address spaces [6]. It consists of two major phases, the binding of an invoking client to an invoked server, and the invocation itself including encoding, transfer, decoding and execution of an invocation as well as the encoding, transfer and decoding of the results of the invoked operation [6]. In general, RPC facilities are integrated into a procedural programming language. Message passing facilities can also be extended to RPC mechanisms by introducing additional stub generators [17]. Important aspects and extensions of the RPC paradigm are summarized below:

Binding: The binding of an invoking client to an invoked RPC server can be done statically at client startup time or dynamically before each remote invocation. In general, a name server is addressed by a client to retrieve the server's address via a logical name matching. Dynamic binding facilitates reconfigurations because anonymous clients recognize changes in the server configuration automatically this way. In addition, alternative servers can be addressed in case of overload or failure situations. However, there is a significant additional runtime overhead associated with it.

Bulk-data support: New RPC extensions enable an integrated efficient transmission of bulk data. This facility requires a throughput-oriented optimization while RPC mechanisms are usually optimized towards short response times. A system example based on remote pipes integrated with remote procedures to transfer bulk data is described in [13].

Asynchronous invocations: To enable additional computations during a remote invocation at the invoker's site, RPCs can be done asynchronously, i.e. in a non-blocking way. The results can later be retrieved via special variables; their values are undefined before the call returns. An example is the promises approach [21] developed at MIT.

Heterogeneity of implementations: In general, the coupling of different RPC implementations is difficult. It can be facilitated, however, by modularized implementations of stub generators, communication managers, and lightweight thread managers as described in [2]. This way, heterogeneous RPC protocols can interact.

Transport protocol support: To increase the efficiency of an RPC mechanism, special transport protocol facilities can be exploited [19]. Stream-oriented bulk data are best supported by connection-oriented protocols while connectionless protocols optimize for short response times. For integrated RPC and bulk data transfer mechanisms, a mixed protocol approach is most suitable.

3.4. Distributed Object-Oriented Approaches

Distributed object-oriented approaches are based on the well-known object-oriented model of computation [32]. They extend this model towards distributed systems in an almost transparent way; a uniform model of computation and communication is achieved. The basic primitive is the location independent *method invocation*, i.e. the invocation of an operation of an object without any syntactic or semantic difference whether the invoked object is local or remote to the invoking object [5]. This location independency is achieved by special object addressing mechanisms enabling remote object references with standard reference semantics. A second important feature of the distributed object-oriented approach is *object mobility*, i.e. the facility to move an object between different system nodes together with its data and with possibly existing invocation segments. Existing approaches can be classified by the following criteria:

Extension of existing system / new development: Distributed object-oriented systems can be based on extensions of existing object-oriented programming languages or on own distributed object-oriented languages. Examples of the first category are *Distributed Smalltalk* [3,10], *Amber* [8] (based on C++), and *LII,* a new extension of Modula-2+. Examples of new languages are *Emerald* [5] and *COMANDOS* [14]. While systems of the first category enable the reuse of existing applications, systems of the second category allow for improved optimization of their implementation.

Object structure: Basically, an object consists of a typed data structure. However, extensions enable a further structuring into global objects and associated, encapsulated local objects [5]. This way, the local objects which are not invoked remotely can be implemented more efficiently. In addition, an object can include active threads of control implemented by lightweight processes. This way, active elements of a distributed application can be represented adequately.

Object addressing mechanism: In general, object addressing is performed in a decentralized way. To achieve location independence of object addresses, special mechanisms are required when objects migrate. The two major possibilities are *forward addressing* [5] and *proxy mechanisms* [3]. With forward addressing, a migrating object leaves a reference to its new location at its previous location. During forthcoming invocations, the forwarding address is used to locate the object; the reference of the invoker at a third location may then be updated. With a proxy mechanism, all referencing objects are informed immediately about the migration of a referenced object; therefore, the migration overhead of this mechanism is higher, but there is no additional invocation overhead.

Object mobility support: Major goals of mobility are the allocation of communicating objects at a common node, load balancing, facilitated data transmission, and fault recovery [16]. The technical realization of object mobility is described in [16], for example. In general, it can be restricted to objects without current invocations (*restricted mobility*) [3]. Moreover, restrictions can result from fixing of objects at their current location and from placement restrictions in heterogeneous systems [28].

3.5. Comparison of Distributed Programming Approaches

The three major distributed programming approaches presented above can be compared by the following criteria (see also table 1):

Distribution transparency: The message passing approach is based on two separate models of computation and communication and can therefore not achieve distribution transparency. As opposed to that, the remote procedure call and the distributed object-oriented approach provide an integrated model of computation and communication. Therefore, distributed object-oriented systems achieve full distribution transparency (except the specification of object migrations); RPC systems at least provide the same syntax for local and remote invocations but do not achieve the same semantics, e.g. concerning reference parameters [31].

Efficiency: As message passing mechanisms can be built directly on top of an underlying transport mechanism, they can be implemented most efficiently. Even the internal copying of message buffers can be avoided by passing buffer references. Remote procedure call and object-oriented mechanisms are less efficient, in general. Therefore, realtime applications may better use efficient but less comfortable message passing facilities.

Bulk-data support: Bulk data are best transmitted by an efficient message passing mechanism. New RPC developments try to integrate such facilities (cf. section 3.3). However, these systems are currently only at an experimental stage.

Heterogeneity support: All of these mechanisms could provide data translation facilities between heterogeneous computers. Their implementation, however, is facilitated by the object-oriented approach as layout descriptions of object data structures are automatically available.

Commercial availability: While message passing and basic RPC mechanisms are already commercially available, distributed object-oriented systems only exist as experimental prototypes at universities or industrial research labs.

In summary, current distributed application developers should use message passing mechanisms when time constraints or bulk data transmissions are important. For more general applications, RPC facilities seem suitable. In the more distant future, distributed application development can be significantly facilitated by distribution-transparent object-oriented mechanisms.

	Message passing	RPC	Object–oriented
Distribution transparency	−	+	+ +
Efficiency	+ +	o	o
Bulk–data support	+	o	o
Heterogeneity support	o	o	+
Commercial availability	+	+	−

++ = very well supported   + = supported   o = possible   − = no support at all

Table 1: Comparison of distributed programming facilities

Therefore, we have selected the object paradigm as the basic model of computation and communication for our research activities in the distributed systems and applications area.

4. MECHANISMS FOR DISTRIBUTED CONFIGURATION MANAGEMENT

While the mechanisms described above support distributed programming-in-the-small tasks concerning computation and communication, distributed configuration mechanisms are focussing on distributed programming-in-the-large. Their major tasks, i.e. structure support and coarse-grained allocation support were already mentioned in section 2.4.

4.1. Classification of Existing Approaches

Existing approaches can be classified according to the criteria given below. In particular, a comparison of process-oriented and object-oriented approaches can be performed this way.

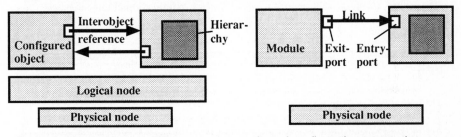

Figure 3: Elements of an object- vs. process-oriented configuration approach

Configuration elements: In process-oriented systems, modules (i.e. operating system processes) of fixed grain are the basic elements of an application configuration [18]. They are allocated to the basic elements of a system configuration, the physical nodes. In object-oriented approaches, configured objects of arbitrary grain are the basic application configuration elements. They are allocated to logical nodes (operating system processes). In both approaches, the basic elements of a configuration can be structured hierarchically (cf. fig. 3).

Communication mechanisms: In process-oriented systems, the modules are communicationg via intermediate exit- and entryports and logical links by exchanging messages. In object-oriented approaches, distribution-transperent interobject references are used as the base for remote method invocations (i.e. invocation of operations offered by an object).

Configuration language: In general, a configuration language can be declarative or operational. A declarative language describes the target configuration directly while an operational language describes the actions how to generate a target configuration. The Conic configuration language [18], for example, is declarative, while the *NETSLA* language of *PRONET* [20] is operational. A declarative language is easier to understand and to use but more difficult to implement.

Management of configuration data: The data about a current configuration can be managed by a central server; this, however, may lead to efficiency and availability problems. Alternatively, this server can be decentralized or the configuration elements can manage other elements which are dependent on them directly. All of these approaches are found in current systems.

Our own work described in section 5 is based on an object-oriented configuration approach to facilitate the integration with the selected object-oriented model of computation and communication.

4.2. Basic Architecture of Full Configuration Management Support

To provide full configuration management support, several specific tools are required (cf. fig. 4). First, the initial configuration notation has to be transformed into an internal representation by a compiler. This representation may be incomplete, e.g. concerning allocation specifications. Therefore, an initial configuration manager using a heuristic algorithm has to resolve implicit allocations and has to update the internal representation.

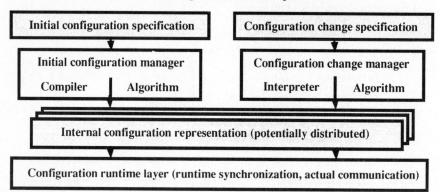

Figure 4: Basic architecture of distributed configuration management support

Then it has to generate and interconnect all system and application elements in the underlying actual distributed system. At this configuration runtime layer, the actual communication between configured elements takes place. Therefore, each element has to be realized by an associated element of the distributed programming approach. The internal representation can itself be distributed to increase the efficiency of read-only accesses and to decentralize the management operations.

At runtime, configuration changes are specified using the change notation and are the interpreted by a configuration change manager. An associated algorithm then performs the changes on the internal representation and at the runtime layer. In addition, a runtime synchronization and consistency check concerning possible conditions the configuration has to obey has to be performed.

5. INTEGRATED SUPPORT: ARCHITECTURE AND PROTOTYPE

To provide fully-integrated support for distributed application development, an architecture of a complete environment has been defined [24]. Its major features comprise a widespectrum (lifecycle-spanning) design language (integrating communication and configuration facilities) and an integrated tool set approach. It is based on the object-oriented paradigm as presented above. The architecture of the environment is shown in fig. 5. It consists of three major layers, the *human interaction layer*, the *functional layer* and the *data layer*. The widespectrum design language is the base to develop a distributed application. A design with this language is generated using synthesis tools of the human interaction layer (e.g. graphical editors). It is then transformed into the data layer representation by language manipulation tools residing at the functional layer. A target runtime system also present at this layer is executing an application at the different stages of design. In addition, a number of workbenches (tool sets) are plugged into the design language representation. Each of them is offering a consistent set of tools to handle a specific problem related to distribution (see section 5.2).

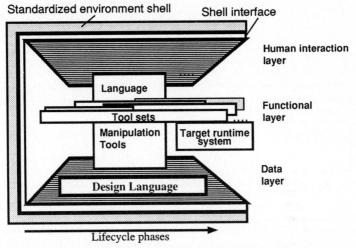

Figure 5: Architecture of the distributed application support environment

The different lifecycle phases are not treated sequentially according to the traditional waterfall lifecycle model but are reflected by a seamless design transformation with arbitrary revision and reflux steps. To support design data management (e.g. persistent storage and versioning), a standardized environment shell (according to current PCTE standardization efforts [12]) is imported via a shell interface. The design language consists of a declarative part describing structural configuration aspects and a procedural part describing computation. It is based on a toplevel object class hierarchy offering generic classes relevant for distributed applications. The three major categories are *configured objects, generated objects* and *relation objects*. Configured objects are separately managed by configuration support mechanisms (cf. section 4) while generated objects are managed by the runtime system only. The language elements associated with these kinds of objects represent a configuration notation and a distributed programming notation, respectively. The relation objects represent semantic relations explicitly. The design language approach achieves two major goals: the explicit representation of semantics and the integration of computation and configuration. The central mechanisms conform to the description given in section 3 and 4, respectively. Different tools of the environment can be integrated into *tool sets* [28] (cf. section 2.4.3). A tool set is oriented towards a *common goal*, uses a *common internal data representation* and should provide a *common look and feel* at its human computer interface [23]. Each tool set is plugged into the design language via a specific relation class representing major semantic information used by its tools. Details of the computation and configuration language parts will be described separately.

6. CONCLUSION

The paper has given an overview and a classification of distributed application support mechanisms. Charateristics and basic requirements of distributed applications have been discussed and distributed programming and configuration mechanisms have be summarized and compared. As a result, an architecture based on an integrated model, language and tool ap-

316

proach has been presented. The integration of a widespectrum design language based on an object-oriented model of structure, computation and communication and of a goal-oriented tool set approach provides a sound base for distributed application development support. The architecture is the base of a prototype which is currently under development. This work is performed in the joint project DOCASE of the University of Karlsruhe and Digital Equipment Corporation [23].

From the practical point of view, future work will focus on the implementation of the environment tools. From the conceptual point of view, the different analyses outlined above will be further detailed. In addition, an integration of extended remote procedure call facilities into an object-oriented environment shall be achieved. Important issues, for example, are the treatment of bulk data transfer and n-party interactions.

REFERENCES

[1]   M. Bhattacharyya, D. Cohrs, B. Miller
        A Visual Process Connector for UNIX
        IEEE Software, July 1988, pp. 43-50

[2]   B.N. Bershad, D.T. Ching, E.D. Lazowska, J. Sanislo, M. Schwartz
        A Remote Procedure Call Facility for Interconnecting Heterogeneous Computer Systems
        IEEE Trans. on Software Engineering, Aug. 1987

[3]   J.K. Bennett
        The Design and Implementation of Distributed Smalltalk
        OOPSLA '87 Proceedings, ACM 1987

[4]   J.S. Banino, J.C. Fabre, M. Guillemont, G. Morisset, M. Rozier
        Some Fault-Tolerant Aspects of the CHORUS Distributed System
        5th Int. Conf. on Distr. Comp. Systems, 1985

[5]   A. Black, N. Hutchinson, E. Jul, H. Levy, L. Carter
        Distribution and Abstract Types in Emerald
        IEEE Trans. on Software Engineering, Jan. 1987

[6]   A.D. Birrell, B.J. Nelson
        Implementing Remote Procedure Calls
        ACM Transactions on Computer Systems, Feb. 1984

[7]   T.J. Le Blanc, S.A. Friedberg
        HPC: A Model of Structure and Change in Distributed Systems
        IEEE Trans. on Computers, Vol. c-34, No. 12, Dec. 1985

[8]   J.S. Chase, F.G. Amador, E.D. Lazowska, H.M. Levy, R.J. Littlefield
        The Amber System: Parallel Programming on a Network of Multiprocessors
        Internal Report, University of Washington, Seattle, 1989

[9]   D.R. Cheriton
        The V Kernel: A software base for distributed systems
        IEEE Software, April 1984

[10]   P.L. McCullough
        Transparent Forwarding: First Steps
        OOPSLA '87 Proceedings, ACM 1987

[11]   H. Eberle, K. Geihs, A. Schill, H. Schöner, H. Schmutz
        Generic Support for Distributed Processing in Heterogeneous Networks
        HECTOR Proceedings, Vol. 2, Springer-Verlag, Berlin 1988

[12]   F. Gallo
        The PCTE Initiative: Towards a European Approach to Software Engineering
        Proc. CRAI Workshop on Software Factories & ADA, Capri, 1986, Springer-Verlag, Berlin 1986

[13]   D.K. Gifford, N. Glasser
        Remote Pipes and Procedures for Efficient Distributed Communication
        ACM Trans. on Computer Systems, Vol. 6, No. 3, Aug. 1988

[14]   C. Horn
        An Object Oriented Model for Distributed Processing
        Workshop on Research into Networks and Distributed Applications, Wien 1988, North Holland, 1988

[15]   Information Processing Systems - Open Systems Interconnection
         Specification of Basic Encoding Rules for Abstract Syntax Notation One (ASN.1)
         ISO/DIS 8825, ISO 1985

[16]   E. Jul, H. Levy, N. Hutchinson, A. Black
         Fine-Grained Mobility in the Emerald System
         ACM Transactions on Computer Systems, Vol. 6, No. 1, Feb. 1988

[17]   M.B. Jones, R.F. Rashid
         Mach and Matchmaker: Kernel and Language Support for Object-Oriented Distributed Systems
         OOPSLA '86 Proceedings, ACM 1987

[18]   J. Kramer, J. Magee
         Dynamic Configuration for Distributed Systems
         IEEE Trans. on Software Engineering, SE-11 (4), April 1985

[19]   B. Liskov, T. Bloom, D. Gifford, R. Scheifler, W. Weihl
         Communication in the Mercury System
         Programming Methodology Group Memo 59-1, MIT, Laboratory for Computer Science, Cambridge, MA 02139

[20]   R.J. LeBlanc, A.B. Maccabe
         The Design of a Programming Language Based on Connectivity Networks
         Proc. IEEE 3rd Intl. Conf. on Distributed Computing Systems, Ft.. Lauderdale, Florida, Oct. 1982

[21]   B. Liskov, L. Shrira
         Promises: Linguistic Support for Efficient Asynchronous Procedure Calls in Distributed Systems
         ACM Sigplan '88 Conference on Programming Language Design and Implementation, June 1988

[22]   J. Magee, J. Kramer, M. Sloman
         Constructing Distributed Systems in Conic
         IEEE Trans. on Software Engineering, Vol. 15, No. 6, June 1989

[23]   M. Mühlhäuser, A. Schill, L. Heuser
         Project DOCASE: Software Engineering for Distributed Applications: An Object-Oriented Approach
         Int. Workshop "Software Engineering and its Applications", Toulouse, 1988

[24]   M. Mühlhäuser, A. Schill, J. Kienhöfer, H. Frank, L. Heuser
         A Software Engineering Environment for Distributed Applications
         Euromicro, Köln 1989

[25]   M. Mühlhäuser
         Software Engineering for Distributed Applications: The DESIGN Project
         Proc. IEEE 10th Intl. Conference on Software Engineering, Singapore, April 1988

[26]   G.J. Popek, G. Walker
         The LOCUS Distributed System Architecture
         The MIT Press, Cambridge/MA, 1985

[27]   A. Schill
         Mobility Control in Distributed Object-Oriented Applications
         IEEE Int. Phoenix Conf. on Computers and Communications, Scottsdale, Arizona, March 1989

[28]   A. Schill
         Objects and Distribution: Advantages, Problems and Solutions
         Int. TOOLS Conf., Paris, Nov. 1989

[29]   L. Svobodova
         Client/Server Model of Distributed Processing
         Kommunikation in verteilten Systemen, Karlsruhe 1985, Springer-Verlag, Berlin 1985

[30]   A.S. Tanenbaum, S.J. Mullender
         Design of a Capability-Based Distributed Operating System
         IR-88, Vrije Universiteit, Amsterdam, 1984

[31]   A.S. Tanenbaum, R. van Renesse
         A Critique of the Remote Procedure Call Paradigm
         Workshop on Research into Networks and Distributed Applications, Wien, April 1988, North Holland 1988

[32]   P. Wegner
         Dimensions of Object-Based Language Design
         OOPSLA '87 Proceedings, ACM 1987

Information Network and Data Communication, III
D. Khakhar and F. Eliassen (Editors)
Elsevier Science Publishers B.V. (North-Holland)
© IFIP, 1990

AFTER OSI - STANDARDIZATION OF OPEN DISTRIBUTED PROCESSING

Peter F. Linington

Computing Laboratory
University of Kent
Canterbury, UK

The definition of the OSI Reference Model has lead to the creation of a broad family
of standards for the different aspects of system interconnection. However, there are
many problem areas which require more than just the consideration of the
interconnection of communicating systems. There is a need for standardization to
support the coordinated use of distributed resources in many different locations and
the description of aspects of system structure other than external communication.

This has lead to the initiation within ISO of a project to agree a new reference model
of Open Distributed Processing (ODP), which is building upon the success of the
OSI work to create a framework to support the newer requirements. Study has also
begun on the needs for standards to support Interfaces for Application Portability,
which would satisfy one of the ODP requirements.

This paper describes the requirements for extensions to the scope of OSI, and the
progress that has been made so far in agreeing a model for ODP. It then outlines the
expected direction for the work in the future. Finally, it draws on current multimedia research at the University of Kent to indicate the kinds of system which such
an extended architecture makes possible.

1. THE OSI PROGRAMME

1.1. The objective of OSI

As everyone now knows, OSI stands for Open Systems Interconnection, and the word
interconnection signifies at once both the strength and the limitations of the OSI approach. OSI
was originally conceived as a programme of standardization with the objective of allowing the
interconnection of computer equipment from many different suppliers. The benefit for users was
ease of communication between the various types of equipment; this would simplify the
operation of multi-sourced systems and thus allow procurement from the full range of suppliers,
avoiding the danger to the user of being locked into one technology.

The computer supply industry accepted this objective, because it recognized the commercial
advantages of more open competition. However, the industry pressed very hard for the exclusion
of any aspect of internal interfacing or system structure from the scope of the standardization.
This is why the OSI standards do not express internal interfaces to the communications

320

subsystem, and do not require conformance to the abstract services provided by a protocol. To do so would limit the freedom of the system designer who might not even wish to make a particular service available as an interface at all, let alone provide it in a standard form.

Strictly speaking then, the only way OSI standards can be applied is to constrain the way a sequence of bits is sent over a communication line joining the two interconnected systems. This limitation was necessary to ease the adoption of OSI standards because it gaves so much more freedom to implementors to fit within existing structures. However, the system is still a monolith; the user must buy a complete system from one supplier, who determines its internal structure.

One effect of this limitation of scope is that the OSI Reference Model, which provides the framework relating the various pieces of OSI standardization, concentrates on the interconnection of two systems. From the viewpoint of the interconnecting medium, the two systems are seen as two halves of the world, filling the horizon and obscuring the view of anything within or beyond themselves. In this model of the world, it is not even possible to make statements about system structure; any structure which leads to the same pattern of communication will do. The distribution of the system which provides a service is not even on the agenda.

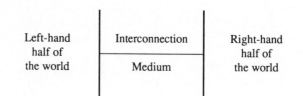

1.2. The limitations of OSI

One consequence of the interconnection-centred view outlined above is that it is difficult to describe the standardized operation of a number of components. Descriptions of this type are needed whenever one system acts as an agent for others, or when the coordinated action of a number of systems must be performed according to a fixed set of rules in order to achieve some purpose.

There are many examples of such requirements, and they tend to be the areas in which clear standards have proved to be most difficult to write. Examples can be seen in message transfer systems, network management, naming and addressing, commitment, concurrency and transaction processing. In each case, the difficulty arises in part from the lack of a clearly agreed architecture for identifying the components of a system and expressing their configuration and the rules which coordinate their interaction.

One example will serve to illustrate the point. The Presentation Layer of the OSI Reference Model was designed to provide any necessary management of data formats and encodings. The service it provides is for the communication of the values of abstract datatypes. The application entities which use it must agree on the set of abstract datatypes the channel between them must support but should be completely unaware of the implementations of these datatypes chosen by the presentation layer. This is a very powerful service for the transfer of information in a way that will lead to its correct interpretation.

Howeer, when we consider the use of such a service in, for example, a message handling application, we need to examine the interrelation of the separate views of communication

a) shared by the originating user agent and its nearest message transfer agent;

b) shared by two cooperating message transfer agents;

c) shared by the recipient user agent and its nearest message transfer agent.

These views may differ. The way they are coordinated will result in different error behaviour when some datatypes are not universally understood. When does the originator receive error notification and from whom? How are rules for service extensibility to be expressed? These are difficult questions to answer from the interconnection viewpoint.

At the same time that such limitations of interconnection-based standardization have become apparent, there has been growing interest in the standardization of much more tightly coupled distributed systems, based on the intimated linking of smaller, more specialized system components.

2. THE ODP PROGRAMME

2.1. Why is ODP needed?

It is not possible to build distributed systems from components produced by a variety of suppliers without publicly agreed standards. The growth of interest in distributed systems arises from technological developments in a number of fields of communication and computing, leading to a much greater overlap between the techniques used to support quite different types of application. The same mechanisms are being applied in administrative, business, scientific and domestic systems with a vast range of objectives.

Increased use of digital techniques is thus leading to integration of services and common solutions to the management of many different kinds of information. Similar methods are now being applied to the transmission and storage of information varying from scientific data to Hi-Fi sound. It is the common core of distributed processing technology which spans all these fields that is the concern of ODP.

To handle the transformation of all kinds of information into digital form and to manage its storage, distribution and manipulation, the skills of the computer scientist and the communications engineer must be brought together to solve problems of software, hardware and systems engineering. The ODP Reference Model provides a framework for the management of this process.

2.2. What is ODP?

The objective of the Reference Model of Open Distributed Processing is to provide a framework for the standardization of distributed systems. This will cover both new areas of standardization and the incorporation and rationalization of a number of existing but disjoint areas of work. As such, it is continuing the process begun several years ago when the ISO committees were reorganized to bring together related strands of Information Technology work.

The target is to provide an architecture within which the functioning of distributed systems can be expressed, covering both the individual components and the overall system design of which they form a part. The work on ODP brings together experts from the fields of OSI protocols, Management, Databases and Graphics to form a team with very wide experience of a range of IT activities.

2.3. Where can the standards be applied?

The creation of specifications for Open Systems Interconnection allows systems to be connected together, with confidence that they will be able to interwork at the point of connection. However, these specifications deliberately avoid constraints on the internal structure of the systems, so as to allow the maximum of freedom to implementors. It is therefore only possible to demand conformance to OSI at the point of connection between systems.

In considering distributed systems, where a logical structure of connected components is built up to achieve the application objectives and then distributed over the available set of physical systems, this restriction to interconnection becomes unacceptable. Constraints need to be placed on all the elements of the system, so that components within a system can be specified and related with the same confidence that OSI gives in communication between systems.

To this end, the ODP Reference Model identifies several types of interface at which standardization may be required. These are

a) programmatic interfaces allowing access to a defined function; an example might be the standardization of database languages;

b) man/machine interfaces, as for example in some graphics standards;

c) interconnection standards, like the familiar OSI standards for communication between systems;

d) external physical storage media specifications, to allow information exchange between systems.

For the first time, the ODP Architecture will allow the general expression of requirements for consistency between the human interface, the programming interface which supports the application and the OSI protocols which convey information between systems. Specific models in areas such as graphics cover some aspects of this interrelationship, but use of a general architecture will greatly facilitate the combination of standards from a number of different areas.

3. FUNCTIONAL DECOMPOSITION

3.1. Identifying aspects

In creating a distributed system, use is made of a range of general functions or aspects which are each needed by a wide range of applications. They are concerned with such things as naming, authentication, security and management. The new Reference Model provides hooks for the incorporation of common mechanisms for handling these functions, allowing implementors to integrate components with a minimum of additional specification.

The formalization of these linkages makes the maintenance of the various components easier by avoiding the need for parallel updating of the different standards. In effect, it extends the advantages of a layered architecture already exploited for communication to the more complex non-layered situations found in distributed processing.

3.2. Structuring Distributed Systems

The specification of distributed systems requires well structured descriptive tools which allow the various information resources involved to be separated clearly, and unpredictable side effects of interaction to be avoided. This has lead to the identification of a series of fundamental transparencies, each representing a system property which may or may not be preserved in a particular distribution mechanism.

Examples are transparency of location, transparency of replication and transparency of component failure, but there are many more. Analysis of the necessary transparencies indicates the form of distribution applicable to the task to be performed, and so aid the design process.

Once the objectives have been established, the distributed mechanisms for achieving them can be analysed in terms of the interactions between components which will be involved. Current thinking is concentrated on the decomposition of systems into interactions at a series of interfaces (providing, for example, client/server interactions) and on the use of an object oriented model of information processing to allow the separate statement of the required properties of each information resource.

4. SEPARATION OF CONCERNS

4.1. Taking a view of the system

Rather than attempt to deal with the full complexity of a distributed system, we consider the system from different viewpoints, each of which is chosen to reflect one set of design concerns. Each viewpoint represents a different abstraction of the original distributed system, without the need to create one large model describing it.

It then becomes necessary to consider the framework which organizes these viewpoints. This framework allows verification of both the completeness of the various descriptions and the consistency between them. Depending on the level of detail, the resulting description will also allow the operational characteristics of the described system to be studied.

Informally therefore, a viewpoint leads to a representation of the system with emphasis on a specific concern. More formally, the resulting representation is an abstraction of the system, that is, a description which recognizes some distinctions (those relevant to the concern) and ignores others (those not relevant to the concern).

4.2. Five viewpoints

The current work on ODP recognizes five viewpoints. These are as follows:

a) the enterprise viewpoint, which is concerned with business policies, management policies and human user roles with respect to the systems and the environment with which they interact;

b) the information viewpoint, which is concerned with information modelling, covering information sources and sinks and the information flows between them;

c) the computational viewpoint, which is concerned with the algorithms and data structures which provide the distributed system function;

d) the engineering viewpoint, which is concerned with the distribution mechanisms and the provision of the various transparencies needed to support distribution;

e) the technology viewpoint, which is concerned with the detail of the components and links from which the distributed system is constructed.

5. THE FORM OF THE ODP REFERENCE MODEL

The Basic Reference model of Open Distributed Processing will be based on precise concepts and, as far as possible, on the use of formal description techniques for specification of the architecture. It will contain a range of precise definitions and supporting material of a more tutorial nature. However, these two types of material will be separated into normative and non-normative parts, so as to make it clear what obligations the standard implies. There will also be a division between the descriptive parts which introduce basic concepts and specification techniques, and prescriptive parts which state the design choices which characterize the particular architecture chosen for ODP.

The model will be published in four parts:

a) Part 1: **Overview**: contains a motivational overview of ODP, giving scoping and explanation of key definitions (with no substantial architectural content), and an enumeration of required areas of standardization expressed in terms of the reference points for conformance identified in Part 3. This part is not normative.

b) Part 2: **Descriptive model**: contains the definition of the concepts and analytical framework and notation for normalized description of (arbitrary) distributed processing systems. This is only to a level of detail sufficient to support Part 3 and to establish requirements for new specification techniques. This part is normative.

c) Part 3: **Prescriptive model**: contains the specification of the required characteristics that qualify distributed processing as open. These are the constraints to which ODP standards must conform. It uses the descriptive techniques from Part 2. This part is normative.

d) Part 4: **User model**: contains a description of the resulting ODP environment from the users' point of view. This part contains explanatory material on how ODP is intended to be viewed by system engineers designing distributed applications to be run in the ODP environment described in Part 3. This part is not normative.

6. MANAGEMENT OF THE ODP WORK

The ODP project is complex and must be expected to take a long time. The first working drafts for some parts of the Reference Model are just appearing, and final publication is still some years off. Consequent detailed standardization will go on beyond this, and maintenance work will also be required.

Experience with other large standardization projects, such as OSI itself, has shown that there will be a steady turn-over of personnel during this time, and that in consequence there will be a tendency to revisit technical decisions taken early in the project and duplicate discussions which had been completed but forgotten. This process can waste a great deal of effort if it goes unchecked.

One of the first steps taken by the ODP group was therefore to establish clear procedures for the management and scheduling of its business, and for the recording of all major technical discussions, covering not only the agreements, but also their rationale and the reasons for rejecting technical alternatives. These logs will provide those joining the group later with the necessary background to the work already completed, without cluttering the standards produced with unnecessary rationale.

The ODP project has, so far, been concentrated on a number of technical topics which were aimed at exploring the major features of the problem and of the techniques for structuring and expressing an architecture for distribution. This phase of the work has progressed well, and the last major ODP meeting began the creation of the ODP Reference Model itself.

7. THE NEXT STEPS

The first working draft to be produced is for part 2 of the model, which deals with the definition of descriptive concepts and introduces specification techniques.

The current text introduces the basic concepts behind any distributed system and them builds upon them progressively more complex architectural concepts related to system structure, evolution and management. An increasing amount of liaison activity is taking place to align this work with the requirements of the existing OSI projects and with work in a parallel activity on a framework for distributed applications (DAF) in CCITT.

Refinement of this text will continue as the draft progresses, but the next major milestone for ODP is the creation of a first draft for the prescriptive part of the model, which will set the style for the eventual systems produced on the basis of ODP standards.

8. DISTRIBUTED SYSTEMS BASED ON ODP

8.1. Multi-media systems

It is clear that future information systems will be expected to handle a wide variety of media, ranging from traditional data through voice and fixed images to high resolution TV. Local area networks operating at Gigabit rates already exist in the laboratory and their exploitation is within sight, so that incorporation of high bandwidth media into an integrated network will soon become technically feasible. These developments will enable new kinds of system which will stretch the evolving ODP architecture to its limits. The author's research group at the University of Kent is exploring the construction of prototype systems in order to validate the architecture.

The final section of this paper reviews some of the areas in which multimedia operation raise particular problems. However, the real test of both the requirements and the quality of the solutions to them is trial implementation and use, and work to do so is currently in progress.

8.2. Objects and interfaces

At a sufficiently abstract level, the interactions in a distributed multimedia system can be described as interactions at the interfaces between distinct abstract objects. Thus the description of a data retrieval application is in terms of an interface between a user and the storage system. Each of these can be considered as a separate object with a specific behaviour.

When a particular realization of this abstract description is considered, it becomes necessary to model explicitly the various components via which the user interacts with the data, describing separately video, audio and data channels and the various display component used to provide them. This will, in general, involve the introduction of additional objects and additional interfaces, leading to a specification in which the original user and storage objects are transformed into a user and a storage provider for those specific forms of information flow.

Similar considerations apply to the introduction of explicit communication in place of the various forms of distribution transparency, leading to the inclusion of communication objects and interfaces to them, the natures of which are determined by the properties of the communication mechanisms available.

8.3. Transformations

There are four basic forms of transformation to the system description. These are transformations of the system description at a single point in time, not to be confused with the evolution of a system over time.

a) replacing an interface specification with a compatible one, so as to introduce additional constraints or details of the operations to be performed. For example, it is possible to replace a requirement for a video display by a specific mechanism associated with a video window.

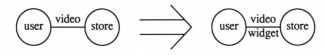

b) dividing an interface into two parts which together meet the original specification. For example, it is possible to replace the specification of a television channel by parallel but separate video and audio channels. Note that, in general, this will include the specification of some additional coordination rules on the two parts, such as constraints that they start and stop together.

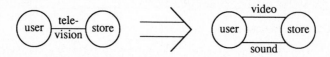

c) replacing an interface with an object offering two compatible, but possibly different interfaces to two users derived from the two users of the original interface. For example, an unspecific interaction may be replaced by the use of a specific network, which provides to the systems linked two geographically separate interfaces, each having some (possibly different) network control functions associated with it.

d) replacing an object by partitioning its function, yielding a specification in which two objects are linked by a new interface, and each existing interface to the previous object is allocated to one or other of the new objects. For example, the division of a computing resource as seen by the user into separate workstation and fileserver.

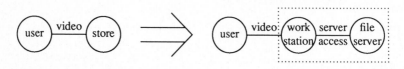

8.4. Configuration

In practice, specifications rarely progress from a single object by repeated refinement. Instead, the designer creates some more complex configuration of objects and interfaces directly, and so tools for the specification of such configurations are needed.

When we turn to the creation of an instance from the specification, there is also a need to specify incremental changes to the configuration, and most configurations are constructed from some more or less simple starting point in a series of steps.

Indeed, at its simplest, the construction process is based on the selection of details of individual interfaces. Complex configurations are established by adding interfaces with stated properties in such an order as to create the configuration desired. If the objects needed are connected in an arbitrary graph, this process requires ingenuity and there may be a need for a specific synchronization step to prevent incorrect operation while the configuration is being built up.

The types of configuration likely to be needed when supporting multi-media activities are complex. For example, the video display interface will be supported by a series consisting of a source object, a video connection object, a video server object to control the screen format, another network object and display object (widget). All these are also interfaced to some control object or objects. This configuration could be set up by a suitable series of separate trading exchanges, but it would probably be much more convenient to request the configuration by name, relying on the infrastructure to create it as a whole and deliver it in a working condition, ready for business.

The consequence of this is that there is a need for a suitable configuration description language. This could be relational in style, specifying a set of tuples each identifying two objects and an interface type. Iterators and arrays would be necessary to provide for the simple declaration of, for example, rings of connected objects. Structured composition would be at least convenient, and probably essential. There would be a need to distinguish in expressing, in either the configuration or the instantiation process, which component objects are to be bound to pre-existing resources, like stores, and which should be dynamically created. There is also the problem of infrastructure operations for mending broken configurations; for example, there may be a need to replace failed objects within an existing configuration.

8.5. Temporal description

One of the characteristics of multimedia applications is their direct modelling of temporal structures. Stored video and audio have an essential time component, and many user interface operations (such as slow speed or reverse play) manipulate the mapping of model time to real time. Even when there is not a regular timebase, there is often some concept of sequence. Even scrollable text has an element of sequence in its local interpretation. The relation of the time lines of the different media require various forms of synchronization.

In categorizing media, it will be important to start with the distinction between real time media (which only have a continuously changing current state) and stored media which have a known temporal structure.

8.6. Synchronization - media specific

The most basic form of synchronization is that which is specific to the media format, such as line or frame synch for video and sample sequence for audio. The systems being developed will generally have sufficient storage at the lowest level for us to regard these problems as essentially point-to-point. Thus, while they pose some interesting engineering challenges, they do not pose additional structural constraints to the writer of applications.

8.7. Synchronization - continuous

When two media are stored, processed or displayed together, their time lines need to be coordinated. This involves establishing common starting conditions and maintaining progress of the two times in step.

There may be separate monitoring objects which signal timing errors to the controllers of the various media, or there may be synchronization of each with respect to a single reference clock.

There is a problem if there is a mixture of storage technologies which do not allow for timing corrections. The application (or worse, the user!) may then have to allow for the possibility of progressive skew.

In addition to time line synchronization, there is a need for time extraction to relate the current display state to a supporting script (relating to interpretation of the medium content).

In addition to the synchronization problems on output, there is a related problem of recording relative timing of structured input.

8.8. Synchronization - points

Significant points during display need to be tagged so that signals can be triggered when they are reached. Examples of this are the changes of image during a tape/slide style presentation, or text comments at points in a video sequence. There may also be a need to start one medium at a defined point during the display of another - or to cut smoothly from the end of one sequence to the start of the next without visible starting delay.

Given that some media have a significant latency in positioning to the start of a sequence, it may be necessary to provide an earlier cue messages indicating when the sequence is going to be needed.

If facilities for starting display at an arbitrary point are supported, there may be a need to do so in the context of a specific checkpoint structure giving the prerequisites for display at that time. This may involve the replay of some events from previous times to provide the necessary background.

9. CONCLUSIONS

This paper has outlined some of the problems which arise if standardization for distributed systems is based on interconnection. It has introduced the way the work on ODP is responding to the requirements by going beyond interconnection, and finally it has tried to give the reader a glimpse of the the kind of new systems that could result from such an architecture.

The work on the ODP Reference Model is still in progress, and will continue for some years to come. However, it seems likely that ODP will have at least as large an impact on system design in the 1990s as OSI had in the 1980s.

Information Network and Data Communication, III
D. Khakhar and F. Eliassen (Editors)
Elsevier Science Publishers B.V. (North-Holland)
© IFIP, 1990

AN INTRAORGANIZATIONAL INTEGRATED NETWORK SYSTEM*

Larry RAILING and Thomas J. HOUSEL
TRW Corporation and
Center for Operations Management and Research Education
University of Southern California
Los Angeles, CA

Overview

TRW's Space and Defense Sector's top management faced a challenge in the
early 1980s: reduce spiraling communication costs and posture itself to
meet the objective of maintaining profitable growth in a highly
competitive marketplace. Increasing telecommunications costs were
perceived as a potential threat to management's goal to make the company
more effective. The need for faster response capabilities was the result
of the turbulent market conditions that characterized the shortening
cycle of the high technology marketplace [1].

The strategy to invest capital assets in a new network infrastructure
was focused to contain communications costs while providing the
flexibility necessary for fast response. Large information intensive
companies, such as TRW, must achieve fast response capabilities, while
reducing overhead, to stay competitive. The flexibility of an
integrated digital network allows the company to quickly reconfigure to
meet the demands of shorter product life cycles.

The Data Services and Telecommunications departments completed the
integrated voice, data, and image digital network on schedule and 10%
under budget after two and one half years of planning and two years of
installation. Creating the new network for TRW's Space Park complex,
consisting of 55 buildings with over 20,000 employees, was no small task
given that it was slated to cost over $50 million and involved the
installation of a

- 30,000 line digital private branch exchange (PBX),

- 25,000 integrated voice and data digital lines,

- security video services,

- 200 communications rooms,

- a campus area backbone network (CABN) containing:

    1. a common, campus-wide, intrabuilding Space Park
        local area network (SPLAN) with the potential for
        30,000 drops
    2. 38,600 feet of coaxial cable for the SPLAN,

*A different version of this paper is under consideration to MIS
Quarterly.

3.   over 700 miles of fiber optic cable, and
4.   10,000 miles of twisted pair wire.

The planning, procurement, and implementation processes described in
this paper will demonstrate how program management techniques can help a
company negotiate the best price for a network that will contain costs
and enable fast response.

1.   TRW BACKGROUND

TRW is a multinational corporation comprised of three business segments
one of which is the Space and Defense Sector. Each of the business
segments operates relatively autonomously within the corporation,
except for financial reporting and overall corporate strategy.

The Space and Defense Sector is driven by its product groups which
contain operating divisions. Project units within these operating
divisions provide revenue, and are also given a great deal of autonomy
because they are major contributors to profit centers. Project teams
are usually housed in a common location and vary in size from 5 to over
400 members. The heavy scientific, engineering, and business
requirements of the Space and Defense Sector's high tech employees makes
easy and quick access to information critical to its mission.

Space and Defense had an average 60% annual move or churn factor. The
approximate aggregate cost of the 60% annual churn factor was $5 to $10
million in hard dollars with an average of $500 for every voice and data
line which had to be moved, added, or changed. The cost in soft dollar
productivity loss, while considerable, was far more difficult to
quantify objectively but probably represented an equal or greater cost.

The network changes to the existing system had to be made manually, with
significant disruptions in the office environments often occurring when
complex line changes were made. As a consequence, this system for
reconfiguring the network was ineffective with poor response time.

Often when a team was assembled for a new project, they would not use
the abandoned network cabling which had supported the computing system
for the prior project. Eventually all of the available network conduit
space became clogged with cables, for which there were no records.
Further time was wasted because the local telephone companies (GTE and
Pacific Bell) moved, added, or changed lines on a time schedule that
suited their priority scheme, not TRW's.

Company Growth

The Space and Defense Sector grew from one billion to three billion in
revenues during the period from 1979 to 1988. This explosive, threefold
growth resulted in an increased demand for more information services.
Within the same time frame, AT&T divested, the telecommunications
industry became more deregulated, and there was an exponential growth in
desk top information technology.

Providing Network Services

The task of providing network services was made even more complex because of the multitude of isolated heterogeneous data processing systems in use. The Sector had IBM, DEC, Prime, Sun, Apollo, and an assortment of other computing systems and data networks. The standard approach of relying on the telephone company for most network services was deemed unfeasible because of the uncertainty brought on by AT&T's divestiture and the escalating costs of local telephone service.

During this turbulent period between 1982 and 1989, Data Services and Telecommunications management had to hit the moving target of a company with constantly changing network needs while undergoing significant management changes. This required a network that would have the flexibility to meet the challenges of an evolving organizational configuration.

An integrated digital network offered an opportunity to enable faster response because it would reduce the costs of assembling project teams. The new network could be reconfigured quickly and easily to suit team members new locations. Instead of moving members to a common location, they could remain at their current location and be connected through the new network.

The end result would be easier network reconfiguration and subsequently, faster response, at a lower cost.

Many technical and organizational obstacles had to be overcome to ensure the network project's success. The technical obstacles, while formidable, were less of a problem in the long run than the organizational culture obstacles.

Corporate Culture

The corporate culture of the Space and Defense sector encourage entrepreneurship and allows the autonomy of action that goes with this philosophy. The potential benefits are fast and innovative responses to market demands [2].

One of the characteristics of this emphasis on autonomy was that the project units wanted a degree of control over their information resources that they felt was only possible when they owned and managed them. This phenomena can be characterized as the "not controlled here" (NCH) syndrome. The result of this NCH syndrome, among the project units, was an adhoc approach to acquiring network resources which led to a proliferation of underutilized and abandoned resources contained in isolated data networks.

Integrating Computing

The integrated network would allow newly formed teams to share the surplus capacity of computing resources from existing project units. (See Figure 1) This would be made possible because of the new network's high speed digital lines which would provide distribution capabilities for any of the existing computing systems at the Space Park complex.

Backbone and Building Network

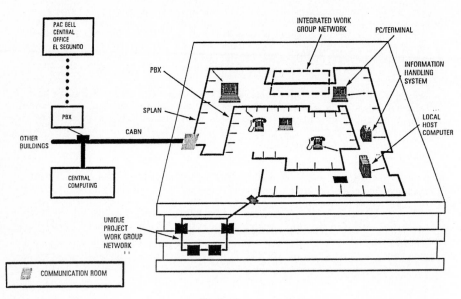

Figure 1

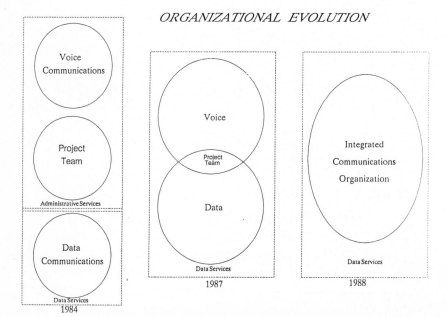

ORGANIZATIONAL EVOLUTION

Figure 2

The same digital links could connect previously isolated project units
to make sharing of database information easier. Even if they had
incompatible computing systems, they could share information because the
network would also provide gateways to ensure system interoperability.

The question facing Data Services and Telecommunications management was
how to meet the disparate networking needs of a multifaceted large
organization while affecting a change in corporate culture so that the
NCH syndrome would not prevent optimal utilization of computing capacity. They also had to change the organization so that information would
be viewed as a common resource that should be available to all units who
stood to benefit from accessing it.

The telecommunications department had centrally managed the voice network through the local telephone companies Centrex offerings. However,
the multiple data networks had not been centrally managed. A move to
centralized network management of voice, data, and image transmissions
required a digital network that could integrate all types of communications.

The new integrated network would provide project teams access to computing resources without controlling how they utilized those resources. In
this manner, the specialized application development that project teams
required remained under their control, while network management would
come under the control of the Data Services Organization. A centralized
digital network facilitated the simultaneous evolution of centralized
common business applications and decentralized project specific applications.

An additional benefit of the proactive network planning was that it
would provide a new basis for cooperation between the Data Services and
Telecommunications departments which had to work more closely together,
and eventually merge under the Data Services Organization. This merger
was stimulated by the network upgrade and occurred over the four year
planning, procurement, and implementation period. (See Figure 2) This
merger also created a new primary role for the Data Services Organization director as **network manager**.

Network Requirements

Data Services management selected an integrated digital network to
create a new network infrastructure. The primary goals for the network
were to

- reduce the cost of doing business in an information intensive
  industry,

- promote movement of information instead of people,

- improve sharing of excess computing capacity,

- create the flexibility to reconfigure the network to meet any
  organizational structure,

- create an envelope containing all communications with a single
  point of demarcation for incoming and outgoing communications,

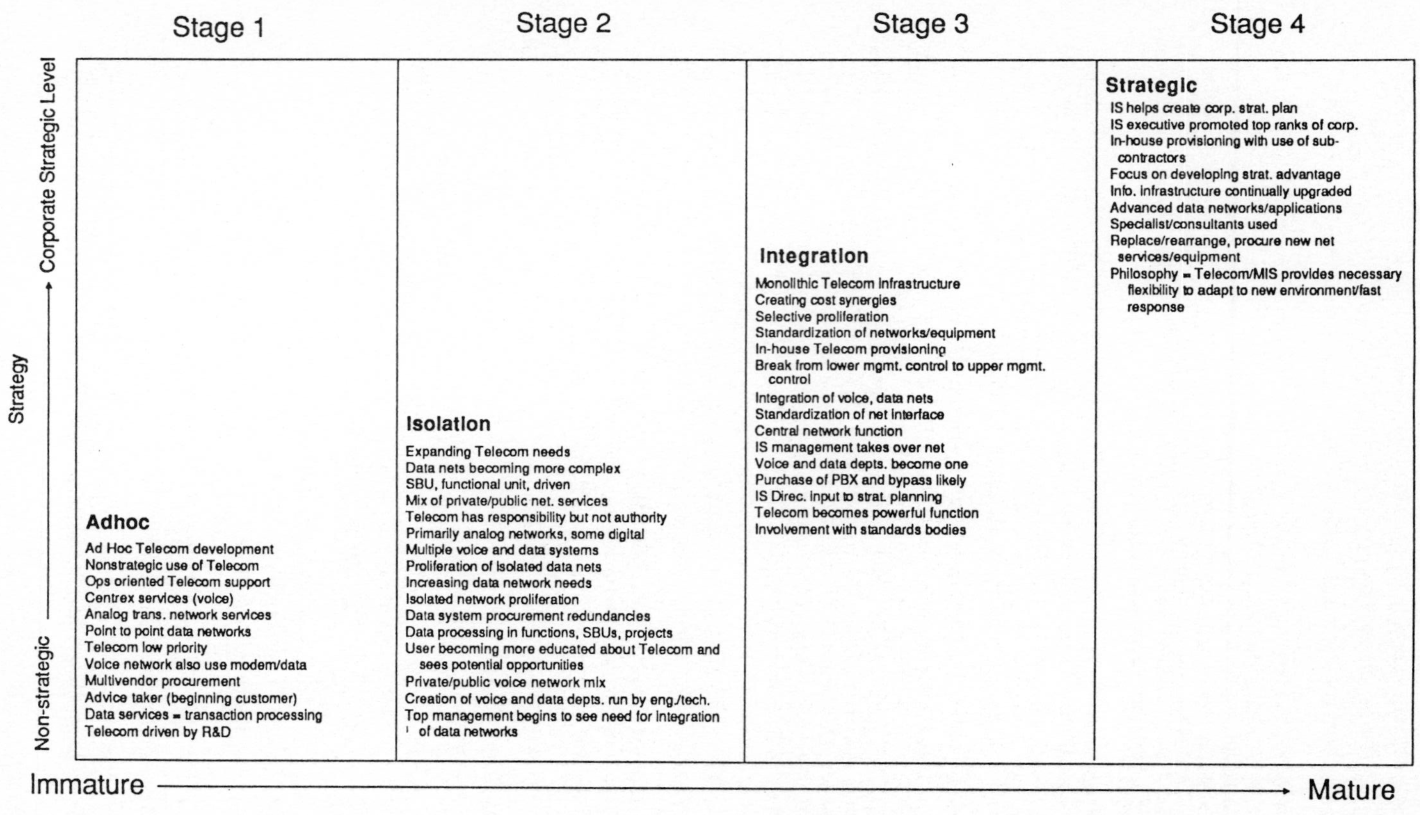

Stage 1	Stage 2	Stage 3	Stage 4
Adhoc Ad Hoc Telecom development Nonstrategic use of Telecom Ops oriented Telecom support Centrex services (voice) Analog trans. network services Point to point data networks Telecom low priority Voice network also use modem/data Multivendor procurement Advice taker (beginning customer) Data services = transaction processing Telecom driven by R&D	**Isolation** Expanding Telecom needs Data nets becoming more complex SBU, functional unit, driven Mix of private/public net. services Telecom has responsibility but not authority Primarily analog networks, some digital Multiple voice and data systems Proliferation of isolated data nets Increasing data network needs Isolated network proliferation Data system procurement redundancies Data processing in functions, SBUs, projects User becoming more educated about Telecom and sees potential opportunities Private/public voice network mix Creation of voice and data depts. run by eng./tech. Top management begins to see need for integration of data networks	**Integration** Monolithic Telecom Infrastructure Creating cost synergies Selective proliferation Standardization of networks/equipment In-house Telecom provisioning Break from lower mgmt. control to upper mgmt. control Integration of voice, data nets Standardization of net interface Central network function IS management takes over net Voice and data depts. become one Purchase of PBX and bypass likely IS Direc. input to strat. planning Telecom becomes powerful function Involvement with standards bodies	**Strategic** IS helps create corp. strat. plan IS executive promoted top ranks of corp. In-house provisioning with use of sub-contractors Focus on developing strat. advantage Info. infrastructure continually upgraded Advanced data networks/applications Specialists/consultants used Replace/rearrange, procure new net services/equipment Philosophy – Telecom/MIS provides necessary flexibility to adapt to new environment/fast response

Strategy

Corporate Strategic Level ←

Non-strategic

Immature ——→ Mature

Figure 3. Network Maturity Cycle

- allow autonomous business units, such as project units, to focus on applications development instead of network procurement and management,

- provide TRW's employees with the best available information technology with the features and functions to help them accomplish their tasks.

One of the first steps in meeting these goals was to analyze where TRW's networks had come from and where they should be going.

Network Maturity Cycle

As a company's network function matures it moves through four stages [2]. During the first stage, or **Adhoc** stage, networks proliferate without the benefit of centralized planning. During the second stage, or **Isolation** stage, networks are planned and controlled by individual project, business, or functional units. In the third stage, or **Integration** stage, management moves to integrate the multiple networks to take advantage of economies of scope and scale and the potential for synergistic collaboration among units and functions. The fourth stage of development, or **Strategic** stage, occurs when voice, data, and image networks become a centrally integrated aspect of the company's strategic plan for beating the competition. (See Figure 3)

Companies can be placed along this rough continuum in terms of their network maturity. TRW, for example, was in the Isolation stage before they implemented their plan to install an integrated network across the Space Park complex.

The network maturity cycle provides a context for understanding how the Sector evolved with multiple, unconnected, and adhoc data networks to isolated networks controlled by the product groups and their project units. The organizational evolution of Data Services and Telecommunications paralleled stages two and three of the network cycle in that these units represented isolated voice and data networks before the upgrade and an integrated network afterwards. The model also predicted that the next step in network maturity was a move to a strategic network.

2. PLANNING AND IMPLEMENTING THE NETWORK

Based on broad cost and benefit forecasts, top management gave the Data Services and Telecommunications departments the go ahead to develop a detailed analysis of the Sector's current network needs. This needs analysis would form the basis for requests for information (RFI), an internal promotional program, and eventually, requests for proposal (RFP). (See Figure 4)

The overall project management team was created to help coordinate the planning, procurement, and implementation of the new network. Drawing on internal expertise, the management team consisted of a team of technical, engineering, and project personnel from the Engineering, Data Services, and Telecommunications organizations.

The procurement processes were the same as those developed for revenue producing programs, such as defense satellite projects. This program

Network Planning, Procurement, Implementation Process

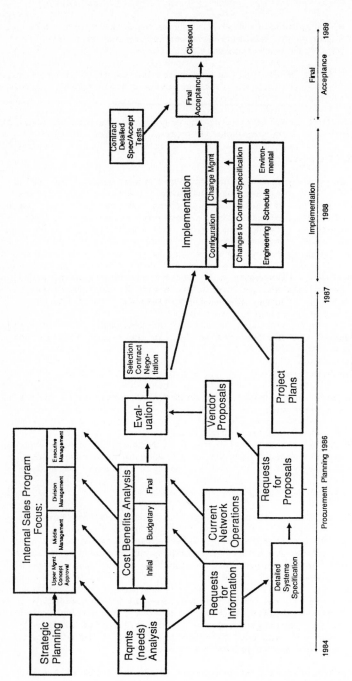

Figure 4

management approach took a large scale, complex procurement, such as the integrated digital network, and broke it into "bite-sized" subprojects. Each subproject team was responsible for a budget and subject to the scrutiny of regularly scheduled (i.e. weekly, monthly) and independent progress and cost reviews. Any changes in baseline progress and cost requirements had to be justified by the project team during the reviews.

Baselines were never changed because the project management team wanted to keep track of how closely they were staying on schedule and within cost parameters. Keeping track of the baselines, also forced subproject management to concentrate on fixing any problems that kept them from meeting baseline requirements.

Vendors had to use program management systems that paralleled TRW's. This allowed the project team to integrate the vendors within TRW's overall network project cost schedule control system. They too, were responsible for regularly scheduled cost and progress reviews with TRW's subproject management teams.

Requirements Analysis

The overall project management team's first task was to perform the detailed requirements analysis which was necessary to accurately estimate costs and identify the needed functionalities of the user communities. The requirements analysis consisted of

- estimating the types and numbers of devices that would use the network,

- gathering data on the characteristics of the user population,

- understanding the current operations necessary to provide network service,

- identifying the existing networks,

- gathering data on the costs for current network services,

- understanding the cultural issues affecting provision of network services, and

- establishing evaluative criteria to judge the network.

The two overriding criteria for the network were that it had to contain escalating telecommunications costs and provide the utility and flex-ibility for rapid reconfiguration to enable fast response. These general criteria were defined in specific network criteria including flexibility, performance, relative cost (e.g. current versus future costs for services), reliability, interoperability, functionality, modularity, maintainability, ease of operation, environmental require-ments, and footprint (e.g. housing will be required for equipment). This list of criteria was used to evaluate current systems and to compare current systems to proposed systems.

The distinct populations that the new network had to serve were administrative, engineers, scientists, management, and support personnel. In 1984, 53% of the user population were engineers and

338

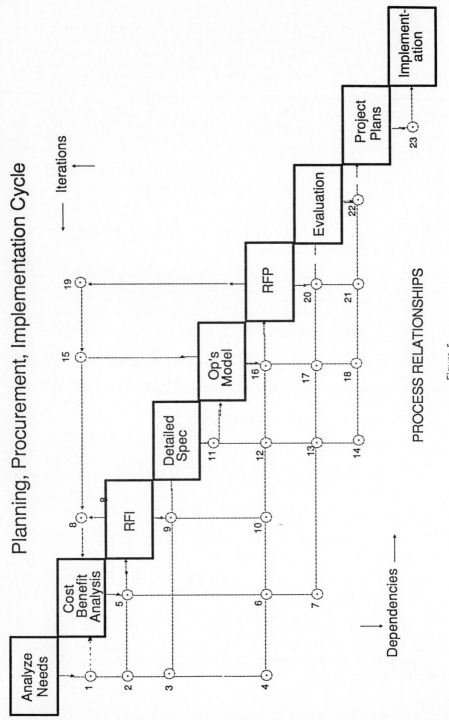

Planning, Procurement, Implementation Cycle

Iterations

Analyze Needs

Cost Benefit Analysis

RFI

Detailed Spec

Op's Model

RFP

Evaluation

Project Plans

Implement-ation

Dependencies

PROCESS RELATIONSHIPS

Figure 5

scientists, 20% were management and administrative, and 27% were support personnel. This population used 85% asynchronous and 15% synchronous data communications. This kind of information was critical in estimating future usage patterns.

The current systems providing network services had to be catalogued in order to understand what it would take to replace and augment them. The current systems included Centrex services for most voice services, several small PBXs, a demanding SNA network, multiple LANs, and point-to-point dedicated data circuits. The new network had to integrate the existing SNA/CAE and LAN networks, provide gateways between systems, and replace the voice and dedicated point-to-point data links supplied by the local telephone companies.

During the analysis, the team collected detailed information on the number and type of data and voice devices. The voice equipment numbers were easy to assemble because most of the this service was purchased from the local telephone companies and was available through the billing information. The number of data devices was much more difficult to determine because, due to independent procurement's, there were no central records for this equipment.

It was necessary to understand the operational activities required to meet the current service needs of the diverse user population. Because the new network would be managed internally, many of the services, which were bundled into the vendors standard charges, needed to be understood.

Current Network Costs

The current costs for providing network services were difficult to obtain because the information was in many different places, e.g. project units, functional units, and telephone companies. However, the following cost data was collected.

- Capital depreciation of existing plant.

- Human resources costs to run the existing systems.

- Access charges for long distance communications.

- Point to point circuit costs.

- Line and station equipment rental and purchase costs.

- Transmission equipment costs (e.g. multiplexers, modems).

- LAN equipment costs.

- Computational support (e.g. mainframe time, PCs, applications software).

- Aggregate numbers of moves, adds, and changes.

While this list is not exhaustive, it represents the primary components of cost that had to be accounted for in order to estimate aggregate network costs.

PROCESS CHECKLIST

Actions	Description
1	Identify initial requirements by examining the top level operations and functions provided by existing services.
2,5	Expand upon requirements, assign priorities and value (from initial cost/benefit analysis), and describe future needs (part of strategic plans) as part of Request For Information (RFI).
3,9	Use expanding requirements base augmented by technologies available per RFI's and prepare detailed systems specification.
8	Iterate the results of the RFI evaluation back to refining the cost/benefit analysis.
15	Evaluate the operations scenario and strategy for employing resources to expand cost/benefit analysis for life cycle impacts.
4,6,10, 12,16	Use expanding requirements, assign value of feature/functions (from cost/benefit analysis), available technologies (RFI), and Detailed Specification as augmented by operations scenario and network management strategy merged with terms and conditions of procurement to prepare the Request For Proposal(s).
19	Iterate and use the vendor proposals to update and refine the cost/benefits analysis to include realistic costs and values of equipment, labor, maintenance, operations, and spares.
7,13, 17,20	Utilize accumulated knowledge and data to evaluate the RFP and make a selection of vendor(s). Include an evaluation matrix approach (See Figure 17, literally or figuratively) to examine acceptability of technical offering, costs and risks.
14,18, 21,22	Utilize accumulated knowledge and data along with specifics and commitments from negotiations with vendor(s) to prepare detailed (living) Project Plan(s).
23	Implement Project Plan using change control and configuration management techniques.

Figure 6

Figure 5, identifies the interrelationships among the sequential steps
in the planning, procurement, and implementation cycle. Figure 6,
represents a checklist that follows the steps in Figure 5. This
checklist should prove useful for companies planning similar network
upgrades.

Network Cost Justification

The project team had to demonstrate that there would be a return on
investment (ROI), after taxes, or that the net present value of the
investment (NPV) would exceed the company's ability to invest the money
in alternative investments, e.g. stock market, long term bonds.

Other financial issues that had to be resolved in making life-cycle
comparisons including leasing versus buying the system, capitalization
versus expensing the investment based on IRS regulations, the
investment's impact on asset utilization measured by return on assets
employed, current year rates, forward pricing (estimated pricing rates
for multi-year contracts) all of which affected the cost of doing
business.

The final cost estimates promised a minimum cost avoidance of eight
percent compared with a projected increase of over 30% if no network
upgrade occurred. The hard dollar savings were projected at more than
$100 million over a ten year period with an estimated soft dollar saving
of $30 million due to productivity increases. Figure 7 segments the
percentage savings from voice and data network services operating costs.

These cost estimates were accurate because the hard dollar savings, to
date, have met projections. If current savings trends continue, since
the network upgrade, these projections will meet future expectations.

3.   THE RFI AND RFP PROCESSES

The project team developed a series of requests for information (RFI)
to invite vendor's to begin the bidding process for the various parts of
the new network contract. There were multiple RFIs because the team
requested information on the PBX, CABN, and SPLAN. The responses to the
RFIs formed the basis for the RFPs to follow. The RFI responses were
helpful to the team in developing basic cost and boundary parameters for
the network's elements.

The RFPs were developed in painstaking, paragraph by paragraph, line by
line detail. The RFPs included detailed specifications on the network's
architecture, standards, network elements (hardware and software),
environmental requirements, vendor relationships, acceptance criteria,
and quality assurance for each aspect of the network.

The architecture specifications required a general description of the
network's design. For example, the team requested a more distributed
architecture to meet system security and availability needs. The
responses to the RFPs had to show how the proposed architecture would
meet growth or contraction contingencies. The team did not want a
network that would "top out" before the 10 year pay back period because
they planned to provide transmission capacity for all growth needs for
the next 20 years.

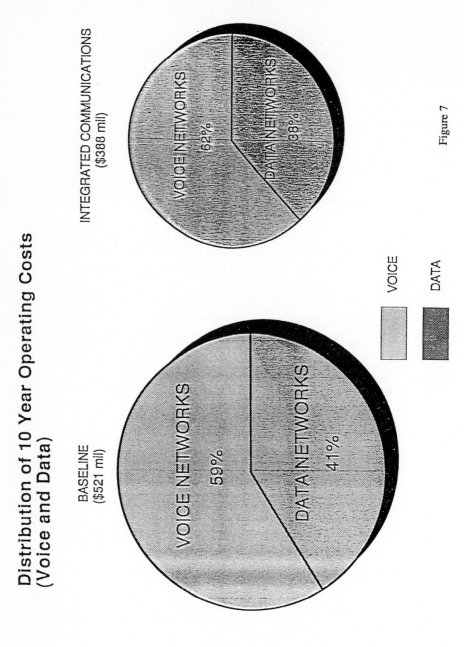

342

Distribution of 10 Year Operating Costs
(Voice and Data)

INTEGRATED COMMUNICATIONS
($388 mil)

VOICE NETWORKS
62%

DATA NETWORKS
38%

BASELINE
($521 mil)

VOICE NETWORKS
59%

DATA NETWORKS
41%

VOICE

DATA

Figure 7

The vendors communicated their architectural approach at the subsystem level so that a management framework could be developed for the more detailed evaluation of the network operations, elements, and standards. The team requested that the vendors unbundle their hardware and software offerings as much as possible to enable a more detailed function versus cost analysis.

Standards

The vendors had to validate how their proposed systems would subscribe to the specific standards for data and voice communications and evolve toward future standards. In addition to responding to the hardware requirements, the vendors had to demonstrate how they would comply with the codes and regulations of city, county, state, and federal governments. These regulations governed rights of way, system safety requirements, and many others.

The features and functions of the software that the vendors must meet were specified. The vendors were also requested to demonstrate how they would help TRW accomplish detailed surveys that are necessary to complete control tables for the PBX. The vendors approaches to providing software safeguards, such as personal identification numbers and passwords, also had to be listed.

Warranties for software and hardware were requested as well as system documentation (owners manual) for each element. Along with the warranty, the level and duration of maintenance and operational support for the network elements had to be included in the contract price as specified against a basic requirement.

A significant cost driver, that can prove expensive if overlooked, is the environmental requirements for a systems installation and operation.

Environmental features include

- space to house switching units and equipment and wiring in communications rooms,

- special air conditioning required for system operation,

- special equipment power requirements, and

- safety features such as bracing (for earthquakes), backup generators, etc.

Vendor Relationship

The vendors had to demonstrate how this interface would be accomplished to perform the network installation tasks. For example, they had to identify what they were responsible for, what the subcontractors were responsible for, and what TRW was responsible for in the network installation.

The vendors had to provide project plans that would show schedules for completion of milestones and what kind of plant changes were necessary to install the network on schedule. These elements of planning were essential to accomplish facilities changes and upgrades and not interfere with the project's overall critical path plan. They also had to show the availability of resources that would be allocated to accomplish these plans so that evaluations could be made as to how realistic the plans were.

Quality Issues

The RFPs made it clear that the vendors would have to test and verify each hardware and software element of the network as it was installed to meet quality assurance criteria. The staged testing and verification provided benchmarks which helped keep the project on schedule. Incoming quality inspection of network hardware and transmission media (e.g. station equipment, wiring, fiber optic cable, conduit) was required. TRW also wanted to ensure that the vendors were providing identical versions/revisions of a given product and that the current version would not become obsolete before it was installed.

The RFP evaluation team was comprised of the overall project management team, accounting personnel, procurement personnel, and price-cost analysts. This group provided a cumulative level of expertise that would not have been possible if a single department, such as the Data Services Department, had completed the evaluation alone.

When the technical evaluations were made, a final evaluation was performed which aggregated the results of the technical evaluations and examined total cost and risk. The risk evaluation centered on whether the vendors

- had developed an adequate management plan,

- could provide the resources to perform the installation on schedule,

- were delivering the type of products proposed,

- could deliver services or products not in their standard offerings,

- had the product inventory and/or ability to produce the required quantities and types of products,

- and whether they were able to identify subcontractor/supplier support mechanisms.

The total cost of each acceptable bid was detailed and extended to reach an overall and final price for the project. This final aggregate price had to be compared with the promised hard dollar cost savings to determine if the network upgrade was worth the price.

Contract Negotiations Plan

Once the final bids had been received and evaluated, the overall project management team and TRW Procurement and Contracts management had to develop a negotiations plan. The plan represented the strategy for getting the lowest "reasonable" price.

4.   INSTALLING THE NETWORK

The detailed RFPs and requirements analysis provided the input to the implementation plan. The plan included

- plan scope,

- technical design criteria,

- the implementation approach (i.e. phased),

- a list of user requirements,

- pre-installation preparations (e.g. user surveys),

- organizational structure of implementation team,

- automation systems requirements (e.g. project planning tools and software)

- conditional and final acceptance test plans,

- facilities plan (e.g. switch and communications rooms),

- operations plan (e.g.how to transition from implementation to an operations environment)

- user support plan (e.g. cutover support, operations, and training),

- security plan (e.g. PINs, passwords),

- chargeback and accounting plans (e.g. PBX line usage, billing), training plan (e.g. user training for new telephones),

- and the network configuration plan (e.g. numbering plan addressing schemes, cable labeling, line assignments, for on-site telephones).

Because the implementation plan was so detailed, the subproject teams were able to keep to a very tight schedule even when problems arose.

Two levels of automation were used to support project implementation. The first level was software designed to provide the detailed day to day scheduling and tracking of tasks and the second level provided consolidation schedules to allow a high level view of scheduling and tracking based on the critical path method. This automation led to flexible project management because it allowed

- examination of ripple effects from any schedule changes,

- logistical experimentation using what-if simulations,

- identification of conflicts in scheduling resources,

- examination of budgetary constraints, and conflicting deadlines.

Unanticipated Savings

One reason most network implementation projects run over budget is that users request many modifications to the system. To limit the impact of this common problem, the team created the Configuration Control Board to limit modifications to the original contracts. The board, which was made up of users and members of the implementation subproject management teams, reviewed all requested changes and were able to keep changes to a minimum.

The Configuration Control Board reviewed each change against the contract to determine if it was outside the contract scope. When changes were justified, they performed a technical and price justification for each change which was then negotiated by procurement and contract support personnel.

Taking into account the likelihood of modifications, the contracts were negotiated in such a way that the implementation teams had windows of time within which network modifications could be made without additional costs to TRW. It was fortunate that these time windows for modifications had been negotiated because some unanticipated resource changes did occur during the two-year period.

The result of having change control management resulted in a 10% savings on the original budget projections for the network upgrade. Since the project budget was based on precise cost estimates and was comparable to similar sized projects in peer companies, coming in 10% under budget represented a true cost savings.

Problems in Data Communications

An unanticipated problem arose during the network installation: the use of PBX lines for prolonged session time, high speed data transmissions impacting sizing and performance estimates. To take advantage of network flexibility, a number of low speed PBX lines were allocated for use by the casual dial-up data user.

A more limited number (i.e. 12 per building) of high speed lines were available for short term data communications so that users could connect these lines temporarily while the user was being connected to the SPLAN or backbone network services which could handle the long session time, high-speed data applications easily.

The PBX lines being new and easy to use, the users did not want to become connected to the SPLAN, and therefore, they were all identified as casual users. Long session times can prove hazardous to PBXs which are set up for short session times (i.e. the average time for a telephone call). Data applications vary widely in terms of transmission speed or bandwidth, network topologies, and session times. This inherent variability makes it very difficult to predict data application usage patterns, which in turn, makes it difficult to size a network for data applications. This is a common problem in many information intensive companies.

A clearly defined network policy about length of use of the special PBX lines was necessary to bring the problem under control. It also required a concerted effort to inform users through a series of educational and informative bulletins.

Throughout the planning, procurement, and implementation process, TRW learned a number of lessons which will benefit other companies faced with the challenge of providing an network infrastructure to enable fast response and contain costs.

5.   CONCLUSIONS

The core characteristics of TRW's network planning, procurement, and implementation processes that kept it on schedule and under budget were

- **proactive strategic planning** that emphasized the long term in maintaining standards that provided flexibility for the inclusion of new information technology without the need for system replacement,

- **detailed requirements analyses** that led to baselines against which current network services could be compared to new network services to ensuring that TRW was on the leading edge --not the bleeding edge--in meeting corporate business objectives,

- **cost-benefit analyses** that were constantly updated and communicated to upper management throughout the iterative network planning, procurement, and implementation processes to ensure upper management's consent and support,

- the generation of **detailed network specifications** that defined requirements, described systems, and defined acceptance criteria in sufficient detail that each requirement could be uniquely defined in a single paragraph in the RFP,

- **RFP processes** that included the detailed network specifica- tions, enumerated terms and conditions permitting TRW implementation modification flexibility, withholding of pay- ments conditional on vendor performance, identification of vendor performance relationships and material warranties, as well as an evaluation plan prepared before the RFPs were released,

- **rigorous** RFP evaluation processes performed by the project team and other, independent reviewers to ensure **objectivity** and prevent "group think" combined with a detailed "what-if", scenario generation method to develop a **negotiation plan**,

- **implementation processes** based on

    1.   exacting project scheduling and performance monitoring,
    2.   timely project reviews,
    3.   independent project management reviews with upper management,

    4. a Configuration Control Board made up of project,
       procurement and contracts, functional management,
       support services, and security personnel
    5. cost/quality/performance tracking against original
       baselines, with changes allowed only in the event of a
       major contract change,
    6. and incremental implementation payments, to
       incentivize vendor performance.

These same processes should help other companies stay on schedule and
within budget provided similar program management techniques are understood and applied.

Apply Program Management Techniques

This report should persuade the information systems executives of other
large companies that the key to success in planning, procuring, and
implementing a network lies in the use of rigorous program management
processes. Applying these generic rules of pushing responsibility to
the subproject level, religiously maintaining baseline requirements,
integrating vendor sub-teams within the overall project plan, controlling contract and network modifications, developing negotiations plan,
and drawing on technical expertise will help ensure success.

Take a Leadership Role

It is very difficult to change a company's culture with regard to
computing and network resources. The best way to accomplish this feat
is to build a concrete case for how the new approach will reduce operating costs, lead to increased productivity, and not threaten users
control over their unique computing applications needs. Information
systems executives need to take a more leading role in helping change
their companies cultures by participating in the formulation of a
general business strategy that demonstrates how a network infrastructure
can help meet strategy objectives, such as fast response and lowering
overhead. By doing so, they will help bring their companies' networks
into the **strategic** phase of network maturity and reap the benefits of
this positive change.

Anticipate - Unanticipated Advantages

While demonstrated cost savings may be a prerequisite for top management
approval of a new information network, it may not represent the greatest
advantages of such a system. With the new network, the Space and
Defense Sector was able to meet customer contract requirements that
could not have been met with the old system. This provided the ability
to meet new contract provisions without investment of significant
capital.

The days of business as usual on outmoded networks are over for the
Space and Defense Sector. Those companies that choose to stay
competitive in the "information age" must make sure they have the
network infrastructure to do so.

REFERENCES

[1]   Bower, J.L. and Hout, T.M. "Fast-Cycle Capability for Competitive
      Power," <u>Harvard Business Review</u> (66:6) November-December 1988,
      pp. 110-118.

[2]   Guterl, F.V. "Goodbye, Old Matrix," <u>Business Month</u>, February 1989,
      pp. 32-38.

[3]   Housel, T.J. "Procuring Telecommunications: A Strategy for User
      Companies," in <u>Purchasing in the 1990s: The Evolution of
      Procurement in the Telecommunications and Information Technology
      Industries</u>, W. Johnson and J. Sheth (eds.), JAI Press, in press.

Information Network and Data Communication, III
D. Khakhar and F. Eliassen (Editors)
Elsevier Science Publishers B.V. (North-Holland)
  IFIP, 1990

INTEGRATED NETWORKS AND THEIR IMPACT ON THE INFRASTRUCTURE

Dieter LAZAK

Siemens AG
München, West Germany

ABSTRACT AND SUMMARY

Integrated telecommunication networks are increasingly influencing the planning and structuring of factories, administration buildings, and even the set up of whole new cities. In this connection the concept of a Teleport has been created. In this connection a Teleport is defined by the physical and logical availability of all existing telecommunication network interfaces (physical) and telematic services (logical) within the geographic (spatial) area covered by the Teleport communication network. Intelligent Buildings (IBs) residing within the Teleport area are by definition providing at any point within the building all these telecommunication facilities e.g. by means of an internal cabling system. In this way a Teleport can be defined as a cluster of IBs served by an integrated telematic service center. The telematic service center is comprising the technological nucleus and the Teleport operator organization. Within such a Teleport new forms of ecoarchitecture are possible allowing e.g. a high degree of energy-, water-, and oxygen-autonomy of IBs on the basis of solar collectors, building-integrated biological ("green") surfaces which are automatical sustained by computerized watering-, heating-, and cooling systems. Those Teleport-based oecotronic buildings are avoiding oecological and in the long term also economical destructive effects on the environment.

1. INTRODUCTION

Telecommunications- and telematic-systems are with growing speed effecting the tactical and strategical behaviour of enterprises and also of social communities. These effects are to be seen within the

- organization
- technology
- infrastructure

of an enterprise.

Looking backward into history of Teleports all those effects could be seen already with the establishment of the first Teleport at the early 1980s in New York. In this case the twin-towers of the World Trade Center (WTC) had been established without thinking of the fully copper wire crammed cable tunnels in Manhatten which were not any more able to take further telecommunication lines as an additional load for the WTC. For this reason the twin towers could not be equipped with enough telecommunication facilities in the beginning and thus not sufficient profitability from real estate business could be gained because not enough customers were moving into the twin towers.

For these reasons the Teleport of New York was founded with a network-center outside Manhatten on Staten Island and linking this center by a glass-fiber cable to the twin towers. In this way enough telecommunication channels were provided for the users of the WTC and nearly 100% of all offices could be rented.

From this example we can see the interlinking of the above mentioned three components:

A. Organizational Unit (Teleport Operator Organization)

In order to provide integrated telematic services to the users within a geographic defined area first of all a Teleport Operator Organization is founded, which is serving as a contractor to the Teleport users.

B. Teleport Network Center (Teleport Technology Concept)

A technological network center managed by the Teleport Operator Organization is providing the telecommunication and telematic services to the users of the Teleport. Especially integrated services like VANS (Value Added Network Services) can be provided and supported in this way.

C. Infrastructural Improvements (Intelligent Buildings IBs)

The integrated networks are servicing a number of IBs and are gaining their financial basis from the tariffs these users are paying to the Teleport Operators Organization.

2. TELEPORTS AND THE ECOLOGICAL ECONOMY (1)

Telematic cities can replace highly polluted areas by groups of clean and intelligent buildings. Because people want to live in those areas real estate companies and micro-scale economical effects have been calculated in (1). The result is that ecology and economy are simultaneously promoted here. Also a lot of permanent new working places are created here which has been calculated quantitatively in (1).

3. TELEPORT OPERATOR ORGANIZATION (TOO)

The TOO is forming the strategical long term backbone of a Teleport. Thus the concept of a Teleport is primarily of a organizational nature. Technology within a Teleport is only the tactical tool for realization.

Besides forming the strategical backbone the TOO is also the basis on which a user of a Teleport can contract for his services he is expecting from the Teleport.

The internal logical structure has several functional levels as can be seen from fig. 3/1:

Level 1: The Teleport Nucleus
It consists of
- the Teleport Network Operator who is performing network-management and -administration functions. Those functions are e.g.
-- network switching
-- service distribution
-- service generation and provision
for information-providers and end-users. The Teleport Nucleus of a TOO can be managed by an Information Manager.

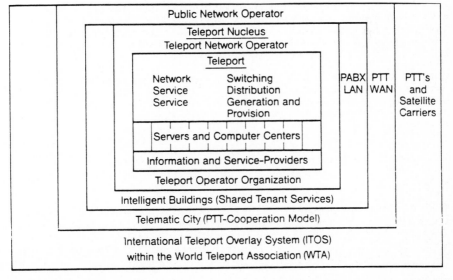

Fig. 3/1: Structure of the Telport Operator Organization (TOO).

Level 2: Public Network Interworking
        Within this functional range the TOO-management has
        to contract with the public network operators opti-
        mal technical and financial conditions for the inter-
        faces obtainable from common and special carriers.

Level 3: User-Interfacing
        The TOO-management should provide the Teleport users
        -if possibly with standardized hardware- and software-
        interfaces of the telematic system in order to esta-
        blish an economical access to the Teleport services.

        Other services of the TOO are the provision of
        - system back up
        - security of access
        - system monitoring
        - system amintenance
        - value added services
        - computer aided system engineering
        - corporate software consulting (prototyping)
        - network design
        - cost- and tariff-management
        - internal and external training
        - etc.

4. TELEPORT TECHNOLOGY CONCEPT (TTC)

The main task of the TTC is to establish for Teleport users the
provision of integrated services. In the ideal case the TTC is
providing all services to the Teleport user by means of only
one technological (=physical and logical) interface. This is
it what makes a Teleport attractive to usersbecause it can
keep things simple. One form of integration of telecommunication networks and telematic services will be in this connection
the Integrated Broadband Communication Network (IBCN) which is
favoured for reasons of cost-effectivness by the public PTTs
because on the basis of the high speed digital data transmission technology any network- and communication-service can be
carried on one transmission system only. The transmission technology may be the so-called Asynchronous Transfer Mode (ATM)
which is a form of fast packet switching.

However for the present time being, a manyfold of technologies
have to be integrated within a hybride Teleport switch, fig.
4/1. A pure IBCN-switch is shown in fig. 4/2. The realization
of a technology concept for a small Teleport is shown in fig.
4/3.

Within the TTC special attention has to be focussed on the development of multifunctional workstations. In principle for an
individual user of a Teleport the multifunctional workstation
(MFW) is the private or individual Teleport of this individual
user. In this way a MFW may also be called an individual or
private User-Teleport. Those User-Teleports can, however, be
efficiently operated on the basis of a well structured combination of a City or regional Teleport comprising the above

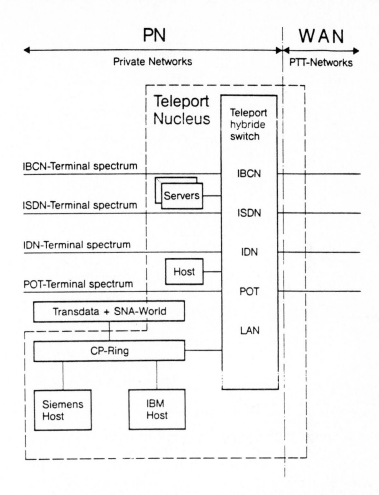

<u>Fig. 4/1</u>: Technology concept of a Teleport-Nucleus, interfacing Private Networks (PN) against public Wide Area Networks (WAN).

mentioned TOO, TTC, and ICT. However in the more distant future the individual point-to-point contact directly between User-Teleports by means of satellite-links, micro-wave facilities, and glassfiber connections may be possible, establishing some sort of direct individual "Teleport-Democraty".

Returning to the concept of an User-Teleport which may be a stationary installed MFW (2), fig. 4/4, this will be basically a single or multiprocessor PC (fig. 4/5), which has additionally a multitude of communication interfaces possibly an IBCN-Interface (fig. 4/6), which is opening access to all physical telecommunication networks and logical telecommunication services.

356

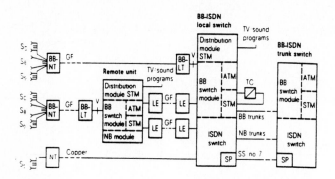

ATM	Asynchronous Transfer Mode	S	S Interface
BBB	Broadband	SP	Signalling Point
GF	Glass Fiber	SS	Signalling System
LE	Line Equipment	STM	Synchronous Transfer Mode
NB	Narrow Band	TC	Transcode
NT	Network Termination	V	V Interface (can be omitted)

<u>Fig. 4/2</u>: Principle structure of an IBCN-switch.

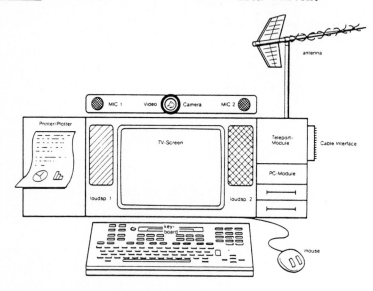

<u>Fig. 4/4</u>: Mobile compact-MFW.

5. INFRASTRUCTURAL CONCEPT OF TELEPORTS (ICT)

As a matter of fact the fast evolution of telecommunication
and telematic technology is causing permanent and quick changes within the infrastructure of those systems. Especially
cables, terminals, switching and host-systems should be easily

**IBCN-Teleport
Type 3**

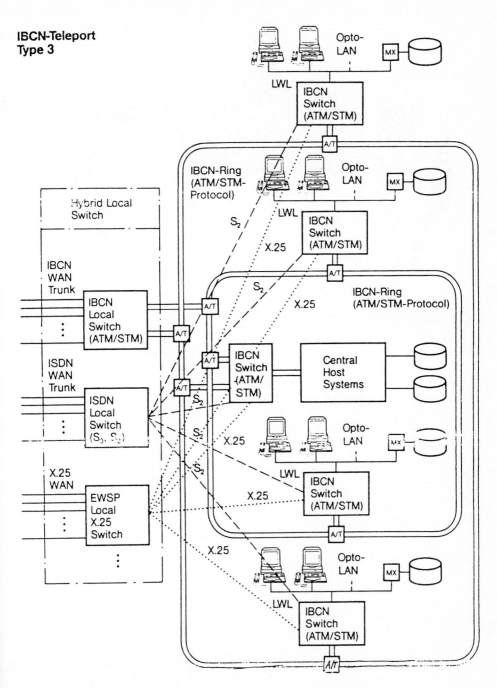

Fig. 4/3: Technology concept of small Teleport.

358

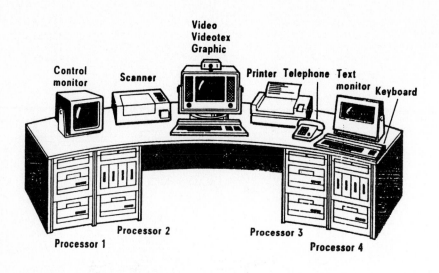

Fig. 4/5: Multiprocessor-Multiscreen-Multifunctional Workstation.

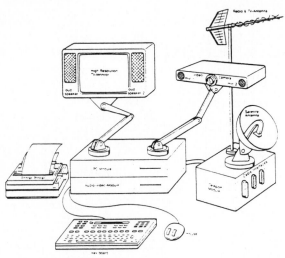

Fig. 4/6: Mobile MFW with the possibility of Cable Interfaces.

changeable and replaceable without disrupting the Teleport-
operations too much. By this permanent evolution and replacement process especially the infrastructure and housing of computer centers, office buildings, manufacturing plants, and
even the infrastructure of the so-called intelligent homes is
continuously affected. Thus a highly flexible infrastructural
concept within those systems has to be applied which is espe-

cially concerned with an effective and flexible cabling and airconditioning of those Intelligent Buildings where Teleports are installed. As a byproduct those telematic systems are allowing a complete building control which in turn is allowing the architect to conceive highly effective ecobuildings, i.e. buildings which are creating more natural environment than the building is destroying by the floorspace of its fundaments. IBs comprising those features of ecoarchitecture will be the most important and on a large scale profitable business of the coming years.

The principle structure of an IB is shown in fig. 5/1. An IB

Intelligent Building

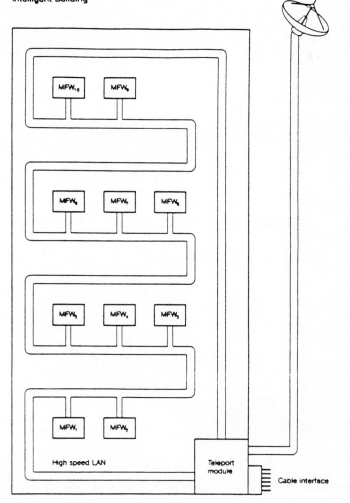

Fig. 5/1: Principle structure of an Intelligent Building (IB).

is defined as a building which is providing at any point within its body any telematic service, a Teleport is able to provide. Preferably multifunctional workstations as mentioned above are offering those services within a IB.

A 3-dimensional picture of such an IB is shown in fig. 5/2. This IB is still a building of conventional architecture.

The Teleport modules of an IB are allowing the installation of a high degree of building automation which can serve among other things for the support of ecological zones on and within these IBs. In fig. 5/3 the elements of such an ecobuilding are shown:

A) The roof and one ecoterrace are already generating more green land than has been destroyed by the fundaments of the building. The highly developped telematic building control system guaranties watering, fire protection, and possible heating of those ecozones.

B) Furthermore the roof is comprising solar collectors for energy production.

This idea of an intelligent ecobuilding is further developed by the building shown in fig. 5/4. In this case the ecolandscape generated by the ecobuilding is even larger than the

PRINCIPLE STRUCTURE OF AN INTELLIGENT BUILDING

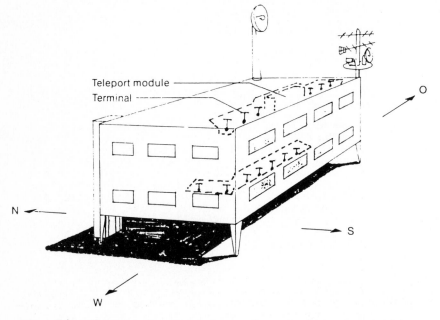

Fig. 5/2: 3-dimensional picture of an IB (T = terminal).

Principle Structure of an Intelligent Oecobuilding

Fig. 5/3: Intelligent Oecobuilding.

ground floor of the building itself. The ecofactor is greater than 1 (ecofactor = ecolandscape of the building/groundfloor of the building). The solar collectors are enlarged and serving simultaneously as shelter against strong winds for the roof gardens. Compared with the ecofactors of contemporary modern architecture which are zero or even less because not only the ground floor is covered by concrete but also the surrounding of it. This eco-architecture will create new biological living zones. Todays architecture can be characterized by a deathfactor (deathfactor = dead building surfaces/groundfloor of the building). The survival of future cities will only be possible if the ecofactor of the city as a whole is at least equal to 1. The quality of cities will be measured by its ecofactor. Also the quality of city architecture and planning will be measured by this factor.

The enlargement of natural environment by intelligent ecoarchitecture can not only be considered in a spatial way, but in a timely way as well as is shown in fig. 5/5. This ecobuilding does include large scaled wintergardens heated by solar collectors. Thus the generation of oxigen by plants does not only prevail in summer time but in winter as well.

Intelligent Building Generating More Green Surfaces than it is Consuming Green Landscape

Fig. 5/4: Enlarged intelligent ecobuilding.

Teleportbased intelligent ecobuildings are not only characterized by high ecofactors but by a very high internal flexibility, fig. 5/6. This is achieved by changeable internal wall-elements and by the high flexibility generated by double floors and hanging ceiling for airconditioning ducts. This form of elementary flexible architecture ("Lego-architecture) is giving the architect maximum freedom in creating new forms of building complexes. Those buildings can be used nearly for any purpose without wragging the building and constructing it anew. In this way it is a very save long term investment and it does not consume energy by an eventual new construction for another building purpose, because it can be used for the new task by simply changing its iternally variable structure.

Intelligent ecobuildings can evoid individual traffic to a large extent by the installation of teleport-based intelligent rooms, fig. 5/7. Those rooms do have all telecommunication facilities provided by small- and wideband telecommunication systems including HDTV-picturephoning and videoconferencing which can be used to avoid individual business travels. In the case of the intelligent room the user is not sitting before but within the terminal.

Intelligent Building with Closed Wintergarden Architecture

Fig. 5/5: Ecobuilding with wintergarden.

Intelligent ecobuildings can be extended to the altitude sky-scrapers. They are not limited in hight, fig. 5/8. The ecofactors are even becoming greater with growing altitude. In this way intelligent ecoarchitecture is not only creating new business opportunities of long term save investments, long term stabile employment situations within economy by providing low-tech- and high-tech-industry jobs and income simultaneously, but is enlarging as the first product in the history of industrial economy the ecosphere of man-kind as well. Every other business of industry and economy in the history of man-kind has destroyed nature. Intelligent ecobuildings are doing the contrary. This is new. This is the business of the future which has been made possible by the conceptual development of Teleports. This will be the ever lasting merit of the World Teleport Association (WTA).

Looking at the cities as they are today creating many hundreds of thousands of tons of dust and smog, ear deafening noise and non reversible energy consumption of coal, gas, and oil re-sources simultaneously, together with millions of people dying of lung cancer and traffic accidents and comparing those urban megacloacas with the possibilities of the multifunctional structure of intelligent ecobuildings (fig. 5/9) one can easily recognize the following facts:

Building Nucleus <u>Internally Fully Flexible</u>

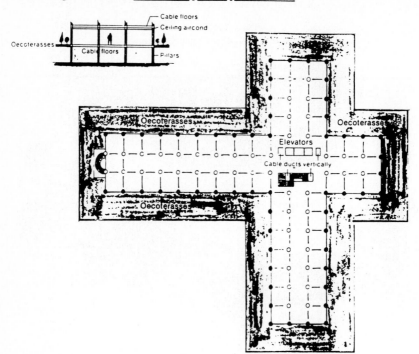

<u>Fig. 5/6</u>: Internally flexible IB.

A) Filterfunctions and revitalization
   The green roofgardens and ecoterraces are acting as dust-,
   smog-, and noise-absorbers. From dust they are creating new
   biological life. Smog is converted into oxigen. And noise
   gets absorbed within the green carpets of ecoterraces.

B) Tunnelling of individual traffic
   As far as individual traffic cannot be avoided, it can be
   enclosed into the lower floors of those buildings including the resting traffic within parking floors.

C) Multifunctionality of buildings
   is allowing to have office space and homes within the same
   architectural structures. Intelligent ecobuildings can be
   used to be constructed above of railway stations and motor-
   highways thus guiding its inhabilitants directly to trains
   and busses without the necessity to use individual cars in
   an extensive way. Car manufacturing industry should as
   strategic long range goal switch into the business of the
   construction of intelligent ecobuildings.

   Using above mentioned intelligent rooms you can move as

Intelligent Room

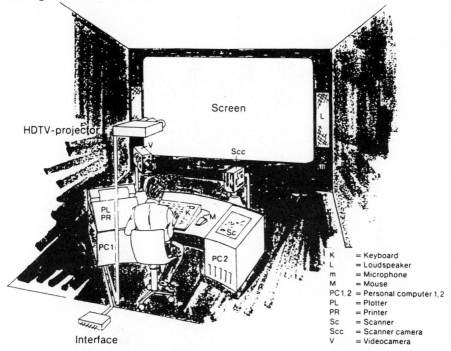

Screen

HDTV-projector

V

Scc

PL
PR

K

M

PC 1

PC 2

Sc

Interface

K	= Keyboard
L	= Loudspeaker
m	= Microphone
M	= Mouse
PC 1, 2	= Personal computer 1, 2
PL	= Plotter
PR	= Printer
Sc	= Scanner
Scc	= Scanner camera
V	= Videocamera

Fig. 5/7: Teleport-based intelligent room within IB.

fast as light in the picturephoning and videoconferencing mode without destroying nature and endangering other people. And above it all, business volume and profits are much higher than on battlegrounds of common car business which is endangered by far east low cost production companies.

On top of all advantages mentioned so far there is not only a reduction of fossil energy consumption to be expected by the construction of Teleport-based intelligent ecobuildings but complete energy autonomy is possible, fig. 5/10. This goal can be reached by a combination of batteries charged by solar cells, hydrogentanks filled by solar electricity, and warmwatertanks heated by solar-collectors and heat-pumping. Thus intelligent ecobuilding can even provide electricity and hydrogen for the cars of the future.

Larger complexes of intelligent buildings are called telematic cities, fig. 5/11. Those structures with integrated inner city-spaces can be placed even in deserts or in outer space. Telematic cities can also be installed to protect its users against outside smog. In contrary to conventional industrial products the ecological advantages are growing with the size of the system. The theory of economical systems has to be re-

General Section of an Intelligent Building

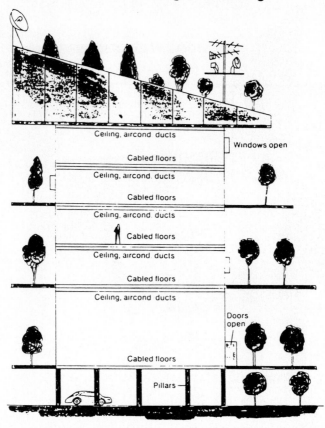

Ceiling, aircond ducts

Windows open

Cabled floors

Ceiling, aircond. ducts

Cabled floors

Ceiling, aircond. ducts

Cabled floors

Ceiling, aircond ducts

Cabled floors

Ceiling, aircond ducts

Doors open

Cabled floors

Pillars

Fig. 5/8: IBs can grow into the altitudes of skyscrapers.

written. So far the profit-function had always to be maximized with inevitable desasterous ecological consequences. Today no industrial system created so far, can avoid this statement, but intelligent ecobuildings because the profit-function of those buildings is coupled to the ecofactor. The higher profit the bigger the ecobuilding and by means of an ecofactor >1 the larger the ecological benefits. No other industrial product in world can do this.

From all these considerations a new landtronic ecoarchitecture does arise, fig. 5/12. The consequences of this teleport based landtronic ecoarchitecture are revolutionary:

1. No consumption of fossile or atomic energy.

2. No environmental pollution.

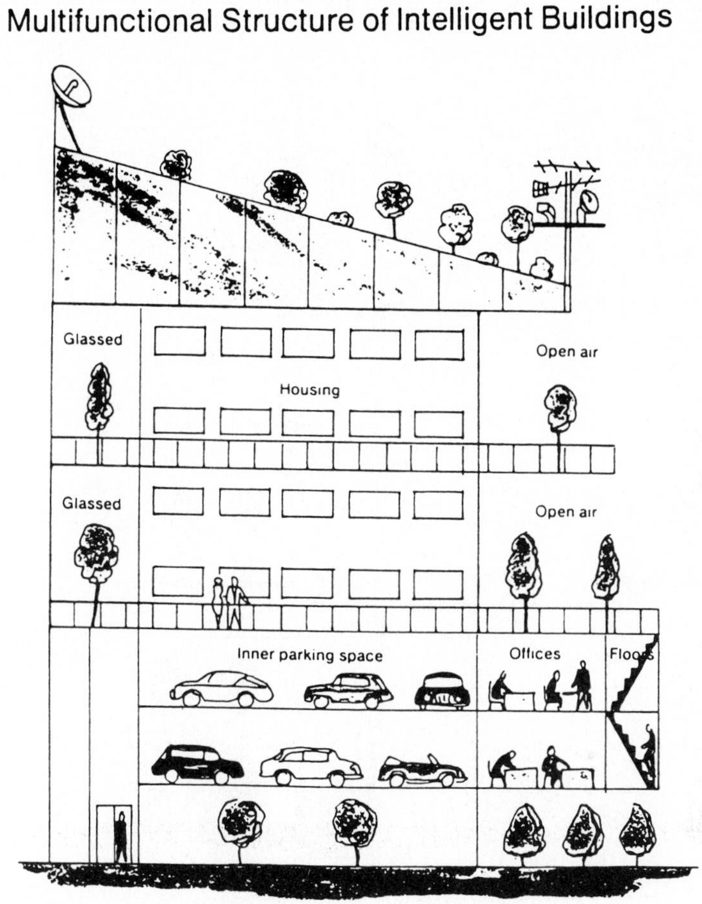

Multifunctional Structure of Intelligent Buildings

Fig. 5/9: Multifunctional Eco-IB.

3. Maximization of new industrial activities because all cities can be renewed.

4. High security against economic crises because people can live by using products created by cityintegrated (building-integrated) agriculture. Also energy is produced by the buildings. Its users can survive even if the economy of the rest of the world is going into bankruptcy.

REFERENCES

(1)   Lazak,D.: ISDN-Entwicklung und Teleportsysteme für nationale und internationale Organisationen. In: CW/CSE (ed,): 3. Europäischer Kongreß über Bürosysteme & Informations Management. München 1986. S. 119-150.

Potential Energy Autonomy of
Intelligent Buildings

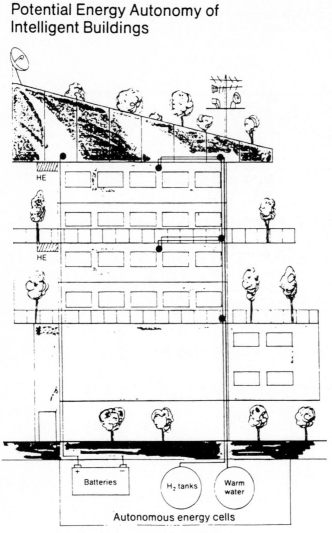

HE = Heat exchange units for thermo pumps

Fig. 5/10: Energy-autonomy of Eco-IBs.

(2) Lazak,D.: Multifunktionale Workstations und künftiges
     Datenfernverarbeitungsmanagement. In: Haberland,U. (ed.):
     Der kaufmännische Geschäftsführer. Landsberg 1985.

(3) Lazak,D.: On Board Eqipment. Proceedings der Jahresta-
     gung der IRU (International Road Transport Union) in
     Istanbul 1988. IRU-Geneva, BP.44/1211 Genève 20/ SUISSE
     1988.

Telematic City Element
Comprising Several Intelligent Buildings

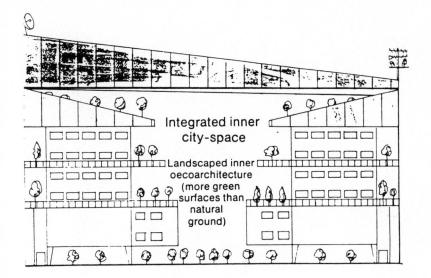

Fig. 5/11: Structure of an element of a Telematic City.

Landtronic Oecoarchitecture

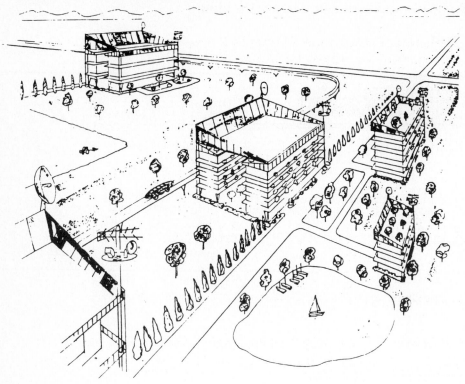

Fig.: 5/12: Example of landtronic ecoarchitecture.

Information Network and Data Communication, III
D. Khakhar and F. Eliassen (Editors)
Elsevier Science Publishers B.V. (North-Holland)
  IFIP, 1990

Telecommunications Trends In Europe:
Towards A Competitive Environment

Peter S Weltevreden
Director, Telecommunications Policy
Commission of the European Communities-DG XIII
Belgium

INTRODUCTION

I would like to start by thanking you for the invitation to address you on the future of the European telecommunications environment as we move towards 1992.

This conference concentrates on the technologies of the emerging networks and services. But a good amount of time has been set aside to look as well at the market and competitive aspects, and at the regulatory framework. In fact, no single approach is enough to ensure that the best and most advanced telecommunications are made available in Europe. The goal must be a pooling of the energies of engineers, of business people, and of regulators, to develop an appropriate framework for growth for our increasingly complex and variegated sector.

In my talk, I shall give an account of where we have reached so far in regulatory terms. On this basis, I shall seek to identify the principal tasks which remain outstanding on the road to a Europe of telecommunications.

In June 1987, the EC Green Paper on the development of telecommunications in the Community ("Towards a Dynamic European Economy - Green Paper on the Development of the Common Market for Telecommunications Services and Equipment", COM(87)290), was issued, launching a broad discussion on the future of telecommunications in the Community. In February 1988, after an in-depth public debate, the Commission published a schedule for the implementation of the Green Paper ("Towards a Competitive Community-wide Telecommunications Market in 1992 - Implementing the Green Paper", COM(88)48).

The broad consensus achieved in the Europe-wide discussion around the EC Green Paper was reflected in the unanimous support given by all the Member States of the Community, in the EC Council of Ministers, to the main proposals of the Green Paper and its overall policy approach, in their resolution of 30 June 1988.

The Community's regulatory actions since that time can best be summed up as the implementation of the programme which these documents defined. This complex process has involved the very different areas of terminal equipment, services, standards, regulatory structures, procurement and type approval. It culminated in December of last year in a comprehensive agreement between the Commission and the EC Council of Ministers, on how to proceed in the liberalisation of the services market, the most important market in telecommunications.

I AFTER THE EC GREEN PAPER

The development of telecommunications regulation in the European Community operates on two, interacting, levels: the level of the Community as a whole, and the level of developments in each Member State.

At Community level, the EC Green Paper and the discussions around it provided a clear picture of a structure that would allow the

opening of telecommunications markets, and at the same time forge
the 12 separate markets of the different Member States into a single
market, in time to merge with the aim of the Community to
establish this single market for the whole of the economy by the end
of 1992.

The reforms at national level therefore lie at the very heart of the
overall reform process.

II MEANING OF 1992

I said that the Community's telecommunications policy is meant as
part of the wider process of building the Single Market of 1992. It is
worth recalling the tasks set by this wider task, and examining their
impact on telecommunications.

The reform of the Treaty of Rome, the so-called Single European
Act, means that achieving a Europe-wide market by the end of 1992
is now a legally binding obligation on all 12 EC Member State
Governments.

1992 therefore means, among the many profound changes which
these goals imply, in particular that the common market will be fully
implemented for some of the up-to-now most regulated sectors in
the European economy : financial and insurance markets, transport
and telecommunications. Within this broad range of services which
represent a large share of the potential for the future growth of the
European service economy, telecommunications plays - in a more
and more communications-based society - a key supportive role.
Free circulation of services in the European Community will mean
more trade.   Trade in services means more freedom of choice for
the user. More freedom of choice for the user requires the
liberalization of structures.

1992 therefore will inevitably expose telecommunications in Europe to a new competitive environment; and 1992 will introduce new demands for a reorganization of telecommunications. Europe's industrial and service enterprises will depend critically on the Europe-wide telecommunications infrastructure for their international operations in the coming Europe-wide market.

III THE ELEMENTS OF CONSENSUS

Let me concentrate on three areas which are key to action at EC level, while at the same time driving the national reform debates in all the Member States.

Liberalization of use

Europe-wide - and world-wide - all countries are confronted with the fact that the enormous new technological possibilities offer a broad range of new activities for both the users and the public telecommunications operators, both in the terminal and in the services field.

In regulatory terms, a clear answer is required, saying whether those involved should be restricted in the use of this vast new potential, or whether they should be allowed to make full use of it for economic and social growth.

In accordance with the general trend in the European debate, the EC Green Paper takes a very clear position on this basic issue. In favour of liberalization - EC-wide - of the market for terminal equipment and far-reaching liberalization of the telecommunications services market, in particular for all value-added services, and of participation of both new private operators and the Telecommunications Administrations in the new markets, with no line of business restrictions.

Separation of regulation and operations - transparency of market rules

As competition emerges, the Telecommunications Administrations who will now be competing with other, new service providers, cannot at the same time set the rules of these new competitive markets. They cannot set standards, allocate frequencies, and define conditions for the use of services, as has been the case in the past.

The creation of transparent market rules, then, calls for a full separation of regulation from operations.

Transborder provision - European dimension of 1992

From a European point of view, it is vital to free up the transborder provision of terminal equipment and - still more importantly - of services within the Community. The aim of 1992 is to produce one single market, not twelve separate markets. This means that it is not enough to allow competitors to enter the 12 markets of the different Member States; new service providers and terminal equipment vendors must be free to supply across the whole of the Community.

IV IMPLEMENTATION STATUS

It is now over two years since the publication of the EC Green Paper. It is under three years till the decisive date of 31 December 1992. How far have we got in the implementation of the regulatory goals set out in the Green Paper?

Let me precede our record with a general remark. One of the most important impacts of the EC Green Paper was that it should contribute towards generating consensus in Europe on the main regulatory issues in telecommunications. It is clear that the EC

Green Paper is serving, across Europe, as the point of reference for the national reform debates and legislative initiatives.

As such, it has already fulfilled one of its major objectives, of 'providing the Community framework as a focus for policy formulation'.

But the European Commission also made it clear from the start that, given the importance of telecommunications for 1992, it would strictly follow up the objectives and proposals set out 'by applying the EC Treaty's competition rules and by submitting proposals to Council'. The proposals can be divided in two categories : Liberalisation (1) and Harmonisation (2), the two faces of the EC's telecommunications policy.

(1) Liberalisation

Terminal equipment

The Commission issued a Directive[1] on 16th May 1988 to open up EC-wide the market for terminal equipment to competition within its mandate under EC-competition law, based on Article 90 of the Treaty. This Directive defines a deadline of the end of 1990 for the opening-up of this market.

Satellite receive-only antennas

The opening of the market for satellite receive-only antennas is included in the Commission Directive on the liberalisation of the terminal market.

---

1 Commission Directive on competition in the markets in telecommunications terminal equipment, 88/301/EEC, Brussels, 16 May 1988.

The services market

Liberalization of the services market was the main item on the agenda of last December's EC Council of Ministers meeting. I will return to this point later.

Cost-related tariffs

The EC Council, in its Resolution of June 30 1988, made clear that Telecommunication Administrations will have to move towards a greater cost orientation for tariffs. The Commission will be conducting a review of progress achieved on this objective by 1 January, 1992.

Separation of regulatory and operational activities

The principle is now generally recognized and integrated in all Member States' reform projects, albeit in varying forms. As regards the separation of terminal equipment approval authorities, this is included in the terminal equipment Directive. As regards authorization of services, this is included in the Commission Directive on services.

Opening of procurement

In August 1989 the Commission submitted to the EC's Council of Ministers revised proposals for a Directive for the opening of procurement procedures, in the areas of telecommunications, water, energy and transport. For telecommunications, this aims at a progressive opening of procurement to bidders from other Member States up to 100% by 1992. The aim is to eliminate undue - and discriminatory - influence on procurement decisions and to base procurement decisions exclusively on commercial criteria.

Last month, the Council reached a common position on this Directive.

(2) Harmonization

Definition of Open Network Provision (ONP)

The ONP Directive is intended to facilitate access for competing service providers to public networks and certain public telecommunications services as far as is necessary for the provision of competitive services.

The definition of ONP is intimately linked to the overall development of the Europe-wide market for services, and the agreement between the Telecommunications Ministers at the December Council, mentioned above.

Establishment of the European Telecommunications Standards Institute

The proposal of the EC Green Paper for the creation of a European Telecommunications Standards Institute (ETSI) has resulted in a major reform of the standards-setting process in the sector. ETSI was founded in April 1988 in Sophia-Antipolis near Nice, France, and is now the main body involved in the production of European telecommunications standards.

Full mutual recognition of type approval for terminal equipment

The Commission will apply the procedures for harmonizing provisions according to Article 100a of the Treaty of Rome as amended by the Single European Act. A draft Directive was submitted to the EC Council of Ministers on 27th July 1989.

V   SERVICES / OPEN NETWORK PROVISION (ONP)

Services :

Let me go into more detail on telecommunications services.

On 7 December last, the Commission and the EC Council of Ministers representing all 12 Member States reached a global compromise on the approach to be taken to the opening of the services market. A good balance has been found between the objective of open markets and the value of public service. This compromise is based on the following elements:

-   rapid and full introduction of competition for all value-added services;

-   progressive liberalization of data communication services:

    -simple resale allowed from 1 January 1993, with possibility of extension of transition period to 1 January 1996 in Member States with undeveloped public data networks;

    -Member States to be able to require providers of data communication services to meet obligations such as quality and coverage - but Commission to scrutinize these obligations to ensure they are based on objective criteria, are non-discriminatory and are proportionate to the objective of general economic interest which motivates the imposition of obligations.

In conjunction with the Services Directive, the Council also gave unanimous support to the ONP-Framework Directive.

Open Network Provision (ONP) - building the future network environment in Europe

The basic principles of ONP are the opening and harmonization of conditions of access to the network infrastructure, for new service providers or for users - a goal complementary to market-opening and fundamental to the development of the services market. This harmonization is to apply in the three areas of technical interfaces, usage conditions and tariff principles. This will open the way for the development of pan-European services, in which service providers will be able to make use of the network in the different Member States according to common principles and forms of access.

- **Openness**

The conditions of Open Network Provision must not restrict access to networks and services except for reasons of general public interest. Any restrictions must be objectively justified, must follow the principle of proportionality and must not be excessive in relation to the aim pursued.

Basic principles are :

- conditions must be based on objective criteria ;

- conditions must be transparent and published in an appropriate matter ;

- conditions must guarantee equality of access, and must be non-discriminatory, in accordance with Community law.

- **The rules of the game**

The rules of the game for the remaining very limited number of access regulations are set by the 'essential requirements'. Essential requirements is a term from Community law, which in telecommunications really refers to ensuring that the necessary rules of the game are defined and applied as competition is introduced. This covers various areas:

- **Network integrity**

Given the special European history of fragmented and incompatible networks, a special emphasis needs to be placed on network integrity. In many cases, this is a matter of creating trans-European network integrity in the first place, rather than simply preserving already existing network integrity.

- **Interoperability**

In the area of services, too, there is a need to ensure that the services that develop allow interoperability.

There is the general principle that technical interfaces and service features will be subject to standards of a *voluntary* nature. Reserve power for Commission to make reference to standards *mandatory* only to the extent necessary to ensure basic interoperability.

- **Data protection and privacy**

As data protection becomes an issue of increasing public concern, it is important to ensure that compatible approaches are taken to the question in the Community. The future development of Europe-wide services will also mean looking at the question of privacy from the Community angle - concerning such problems as unwanted or 'junk' fax.

The ONP programme

There will be specific ONP Directives for leased lines and for voice telephony. ONP conditions will be adopted in the form of recommendations for packet-switched data transmission and for the ISDN by 1 July 1991 and by 1 January 1992 respectively.

VI CURRENT POSITION

With the December compromise on services and ONP, all the action areas set out in the EC Green Paper are now underway. All the measures required for the single market in telecommunications have now been submitted to the EC Council, while common positions have now been reached on the way of implementing this market in the different areas of telecommunications.

VII NATIONAL REFORMS IN EUROPE

As a result of the national discussions, the Green Paper process, the emerging 1992 market, and the related EC-legislation, the European telecommunications market is now in the middle of a comprehensive transformation.

In the Member States, the moves to transform the structure of telecommunications in individual countries have merged into a vast Europe-wide movement for reform, which gives the background also for the reform of the sector underway in this country.

Let me recall the major milestones which have been reached so far:

-      in the Netherlands, the new law entered into force at the start of 1989, liberalizing the telecommunications sector ;

-      in the Federal Republic of Germany, July 1989 saw the fundamental reform of the sector in place, with the reorganisation of the Bundespost and extensive introduction of full competition, as well as the liberalization of mobile communications ;

- in France, major steps have been taken towards the liberalization of value-added services and of mobile communications. Over the past year a broad public debate has taken place over the future of the sector. Legislation has been announced for this summer ;

- in the UK the sector has been further liberalized, in particular with the liberalization of satellite communications of 1988 and of simple resale of 1989;

- Spain has adopted its telecommunications law in 1987 and is adjusting its implementation to the 1992 goals ;

- in Italy, Belgium and Portugal, major steps are being taken in the direction of a structural reform of the sector ;

Beyond the Community, in the larger European dimension, other members of the European Conference of Postal and Telecommunications Administrations - the CEPT - have initiated important telecommunications reforms. Norway, as well as Switzerland and Sweden, should be cited in this regard. More recently, in the context of the global change in Eastern Europe, telecommunications reform is beginning to enter the Eastern part of our continent as well.

VIII OUTLOOK

The 90 ies will be a very dynamic and very important decade. The comprehensive transformation of the European Telecommunications Market which is now under way will lead to a substantially different pattern of relationships between all the actors.

A lot of work has still to be done to achieve the objectives as set out in the Green Paper in all regions of Europe. However, the objectives are certainly worth the effort. The challenges are enormous for European operators and suppliers of equipment and services. On the Single Market, once realised, they will have to achieve a sustainable market position on the basis of their competitive strength only. That this can be done is already shown in the area of mobile telephony. Anyway, the EC will do whatever is in its power to make sure that Europe will get a fair return on its investment.

Information Network and Data Communication, III
D. Khakhar and F. Eliassen (Editors)
Elsevier Science Publishers B.V. (North-Holland)
© IFIP, 1990

PERSPECTIVE ON POLITICAL PROCESSES EVOLVING FROM THE NEW TELEPOLICY IN EUROPE - THE SWEDISH APPROACH

Olof NORDLING

Corporate Planning, International Affairs
Swedish Telecom
Farsta, Sweden

The Swedish telecom market is already one of the most liberal in the world. Telepolicy develops rapidly in both the EC and the US, and these changes are of obvious interest to Sweden. A general harmonization with the EC is also an adopted general objective in Sweden. The telepolicy development abroad has served as an important input to the process of further liberalization of the Swedish telecom market, while taking into account the specific domestic situation. The outcome is a quite interesting combination of maximum liberalization with minimum specific telecom regulation. This paper outlines the Swedish background and describes planned changes.

1. GENERAL BACKGROUND

The general situation for telecommunications in Sweden today differs in important respects from the situation in most other countries. Such differences are not always well known abroad, and sometimes appear to be surprising. Conventional wisdom may for example have it that Sweden is a thoroughly regulated society. This is true in some areas, but false when it comes to telecommunications. Unlike most other nations, Sweden has had a minimum of specific telecom regulation ever since telecom services were introduced. Telecom is thus governed by the general rules applicable to all business activities in Sweden. Important characteristics of telecom in Sweden are highlighted below.

1.1. Separation of Agencies from Ministries

Swedish Telecom is a commercial agency and operates like a company. Its finances are completely separated from the national budget and the decision

Olof Nordling, Coordinator International Affairs
Swedish Telecom   Telephone   +46 8 713 36 47
S-123 86 FARSTA   Telefax   +46 8 713 36 36
Sweden   (Contribution presented at the INDC 90 Conference)

power lies with the board of Swedish Telecom. The Ministry of Communications defines general policy objectives and approves rates for household telephony, but does not intervene in daily operations of Swedish Telecom. As a matter of fact, the first rule to give agencies a large measure of autonomy was introduced already in 1634 by the governor Axel Oxenstierna. This occurred during the infancy of queen Christina, when Oxenstierna sought to protect the operations of the agencies from any whims of future monarchs.

1.2. Separation of telecom and postal services

Swedish Telecom was never amalgamated with the Swedish Postal Administration. In fact, what was eventually to become Swedish Telecom once originated from the military signal corps. This historical perspective explains why it was never associated with the postal service.

1.3. Separation of regulatory functions from operator activities

Like most countries, Sweden has had type approval and frequency administration integrated with the Telecom Administration. This has been deemed unacceptable in a competitive environment. In 1989 a new independent authority, STN (the National Telecom Council), was given the responsibility for defining technical requirements and handling type approvals. At the same time the type approval procedure was simplified to what is now called "registration", in order to speed up market introduction of new products.

The frequency administration still remains organization-wise as an entity within the Swedish Telecom Radio Division, but with a separate outside appeals procedure. A complete separation of the frequency administration from the Swedish Telecom Group has been decided and is currently under preparation.

1.4. Absence of de jure telecom monopoly

Sweden never had any formal telecom monopoly, neither on telecoms infrastructure nor on any telecom services. A political debate on a possible monopoly took place already a century ago, while Swedish Telecom emerged as the dominant operator on the Swedish market. The debate was animated at the time, but after some ten years the final verdict was clear: no formal telecom monopoly in Sweden. Specific telecom regulation was kept at an absolute minimum and has stayed so ever since.

1.5. Completely open CPE market

Up to 1980, Swedish Telecom maintained exclusive rights for provision of equipment to be connected to the PSTN. The CPE market has since been liberalized gradually during a ten year period. The last remainders of the Swedish Telecom exclusive rights, for high-speed modems and large PBX's, were abolished in 1989. The Swedish CPE market (in a wide sense, including VSAT terminals, pay-phones etc.) is thus completely open today.

1.6. Positive experience from competition

The experience from telecom competition is quite encouraging in Sweden, also for Swedish Telecom. A fundamental insight is that a competitive market shouldn't be interpreted as a zero-sum game. Competition has improved Swedish Telecom performance, enlarged the total market, given focus to the activities and has at the same time relaxed the implicit demand on any agency in Sweden to provide everyone with anything, anywhere, anytime, and preferrably free of charge. Market niches overlooked by Swedish Telecom, as operating credit card pay-phones, have been filled more rapidly by the competition, to the benefit of the users.

1.7. Surveillance of fair trade

Our Swedish language has rarely contributed to the international vocabulary. One exception is "ombudsman", a word that doesn't translate easily, meaning approximately "someone to advocate the public interest". Sweden counts numerous specialized "ombudsmän", organized to care for issues as diverse as consumer protection, promotion of fair trade and equality between the sexes, just to mention a few. The major task of the fair trade ombudsman, called NO, is to take on cases of suspected unfair practices in all business sectors, including telecommunications. A similar role is performed by SPK, the National Price and Competition Authority. Thus, Sweden has got general tools for supervision of all business activities, and these tools apply to telecom as well.

1.8. Supervision of organization and of financial transactions

RRV, the National Audit Agency, was organized by King Gustaf I in the 16th century and has scrutinized both the accounts and the activities of all government agencies ever since. In the area of telecommunications, RRV recommends organizational changes of the Swedish Telecom Group and acts as a watchdog to pinpoint any undue cross-subsidies. The Swedish rules on structural separation and internal financial flows are roughly similar to Computer III conditions in the US. Swedish Telecom is allowed to compete in all areas of telecommunications, but revenues from the telephony service may not subsidize other activities within the Swedish Telecom Group.

1.9. Internal subsidies

The principle of realigning tariffs with costs enjoys full political support in Sweden. This realignment must however take place gradually, without too drastic changes for the citizen. Major tariff changes for Swedish Telecom household telephony service have furthermore to be approved by the government. For the time being household subscription rates are still too low, implying a cross-subsidy within the telephony service from business customers to households. Swedish Telecom puts high priority on eliminating this subsidy, since it distorts competition. Possible remaining subsidies within the household sector itself would not have the same effect and will probably remain for quite some time.

1.10. No external cross-subsidies

There are no cross-subsidies to other government activities from Swedish Telecom revenues. Swedish Telecom tariffs are among the lowest in the world, as the statistics from Logica and the comparisons from OECD prove. For the Swedish Telecom Group, gross yearly revenues amount to some 23 GSEK, investments account for roughly 9 GSEK per annum, and we pay back some 200 MSEK each year as return on equity to our owner, the government.

1.11. Harmonization with the EC

Sweden is not a member of the EC, but most active within the EFTA to build the European Economic Space, EES, together with the EC. It also deserves to be mentioned that the Swedish Government has adopted a general policy of harmonizing with the EC in all areas, with the exceptions of foreign policy and defence. A special organization is charged with analyzing and orchestrating the needs for change. Among the multitude of areas covered by the current analysis, telecom seems to be an area where harmonization with the EC is readily achieved.

1.12. A sound basis

The absence of a formal telecom monopoly, the structure and operation of a Swedish commercial agency and the policy of general regulation (rather than specific telecom regulation), together account for the major differences in tele-policy between Sweden and other countries. It might also be important to note that Sweden has a long-standing tradition of a consensus building approach in most areas, trying to reconcile different interests towards pragmatic objectives. Whether the current situation outlined above is a result of this consensus tradition, or of unusual foresight displayed by our ancestors, or a matter of sheer luck, is hard to tell. Anyway, Sweden finds itself in a quite fortunate position. Our country has thus escaped much of the current time-consuming debate elsewhere, for example on separating postal service from telecommunications and on reorganizing the telecom administration more like a company. Such feats were already accomplished in Sweden, enabling us to concentrate on market and customer issues.

There were certainly additional important issues that called for attention. First of all, the time was ripe for a further liberalization of the rules for interconnection of telecom service operators to the Swedish Telecom network. Certain cases also demonstrated a need for improved clarity in the rules. This called for an appropriate concept for a completely open network.

2. APPLICATION OF THE OPEN NETWORK CONCEPTS

The Open Network Provision suggested by the EC is currently expressed as fairly general principles, with more precise interpretations for individual areas still to be defined. The Open Network Architecture of the US is however implemented and gives additional guidance to the possible ramifications of telepolicy. How could such concepts be applied to the Swedish background? A study group with all interests represented was set up by the Ministry of Communications in the summer of 1989 to elaborate particularly on the ONP concept and come up with suggestions for change in Sweden. The objective was to open the market in a clear way for all telecom services. Some relevant facts found initially by this group are described below.

2.1. Existing third party traffic

Sweden already accepted so called "third party traffic", in particular for VANS, but also for certain voice services. A private mobile telephony operator was connected to the PSTN in 1981, to compete with the Swedish Telecom mobile telephony service. Numerous VANS providers are operating, without any need for a service license. The rules, in particular those for leased lines, left however room for interpretation. The application of the rules was not always consistent. This created a grey zone of "tolerated" third party traffic, and consequently a certain degree of ambiguity.

2.2. Absence of license procedures

Since there is no formal telecom monopoly there are no license procedures necessary to operate competing networks. VANS providers and other operators have established themselves freely, without any barriers to entry. The absence of license procedures is generally percieved on the market as a major advantage.

2.3. Need for clear operator conditions

Sweden lacked a definition of network operators and clearly defined conditions for operators to be connected to the PSTN. The interconnection of the private mobile telephony operator was performed as an ad hoc solution in the past. The request from a competitor, Comvik, to interconnect its future international satellite service, "Comvik Skyport", to the Swedish Telecom network emphasized the need to find a generalized solution to this and future requests.

2.4. Leased lines in competition

To offer leased lines within Sweden is an activity exposed to competition, since there is no network monopoly. A customer or an operator could choose between leasing a Swedish Telecom circuit, or using a connection via the Tele-X satellite operated by the Swedish Space Corporation (not related to the Swedish Telecom Group), or buying a radio link equipment from any supplier. Even leasing circuits from the Swedish Railroads has lately turned out to be an alternative solution. This means that any surcharge applied by Swedish Tele-com and related to the type of traffic (i.e. surcharge for third party traffic or volume sensitive tariffing) would simply have the effect of making the Swedish Telecom offer non-competitive.

3.   PROPOSED CHANGES

Consequently, the analysis boiled down to clarifying the rules and solving the question of operator connection to the PSTN operated by Swedish Telecom. Here some key trade policy concepts were applicable, notably "transparency" and "non-discrimination". Following the Swedish consensus tradition, the study group reached an agreement upon the following as a proposed frame-work.

3.1.   No license procedures

No change, but only a clarification of the existing situation. VANS operators (in the US sense, i.e. including data communication networks) to be connected as ordinary business customers with ordinary business conditions. No licenses needed and no surcharges applied.

In fact, to introduce a licensing or concession scheme would call for additional restrictions to be enforced first in order to be able to grant exemptions from them. This has a somewhat absurd flavour. A debate for additional restrictions, let alone a monopoly, would probably have the same outcome as a century ago. There were different opinions in the group on this issue, though, so future modifications are possible.

3.2.   Abandoned restrictions on leased lines

No traffic restrictions on leased lines. The same normal flat rate should apply to all customers regardless of usage or traffic type. This measure will have the additional benefit of eliminating the previous ambiguities in this field.

3.3.   Operator concept

Addition of a new concept of voice operators, to have specific operator conditions for connection to the PSTN in analogy with telecom operators abroad. The operator concept would be applicable to operators with a substantial volume of voice services utilizing the PSTN.

3.4.   Operator conditions

Operator conditions based on the international situation, using the existing international calculations of cost elements for pricing national extension. Unitary tariff per minute for reaching any point in Sweden through the PSTN.

3.5.   Equal treatment

Transparency in conditions and non-discrimination should apply to all operators, whether part of the Swedish Telecom Group or not, and whether international or domestic.

3.6.   Realignment of tariffs with costs

Cost-oriented tariffs are a prerequisite for undistorted competition. The realignment of household subscription rates with costs should be continued. This will also facilitate the necessary continued rebalancing of international and long distance tariffs to better reflect actual costs. Swedish Telecom has repeatedly suggested a general lowering of the international rates, that remain too high. Swedish Telecom has also trimmed its own collection rates for international traffic substantially.

3.7.   Additional external measures

The ombudsman for fair trade practices (NO) recognizes a need for additional special competence for telecom questions. This special competence could be added by a supporting council of experts from the parties involved, or by adjoining a suitable existing organization, like STN, to give expert technical advice when needed. However, no creation of any additional supervising agency specifically for telecom is envisaged, at least not for the time being.

3.8.   Additional internal measures

Interconnection requests from operators should be handled by Swedish Telecom Group headquarters in order to ensure equal treatment. The already existing possibilities to appeal to the government or to NO will of course remain to solve possible disputed cases.

Technical information to and from interconnected operators on planned network changes etc should be handled in a timely way by separate Swedish Telecom staff. For obvious reasons this activity must be clearly separated from the normal marketing activities of Swedish Telecom.

4.   FINAL REMARKS

The above proposals can be implemented rapidly. It seems possible to do this without any increase in regulation, and without any need to even modify the current law. The established Swedish way, regarding telecom as a normal business activity, subject to the same laws and procedures as any other business, seems to work well also for the future. Telecom is an area that is changing too quickly to be emprisoned in too detailed regulation, which could also put market development in a straight-jacket.

The Swedish approach outlined above is in agreement with the EC telepolicy concerning service liberalization and ONP principles. In addition it opens up the market for interconnection of voice operators. We believe this approach to be an appropriate framework for an open telecom service market. Hopefully this framework will also be capable of accommodating successive detailed improvements in the future. Telepolicy will certainly continue to evolve together with market and technical development.

Information Network and Data Communication, III
D. Khakhar and F. Eliassen (Editors)
Elsevier Science Publishers B.V. (North-Holland)
IFIP, 1990

PROSPECTS OF THE TELECOMS WITHIN A NEW EUROPEAN TELEPOLICY

Dr Nic KNUDTZON

Norwegian Telecom

Based on the previous presentations of this session on:
- the opening of the European market
- the activities of the European Community (EC)
- the political processes
- the European Telecommunications Standards Institute (ETSI)
- the regulatory issues,

and prior to the presentation on:
- the industrial aspects,

I shall deal with the prospects of the Telecoms.

My presentation will consist of four parts:
- Developments within the "Conférence Européenne des Administrations des Postes et Télécommunications" (CEPT)
- The establishment of the European Institute for Research and Strategic Studies in Telecommunications (EURESCOM)
- Challenges and threats facing the telecoms
- Conclusion.

Conférence Européenne des Postes et Télécommunications (CEPT)

CEPT was established in 1959 as a body essentially of government departments providing postal and telecommunications services as monopolies, with the aim of harmonizing their admin-istrative and technical services.

CEPT currently represents 26 countries in Europe.

A simplified organigram of CEPT today is shown in Figure 1. It consists of:
- the Postal Commission (Com P)
- the Telecommunications Commission (Com T).

The Com T comprises Committees, each of which have several Working Groups (not shown in this figure).

Recent and prospective external developments call for a review of CEPT's telecommunications activities:
- Posts and Telecoms have been or will be divided in many of the European countries.

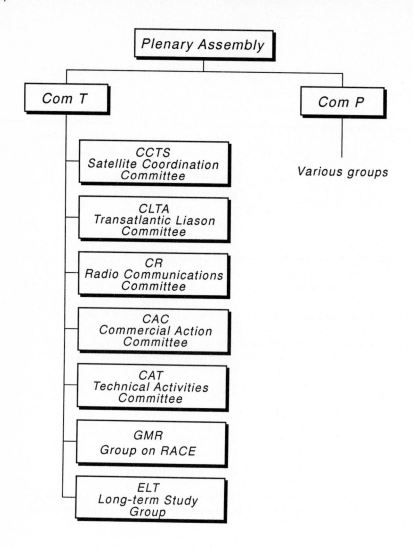

Figure 1: Simplified CEPT organigram

- *Network operators* and *regulators* will soon be separated in many countries.
- Several Eastern-European countries wish to join CEPT.
- Networks and services will in the future be provided by an increasing range of players. They can be broadly classified as:
  · main network operators providing national and international public fixed networks with special or exclusive rights for the provision of basic services,

- other network operators for mobile, cable TV, etc,
- other service operators.

However, the patterns are not the same and they develop at different rates in the various countries. Furthermore, the future developments may follow two trends:
- closer integration of national networks
- competition on long-distance networks across Europe.

Com T has played a major role in the development of telecommunications in Europe. However, Com T's influence is clearly declining for several reasons, inter alia:
- the earlier monopoly responsibilities are being spread over more entities, the EC being a major promoter in this development,
- Com T is perceived by many as a "closed shop", not open to consultation with customers and others. Thus, other interest groups seek to bypass it.

In order to meet the future needs, Com T must therefore now respond to the changing circumstances. At their meetings during the last years, Com T has discussed how to move for better use of telecommunications in Europe, and at the meeting in London 21-22 February 1990 some major steps for the short-term period 1990-1992 were decided upon:
- It was recognized that there is no good practical reason for keeping Posts and Telecoms combined in CEPT. A proposal for a future split will therefore be taken up with Com P.
- Com T set up new arrangements to influence radio frequency spectrum use and allocations. Under the new European Radiocommunications Committee
  - a European Communications Office with a permanent group of experts will carry out studies and propose strategies,
  - all interested parties will be consulted before decisions are made,
  - decisions will be taken only by government representatives, because they alone can decide national policies,
  - decisions will be binding to ensure that agreed plans will be implemented consistently throughout Europe.
- The work of the Com T (possibly renamed CEPT Telecom) will be divided more clearly between the activities appropriate to the *main operators* and the activities for which the *regulators* are responsible. Specifically,
  - the CCTS, CLTA, CAC, CAT, GMR and ELT committees (reference Figure 1) will belong to the *operator* part, but with revised mandates,
  - a new Regulatory Committee to provide a forum for considering Europe-wide regulatory issues, and the European Radio Communications Committee will belong to the *regulator* part.
- Com T will consult much more widely with other bodies concerned with the development of telecommunications in Europe to ensure more effective decision-making in its current activities.
- The present series of regular meetings with the EC and the European Free Trade Association (EFTA) will continue.
- Working arrangements, including decision-making and a permanent secretariat, will be discussed further.

The objective of EURESCOM is to support the development and provision of harmonized Europe-wide public telecommunications networks and services. For this purpose the activities shall:
- enable the development of harmonized strategies by its members for the planning and the provision of the future European public telecommunications network infrastructure and services,
- stimulate and coordinate the common participation of its members in precompetitive and prenormative research projects,
- stimulate and coordinate field trials and pilot projects to be carried out by its members,
- contribute to European and worldwide standardization,
- contribute to the work of CEPT, EC, EFTA and relevant European R&D programs.

A list of possible common projects include:
- Public network and services
  · Network evolution
  · Electronic highways
  · Open services architechture
  · Generalized communication protocol reference model
  · Analysis of facility priorities
  · Intelligent networks and intelligent architechture
  · Telecommunications management network.
- Precompetitive and prenormative research
  · Coordination and management of the participation of the members in the projects within the EC framework program
  · Computer-aided network planning
  · Electromagnetic compatibility
  · Market research
  · Socio-economic research
- Field trials
  · Projects within the EC framework program
  · Advanced network experiments
- Standardization
  · Validation and evaluation of proposed and adapted standards
  · Conformance testing
- Miscellaneous
  · Intellectual property rights
  · Quality.

This list contains many of the items which are now being studied by the Com T Committees and Working Groups, and which may be transferred to EURESCOM.

Furthermore, it should be mentioned that the EC has set up a working party to study the possibility of establishing an appropriate structure to pursue the R&D programs of the EC in the field of broad-band telecommunications. The purpose is to facilitate conserted action among telecommunications operators, manufacturers and users, in order to prepare for the introduction of broad-band communications services throughout the EC. Furthermore, it should define the advantage and role of such a structure in implementing projects within the EC framework program.

Challenges and Threats Facing the Telecoms

As a general observation on the prospects within the new European telepolicy, I will state that the telecoms should have a good starting position. After all, they have in many cases designed and established services before the customers became aware of their needs. Examples are the Nordic Mobile Telephone systems NMT-450 and NMT-900 developed by the Nordic telecoms, which have a subscriber penetration (in the case of Norway 40 subscribers per 1000 inhabitants) of about ten times that of the central European countries. Furthermore, within Com T a large number of the telecoms have signed memoranda of understanding for the implementation of the pan-European GSM mobile system by 1991 and of the Integrated Services Digital Networks (ISDN) by 1992, and for a European Broadband Interconnection Trial (EBIT).

However, the telecoms have hitherto been able to set their own pace for these developments. In the new dynamic environment with competitors and increasingly knowledgeable customers, the telecoms will come under time pressure.

I will now consider *some* of the challenges and threats facing the telecoms in two areas:
- Networks and services
- Personnel.

Networks and Services

Challenges:
- To plan, implement and maintain reliable basic networks in a techno-economically optimal way. Even if the telecoms do not supply all services, they will get revenues from providing network infrastructures.
- To establish long-term standardized systems and networks such as ISDN and Intelligent Networks (IN) with an open provision for all value-added users and suppliers, both nationally and internationally.
- To provide services tailor-made to meet particular needs of special users, in addition to the long-term standardized solutions.
- To introduce cost-based tariffs as soon as possible.
- To have an open and market-oriented attitude to all customers.
- To provide "one-stop shopping" solutions, both nationally and internationally. The latter requires agreements and close cooperation between the telecoms of the various countries.
- To pay special attention to the participation and cooperation in the field of mobile systems, both the GSM system and the supplementary personal communications networks. Together these will form one of the fastest growing markets in telecommunications.
- To assist eachother in the implementation and operation of Very Small Aperture Satellite (VSAT) systems with terminals located in various countries.
- To introduce a wide variety of ISDN services, including teleaction services.

- To include the Eastern-European countries in the telecom family and establish cooperation with them.
- To follow the developments and prepare for the outcome of the "Uruguay round" of the General Agreements on Tariffs and Trade (GATT), which considers trade in *services* as a separate category. The aim is to establish a more liberal regime for international trade in services. Althought statistics are highly deficient, it is recognized that telecommunications constitutes a large and increasing part of the total trade in services. The policy on liberalization adapted by the EC is expected to become a model for the rest of the world.

Threats:
- To have limited financial freedom to operate dynamically in the rapidly changing markets. The Norwegian Telecom is one of the few telecoms in Western Europe whose funding is part of the national budgetary process, which implies a wandering of more than one year before the Stortinget (the national assembly) takes the final decision. Telecoms which are subject to such procedures, are seriously handicapped compared with competitors having greater financial freedom.
- To be prevented by the authorities in competing with other suppliers on equal terms.
  · Excessive social obligations. This is in fact an area which requires a thorough financial analysis.
  · Schemes which would enable competitors' bypassing and cream skimming.
  · The underlying ruling ghost is the fear of cross-subsidizing within the telecoms, whereas this aspect is not taken into account for the competing suppliers. Thus, terminal suppliers may sell their equipment, if necessary at dumping price, together with appurtenant private networks, and later with the customer "on the hook" increase at their own will the costs for additional equipment and network rental. Such vendor-controlled solutions do not represent Open Network Provision (ONP) and are not in the interest of the users. On the other hand, the telecoms provide standardized networks and interfaces with free choice of terminal equipment. However, they may not deliver complete solutions including terminals. Such discrimination is clearly detrimental to the development of good total solutions for business communications.
  · In Norway we have the rather peculiar situation that the Stortinget (the national assembly) has decided that the Norwegian Telecom can take part in the competition on value-added services from June 1989, if they are provided through special limited companies (or under separate book-keeping). However, the Ministry of Transport has as yet not granted the permission for establishing such limited companies.
- Too fierce competition between the national telecoms.

Personnel

Challenges:
- To establish, continously update and carry through a long-term plan for training and efficient use of the personnel for administrative, commercial, financial and technological aspects of the implementation and operation in the rapidly changing telecommunications world, coupled with appropriate incentives.
- To handle diligently the present situation with a surplus of personnel in many European telecoms. Competition requires high productivity, which again implies reduced personnel costs. This is an area where short-term considerations easily may overrule a favorable long-term solution. As far as possible, the present situation should be managed by limited replacements of retirements, early retirement schemes and mobility arrangements. It should be kept in mind that - according to the estimates of the EC - the telecommunications business is expected to grow from 2 % of the GNP in 1988 to 7 % by the year 2000. Thus, although the personnel required per bit/second is going down, it must be the *common* challenge of the telecoms and their personnel unions to achieve a market share, which - after the consolidation of the present transitional situation - could maintain or even increase the staff. At the same time the general quality level will continuously have to be raised.

Threats:
- To be unable to provide the appropriate incentives for keeping the staff, as is the case in Norway where the Norwegian Telecom has to follow the government salary scale.

Conclusion

If allowed by their national authorities to compete with others on equal terms, I conclude that the European telecoms are in a good position to pursue the challenges of the bold new telecommunications world.

Information Network and Data Communication, III
D. Khakhar and F. Eliassen (Editors)
Elsevier Science Publishers B.V. (North-Holland)
© IFIP, 1990

EXPECTATIONS BY EUROPEAN IT-INDUSTRY

Ivar Ørbeck

Alcatel STK
Norway

1. INTRODUCTION

Europe is in the melting pot. Information technology is fuelling the process, and the process itself is affecting the information technology policy for Europe.

The IT industry, in its fullest sense, is undergoing a period of almost revolutionary change. Not only are companies, technology and markets transforming at a high speed, also European PTT's and institutions are undergoing vast changes.

What are so the expectations by the European IT industry? I do not think there is an unanimous answer in the industry to that question. It is easy to be tempted to construct predictions, set up scenarios and provide roadmaps of the future. The likelihood of such predictions becoming accurate is, however, small. That we know from past experience.

In the early 1980's, that decade was named the "age of discontinuity". Now at the turn of the decade we can account that there have been more transformation, more changes in technology, business, politics and human endeavour than what was expected. Particularly the last part of the decade has been years of confusion and continuous turbulence in world politics, and in world economy. This we bring with us into this decade, but we also bring with us the great enthusiasm based upon the potential which is present and real.

2. THE IMPACT OF NEW TECHNOLOGY

For our industry the necessary technologies and tools are available, and they are ready to be further exploited. The level of readiness is tremendous. The fibre optics evolution is providing an explosion of band-width capacity. We know that in the next 10 years there will be a web of fibre cables networking the continents with open provision for information transfer. The cost for bit transportation will drop dramatically. Let us also mention telecommunication satellites.

Data and telecommunications will be integrated, the process
is already on the way. The transformation of the networks
from electro-mechanical to digital will be completed in our
part of the industrialized world in this decade. Voice,
text and image will all be handled and transported as
digital data. Telecommunication switches are complex data
processors, and traditional data processing, EDP, will be
networks rather than central installations as in the past.

Further evolution in micro-electronics will give us at
least a tenfold in speed, circuits per chip and cost efficiency. For the users, systems, equipment and user applications software are becoming available on the shelves, but
in this area we only see the beginning, perhaps only the
beginning of the beginning. We know the new generations
which are in the pipeline, and we know that equipment
generation life will be shorter with a high rate of evolution and decreasing cost.

What is, and has been the bottleneck, is standardization.
I believe that this will be the major limiting factor also
in the years to come, but we have passed important milestones. Standards have come a long way at the end of the
last decade, and results are coming out which will accelerate the information technology evolution. Coordinated
introduction of ISDN, Open Network Provision to service
providers and users are perhaps the most important of the
forthcoming events, but there is more to follow.

The establishment and results of ETSI will play a major
role. Stimulation and development of transnational value
added services will be open to users on a standardized
basis and be available across national and organisational
borders. A multitude of user-orientated virtual networks in
open network configuration will emerge.

The technology will push the market and the market will
pull the service and network providers.

The need for more capacity for transportation, handling and
storing of information will most likely push forward an
early introduction of the broadband network, ATM, in the
second half of this decade. Again standards and international agreements will be the limiting factors.

3.   NEW AND EMERGING MARKETS

For the telecommunication industry the emphasis will be
focused on the ability to provide systems rather than boxes
and equipment. New and emerging markets are building up.
ISDN, Intelligent Networks, mobile networks, business
communication network will provide business opportunities,
but will also open up for Value Added Services as a new
business segment.

These potentials are reflected in forecasted growth of the
telecommunication market. The EEC commission is estimating
that by the end of the century up to seven per cent of the
Gross Domestic Product of the Community will result from
telecommunications, as against over two per cent today. The
combined world equipment and services market for telecommunications and information technology already represents
more than 500 billion ECU. It is estimated that via information technology, more than 60% of Community employment
may depend on telecommunications by the end of the century.

Yet, it is hard to understand the parameters which will
influence the process that will shape the future.
Economists and politicians are today swinging from one
prediction to another. From great depression to optimistic
forecast of a period of high growth. Eastern Europe scenarios are swinging from democratisation with full growth
and potentials for trade and expansion to that of chaos and
low trade. A rumour about Gorbatsjov's position can make
the New York Stock Exchange swing like a pendulum.

We have to face that the contradiction, discontinuity and
instability will follow us into the 90's, perhaps even more
so than in the 1980's.

4.   THE OPENING OF THE EUROPEAN MARKET

There are, however, fermer trends we can predict more
accurately. I have mentioned technology and telecommunication evolution. The process of market integration and the
opening of the European market by 1992 are also firm. The
1992 process is irreversible and will have major effects on
European telecom structure and markets. The terminal market
liberalisation trends are constantly creating more and more
open markets.

The new European norms being developed by ETSI are con-
tributing to the fast opening of the European markets.

The re-regulation of PTT's and the new operators which are
emerging, are trends which the telecom industry must be
able to respond to. There will be requirements of those
operators for more efficient management systems for their
network, and there will be needs for new subscriber
services.

The telecommunication industry, which I represent, will
have to adapt to a new way of conducting business. The
distribution problem is a major challenge, because whereas
in the past very often they went through PTT's to distribute terminals and customer premises equipment, today they
must be able to sell through their own direct distribution
channels. We are forced to be more competitive and to give
more and more differentiating features to our products and
renew our products more often. There is thus a premium on

innovation to gain competitive advantage.

The opening of public procurement rules forces companies to become more and more price competitive. Experience from my own company shows that even from a high cost country like Norway, we are able to compete on the international market with switching equipment because we were exposed to international procurement several years ago. We had to adapt and bring our cost below that of most other countries in Europe. It was a painful process, but it has made us able to meet open market prices and be able to compete on the international market.

Alcatel STK has signed contracts for public networks with China and export to other European Alcatel houses is taking place.

With the opening of the inner market in Europe there will be major changes in the telecommunication industry. There will be a gradual change from national to a pan-European telecom market which will influence the structure of the industry. It is estimated that the total "gain" to the Community in the telecom sector will be between 2.5 and 4.2 BECU of which PTT procurement counts for 30% and the gains from standardization represent 25%.

From industry point of view it is important to be aware that it will mainly be the telecommunication industry that will be forced to provide the cost reduction that represents the "gain" of the open market. It will follow that industry will have to restructure and rationalize. There will be lower prices, less margins for R&D and less employment in the industry. This will be a tremendous challenge to the industry, but it will offer advantages on the export markets.

Telecommunications have been a key target for the 1992 reform. There are several reasons for this:

-   Compared with US and Japan, the markets are very fragmented.

-   Strong national procurement practices.

-   There are great barriers in standards and tariffs.

-   Too many product varieties, too many factories and suppliers.

-   Information network integration is a key to European integration.

-   Telecom and IT have a high symbolic value. Transformation from national to pan-European networks can be made visual and can be realized within few years.

- There is a high growth potential in pan-European
  services.

Towards a more integrated all-European market and open
networks there will be less national differences in
services and equipment. As it is now, different countries
have developed special services and network concepts like
NMT in Scandinavia and Minitel in France. Open networks
will have snowball effects when different national services
are adapted into pan-European networks. Let me mention one
example: The mobile telephone density in Norway is about 45
per 1000 inhabitants. In France there is about 1 per 1000.
For the videotex system the pattern is the reverse. France
has 80 Minitel terminals per 1000 inhabitants compared with
less than 1 videotex terminal per 1000 for Norway. If the
rest of Europe reaches the level of Norway and France in
these two areas, it represents a potential of 15 million
mobile telephones and 25 million videotex terminals respectively. These figures will most likely be surpassed for
Europe by the end of the decade. As regards the mobile
telephone, it is most likely that figures will be considerably higher due to several factors:

- Introduction of GSM

- Reduced equipment cost

- Lower tariffs

- Introduction of Telepoint, PABX cordless, residential
  cordless.

5.   THE POTENTIAL FOR THE INDUSTRY

Let us have a look at the future trend of our telecommunication industry. As the network becomes more integrated and
more complex, with built-in intelligence and services, this
will effect the telecom equipment manufacturers significantly. To be able to provide such networks, there will be
a need for closer cooperation between the network providers
and the network operators.

The suppliers' contents will change from boxes and hardware
modules to systems, networks and information services. The
network will change from being a channel through which
information can be conducted, to becoming a network for
information handling including storage, message handling
and information services.

As EDI (Electronic Data Interchange) takes off, it will
require capability for storing and retrieval. Operation and
maintenance and securing of network equipment and
operation, will gain importance. The network must also be
able to provide secure transportation and storage of user

information.

These demands and requirements will call for more functionality in our products and lead us into total network
and service contents. The trend will thus in one dimension
be from boxes to services and user application and in the
other dimension from simple information transport mechanism
to integrated system concepts.

6.   THE TRIAD

European suppliers have a strong competitive position in
telecommunications. European industry serves a competitive
telecommunication market in Europe and has a two-thirds
share of the world market outside the Triad (North America,
Europe and Japan). It is in the interest of Europe to see
to it that policies are established which benefit the user,
balance the trade in favour of Europe and secure the
employment and the technology base to maintain its industries. This must be achieved within the framework of the
single European market involving both EC and EFTA.

The telecommunications open market should thus stimulate
the telecommunication industry in the following way:

-   It should provide a high level of service to the Euro-
    pean telecom's users.

-   It must stimulate the establishment and maintenance of
    a high technology level base shared by industry
    operators and the users.

-   It should stimulate European business.

The pan-European R&D projects set up by the commission, but
now also open for EFTA participation, are important tools
to stimulate these objectives. In my own company, Alcatel
STK in Norway, we participate the RACE, ESPRIT and EUREKA
programs in collaboration with European industry and PTT's.
This opens up for developing partnerships and strategic
alliances.

A telecommunication open market poses a key problem for
almost all companies which are able to obtain scale of
economy and still are maintaining the flexibility and
innovation encouraged by small units. For smaller companies
it becomes important to participate pan-European alliances
and to select market niches where it is possible to grow
global competitiveness. In these niches we must obtain
international leadership in technology in order to secure
production and market share.

At present the European telecom equipment supply industry
ranks first in the world. This position should be main-

tained. There are several reasons for this:

- The European market is the world largest market with a population equal to USA and Japan combined.

- The telecommunication and technology base of Europe is the world leading with large potential for rationalization with the introduction of the open market.

- Five of the top ten equipment suppliers are European, they also have a two-thirds share of the world market outside the Triad.

- An open, single market with standardized products and services should give Europe the benefit USA and Japan already have at hand.

But to succeed, there must be fair competition within the Triad. There must be reciprocity of opportunity. Europe cannot open its markets if Japan and America remain closed to the European manufacturers. It will be in the interest of Europe to obtain equal treatment rather than exclude foreign protectionist countries from the European market.

The Green Paper has established the policy for the development of the common market for telecommunication services and equipment. This is a foundation stone for the architecture of future European telecommunications.

From industry point of view these policies must be implemented in such a way that our competitive position is maintained particularly towards USA and Japan. A threat to Europe compared with America, is that US suppliers also are network operators. This offers cross-subsidization and provides R&D programs funding to US telecom industry that does not exist in Europe. USA also has strong national R&D programs which are aiming beyond precompetitive milestones.

In Japan there is a very strong knit between governmental R&D funding, industry and network operators. Japan is still strongly protectionist. Purchases of telecom equipment by Japan from European suppliers amounted only to 30 M $ in 1988, which is about 0,3% of the total Japanese telecom equipment market. The import, however, by Europe of Japanese telecom products amounted to 1000 M$.

Contrary to Japan, North America is not by nature a protectionist country, and most of the telecom markets are open even if very hard to penetrate. However, some North-American markets are virtually closed to European suppliers. ATT buys 88% of its telecom equipment and 100% of its switching equipment from its division ATT Network System. Bell of Canada buys 77% of its equipment from its subsidiary Northern Telecom.

Mixing within the same entity of equipment supply and telecom services operation opens for heavy presumptions of cross-subsidization. ATT's ratio of R&D expenses to equipment sales is estimated to be twice the figure of its main European competitors.

European industry needs strong and efficient Telecommunication Administrations. Their role to provide network infrastructure must be safeguarded in order to allow them to enhance their public service mandate.

Provided that regulatory responsibilities are separated from operational responsibility, PTT's should be allowed to participate in the emerging competitive services and terminal equipment market. There is a substantial potential embedded in utilizing the network infrastructure for new services, and to enhance services in the user application field.

The synergy effects of close cooperation between the telecommunication operators and the industry should be of major concern for the telecommunication policy for Europe.

7.   SUMMARY AND PROPOSALS

The open market offers more opportunity than threats to the European telecommunication industry.

The main purpose of the open market must be to provide high standard services at the lowest possible cost to the user.

In opening of the market by 1993, telecommunications will play a major role:

-    Information technology is key to industrial and welfare growth.

-    Change from national networks with different standards and configurations, to a pan-European standardized borderless network, will strongly contribute to integrate Europe.

Shall Europe succeed there must be established "federative" projects to balance those of USA and Japan. Research programs such as RACE and ESPRIT will be a first step, but much more committing industrial and operational programs must be realized. Some potential programs where EFTA countries, and particularly the Nordic countries, could take a lead, could be as follows:

-    Establishment of a pan-European broadband network interlinking all major European cities. A program planned and financed by a model similar to the ESA space projets.

- National or regional programs focusing on user applications and aiming at international applications.

- Increased use of precompetitive and industrial development contracts. European R&D programs following
  RACE and ESPRIT, should be carried out in a close
  cooperation between the PTT's and industry.

- Joint research centres by the European PTT's and
  industry on the model of ETSI and ESA. Norway could
  take an initiative, perhaps by utilizing the IT installation and infrastructure at Lillehammer Olympic
  Games in 1994.

For the European telecommunication industry the 1990's will
be the years of challenge, but most of all they will be the
years of opportunity.